the LAST BATTLE

the LAST BATTLE

THE *MAYAGUEZ* INCIDENT
and the
END OF THE VIETNAM WAR

RALPH WETTERHAHN

CARROLL & GRAF PUBLISHERS, INC.
NEW YORK

First Carroll & Graf edition 2001

Carroll & Graf Publishers, Inc.
An Imprint of Avalon Publishing Group
19 West 21st Street
New York, NY 10010-6805

Library of Congress Cataloging-in-Publication Data is available.
ISBN: 0-7867-0858-1

Manufactured in the United States of America

for
Joseph, Gary, and Danny
and all those who risked or gave their lives to save the
Mayaguez
and for
Carol
who helped bring
about a full accounting

Acknowledgements

Heartfelt thanks go to the most determined—and emotional—agent on the planet, Nancy Ellis-Bell; my patient interpreter Noma Sarvong; superb Executive Editor Philip Turner, eagle-eyed copy editor Muriel Jorgenson; and Herman Graf, who took the big chance, declaring this work a lead book at Carroll & Graf after reading only four chapters and an outline.

I would like to thank the families of the missing, who have carried the heaviest burden for twenty-six years. Especially included are Mrs. Charlotte Hargrove, Gail Hargrove, Kochise Hargrove, Sandy Hargrove, Doug Hargrove, Mrs. Norma Hall, Jane Hall, Mrs. Faye Marshall, and Teleah Cross.

ACKNOWLEDGEMENTS

During the five years it took to complete this investigation and produce a manuscript, I was helped by an enormous number of people. I would like to start with a grateful remembrance of the late Paul Gillette, my teacher, mentor, and guiding light, even after death. My journalism instructor Professor Clancy Sigal, drill sergeant of USC's "boot camp for the brain," gave me the tools to enter the dicey world of journalism. I came out bloody from those "Tuesdays with Clancy," but he taught us how to lick our wounds and press on. I want to also remember that pirate and poet, the late Willard Bascom.

Thanks also go to the writer's workshop, whose members read my stilted prose and fired back with great erudition: Marjorie Aaron, Rudd Brown, Carolyn Coker, Candace Coster, Warren Hamilton Jr., Norvelle Harris, Stephanie Kegan, Brian Keefe, Chuck Larson, Richard MacNaughton, Harold Metz, Jim Morgan, Rulon Openshaw, Daniel Rhodes, Jean Sapin, Robert Schechter, and R.C. Williams.

Special thanks goes to Tom Clancy for help in locator research, Ambassador Kenneth Quinn for support and encouragement, and Wayne Stewart for his great photographs. David Jones and David Sammons were also kind enough to give me their time and recollections. Special appreciation goes to Producer William Howard and Historian John Warren from Henninger Productions, and Michael Wetterhahn for graphics.

I cannot overlook the contribution of author Jimmie Butler, classmate and friend who got me started in my writing career. Thanks also goes to my long-suffering magazine editors, Dawn Stover at *Popular Science*, Warren Lacy, Julia Leigh, Joanne Hodges, Heather Lyons, Molly Wyman, Donna Budjenska at *The Retired Officers Magazine*, George Larson, Linda Shiner, Perry Turner, John Sotham at *Air& Space, Smithsonian*, Walt Ford at *Leatherneck*, and Dwight Swift and Don McLean at *Soldier of Fortune*.

I could not have completed this work without the groundwork laid by Roy Rowan in *The Four Days of Mayaguez*, John F. Guilmartin Jr. in *A Very Short War*, Thomas D. Des Brisay in *Fourteen Hours at Koh Tang*, and Daniel P.Bolger in *Americans at War 1975-1986, An Era of*

ACKNOWLEDGEMENTS

Violent Peace. I want to also acknowledge the Gerald R. Ford Foundation for their generous grant, former President Gerald R. Ford for answering my query, and staff archivists Karen Holzhausen and Geir Gundersen.

To the marines, soldiers, sailors, and airmen whose names appear throughout the book, thanks for sharing your stories, tears, and joy with me. Special thanks goes to Gale Rogers, Clark Hale, Larry Barnett, Curtis Myrick, Dale Clark, Lester McNemar, James H. Davis, James W. Davis, Michael Cicere, Tim Trebil, Randall W. Austin, William J. Thornton, Rusty Bidgood, Jerry Gettelfinger, James Gregory, John Sargeant, Bill Smith, Alan D. Wyatt, Mykle Stahl, Gen. J.J. Burns, Gen. Ron Rand, Al Corson, Greg Wilson, Wayne Fisk, Chris Brims (widow of Richard C. Brims), Mike Rodgers, Robert Peterson, Steve Poore, Em Son, Rot Leng, Mau Run, Som Sok, Chum Soyath, Noun Sareth, Kim Chanee.

To the hundreds of brave and hardworking members of JTF-FA and CIL-HI, thanks for taking such good care of me and carrying on the work of bringing our service members home. Of special note are public affairs officers Colonel Roger King, Major Joe Davis and Lieutenant Colonel Franklin Childress, all of whom went the extra mile. A thumbs-up goes to the smoothest pilots in Asia from Loa West Coast helicopters, Mark Kershaw, Steven Spooner, and Eric Thum.

I would have been lost without safe havens in Bangkok at Joanna Brown, Sompong Chaivaranon and Anastasia Brown's "Thai palace;" in Washington at Michael Fonte and Berta Romero's home; in Chicago with Marvin and Gayle Altur; in New York with John and Arline Wetterhahn; and in Hawaii at Michael Cavanaugh's pad.

Thanks go to all the relatives and members of my family, but most of all to my wife, Carol, who stood by, encouraged me, and without whom this undertaking would have never proceeded.

Finally, thanks go to former President George H. W. Bush, for getting me bumped from that helicopter back in 1995.

Contents

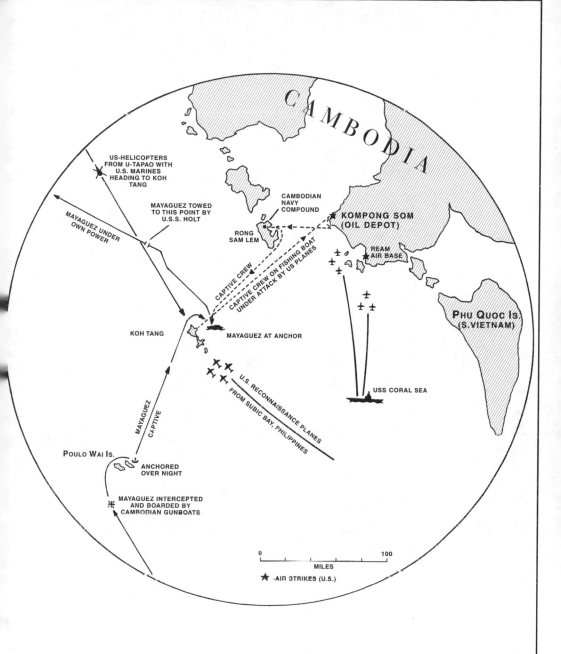

LOCAL AREA MAP

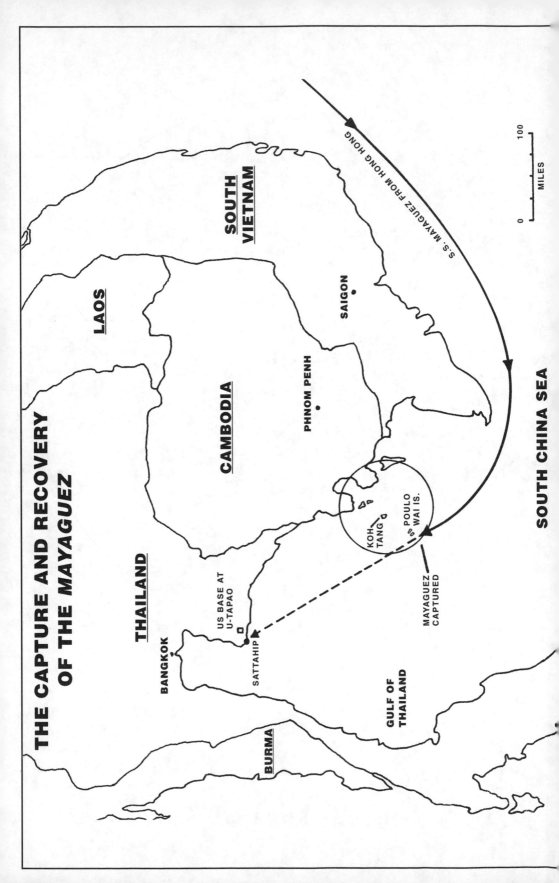

THE CAPTURE AND RECOVERY OF THE MAYAGUEZ

BURMA

THAILAND

BANGKOK

US BASE AT U-TAPAO

SATTAHIP

GULF OF THAILAND

LAOS

CAMBODIA

PHNOM PENH

KOH TANG

POULO WAI IS.

MAYAGUEZ CAPTURED

SOUTH VIETNAM

SAIGON

S.S. MAYAGUEZ FROM HONG KONG

SOUTH CHINA SEA

0   50   100

MILES

PART I

THE QUESTION

1

RETURN TO KOH TANG

Regard your soldiers as your children, and they will follow you into the deepest valleys; look on them as your own beloved sons, and they will stand by you even unto death.

Sun Tzu, *The Art of War*

For me it all began quite by chance on a hot September morning in 1995 when I showed up at Detachment-One Headquarters of the Joint Task Force for Full Accounting (JTF-FA) at the U.S. embassy in Bangkok, Thailand. The Task Force mission is to repatriate missing-in-action (MIA) remains of casualties from the Vietnam War.

At that Bangkok meeting, I met U.S. Army lieutenant colonel Roger L. King, chief of public affairs at JTF-FA. He had flown in from Honolulu. I had come as a freelance writer ostensibly to join him for a plane ride to Hanoi, Vietnam. From Hanoi we planned to board a helicopter that would take us to an F-4 Phantom crash site near Dien Bien

Phu. JTF-FA was conducting one of their bone-recovery operations there. Its 150 members are typically spread throughout Laos, Vietnam, and Cambodia on recovery operations. Teams are made up of forensics experts, mortuary-affairs specialists, bomb-disposal technicians, medics, photographers, radio operators, and scuba divers.

In the midst of writing a novel, I was using the opportunity to research this particular brand of archaeology and its attendant discipline, forensic anthropology. Both weighed heavily in the plot of my fiction. I was on spec, paying my own way, in hopes of spinning off a magazine article or two to help defray expenses.

Lieutenant Colonel King's role was to escort me to the wreckage, make sure I stayed the hell out of the way, and ensure that I did not violate any of the many rules mandated by the U.S. Congress, the Department of Defense, and the Vietnamese government.

"We're not going," King said after we shook hands.

My mouth opened, but no sound came out. I had just traveled nearly seven thousand miles from Long Beach, California, with the idea that we *were* going.

"[Ex]President Bush has taken our seats on the helicopter," King went on to explain. "I didn't know before you left, and I couldn't tell you once I knew because Bush's itinerary is close-hold for security reasons." Bush was on a fact-finding mission to Vietnam. His arrival had just that day been announced to the media.

King must have seen my shoulders sag.

"Tell you what," he added. "A month from now we're doing a recovery in Cambodia. It involves searching for remains of MIAs from the *Mayaguez* Incident in 1975. If you care to join the expedition, I'll reserve the first available seat for you on the helicopter."

As an air force major back in 1975, I had been assigned to the Pacific Air Force Headquarters at Hickam Air Force Base in Hawaii and had actually spent a shift on the crisis team hastily set up in the command post during the *Mayaguez* Incident. My memory of details was sketchy, although I recalled it had involved the rescue of a hijacked commercial ship and the conduct of an island campaign. The outcome was considered successful, albeit a harrowing ordeal with high casualties.

"Let me take a look at what's been written on it," I told King. "I'll let you know my decision in a week or so." With that, I headed home to Long Beach where I began reading everything published about the event. I discovered that although it took place on Cambodian territory, the fourteen hours of combat on May 15, 1975, constituted the last official American battle of the Vietnam conflict. The casualty names became the final ones inscribed on the Vietnam Veterans Memorial Wall in Washington, D.C. I learned that the tentacles of the event stretched from the White House to the deadly sands of an obscure island off Cambodia. What happened there seemed to serve as a metaphor for the entire Vietnam War. Entered into for noble purposes, events quickly turned ugly, a military debacle, yet for America the positive outcome of the *Mayaguez* Incident and the negative result of the Vietnam War have impacted our politics ever since.

A week after our conversation in Bangkok, I called King and signed up. On November 9, 1995, I arrived in Phnom Penh along with King. He turned out to be an affable sort, competent, and very clearly in his element working with the media. "The team is staying on the island in tents," King said. "They've got one for us, too . . . I think."

At the time, Cambodia was being governed by a multi-party coalition that included the Vietnamese-sponsored Communist Peoples Party (CPP) and the National United Front for an Independent, Peaceful, and Cooperative Cambodia (known by the French acronym FUNCINPEC); the Khmer Rouge were isolated. Skirmishes were still going on in the countryside, even though the United Nations had moved a sizable force in during the early '90s hoping to broker peace. Travel by road was risky.

We boarded a French-made helicopter that had arrived from Vientiane, Laos. It was leased from Lao West Coast Helicopters, a company name I found interesting, since Laos has no coast, let alone a western one. To complete the multinational inventory, the helicopter was flown by Mark Kershaw, a New Zealander. Mark placed me in the left front seat in the event there arose an opportunity for some good aerial photos.

Ragged clouds brewed above us as we left the capital. A typhoon was dumping heavy rains on Vietnam, and the edge of the storm front had shoved its way over the Southeast Asian landmass as we headed west toward the port city of Kompong Som, also known as

Sihanoukville, to refuel and pick up escorts. Strong winds buffeted the helicopter as Kershaw leveled it beneath a low ceiling. Rain from racing clouds peppered the Plexiglas windscreen. The country looked green yet barren, with few people and even fewer vehicles on the roads. I discerned hills to the north and south, their peaks muted by rain and fog. Forty minutes later we swung over Kompong Som and Kershaw pointed to still-visible hulks of two patrol boats lying on the bottom of the harbor. They had been sunk by the U.S. Navy in 1975 during the affair. I photographed the scene as we circled to land at a military installation to pick up the rest of our entourage.

With two Cambodian escorts now aboard, the helicopter lifted off and headed over water. As if on command, the sun broke through to the west for a perfect photo op as a wide shaft of sunlight beamed down onto Koh Tang.

The island looked hospitable enough, with swaying palms and lazy swells of azure water undulating over coral formations at the entrances of three beaches, one in the center and two northern ones opposite each other on the east and west sides of the island. The violence that took place here was hard to imagine until the pilot mentioned it as he banked the helicopter above the twin engines of a Khmer Rouge patrol boat lying side by side on the ocean floor. Near a small knoll on the island, an odd circular clearing was still distinct. From the accounts I had read, I wondered if that was where a 15,000-pound BLU-82 "daisy cutter" bomb had been dropped. It certainly looked like we had come to the right place.

Just off the north tip of the island, a ship lay at anchor—a surreal sight—right at the place where the *Mayaguez* was reported to have been held twenty years earlier. This ship was the USS *Brunswick*, an American salvage rig. The *Brunswick* was the first U.S. Navy vessel allowed to penetrate Cambodian waters since the close of the war. On this breakthrough mission, 110 personnel from the *Brunswick* and 22 from the JTF-FA were there to attempt recovery of the remains of eighteen MIAs left behind after the battle launched to free the *Mayaguez*.

As we circled the island, I noticed a row of blue tents lined up along the eastern beach. The whole setup looked oddly idyllic, and I could not help but hope one of those beachfront bedrooms was reserved for

Lieutenant Colonel King and me. My eyes then swept across the beaches where, according to accounts, the battle had raged arguably as fiercely as any that our military has encountered. We landed beside an Mi-6 helicopter, a Soviet-built aircraft flown by the Cambodian Air Force. It had brought local military personnel for a briefing.

Lieutenant Colonel King and I were met by air force captain John Collie, the JTF-FA detachment commander, and as we were led past the Mi-6 toward our tent, Collie briefed us on the living conditions and rules. A gravity-feed shower was set up behind a sand berm and a privy was fifty yards away from that. He pointed out the areas that had been swept by Explosive Ordnance Disposal (EOD) for mines, telling me where I could and could not go.

The last tent in the chain was indeed reserved for us. The shelter was a sturdy-looking walled affair with two cots and a pair of folding chairs inside. Zippered access included a mosquito screen.

Standing outside nearby were four Cambodian guards, armed with AK-47s. Some sixty Cambodians were involved in guarding the island and providing work details for the recovery operation. We tossed our gear on the cots and folding chairs, and then I grabbed a pack of Marlboros from my camera bag. I do not smoke, but it seems most Asian males do. There is no stigma to smoking here, and I've learned that the offering of a cigarette, or better yet a pack, can avoid a good amount of unpleasantness. I approached the guards, and considering the proximity to Thailand, spoke some Thai to them. To my delight, one of them answered immediately. It turned out his mother was Thai. I asked about duty on the island. The Thai-speaker said, "No good. We get paid [nine dollars] a month, and there are no women here." He said the troops did a three-month stint on the island before returning to the naval garrison at Ream. I mentioned how nice the view was, then produced the Marlboro pack. Their faces broke into grins.

Having made a stab at bonding with the security personnel, I began to explore the island with Lieutenant Colonel King.

As we walked the battlefield that day, I felt as though time had been suspended for two decades. Ringing the east beach were fortifications, machine-gun pits, bunkers, and trenches—overgrown with vegetation but basically undisturbed. One bunker had the remnants of a substantial tree next to it that been hit by an artillery round. Burn marks started about three feet from the ground. The trunk had been severed and the rest had fallen into the gun pit. Cambodians had likely perished there.

Along the trench lines, shell casings, shrapnel, mortar rounds, and artillery ammunition were everywhere. Palm trees pocked with bullet holes surrounded a clearing where a Khmer Rouge camp had been. One tree had a six-inch hole blasted through the trunk, but remarkably remained alive. Another had bullet holes from a machine gun running up its trunk and larger holes that went clear through. It had not survived.

Just off the beach, the rotor head from a helicopter jutted from the surf at low tide. Farther south, what was left of another one lay under gentle swells that lapped the shore.

Here a fierce battle had taken place, one involving only combatants. No civilians were killed in any cross fire, no homes destroyed, no hospitals hit. Along this bitterly contested beach, brave men on both sides had fought for every grain of sand.

The salvage crew from the USS *Brunswick* had donned flak vests and scuba gear. They were diving in shallow surf 150 feet from shore where the main wreckage from one of the helicopters had been located. A lot of wreckage had already been hauled ashore and was spread out along the beach.

The *Brunswick* crew used a block and tackle to pull big pieces in. On a charred section of helicopter tail-ramp, white phosphorous from a leaky mortar round had collected. As the phosphorous dried in the sun, it mixed with ambient oxygen and the ramp burst into flames. After twenty years, the hulk of this helicopter was not through burning! The fire was quickly brought under control, but an ominous stench hung in the air.

The salvage crew went back to work. Over the recovery site, they had placed cofferdams, boxes eight by sixteen feet in size that were open on top and bottom. The contraptions were made of quarter-inch steel plates and were lowered into the water. They stabilized the search area, preventing outside sand from backfilling as coral, sand, and wreckage were withdrawn for inspection. Near the cofferdams, two workboats containing diesel-driven pumps drew layer after layer of debris and sand from inside the steel coffers. The mixture was drawn via a suction process to screening tables set up on makeshift barges.

The complete list of the missing had been publicized neither in 1975, nor for many years thereafter, but I did have the names and locations of the Air Force losses and of one marine killed on the west beach. Having read a published account that listed the number of casualties in the burned helicopter, call sign *Knife-31*, I did the math and by lunchtime could account for the location of fifteen of the eighteen fatalities.

Lieutenant Colonel King led me to the mess tent, where I was introduced to navy lieutenant commander Robert Morash, the team medic. I asked him how things were going. "Not bad. I've treated two cases of malaria among the Cambodian security force and twenty or so cases of VD." I met Joel Patterson, a retired marine who was part of the scuba team. He was having lunch, along with the *Brunswick*'s skipper, Lieutenant Commander Paul Ricciuti, and Captain Collie. Patterson cut a dashing figure; he was tall, with thick black hair and bronze skin. He agreed to have one of the divers take me out into the bay later for an underwater look. The wind was out of the east and one-and-a-half-foot waves were breaking near the shore.

Ricciuti suggested I wait a few hours before going. "It's a little rough right now, but in an hour it'll be smooth as glass."

I sat next to Collie, who had resumed eating. Chatting with him was like listening to someone recite a speech. He had the military jargon down pat. "Our mission here with the Joint Task Force is . . ." After a while, I mentioned how I had no clue where three of the MIAs were lost. "Can you give me the names and what units they belonged to," I asked. Collie opened a looseleaf binder as if to look it up. I leaned toward him, thinking he was going to show me a list. He shut the binder. When I resumed my original position, he opened it again, stared at the page, then looked over at me. "I don't know," he said, then shut the binder with an air of finality.

One of the noncommissioned officers standing nearby turned away.

Collie obviously had a casualty list in that binder but simply could not or would not discuss details. The fact that he had something to hide greatly provoked my interest. I had returned to eating my tuna and saltines while pondering this intrigue when I overheard the sergeant who had turned away. He was talking to one of the marines standing near the food locker. He mentioned the term "machine-gun crew."

After lunch, I walked with King toward our tent, wondering if he had heard the machine-gun-crew comment.

In front of our tent, I asked, "How many in a machine-gun crew?"

He gave me a long stare. "Three . . . gunner, assistant, and ammo carrier."

"Thanks," I said and went inside, puzzled that he did not ask why I was interested in the matter. My curiosity had been piqued, and I was overwhelmed by a gnawing suspicion that those two exchanges might become the launchpad for a new direction in my life.

Thirty minutes later I peered out the tent flap. The surf was even higher than at lunchtime. Eager to get to the action, I found Patterson and declared I was ready, "smooth as *Ricciuti* glass" or not.

Patterson handed me a flak vest and snorkel mask. "Regulations," he said as he put his vest on. "In case you touch something and it goes off. Trouble is, the vest won't protect you from the concussion, and the concussion is what'll kill you. The guy that wrote the rules didn't think of that." He shrugged. "Regulations."

I wiggled into the flak vest, looped the strap of my Canon underwater camera over my head, then followed Patterson and one of the other divers to the shore.

Once underwater, it became immediately evident that this was dangerous work. The water turned murky as soon as the suction process began. As I watched and photographed the navy divers who handled the six-inch suction hoses, I kept banging into the side of the cofferdam and its strengtheners, two-inch angle iron rods that crossed from end to side in the corners.

After twenty minutes of bruising and scraping, I hauled myself over the side of the last steel coffer, swam to the sifting barge, and climbed aboard. Anthropologist Scott Law was hovering over one of the screening tables, spraying detritus from the suction hose onto a screen.

What was coming up after twenty years was astonishing.

Inside and from under sections of the helicopter came teeth, as well as arms, legs, fingers, ribs, and jawbones. The team brought up a total of 161 pieces of human remains, plus personal effects mixed in with live and exploded ammunition.

One thigh bone had shattered six inches below the hip. "The injury was perimortem," occurring before or at the time of death, according to anthropologist Law. He pointed to a tiny triangular gap in the fracture. "Hit right here, by a bullet or piece of shrapnel with high energy," he said. Holding this relic in my hand quickly brought home the level of suffering these men endured in their last moments. In addition to bodily remains, 144 personal items and 101 pieces of equipment were recovered.

Law also mentioned that technicians at the army's Central Identification Laboratory in Hawaii and at the Armed Forces DNA Identification Laboratory in Maryland would try to confirm the identities of the recovered remains. They use dental records and a sophisticated process that matches mitochondria DNA from recovered bones with that of maternal relatives of the deceased (see Appendix A).

Found with the remains were ten G.I. helmets covered with barnacles. Inside, however, some of the helmet liners looked ready to wear. Nearby were half of a glove, a T-shirt, a sock, a marine's .45 automatic, the .38 revolver belonging to the deceased copilot, Second Lieutenant Richard Vandegeer, a radio headset, a flashlight, M-16 rifle parts that had warped in the heat, and an armory's worth of ammunition. A crew member's checklist came up, still readable after twenty years in salt water. A cockpit seat was pulled to the surface and brought ashore to somber viewing. The positioning of the armor on one side indicated that it was Second Lieutenant Vandegeer's seat.

Most of the friendly ordnance onboard had detonated in the blazing inferno that consumed the chopper. The rotor head rose out of the depths toned to a macabre blue tint from a high-temperature magnesium fire. There were enemy AK-47 and .30- and .50-caliber machine-gun bullets plus rocket-propelled-grenade fragments, including two rounds that had not exploded. As I watched items come up, the barge tilted ominously. The sea had become rougher, and the wind shifted from out of the east. Diesel fumes from the workboats blew right on us, no matter where we stood on the barge. After fifteen minutes, I began to feel woozy, so I snapped a few more photos, then dove over the side for shore.

The underwater recovery operation was put on hold at 4:00 P.M. The team quit early, intending to watch a recorded video message sent in that morning by the commandant of the Marine Corps on the occasion of the Corps's 220th birthday. The tape was mandatory viewing for all marines. The *Brunswick*'s skipper, Lieutenant Commander Ricciuti, and his executive officer, Lieutenant Neil Voje, returned in duty whites for the occasion. As the tape celebrating marine accomplishments was being set up, dark slate clouds slid overhead from the east, erasing any notion of a festive mood. The air became leaden and moist. Fronds of coconut trees hung limp, their leaves drooping and languid above the tent row. Then a breath of wind picked up, slowly but with increasing tempo. The sea turned ugly as waves came rolling in, breaking right over the stern of the workboats. In minutes, the two boats were swamped and high surf began tearing one of the barges loose.

"All hands turn to," someone shouted.

Navy and JTF-FA personnel went to work. Suction pumps on the workboats were turned on full blast in an attempt to bail the craft. Towering streams of water gushed from the pumps skyward and got whipped into froth by the rising wind. Every few seconds, another swell would roll through, dumping a fresh load of seawater inside the boats. The *Brunswick*'s skipper and his exec waded in to help, white uniforms, ribbons, and all. Lieutenant Voje tried to stabilize the sifting raft and wound up getting his leg tangled in ropes. The raft swung perilously toward an A-frame barge. A few tense moments later, another seaman managed to shove the barge clear and free the lieutenant.

The sky was almost black now with the impending typhoon. Rain came on softly at first as the men tried to keep the boats afloat, but as the sun disappeared, so did the workboats, down to the bottom of the cove. The men hauled lines out from shore, tying them to the submerged bow and stern of each boat, then lashing the ends to tree trunks and rocks on the beach. Using block and tackle, brawn and human ingenuity, they labored long into the night in a man-versus-nature tug-of-war trying to pull the workboats to shore.

Then forty-knot winds and driving rain arrived. Tents swayed. Portable power went out. Still the men toiled in diesel-covered surf trying to keep their craft from being taken by the sea and storm.

"Just tie 'em in," someone shouted above the din.

I joined the effort along with Lieutenant Colonel King, and we found ourselves quickly covered in a film of diesel fuel. As each wave passed, torsos got exposed to the driving wind. Pores raged at the assault, and lungs burned from inhaled fumes. Still we pulled on the ropes, trying to ease the boats ashore.

By 10:00 P.M. both Lieutenant Colonel King and I were spent. Lines had been secured to the sunken vessels and barges. Nothing more could be done until daylight.

"I'm army," King said, followed by a sigh, "and you're air force. This is navy business." We staggered to our tent and crawled onto our cots, not that sleep was in the picture.

Lightning exploded overhead.

"Man, that was close," King said.

Dime-sized drops began drumming against the tent. Then the rain drove harder. It thrashed in furious sheets, pinging like hail against the sides of the shelter. I got onto my cot and shoved my back against the wall of the tent to keep it from collapsing. The tent began to sway and the poles strained. I was just beginning to wonder how safe we really were this close to the water's edge when suddenly a tremendous weight—like a linebacker's—landed on me and pinned me to the cot. I could hear canvas begin to rip, and the cot frame creaked from the strain.

"Roger," I announced, "I can't move."

Lieutenant Colonel King spun in his cot and shoved his feet against the tent roof, which had filled with water and collapsed on top of me. It triggered a case of the giggles in King as he pushed water out of the canvas folds. Several long seconds later, enough water had cleared that I could raise myself to a seated position on the cot. I groped around for my camera and took one photo as the ridgepole tore itself from the floor. A folding chair went flying, and the whole tent collapsed on top of us.

We wallowed stupidly for a few moments until I found the end of my cot. I pushed off it, crawling in pitch blackness toward where I thought the opening was located. Finding a zipper, I pulled it open and squeezed outside. The entire bivouac was leveled, a flattened mass across which wind and rain streamed, beating upon loose tent fabric that flailed in protest like wounded birds.

"Stay put!" I suggested to King. "We need some weight to keep this thing from leaving town!" The lieutenant colonel had no problem with that.

Amid the blackness above, lightning crackled and thunder boomed. I caught momentary glimpses of wind and wave sweeping the beach. Blowing sand stung my eyes. The rain was icy cold. In seconds I was soaked to the bone and shivering. A line of coconut trunks swayed as their fronds battled to stay attached to the tops. Near shore, I saw a shadow of a man bent low and staggering in the night like someone under a flickering disco strobe light. I yelled at him, but he could not hear me above the raging storm, so I made my way over and grabbed onto him. He faced me with eyes that seemed vacant, unconcerned.

"I need help," I yelled. "Our tent has blown over."

"They're *all* flat," he answered. "Wait until it blows over!"

"Huh? This is a goddam typhoon!"

He shrugged but followed me to the side of the tent. A pile of filled sandbags had been stacked nearby. We hauled two over, then pounded the tent pegs into waterlogged sand and threw the bags on top. We tried to raise the tent, with Roger King straightening the poles from inside. The wind ripped the pegs from underneath the sandbags, and again the tent blew over. We got more bags, pulled the tent up, and pounded the pegs in again. Next we stacked two or three sandbags on each tent peg. The shelter strained with the wind but held fast. I thanked my phantomlike helper and asked if he needed aid with his tent. He waved me off and disappeared into the deluge, so I crawled inside the tent, righted my cot, and fell on it. Everything was soaked, caked with sand, but I couldn't have cared less. The rest of the night became one long, fitful attempt at sleep.

By sunrise, the island looked like the morning after a hobo reunion. Drenched men were staggering around dazed and exhausted. Most had slept on the ground under collapsed tents. Scott Law was asleep on a food locker inside the still-standing mess tent. I learned the man who helped me during the night was army staff sergeant Clark Sorenson.

Our efforts of the previous evening and during the tent affair had helped King and me blend in with the recovery team. Now I mostly kept quiet and stayed out of the way. I did not want to be airlifted or shipped back to the mainland because of the sudden shortage of tents.

Looking seaward, the lines we had tied were still attached to the workboats, their tops barely visible above the somewhat calmer surf. It took two hours at low tide to get the first boat afloat. It was hauled to the side of the *Brunswick*. Then the other one was brought up and towed to the ship. The barges were pulled ashore, while the team prepared for a media visit scheduled for 10:00 A.M.

A boat was on its way from the mainland with Michael Hayes, editor of the *Phnom Penh Post*, photographers, and stringers from the *Bangkok Post* and *CBS News*. Hayes is an American ex-pat, who with his former wife Kathleen edits and publishes one of two biweekly English-language newspapers in the Cambodian capital. Hayes and his ex tolerate each other while their views of government and corruption are barely tolerated by the Phnom Penh power structure. That toleration is tenuous, and these two publish at no small peril.

With the workboats out of action, the JTF-FA team set up their workstations on the beach.

"We're going to fake it," Lieutenant Colonel King told me.

Screening tables were lined up and various items from the recovery were placed on tables. The briefing tent, a parachute strung between three trees, had been ripped to pieces by the storm, so the briefing was moved inside the mess tent.

At 10:30, a fishing trawler arrived with the media. All of the news reps, four men and one woman, staggered onto the beach, seasick from a turbulent ride on the still-roiling sea. They did not seem to notice the diesel smell wafting in from the surf, nor the barges strewn along the beach. They focused on the wreckage piled on the sand.

Lieutenant Colonel King had suggested I not mention the absent workboats. The unspoken message was clear: my stay would be over if I chose not to follow his wishes. So I stood among the media, mouth tightly closed, as we were briefed by King on the items so far accumulated, then watched a demonstration of the sand-screening process. No bones were displayed since the JTF-FA has a rule against photography of remains. The media reps took notes of the progress made and photos of the helmets and other paraphernalia displayed on the tables outside the mess tent. The whole visit lasted an hour and a half before the boat headed back to Kompong Som with its weary passengers aboard. Thankfully, I was not among them.

The afternoon was spent continuing the repair of the site. Salvage efforts resumed the next day using one workboat, since the engine of the other craft refused to run. Only a few bone fragments came up. Two days later, the search shifted to a beach on the west side. We crossed from the east through tall grass, then into thick brush. I followed King as he bulled his way through. Then we hit a path that ended at a berm. Topping the berm, I was able to see a narrow stretch of shoreline. From the accounts, this was where an air force helicopter had brought in the first group of marines, only to crash offshore while trying to escape a determined Khmer cross fire. Here was where a frantic night pullout by the marine force had taken place.

A corroded shell case lay on the ground in front of a Khmer bunker. Under the sand near the rocky outcropping a few yards away was an empty M-16 cartridge. One could almost smell the fear and hear the echo of AK-47 rounds pinging off the rocks and visualize exhausted marines struggling through surf, firing as they lunged onto the ramp of a rescue helicopter.

Somewhere a mile or more offshore, the remnants of the downed helicopter lay in deep water. As I watched, Joel Patterson and the team in full scuba gear went diving from a Zodiac in search of the wreckage and its missing flight mechanic, Staff Sergeant Elwood Rumbaugh. He had drowned after saving his copilot, Lieutenant Karl W. Poulsen. Rumbaugh was posthumously awarded the Air Force Cross.

After three hours, the divers gave up the search. No other formal exploration was conducted on the western side of Koh Tang while I was on the island.

Back in the mess tent, a new subject had come up about a witness report from 1985. A Cambodian source had related that an American had been wounded sometime after the Koh Tang assault and was then executed.

The witness provided unusually specific details regarding the burial, stating that the body was located "close to a stream, on the eastern side of the island between a well and two *sone* (fruit) trees."

Hearing this, I wondered if this tale might be about one of the three unaccounted-for MIAs? Captain Collie was unwilling to provide further details.

A brick-lined well, partly covered with thick weeds, was found later by Master Sergeant Robert Maves. The Cambodians pointed out one tree they claimed was a *sone*, but it had no fruit. Regardless, JTF-FA personnel staked out the area from the tree back to the well and began an excavation. Six trenches about five feet apart were sectioned off, the idea being that an average adult Caucasian body would project into the trench unless it was aligned with the trench cut. If nothing was found, then new trenches would be cut perpendicular to the old ones, making a crosshatched grid from which no prone human body could escape detection.

Cambodian laborers dug the sand and carried it in buckets to a screening table set up just offshore. One of the troops from the JTF-FA unit manned the table. A decidedly low level of enthusiasm accompanied the effort. The effects of the storm, the lingering odor of diesel fuel, and the sight of the once pristine cove turned murky with silt from the screening table kept everyone in a gloomy state.

By this time, the recovery team members had seen plenty of sun, wind, and rain and sucked in more than enough fumes. At noon I was told to be ready to return to the mainland the next morning. Closure of the recovery operation had been advanced from the end of the month to the fifteenth, the next day.

I decided to visit the west beach one more time to see if I could figure out where a machine gun might have been positioned. Having no wish to slog my way through the jungle again, I went to the guard near my tent, the one that spoke Thai. I pointed west and asked him if a path I'd spotted south of our tent went to the beach.

"Yes" was the answer.

I thanked him, handed him the last pack of Marlboros I had on me, slung my camera bag over a shoulder, and headed off. Having walked fifty yards, I was under a dense canopy of leaves. After a few turns in the route, I had no idea which direction I was headed. With the beach only about three hundred yards distant from my start point, I was certain I would hit the coast sometime soon. I pushed on another two hundred yards and saw no sign of any beach up ahead. I stopped to get my bearings, wondering if it were best to just turn around and retrace my steps. Maybe I had missed a junction in the trail. A sound from behind caught my attention. Glancing back, I froze. Not ten yards behind me on the trail stood a Cambodian I had not seen before. He wore flip-flops and a ragtag uniform unlike the ones seen in camp. A shiver ran through me. Where was the Marlboro man when you really needed him?

The Cambodian continued to stand in the center of the trail, his AK-47 at the ready, but not pointing at me. The Khmer Rouge were still very much active in the country, and this guy looked like he could be part of that group. He certainly did not seem amused at my presence. Maybe he spoke Thai.

"*Poud passa Thai?*" I asked. (Do you speak Thai?)

He looked around, as if to be sure there was no one within earshot. "A little," he finally said, sounding like a native Thai.

I told him I was looking for the beach, but was lost.

"Follow me," he ordered.

He had the gun, so I followed.

The Cambodian moved past me on the trail, which turned left, then dropped down a short slope before leveling out again. We moved at a brisk pace with him looking over his shoulder at each trail intersection to see that I was still with him. After about a quarter of a mile, a clearing appeared. There were three structures, houses of some sort, in the clearing, but no one was around. By now, I was able to determine we were headed south. I told the Cambodian I was looking for the west beach. He paid me no heed, instead pointing with his rifle straight ahead where the trail continued south. I had some concern about land mines, but from the look of the trail, it was well traveled. Of course, that's where you'd put a land mine if you were so disposed.

After a quarter of a mile, we came upon another clearing, a compound of sorts. I saw a radio antenna strung up on a long pole above what looked like a communications shack. Nearby was a house on stilts. Underneath the house stood five Cambodians. Against a back wall leaned a group of AK-47s, B-40 grenade launchers, and a pair of M-16s. I relaxed, realizing that these guys were probably part of the security force and this was in all likelihood the main island headquarters.

My Cambodian companion told me to stay below. He then took the steps to the upper level. Meanwhile, I became the subject of discussion among the Cambodians. I had kept my cameras out of sight and had no intention of making anything of value visible. I certainly had nothing to offer in the way of hospitality. After what seemed like a long five minutes, my Cambodian guide came back down the steps ahead of another man, dressed in civilian clothes. The new man had a dark unshaven chin. It was obvious he had just awakened, and what was also obvious was the fact that he was unhappy with the interruption.

The new man was apparently the leader of the unit. I stuck out my hand and he hesitated, then gave the weakest of handshakes. He offered no courtesies, no invitation inside, no tea, nothing. He did not respond to my Thai, speaking only Cambodian to the guard who led me there. He wanted to know why I was here. "On my way to the beach," I answered. More discussion followed, the gist of which seemed to be that I did not belong in the interior of the island. I was getting a little spooked. They all had guns. I had a pair of cameras and a notebook. I spotted another path that seemed to be headed east, so I asked if the beach was in that direction, hoping I might get there, turn north, and find myself back at the campsite unscathed.

"The beach is there," my Cambodian escort said.

"Fine. I'll be leaving now." I simply walked away from the group, feeling very vulnerable. No one tried to stop me. When I was well out of sight of the compound, I looked back. My escort was closing the distance as I pushed ahead. A minute later, I reached shore. A white strand of coastline curved away in both directions. It was a beach I had seen from the air, to the south of where we landed. To the north, it gradually swung around to where the island jutted out into the sea. I headed that way along the coast until I was certain I was near our camp. Then I moved into the jungle, mines be damned. The guard stayed right behind me. After another twenty minutes thrashing my way through vines and brush, I broke out into an open marsh. On the other side, I could see the blue tents of our bivouac. A look over my shoulder revealed the guard had turned back.

I was relieved at having gotten back in one piece but felt frustrated at failing in my attempt to discover where a machine-gun team might have been located. Disappointment only served to heighten my interest. If a machine-gun crew had died during the battle, why the secrecy?

Later that afternoon a harness belt was found at the dig site near the *sone* tree. It was a stout-looking strap, probably from one of the helicopters. The digging intensified.

The next morning, most team members were loading gear for the return home when bones were discovered near the well. These were taken for analysis by another anthropologist, Bruce Anderson, who had just arrived that day. Digging continued, but the majority of the personnel busied themselves with packing for departure.

At noon, I bid farewell to my Thai-speaking guard, and gave him one last pack of Marlboros, which I had found stashed in our tent. He tucked the pack in his shirt pocket then looked around at the magnitude of the recovery operation unwinding on the beach. "Cambodian bones very cheap. American bones very expensive," he said.

We boarded the Lao West Coast helicopter for Phnom Penh, but after we landed, King got an urgent call on his cell phone. His two-star boss had arrived, intending to visit the island, and went ballistic when he discovered the site had been closed. I said my good-byes as King and several team members headed for the helicopter to make ready for an impromptu backtrack to the island. The general was going to see Koh Tang no matter what.

Upon my return from Asia, I continued my search for more details regarding the three MIAs whose locations at death were still a mystery. It took two tries before Lieutenant Colonel King from the Public Affairs Office at JTF-FA returned my call and revealed that the three individuals were in fact a machine-gun crew from 3rd Platoon, E Company that had landed on the western shore. They had been inadvertently left behind but were presumed to have been killed before the pullout. Then why the secrecy? One other casualty, Lance Corporal Ashton Loney, was shot and killed while on patrol during the battle and his body had not been brought out. That was no secret.

If everyone left behind was dead, how come there was the 1985 account describing the killing of an American soldier? Then I was told by the Public Affairs Office that maybe the three had not died during the battle, and there was sensitivity over anyone claiming that those marines had been abandoned. I learned that the bones found near the *sone* trees were not of human origin, but I felt that somewhere in the thick jungle cover of Koh Tang there surely lay factual clues to what did happen. Everything else seemed to still be there. I had the unsettling knowledge that information had been suppressed during the recovery operation and not nearly enough had been done to clear things up in the years since, all of which pushed me toward trying to find out what had really happened in 1975.

Researching a ship seizure, a battle, and the final weeks in the lives of three men who disappeared one terrible night two decades earlier might seem like a straightforward undertaking. It could have turned out that way, but instead I found myself venturing forth against legend and the faded memories of still-wary witnesses. Many neither wanted to tell their story nor wanted this story made public, for various reasons, yet I have tried to piece together the events as accurately as possible.

This book covers four days of intense activity surrounding the capture and eventual recovery of the container ship SS *Mayaguez* plus events during the ensuing weeks and years. I used material available in archives, recorded notes, and the personal recollections of those who were there on both sides of the politics and combat. As the years rolled by in my research, I began to see patterns in the testimony from American and Cambodian veterans, patterns that explained what one side or the other *perceived* was happening. In some cases I encountered conflicting testimony, and when that occurred I peered through the fog of war and postulated what most likely *did* happen (all postulations are clearly noted as such). Anything in direct quotes is either based on the work of other individuals and recorded in their writings, or was sourced by me in a formal interview, either in person or over the telephone. Some editing liberty has been taken for grammar and clarity. For a Khmer Rouge soldier to speak a word of English often meant being "sent up" to a reeducation camp from where none returned. As a result, there is no report of any substantial conversation occurring between Cambodian troops and American prisoners.

For the U.S. Marines to abandon their dead or wounded was to fly in the face of over two hundred years of tradition and heritage. The Marine Corps is understandably embarrassed by certain aspects of this history, but brave men made the ultimate sacrifice and have until now received no recognition for their heroism.

The search started on the island in 1995. Years later it shifted to the mainland and a beach grotto, then jumped a mile away to a grassy field near a dilapidated building. A weathered sign above the entrance read in English, VICTORY SIDE. Within the oval structure was a rotunda devoid of furniture, hollow really, much like the victory proclaimed by both sides.

Like the disintegrating building, the tale of the SS *Mayaguez* has not yet been washed from our memories. It began one quiet Monday in May, back in 1975. . . .

PART II

THE INCIDENT

2

THE SEIZURE OF THE *MAYAGUEZ*, MONDAY, MAY 12, 1975

The seas cannot constitute property because they cannot be occupied in the sense in which land can be occupied and that they are therefore free to all nations and subject to none.

Grotius, *Mare Liberum (Free Sea*, 1609), based on the Roman legal principle

She was a battered old hulk, the SS *Mayaguez*, black-sided and rusty from thirty-one years plying the sea-lanes. In her hold and on her cramped deck were 274 shipping containers filled with general cargo bound for the port at Sattahip in Thailand.

Onboard, Third Mate Burton B. Coombes was on watch outside the wheelhouse high above deck on a protrusion called the starboard wing. Gray-haired Coombes, at fifty-five, showed even more effects of years at sea than the ship. A convoy veteran who saw action in Lingayen Gulf during MacArthur's landing in World War II, Coombes's once-brawny chest had slid south years ago, now overlapping the belt on his khaki shorts. With his right leg shorter than his left, Coombes walked with a starboard list on tan Hush Puppies spattered with paint drippings. He had come to the starboard wing to take a bearing.

The ship was making twelve and a half knots as it steered clear of Poulo Wai, a tiny spit of land some sixty miles from the Cambodian coast and even farther from Thailand to the northwest and Vietnam to the east. Rumors of oil deposits had made all three countries pursue claims to the island. At the moment, Cambodians were the landlords. The weather was sunny, hot really, except for the constant breeze that blew over the steel containers, stacked like shoe boxes, two high and six abreast on the deck.

At 2:18 in the afternoon, Coombes bent over an azimuth circle mounted on the wing platform, intent on taking a navigation fix. He lined the crosshair on the western tip of the island, took a reading, and swung the circle a few degrees to the eastern side, spotting a patch of white on the water's surface near the island. As he finished taking the second bearing, he looked through his binoculars at what he guessed was the wake of a fishing boat. Spray was being thrown from her bow, and a red flag flapped furiously from her mast. It was no fishing boat. Coombes stepped inside the pilothouse and picked up the phone.

Sixty-two-year-old captain Charles T. Miller was in his cabin, safe door open with $21,953 stacked inside. He was counting out $5,000 in shore pay for his crew when the phone rang.

"There's a launch with a red flag comin' at us, Capt'n," Coombes announced.

"I'll be right up," Miller replied, then tossed the money back in his safe, which he left open. He had a head full of wavy salt-and-pepper hair above a weathered face and a long prominent chin. He was still spry for his age, taking the steps two at a time from his cabin to the bridge.

As Miller made his way into the wheelhouse, he saw Coombes leaning out the open starboard window, binoculars steady-on. Miller then saw the boat, still a mile away, churning its way toward the ship. He picked up his own binoculars, and the gray sliver that popped into view was easily recognized—a gunboat. He could make out a machine gun atop the pilothouse. Then he heard fifteen to twenty *pops* as tracers whipped across the *Mayaguez* bow.

"Give me maneuvering speed!" Miller ordered. Then he yelled to the crew members that were working on deck, "Get off the deck! Everybody inside."

Coombes lowered his binoculars. Maneuvering speed was used to slow the ship for tight steerage into and out of port. He jerked the engine room telephone off the bulkhead. "Maneuvering speed," he barked, then hung up the phone as another burst of gunfire rang out.

The gunboat turned to parallel the *Mayaguez* course as the ship's speed decreased. Suddenly a dark blur hurtled past the bow.

"Capt'n, there goes a goddamn rocket!" Coombes shouted. A rocket-propelled grenade (RPG) exploded, sending a geyser of water over the bow.

Miller ordered Coombes to call Wilbert "Sparks" Bock in the radio room to send out an SOS. Coombes called the radio room and gave Bock the captain's orders. He then plotted the ship's position based on the fix he had just taken and headed toward the radio room, meeting Bock coming up the ladder. Bock's hands were shaking and his voice was jittery. Coombes knew that without the coordinates an SOS would have little value, so he gave them to Bock who headed back to the radio room.

Belowdecks, First Engineer Vern Greenlin crossed the catwalk on his way to the electrical shop. He heard the insistent buzzer of the engine room telephone forty feet below. With thirty-six years' experience working in engine rooms, Greenlin assumed it was merely another routine call. He continued to the shop, then heard a bell—the stop-engines signal. Peering down through a maze of pipes and catwalks, he could see Third Engineer Al Minichiello begin to turn the throttle to the right, closing off steam to the high-pressure turbine. A stop-engines order at sea was unusual. Deep memories stirred. Twice before Greenlin had been in a tight spot, once when a Japanese torpedo blew his ship out of the water and another time when his ship ran aground and sank. Now, with a surge of adrenaline running through him, he sped down the ladder toward the engine room. His shoes hit the steel floor-plates at the bottom with a whack. Greenlin caught sight of Minichiello opening the guardian valve and red astern throttle used to brake the high-pressure turbine.

The telephone buzzer brayed again. Greenlin grabbed it.

"We're being fired upon by a Cambodian gunboat," Coombes said, then hung up.

The steam was shut down on the turbine, but the ship was still shuddering as it coasted forward. The force of the water kept turning the nineteen-foot propeller.

Greenlin and the other engine room workers who were now gathering below peered upward through seven levels of multicolored pipes and catwalks, wondering what was happening on deck.

In the wheelhouse, Captain Miller felt the pulse of the ship weaken as the *Mayaguez* slowed. Finally, all he could hear was the faint hiss of the hull as it drifted through tropical water. He was more indignant than scared as he watched the gunboat, weapons bristling, make an arrogant sweep in front of the ship.

It was an American-built PCF (patrol craft fast) or Swift boat, designed for Vietnamese river patrols. Unknown to Miller and his crew, this was one of several boats that had fallen into Khmer Rouge hands when the Lon Nol government of Cambodia collapsed nearly a month before. In the intervening time, South Vietnam had fallen to the Communists. Now both countries were trying to secure their borders and islands and take control of the massive stores of American arms and supplies left behind in the wake of their victories.

The Khmer Rouge had a two-week head start on the Vietnamese and they were wasting no time in island grabbing. They commandeered the Swift boats and quickly put all of them to use. Troops and arms were dispatched to all the islands Cambodia claimed. The Swift boat fleet seized seven Thai fishing trawlers on May 2, shot up a Korean freighter on May 4, took over seven escaping South Vietnamese vessels on May 6, and held a Panamanian ship for thirty-five hours on May 7–8.

On the prow of this particular Swift boat stood an edgy-looking Cambodian boy. He was dressed in what Westerners often call black pajamas, a shirt and baggy trousers typical in Southeast Asia among rural inhabitants. The Khmer, looking no older than fourteen or fifteen, stood spread-legged, clutching the handles of a twin .50-caliber machine gun. The barrels swung in response to the tossing of the boat as it pulled alongside the *Mayaguez*.

On the *Mayaguez* deck, Ordinary Seaman Anastasio C. Sereno heard Chief Mate James P. Newman's order, "Lower the pilot ladder."

Sereno released the ladder and it clattered against the steel sponsons as it stretched toward water.

Another boy, dressed in black garb, red headband, and sandals, leaped onto the ladder. He had a rifle slung over his shoulder. As he climbed, the gun butt banged against the ship. Then a second and third boy caught the ladder and started up. The third one lugged an RPG launcher. Four more armed Cambodians followed.

Miller watched from the starboard wing as the seven Cambodians spread out on the deck of his ship and headed his way. He stepped back into the wheelhouse. "We'll find out soon enough what these bastards want!" Then he snapped at Coombes, "Did Sparks get out the SOS?"

"I gave Sparks our position, Capt'n."

"But did he get the SOS out?"

"Sparks said he got it out . . . two or three times. Said an English ship and a Norwegian ship had received it."

Miller got on the phone to Bock and told him to use the single sideband radio and put out a Mayday.

Bock told Miller, "Jeeze, I can't take a chance. If they catch me they're going to shoot me."

"Get in and lock the door," Miller said. "Don't use the CW [continuous wave radio]. Talk on the single sideband; it makes no noise outside of [your] voice."

The first Cambodian to come through the wheelhouse door was Khmer Rouge battalion commander Sa Mean. He was Miller's height, about five-foot six. Sa Mean seemed older than the other ones who came up the ladder, in his mid-thirties, and he was definitely in charge. An AK-47 was slung over his shoulder and he carried a U.S. Army field pack radio. Three others followed him into the wheelhouse.

"Speak English?" Miller asked.

Sa Mean shook his head.

"*Parlez-vous Français?*"

Again the Khmer shook his head. He inspected the radar, which was off because it was broken, then examined the telemotor and gyropilot. Finally, he pointed to the chart room next door and motioned for Miller to go in.

Inside, Sa Mean glanced at the navigation chart. He put his finger on Poulo Wai, the nearby island. Then he picked up a pencil and drew a small anchor behind the island indicating where he wanted Miller to take the ship. They returned to the wheelhouse and the Cambodian pointed at the gunboat, which was already moving toward the island. He meant for Miller to follow.

"Keep her pointed at the stern of that gunboat," Miller ordered the helmsman. Miller then reached for the telephone, but Sa Mean waved the barrel of his gun and shook his head. Miller decided the Cambodian must think it was a radio, so instead he reached for the ship's manual telegraph, which was connected by cable to the engine room. He shoved the arm forward to the half-ahead position. A few moments later, Miller felt faint vibrations as the ship got under way. Half-ahead would not be enough to keep up with the gunboat, but Miller was in no hurry to anchor.

Third Mate David C. English was a twenty-eight-year-old ex-Marine who had been shot twice during combat in Vietnam. At 250 pounds, with carrot-colored hair no better organized than the grass in a vacant lot, English had a temper that flared easily. He saw the boarding party clamber aboard and had already decided not to take any crap off any Cambodians. Upon reaching the wheelhouse, though, he saw Miller dealing with four armed Khmers, so English slipped away. He would need more than brawn to turn things around there. He decided he wanted first to be sure that Sparks had gotten off a good SOS.

As soon as English was out of sight of the Cambodians, he beat feet down to the radio shack. There was no lock on the door, so English bulled his way in.

"Be quiet," Sparks whispered, his hands shaking. "They'll come in here and kill us."

English looked at the log. Blank. Sparks swore he had gotten out an auto alarm, which triggers all ships' alarms within radio range. English was not sure Sparks had come up on the air to tell the ships what the problem was. The auto alarm would simply tell that the *Mayaguez* was in distress and what the coordinates were. English grabbed the mike on the single sideband radio and shouted, "Mayday, Mayday, Mayday."

English waited for a reply. A Philippine tugboat came up first, but the operator had difficulty understanding him. A moment later, an

Australian came on the air. English read the coordinates and radioed, "Call the American authorities. Call anywhere you can." Then English heard the Aussie relay the *Mayaguez* position.

English listened to be sure that the coordinates were right, then he transmitted again. "You may be the last English voice I hear for a long time."

"Things can't be that bad, mate," replied the Australian.

English took another look at Sparks, then shook his head as he began giving continuous updates to anyone who would listen.

The *Mayaguez* began making four knots behind the gunboat, which led the way to the east side of Poulo Wai. Meanwhile Miller slipped out of the wheelhouse and made his way back to his cabin. He wanted to destroy his "alfa envelope," a classified message issued to U.S. mariners by Washington that tells a captain where to sail his boat in time of war. When he got to his cabin, he took the envelope and poured lighter fluid on it, then set it afire in a metal trash can. He saw that his safe was still open, so he took seventeen thousand dollars out, leaving only five thousand dollars inside before locking it. He hid the rest under a wooden drawer.

As the ship came around in deep water just off the island, Miller made it back to the wheelhouse. He could see a tower from which the Cambodians apparently kept lookout for passing ships. The gunboat sped off, dropping anchor next to a bamboo jetty. Twenty men in black pajamas streamed aboard the gunboat.

By now it was after four. Miller hoped to drop anchor as far away from the island as possible, but the Cambodian wanted the ship in closer. Miller led Sa Mean into the chart room and pointed to a spot on the map where he intended to anchor. The Cambodian was unconvinced, but Miller had the bosun start lowering the anchor chain anyway. Sa Mean began to get agitated, now wanting Miller to take the ship to the port at Ream, near Kompong Som on the coast. Miller wanted no part of that since the radar was out and he would be going into an unfamiliar port without it. He turned on the radar in an attempt to show that it did not work and that travel at night would be too dangerous. Still, Sa Mean was unconvinced. He began stabbing his finger at Ream on the chart. By now, the new batch of armed Khmers were scampering aboard the *Mayaguez* and fanning out on deck.

Miller could see that he was on the losing end of the argument, so he had the bosun begin hauling up the anchor. Then Miller tried once again to convey the hazard involved in sailing at night without radar. With his hands, he pantomimed the ship hitting rocks and sinking.

The Cambodian finally got the message. He made a call on his field-pack radio, after which he said to Miller, "Okay."

With that, Miller once again ordered the bosun to drop anchor. At 4:55 in the afternoon, the ship's anchor splashed into the sea. The SS *Mayaguez* had been seized.

3

THE WHITE HOUSE RESPONDS

Who desires peace, should prepare for war . . . no one dare
offend or insult a power of recognized superiority in action.

Vegetius, *Military Institutions of the Romans*

Oil survey employee John Neal of Delta Exploration Company was sitting in the company radio room in Jakarta, Indonesia, Monday afternoon of May 12 when he heard a panic call over the radio: "Have been fired upon and boarded by Cambodian armed forces at nine degrees forty-eight minutes north/one hundred two degrees fifty-three minutes east. Ship is being towed to unknown Cambodian port." Neal notified the U.S. embassy in Jakarta and maintained intermittent contact with the ship for almost two hours until transmissions finally faded. Simultaneously, reports were also being relayed by other radio listeners, including the Defense Attaché Office in Manila. By 5:12 A.M.

Eastern Standard Time, the first dispatch reached the National Military Command Center (NMCC) in Washington.

The news worked its way up the chain of command, taking another two hours to reach the Situation Room at the White House. President Gerald Ford got his first inkling of a predicament during his morning briefing from Brent Scowcroft, then his deputy assistant for national security affairs, and David Peterson, the CIA representative responsible for the president's daily intelligence report.

Scowcroft, a West Point graduate and an air force lieutenant general, was highly regarded by both Ford and the White House staff. He gave the president a rundown on recent Cambodian incidents at sea before relating the current dilemma. The briefing took twenty minutes.

"We've got a little crisis," President Ford said. "I don't know why it is, but these crises always seem to occur on Monday." Ford looked fit and relaxed after a weekend of golf, tennis, and swimming. Very quickly, however, his demeanor changed to one seriously focused on the problem at hand.

In assessing the mood or intentions of the Cambodians, Ford was given little to go on. The identities of the Khmer Rouge leaders were still uncertain. What was known was the rapidity with which they had expelled Westerners from Phnom Penh along with the city's population and the reports of seizures or harassment of shipping the preceding weeks. The president also had recently learned from intelligence accounts that the Khmer Rouge ordered the killing of all officials of the defunct pro-West Lon Nol government, including family members. In fact, executions were being expanded to include virtually anyone with "bourgeois" education.

"My feeling is," Ford continued, "if they are going to take control not only of the ship, but of the personnel, it is a serious matter."

Over in the State Department building Secretary of State and National Security Adviser Henry Kissinger arrived at 8:00 A.M. for his twice-weekly staff meeting. Twenty or so assistants and undersecretaries waited as Kissinger bustled in for the routine session. Going around the table Kissinger asked each bureau head to update him on key issues facing their office. When he came to J. Owen Zurhellen, Jr., the deputy assistant secretary of state for East Asia, he reported, "An American ship has been captured by Cambodians about a hundred miles off the coast and is proceeding into Sihanoukville under Cambodian troop guard."

Kissinger was astounded. "How can that be?" His question was addressed as much to the event as to the casual way the information was relayed.

Zurhellen soon realized the importance Kissinger placed on the revelation as he got bombarded with questions from an increasingly testy secretary of state. When Kissinger learned that Zurhellen was informed of the hijacking only two minutes prior to the meeting, the secretary asked that a call be placed to Scowcroft at the White House. Kissinger closed the meeting with, "I know you damned well cannot let Cambodia capture a ship a hundred miles at sea and do nothing."

Meanwhile, White House press secretary Ron Nessen showed up at the Oval Office for his daily session with President Ford to discuss the day's anticipated media questions.

Ford announced, "Well, I have some bad news to give you." He filled Nessen in on the crisis, then asked, "What would you do? Would you go in there and bomb the Cambodian boat and take a chance of the Americans being killed? Would you send helicopters in there? Would you mine every harbor in Cambodia?"

Nessen offered no answers, sensing that all the president wanted to do was make the point that being president meant he alone had the responsibility for the tough calls.

At 9:20 A.M. Kissinger arrived at the White House to meet with the president and was joined by Scowcroft.

Meanwhile, the National Military Command Center in the Pentagon had not remained idle. Orders had already been given to Admiral Noel Gayler, commander in chief of the U.S. Pacific Command (PACOM) in Hawaii, to launch reconnaissance flights in an effort to locate the *Mayaguez*.

Shortly after nine-thirty that morning, Ford finished consulting with Kissinger and Scowcroft and decided to call a meeting of the National Security Council (NSC). The council convened at 12:05 P.M. and included the president's inner circle: Kissinger, Scowcroft, Vice President Nelson Rockefeller; Secretary of Defense James R. Schlesinger and Deputy Defense Secretary William Clements; CIA director William Colby; Deputy Secretary of State Robert Ingersoll; the NSC staff member responsible for East Asia, W. Richard Smyser; White House chief of staff Donald Rumsfeld; and air force chief of staff David C. Jones. Jones was substituting for JCS chairman General George S. Brown who was in Europe on a NATO inspection.

At this, the first of several NSC meetings, powerful personalities, often at odds with each other, began grappling with the problem.

Colby reported that the hijacked ship was proceeding under her own power, estimated at ten miles an hour, and "would be in or near the port now." At that point, Schlesinger piped in with, "When I left the Pentagon, the ship was already about ten miles out."

The information had been forwarded up the chain of command where staffers had condensed and refined it. Initial questions about how far from the nearest Cambodian port the incident occurred and how fast the ship travels were researched and answered: "Sixty miles to Kompong Som and ten knots." Someone looked at a watch, did a little arithmetic, and the location passed to Colby soon became "in or near the port now," finally refined to Schlesinger as precisely "ten miles out." In this case an educated guess had quickly been upgraded to the level of being stated as a fact. Actually, at the time of this meeting no one in the communication link had a clear idea where the ship was or if it was still under power, but vague answers show weakness and no one wanted to appear weak. Later Kissinger would remark, "We were treated to a detailed intelligence briefing by Colby which turned out to be wrong in every detail."

Kissinger and Schlesinger began an exchange over what should be done to free the crew. With the instincts of a politician, Kissinger opened with, "I think we should make a strong statement and give a note to the Cambodians, via the Chinese, so that we can get some credit if the boat is released. I also suggest some show of force." Then he said, "Perhaps we can seize a Cambodian ship on the high seas." When Schlesinger expressed doubts that the Cambodians had any ships, Kissinger shifted to suggesting the mining of the Cambodian harbor at Kompong Som. Schlesinger said without any hesitation, "We can get mines in within twenty-four hours." The fact that the mines in question were carried by Navy aircraft and the carrier would not be near the scene for days was overlooked by Schlesinger. General Jones noted that his B-52s could deliver mines, but Schlesinger pointed out, "The mines are in Subic; the B-52s are in Thailand." However, in 1975 no B-52s were even there.

Schlesinger was still sensitive over the military debacles in Saigon and Phnom Penh weeks earlier. He proceeded cautiously, answering questions while offering little in the way of suggestions.

Kissinger pegged Schlesinger as being clearly repulsed by the idea of reengaging in Indochina so soon. Kissinger felt the Pentagon, being less than enthusiastic, would fulfill orders without any additional initiative on their part, the practical effect being the same as procrastination.

The absence of General Brown, JCS chairman, magnified the problem because his stand-in, General Jones, would be reluctant to use direct access to the president, which is the chairman's prerogative by law. As a result, anything the generals and admirals had in mind would first go through Schlesinger's ambivalent filter.

Vice President Rockefeller chimed in with the broader political impact that might result from a strong response. "Getting out a message and getting people ready will not do it," he said. North Korea had been sounding more belligerent in the wake of the collapse of Saigon and Phnom Penh. "I think a violent response is in order." To Rockefeller the possibility of a second Korean War loomed. "There is an old Chinese saying about a dagger hitting steel and withdrawing when it hits . . . and that is the impression that we should convey." Never mind that "steel" was not around in old China, the point was made on Ford.

Referring to Rockefeller's "violent response," Ford said, "I think that is what we will do. We will turn around the *Coral Sea*. We will get the mining ready. We will take action."

Ford's "I think," and "get . . . ready" sounded too indecisive for Kissinger. He felt the need to personally turn it into *specific* action and on *his* order. "If it is not released by Wednesday," Kissinger announced, "we will mine."

The secretary of defense was backed by General Jones, who wanted time to "get our contingency plans together," to provide practical options. Both men avoided suggesting force as the way to get the crew freed, while Kissinger and the vice president proposed bold military measures. "Henry was an incorrigible signal-sender, even when it might [be] dangerous," Schlesinger later recalled.

Not satisfied with simply giving orders, Kissinger leaned forward, his words coming with emotion, carefully chosen for the dramatic: "We should get our military actions lined up. My expectation is that we should do it on a large scale. We should not look as though we want to pop somebody, but we should give the impression that we are not to be trifled with."

Rockefeller drew a parallel between the current problem and the *Pueblo* Incident. Ford was well aware of the failure to use force to recover the USS *Pueblo* from North Korea in 1968 and the ensuing eleven-month agony during which eighty-two navy survivors were tortured to extract bogus "spying" confessions. It took a humiliating apology to the Koreans to finally get the crew released. Ford knew the Khmer Rouge were capable of brutal and irrational acts, too, so he was not about to allow this latest hijacking to continue unanswered. The failure during the *Pueblo* Incident was that nearby U.S. air and naval forces were not used promptly by the Johnson administration to halt the hijacking. Once the *Pueblo* reached port, a military operation would have likely triggered a full-scale war. So Ford sided with Kissinger and called for determined action. A White House aide later explained, "The aim was for our action to be read by North Korean president Kim Il Sung as well as by the Cambodians."

In the minds of the decision makers in Washington, the *Mayaguez* crisis was not about Cambodia, but rather about what the rest of the world thought of American power. For the administration, the outcome had to demonstrate that resolve and decisive action garnered success if it were to be of any value at all. To Ford, it represented more: a chance to prove himself.

Ford had become president not by election, but by chance. He had been chosen to replace Vice President Spiro Agnew when scandal drove Agnew to resign on October 15, 1973. Then on August 9, 1974, President Richard Nixon was forced to step down over Watergate, and Ford found himself head of the most powerful country on Earth. Nine months later, by the time of the *Mayaguez* hijacking, Ford had racked up a number of diplomatic reversals. He had appeared helpless in preventing the loss of South Vietnam, Laos, and Cambodia to communism. The media made snide remarks, often including comic derision about his intellectual ability. Ford's speechwriters tried to protect him by omitting troublesome words that he mispronounced, but the president kept putting them back in his drafts. "Judgment" was one of them. The president pronounced it "judge-a-ment." His own writers called that "the

Italian pronunciation." Even more legendary was the danger zone to humanity in the vicinity of Ford when he had a golf club in his hands.

Now the president faced the *Mayaguez* issue: a ship and forty American crew members captured by a little backwater nation that had shut itself off from the world and did not yet know what to call itself. The dilemma for Ford was straightforward: release the ship and its crew or we fight. No need to bring in the think-tank crowd at the Rand Corporation to figure this one out. Ford would call the shots. He had the *Pueblo* Incident to use as guidance about how not to proceed. So first and foremost, a positive outcome depended on keeping the ship away from the Cambodian mainland.

The only suitable staging area for a military assault was in Thailand. The nearest adequate airfield was at U-Tapao, some two hundred miles north of the incident area. U.S. Air Force fighter bombers were available at several other fields in Thailand. Ford wanted them all readied for use, but Kissinger warned, "I do not believe we can run military operations from there." He was well aware that the Thai government would not remain sanguine about the unapproved use of its airstrips. The government was already complaining about the ongoing influx of thousands of Hmong and Lao refugees pouring across the Thai border in boats, in planes, and on foot from Laos. American units were no longer welcome as the Thais tried to figure out how to deal with unwanted refugees and the newly "victorious" neighbors to the north, east, and south.

Ford ignored Kissinger's comment, even when the expected Thai stance was brought up again by the vice president. Ford's attitude was very clear on the Thai situation. Until the *Mayaguez* and her crew were safe, he did not "give a damn about offending their sensibilities."

Although the American elephant was ready to trample on Thai grass with not so much as a by-your-leave, Ford had not given up on diplomacy elsewhere. He instructed Kissinger to urge the People's Republic of China (the United States had no diplomatic mission in Cambodia since the fall of Phnom Penh in April) to intercede in persuading Cambodia to release the crew.

Kissinger summed up his feelings in a concluding comment: "We should know what we are doing. I am more in favor of seizing something, be it the island, the ship, or Kompong Som."

Following the meeting, Nessen issued a press release stating that the president "considers the seizure an act of piracy." At 1:50 P.M. Nessen held a news conference at the White House. He handed out a prepared statement with a map attached. While taking questions, Nessen covered what little information was known about the ship, its location (in or approaching Kompong Som), destination (Thailand), and cargo (unknown commercial).

Schlesinger expanded on what Ford wanted done by instructing the military to find the ship and halt its movement if it was not yet at Kompong Som. He authorized the armed forces to employ munitions in the vicinity of the *Mayaguez* to prevent the ship's movement toward the coast, even okaying the preparation of sea mines for use as barriers, if needed. Jet fighters could make low passes and fire near any small craft in the seizure area. Riot-control gas (tear gas) was approved for use in any recovery attempt.

Kissinger had his deputy convey a message to Huang Zhen, chief of the Chinese Liaison Office in Washington, demanding the immediate release of the *Mayaguez* and her crew. Zhen refused to accept the note. Then Kissinger asked George Bush, head of the U.S. Liaison Office in Beijing, to deliver the same message to the Chinese foreign ministry in Beijing. Kissinger told Bush to escalate the rhetoric by adding an "unsigned" oral note:

> The Government of the United States demands
> the immediate release of the vessel and of
> the full crew. If that release does not
> immediately take place, the authorities
> in Phnom Penh will be responsible for the
> consequences.

Bush delivered both messages, and in the diplomatic parlance of assigning of responsibility, the United States meant that military action was likely if the demands were not met.

None of the NSC decisions or orders was publicly disclosed. In fact, Henry Kissinger ordered a clampdown on any but White House briefings to the media. Part of the reason for this was that Ford wanted it made plain that he was in full control. The clampdown would be step one in quelling the scuttlebutt around Washington that Ford was a lightweight, unsuited for the job as president, and totally dependent on his more capable advisers. This time, State and Defense were there to provide support. And yet, Kissinger was quick to go around Ford by ordering Scowcroft to route any news release through State before it went to Ron Nessen. Kissinger offered to cancel a scheduled speaking engagement in Missouri in order to stay on top of the crisis, but Ford wanted to be in charge, not merely lip-synch the line provided by Kissinger. He told Kissinger to go. So, giving the situation an air of business as usual, Kissinger departed Washington for Missouri.

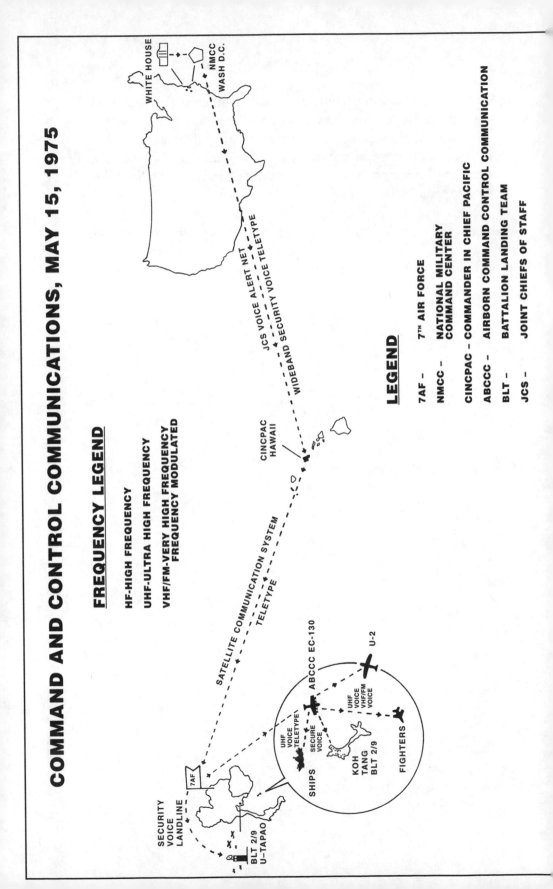

COMMAND AND CONTROL COMMUNICATIONS, MAY 15, 1975

FREQUENCY LEGEND

HF-HIGH FREQUENCY

UHF-ULTRA HIGH FREQUENCY

VHF/FM-VERY HIGH FREQUENCY
FREQUENCY MODULATED

WHITE HOUSE

NMCC
WASH D.C.

JCS VOICE ALERT NET

WIDEBAND SECURITY VOICE TELETYPE

CINCPAC
HAWAII

SATELLITE COMMUNICATION SYSTEM
TELETYPE

SECURITY
VOICE
LANDLINE

7AF

BLT 2/9
U-TAPAO

UHF
VOICE
TELETYPE

ABCCC EC-130

U-2

SHIPS

SECURE
VOICE

UHF
VOICE
VHF/FM
VOICE

KOH
TANG
BLT 2/9

FIGHTERS

LEGEND

7AF – 7TH AIR FORCE

NMCC – NATIONAL MILITARY
COMMAND CENTER

CINCPAC – COMMANDER IN CHIEF PACIFIC

ABCCC – AIRBORN COMMAND CONTROL COMMUNICATION

BLT – BATTALION LANDING TEAM

JCS – JOINT CHIEFS OF STAFF

4

THE FORCES CONVERGE

U.S. pilots during the Vietnam War "can't even bomb an out-house without my approval."

President Lyndon B. Johnson

Secretary of Defense Schlesinger wasted no time setting the military gears in motion. P-3 Orion antisubmarine planes based in the Philippines were ordered aloft to locate the ship. High-altitude U-2 reconnaissance planes were directed to prepare to provide airborne radio relay between the U.S. Support Activities Group/7th Air Force (USSAG/7AF) at Nakhon Phanom Royal Thai Air Base in Thailand and the forces that were soon to be operating over Cambodian territory. USSAG/7AF was the remnant of the Military Assistance Command, Vietnam, which had been relocated to Thailand after the Paris Peace Accords were signed in 1973.[*]

The aircraft carrier USS *Coral Sea*, en route to Australia for the second time in a month, was turned around by Seventh Fleet commander,

---

[*]Since USSAD/7AF's head was an air force general whose command largely involved aircraft, it will be referred to simply as the 7th Air Force from this point on.

Vice Admiral George P. Steele, and ordered to proceed into the Gulf of Thailand. In April the carrier had been diverted to assist in the evacuation of Saigon. But the *Coral Sea* was not the only ship that swung its bow to aid the *Mayaguez*.

Commander Robert A. Peterson stood looking out into the darkness from the helm on the destroyer escort USS *Harold E. Holt*. The afternoon had been pleasant and the ship was on routine maneuvers in the Philippine Sea just outside Subic Bay. Peterson, a trim, no-nonsense career officer, had been in charge of the ship since September 1973. Direct U.S. involvement in Vietnam had ended eight months earlier with the signing of the Paris Peace Accords, so Peterson's tour as captain of a fighting ship had been somewhat benign. Then came the evacuation of Saigon, but the *Holt* found itself diverted to assist a South Vietnamese ship reported to be sinking in the South China Sea, a necessary task, but not the stuff of legend for Peterson. By May 1975, four months short of his scheduled change of command, it seemed likely his tour would end without his ship ever firing its guns in anger, not that his big cannon could fire. The twenty-four-volt power supply to one of the circuit boards was malfunctioning.

The sun was just setting as Peterson was handed a dispatch from his headquarters at Subic Bay. He read it and minutes later swung the ship at full speed onto a new course toward the location of the *Mayaguez* hijacking. Peterson then relayed the disturbing message to Subic that his 5-inch gun was out of service. Somehow though, Peterson, a one-time gunnery officer, was determined to get the weapon working.

One hundred and fifty miles to the west, the guided missile destroyer USS *Henry B. Wilson* was running steady toward Subic Bay. Commander Mike Rodgers, captain of the *Wilson*, had been an English literature major while at Bowdoin College and a chess enthusiast all his adult life. Rodgers prided himself on staying in control, exerting mind over matter. For the past two months, he and his ship had been tested. From March 25 until April 17, the *Wilson* had been positioned off the Cambodian mainland near Kompong Som, providing support for the evacuation of Phnom Penh. As soon as that operation wound down, the ship was ordered off Vietnam's Vung Tao Peninsula to assist in the evacuation of Saigon. On April 30, as the capital was being overrun, refugees streamed seaward on anything that would float. Artillery from the beach began shelling the barges and flimsy craft slowly made their way out of the Mekong Delta. That was more than enough to rile Rodgers. He set all four boilers at full speed ahead. The *Wilson* went hammering through swells at thirty-one knots, her general-quarters bells clanging and 5-inch guns blasting away. Before the shore batteries fell silent, Rodgers counted twenty-six incoming rounds that splashed harmlessly around his ship. These would be the final shots fired at an American vessel during the collapse of South Vietnam.

Near midnight on May 12, the *Wilson* received orders once again to proceed at full speed toward Kompong Som. Rodgers brought his ship alongside the USS *Ashtabula*, a replenishment ship. Ninety minutes later, her tanks refilled with fuel, Rodgers put all seventy thousand available horsepower to driving the *Wilson*'s turbines on course for harm's way.

As the ships began moving to the scene, an alert order was passed to elements of the 1st Battalion, 4th Marines in the Philippines and 2nd Battalion, 9th Marines based on Okinawa.

From the Philippines, a reinforced company including five officers headed by Major Raymond E. Porter and 115 men was ordered to assemble at Cubi Point for airlift to Thailand. Joining them were six volunteers from Military Sealift Command, who might be needed to operate the *Mayaguez* if it were retaken. From Okinawa, an eleven-hundred-man battalion landing team (BLT) was ordered to assemble.

By now the critical preparations had been set in motion for a military option, each step approved by the president. It is important to recall that a few years earlier, President Lyndon B. Johnson had claimed he was so in control of the Vietnam War that U.S. pilots "can't even bomb an outhouse without my approval." Command and control were even tighter by 1975 with communication coming directly into the White House Situation Room via satellite relay. Pilots could now be contacted while still in the air. Much of the information, however, was passed by voice and sifted through numerous levels of command where details were stripped away as other inputs got overlaid. By the time the necessary reports got merged at the highest level of decision making, accounts often lacked important information. The person with the least on-scene knowledge and barest information was making the call simply because the system could do it, not because it brought about the best result. The admirals and generals could, would, and, in some cases, had to pass the buck all the way to the White House.

Once all the forces got into Cambodian waters, Ford would be able to top LBJ by telling the combatants not only what to shoot at but also when to squeeze the trigger.

5

SHOTS IN THE NIGHT

Be sure you are right, then go ahead.

The motto of Davy Crockett in the War of 1812.

Aboard the *Mayaguez,* Captain Miller decided that hospitality might turn things around. If the Cambodians were just a renegade bunch out to better their standard of living, why not bend a little and make that happen. Miller had his thirty-one-year-old South Yemeni messman, Munasseer Thabit Omer, break open the food locker and bring food up on deck. The slight, curly-headed Omer began handing out apples and oranges to the Khmer gunmen. Miller also had Omer open some cartons of Camel cigarettes to give away. Omer knew why Miller chose those. Camels were the slowest sellers in the slop chest. One case had been there almost a year and had gone stale. Miller also had some Kool-Aid mixed up in a bucket and brought up, but the Cambodians would not touch it.

"They think it's poisoned," Miller said as he picked up a plastic foam cup and dipped it in the bright orange liquid. "Very good," he said licking his lips and rubbing his stomach. Then he dipped another cup and handed it to Second Mate Jerry Myregard. Miller watched as Myregard downed the drink and rubbed his stomach, too. The Cambodians joined in. Ten minutes later, the five-gallon bucket was empty.

Miller pointed at the bucket as he spoke to Omer. "Go back down and fill it with ice water. I think these fellas are getting a little friendlier."

Third Mate Dave English, the marine veteran, had watched much of this and was struck by the laxness of his captors. Two of the younger Cambodians were sprawled out asleep on the starboard wing, their AK-47s scattered on the deck beside them. The only really alert one seemed to be the big shot, propped in the chair behind the inoperative radar, his hand resting on the gun at his lap.

English worked out a two-part plan. He wanted to appear easygoing, even friendly, to the Cambodians so they would relax and get used to his coming and goings. He went below, got some more apples and oranges, and passed them out. Then he reached for the phone to the engine room, pausing just long enough to see if this got a rise out of the Khmers. He did not want to get shot over an intercom call. No one paid him any attention, so he dialed the engine room and started gabbing. The second part of his plan involved getting a gun.

English walked out to where Jerry Myregard was standing on the port wing. English had gotten along with the second mate ever since they joined the ship together back in April. English mentioned getting a weapon. Myregard was like-minded.

English scanned the deck. "Let's find out where these bastards are and what they're armed with." They split up to canvass the ship. Up forward on the forepeak, about half a dozen Khmers had hung their AK-47s from stanchions. English figured the group could easily be overpowered and thrown overboard, but that was not the real problem. One of the gunboats was tied off the stern of the *Mayaguez*. The crew would have to wait until it went ashore before trying anything. Then English went back to Captain Miller and reported what he'd found. "Throw 'em overboard," English argued, "then slip anchor and make a run for it."

Miller said nothing. He eyed English with a long, not unfriendly stare. That was okay with English. The seed had been planted.

As darkness settled, the scene two decks below took on a circus sideshow atmosphere. Messman William F. Bellinger watched as one Khmer squatted on a washbasin. Bellinger tried to explain how to use the facilities, but got nowhere regarding the use of Western flush toilets. The Khmers were used to Asian toilets, which are installed at ground level. One squats to use them. The Cambodians could not fathom how standing toilets worked so they stood on the seat rims, then squatted to relieve themselves. The shower was a big hit. One guy held the gun, and the rest piled in under the nozzle. The Khmers showed misgivings about things they did not fully understand. They would not let anyone touch the typewriter, probably because they believed it might be used for sending messages. In the mess, others dug into the rice that Bellinger and Omer had prepared, avoiding the mashed potatoes altogether.

Meanwhile up on the port wing, Charlie Miller stepped out into the quiet, moonless night. He was worn out by the afternoon's events and a little unnerved about having gone from master seaman to prisoner on his own ship. He was worried that the Khmers might decide to get nasty, or worse, that some of his own crew might take things into their own hands and drive the Khmers to violence.

Suddenly Miller flinched. The Cambodian leader stood inches from his face, prodding him.

"Go sleep," Sa Mean said.

Miller nodded. The Cambodian escorted him to his cabin, then headed back to the bridge after Miller went inside. Miller laid down, but his sleep was fitful. He was worried about "this Marine of mine, that powerful son-of-a-bitch" English and his buddy Myregard. They were ex-military and while Miller slept he feared the two might enlist the other crew members into taking on the Cambodians and wind up getting everyone killed.

Reconnaissance orders from Washington seeped down through the command layers, stopping finally in the Philippines at Navy Task Group 72.3. The task group was a long-range patrol force supported primarily by fourteen P-3 Orion patrol planes. The P-3 was a four-engine turboprop, a derivative of the Lockheed Electra, designed for antisubmarine warfare. Commander J. A. Messegee's P-3 squadron at Cubi Point got the first warning order at 8:00 P.M. Messegee had one P-3 on alert in the Philippines, and his deputy, Lieutenant Commander J. Le Doux, had another deployed on four-hour standby at U-Tapao Naval Base in Thailand. The Cubi Point plane could get airborne faster, but would take almost four hours to get over Poulo Wai, where the *Mayaguez* was last reported. The choice seemed a coin toss, but Messegee postponed his decision by alerting both crews to prepare for launch.

Messegee did not take into account the resourcefulness of his deputy at U-Tapao. When notified, Le Doux promised to have his plane in the air in forty minutes. Messegee was skeptical, given the fact that it would take twenty minutes just to refuel the plane, not to mention rounding up a crew and completing a briefing and preflight. Messegee solved his dilemma by ordering both planes into the air with tasking orders sent at 8:30 P.M. Cubi time.

The U-Tapao pilot raised his gear handle just twenty-seven minutes after receipt of the launch command. Eighteen minutes later, the Cubi Point P-3 got airborne with Lieutenant Jim Larkins at the controls. Larkins's P-3 was still in a climb fifteen minutes later when the Orion Le Doux had launched from U-Tapao began painting Poulo Wai on radar.

Messegee had imposed a minimum altitude of six thousand feet to keep the lumbering turboprops above small arms and light antiaircraft artillery range. He was not particularly worried about fighter opposition, the Khmers having captured only a handful of propeller-driven T-28s at Phnom Penh. "But," Messegee cautioned his men, "play heads up!"

The U-Tapao Orion began a systematic search, dropping flares among the profusion of blips that appeared on the radar screen between Poulo Wai and Kompong Som, the apparent destination of the *Mayaguez*, according to intelligence passed from Navy headquarters in Hawaii. By the time the Cubi Point P-3 arrived on station some three and a half hours later, the *Mayaguez* had still not been pinpointed. The two P-3s joined forces at 1:15 A.M., on the morning of May 13 over Poulo Wai. Of the myriad contacts, two large radar returns were prime suspects. The P-3s moved closer and dropped flares. The first of the two was dead in the water and had two patrol boats tied up alongside, but it was too dark to be sure it was the *Mayaguez*. The P-3s got authorization to drop to three hundred feet above and one thousand yards abeam. The Cubi P-3 nosed on over.

Third Mate David English had tried to get some sleep in his cabin, but found it impossible. He could not get the thought out of his mind of winding up a prisoner of war after mustering out of the Marine Corps. Well, if he was going to be in Cambodia for the long haul, he wanted to be ready. He pulled out a pair of rugged jeans, a long-sleeved shirt, high-back shoes, and a hat. Then he stuffed his pockets with vitamin pills and headed topside to stand watch. When he got to the bridge, English saw a four-engine plane sweep past the ship, about five hundred feet off the water. Suddenly, the night sky filled with tracers from the two nearby gunboats, and the deck of the *Mayaguez* sparkled with muzzle blasts as some forty Khmers onboard opened up with AK-47s, M-16s, and M-79 grenade launchers. Within seconds the Khmers were all slipping and sliding around on the spent cartridges. On the beach, one .50-caliber volley after another arced upward in search of the intruding P-3.

Lieutenant Larkins flying the Cubi Point P-3 watched as the deck of the ship he approached lit up like a string of firecrackers had just gone off. He pulled up and turned, trying to ruin the gunners' aims. Tracers sailed toward him in the night from the nearby island. He'd seen enough to convince himself that he had found the *Mayaguez*, but he was not able to absolutely guarantee it to headquarters. Regardless, the Cambodians had something down there they were unwilling to let anyone see without a fight. With fuel getting low, Larkins radioed what he had found and headed for home as a third P-3 from Messegee's unit reported it was inbound to Poulo Wai.

The new Orion was from Patrol Squadron 17 out of Cubi Point. The pilot set up an orbit but waited until daylight before dropping low over the target. At 8:16 A.M. the P-3 roared by alongside the ship. The Khmers responded with a fusillade of small arms and .50-caliber machine-gun fire. One round punched a hole in the P-3's tail. As the pilot pulled up and away, his crew read the name in white block letters on bow and stern: MAYAGUEZ.

6

ON THE MOVE AGAIN

Hold the fort! I am coming!

Gen. William T. Sherman, as signaled to General Corse in
Allatoona, Georgia, from the top of Kennesaw Mountain,
October 5, 1864

The close pass after dawn by the Navy P-3 got the Khmers' attention. Unsure what it meant, the captors of the ship were not about to sit by in daylight while the Americans hatched some clever rescue plot.

A few minutes after the low flyby, Captain Miller got orders from the Khmer leader, Sa Mean, to weigh anchor and get under way. He rang the half-ahead bell down to the engine room. Another fifteen minutes passed before the screw began churning a wake behind the ship at 8:45 A.M. The Khmer ordered a 022-degree course to the northeast, as one of the gunboats took the lead. The heading was not directly at Kompong Som, but instead aimed at a chain of small islands on the way to the mainland. Miller figured the Cambodians probably wanted to be near reinforcements should the American military try something.

Meanwhile, Juan Sanchez, an engine man, had just come off watch. He had breakfast, then, as he did most mornings, went to his stateroom and turned on his shortwave radio. He tuned to the *Voice of America* frequency. The first news he heard made him sit bolt upright. President Ford's "act of piracy" statement was read along with a demand that the Cambodians release the crew or face the consequences. Sanchez dashed from his cabin looking for other members of the crew. Minutes later, Bosun Jack Mullis, Steward Erv Anderson, and several others huddled in Sanchez's stateroom listening to a VOA repeat broadcast. Sanchez pounded his fists together. "We're going to get help now."

Above the scene the aviators in the P-3 watched from altitude as the *Mayaguez* began moving. Based on the estimated speed of the vessel, the crew radioed back to Cubi Point that the ship was headed toward Kompong Som and, if it continued on its current course, would arrive there in about six hours. The P-3 trailed the ship, occasionally losing sight of it as a line of thunderstorms passed through the area. At 10:37 A.M. the *Mayaguez* was sighted again with two Swift patrol boats still escorting it. By that time, word of the ship's status had been relayed by Cubi Point authorities to Pacific Command Headquarters in Hawaii. From there, Admiral Noel Gayler passed orders down through his chain of command to have combat aircraft proceed to the crisis area. That order reached the desk of air force lieutenant general John J. Burns, commander 7th Air Force, located at Nakhon Phanom, Thailand. Along with the orders came assignment of General Burns as on-scene commander over all inbound men, ships, and planes. Burns directed his in-country wing commanders at nearby Takhli and Korat Air Bases to arm their F-4 Phantom, A-7 Corsair, and F-111 fighters and get them airborne. From Udorn Royal Thai Air Base, he dispatched RF-4C reconnaissance planes. Burns learned about two F-111s that were currently aloft, led by Major Roger Bogard from Takhli Air Base. The F-111 is a swing-wing fighter, designed for high-speed precision bombing, but Bogard's two planes were unarmed. General Burns had his command post divert them anyway. By radio,

Bogard was instructed to proceed to the hijacked ship's location. At half past noon, he swung the formation southeast and began a climb.

Meanwhile the first RF-4C took to the air, headed south, and went screaming over Poulo Wai, taking excellent pictures. These proved useless since the ship had been moved. The next three reconnaissance planes managed to fly a track that swept from Kompong Som over Koh Tang and on out to Poulo Wai. These photos were excellent, too, but their interpretation and dissemination would leave much to be desired as events unfolded.

On the bridge of the *Mayaguez*, Captain Miller had been hearing the Cambodian leader constantly repeat his order, "Go Ream, Baye de Ream, wharf number two!" Ream is what was written on Miller's chart at the port of Kompong Som. Miller was not eager to go anywhere near the coast, so he kept the speed at seven knots, hoping his delaying would not get the attention of the Khmer leader. He would occasionally look skyward, noting the presence of the P-3 Orion as it circled the ship. As 1:00 P.M. neared, Miller looked up again just in time to see Major Bogard's two F-111 aircraft make a screaming dive, passing at what seemed like eye level alongside the ship. Again, the Cambodians got excited, firing on the planes as they made pass after pass at near supersonic speed a few hundred yards abeam the *Mayaguez*.

The ship was approaching Koh Tang, a small island thirty miles off the coast.

As the air activity changed with the appearance of combat aircraft, Sa Mean had a change of heart. As soon as the F-111s departed, he ordered Miller to follow the patrol boats, which were diverting around Koh Tang to a position about one mile north of the island. There, to some measure of relief, Miller dropped anchor in about a hundred feet of water. His relief was short-lived, however, as no sooner had the anchor touched bottom than a gaggle of fighters appeared, diving near the ship.

First in were two F-4 Phantoms from Korat, Thailand. They opened fire with their 20-mm gatling guns, strafing in front of the ship. Huge plumes of spray shot into the air, and the Cambodians scurried for cover. To Miller it had become apparent that the American reaction was no longer one of look-and-see. Next came the A-7s and F-111s shooting both in front of and behind the ship. The Cambodians fired back as best they could while trying to avoid being hit by shrapnel that peppered the water nearby.

Miller stayed in the wheelhouse, watching the display of marksmanship as the fighters made close passes without a round ever touching the ship. Obviously, the intent was to halt movement of the *Mayaguez*, but that was already a fact ordered by Sa Mean. Miller worried that he would be given orders to weigh anchor and move closer to the mainland. Before he could dwell on the matter, Sa Mean motioned for him to leave the bridge. He escorted Miller at gunpoint to his cabin where he made Miller open his safe. Once unlocked, the five thousand U.S. dollars Miller had left there were easily visible, stacked in a neat little bundle inside. Sa Mean ignored the cash, moving to Miller's file cabinet, which Miller opened next. Nothing was removed, but the Khmer wanted everything left open. Miller was then led back to the bridge. Overhead, he could see the P-3 continuing to circle and fighters buzzing around in orbit as if ready to pounce.

Meanwhile, in the officer's saloon, former marine Dave English, radio operator "Sparks" Bock, and Third Engineer Al Minichiello were grumbling in low tones. English was adamant about not wanting to go "like a lamb to slaughter." He told his fellow sailors about what he found inside a hamlet when his marine unit recaptured it after the 1968 Hue offensive in Vietnam. "Nineteen Americans with their hands tied behind their backs and their heads chopped off. They were just sitting there. I had to go around and untie them."

Everyone stopped talking.

At 4:15 with jets still roaring high overhead, the Cambodian leader used hand signals to indicate that Captain Miller and Second Mate Jared "Jerry" Myregard were going to be handcuffed and taken to the island. Burton Coombes was in the wheelhouse too, but he was not singled out. "It looks like you and me, Jerry," Miller said.

Word quickly spread that part of the crew were to disembark. Within minutes, English, Bock, and Minichiello had heard. Minichiello got up and made tracks for the engine room. Bock followed him. English headed for his cabin to get the hat and vitamin pills he had set out.

Down below in the engine room, Chief Engineer Cliff Harrington saw Minichiello descending the ladder with Bock right behind him.

"They're taking us off the ship," Minichiello announced.

Bock stepped from the ladder and immediately began poking around the engine room, trying to lift the steel floor-plates, looking for a place to hide as Minichiello repeated English's Hue atrocity.

Harrington glanced upward. Armed men in black were descending the series of ladders. "They're coming down now!" Harrington and his men swung into action, closing off the fuel-oil service pump and the burners in each boiler, then shutting the sea suction valves just as the Cambodians reached the bottom level. With guns pointed, the Cambodians signaled for everyone to go topside. Harrington took a moment to make sure feed water was still going to the boilers so they would not melt. Then with the boilers shutting down, the others, including Bock, started up. Harrington was last, ahead of the Cambodians. As he climbed, Harrington felt his knees turn to jelly at the thought of what might lay ahead.

Shutting down the power plant caused a short burst of steam and smoke to rise from the stacks above deck. This was observed by the two A-7 pilots flying overhead. After a quick discussion with the orbiting P-3, it was thought the *Mayaguez* might be preparing to get under way. The A-7s were told to make a low pass for a closer look.

Meanwhile, English had reached his cabin. He was about to change into the jeans whose pockets he had stuffed with those vitamins when two Cambodians barged in and used their rifles to prod him to the exit and down the companionway. With the barrel of an AK-47 nudging him in the back, English made his way toward the deck. He did not think he was going ashore, since the word was that only the captain and second mate were being taken there. When he got to the deck rail, he peered over. Beneath the pilot ladder, Captain Miller and the second mate were standing on the bobbing deck of a gray fifty-foot fishing trawler. Sa Mean was on a gunboat beside the trawler. Another fishing boat with its armed escort floated nearby, and to English's surprise the rest of the crew were on it. Then English heard the roar of explosions. A jet fighter swept overhead, strafing in front of the ship. The Cambodians on deck scattered, firing wildly as the plane zoomed away. Then another fighter rolled in. Red tracers from .50-caliber machine guns sprayed from the island as the plane made another strafe run. English watched as a Cambodian boy braced himself on the ship's starboard wing while he manhandled an M-79 grenade launcher upward and launched a round. The grenade arced skyward, much too slowly to hit the speeding jet.

English shook his head at the sight, then looked over the side again. One fishing boat had gotten under way, led by its gunboat. He heard someone approach from behind, so he glimpsed over his shoulder. A Khmer waved his gun, motioning for him to get off, so English scampered down the ladder and boarded the smaller of the two trawlers. Then with its gunboat in the lead, the rest of the crew headed for the northeastern side of the island.

Standing on the deck of the lead fishing trawler, Miller glanced back at the ship. He wondered if he would ever set foot on her again. The sky above was clear. The fighters must be up there, though, he guessed. He pondered what their next step would be as he turned his gaze ahead to the island. On both sides stretched a white sand beach, arcing around a small cove. Beyond the beach, palm trees swayed eastward in a light breeze. As the water shallowed, it shimmered to a clear tropical blue. Light faded as the sun dipped behind a small rise in the center of the island, but Miller could still make out a cluster of shacks on stilts tucked just beyond the tree line, midway along the beach. Not a sound could be heard above the hum of the trawler motor as he scanned the placid scene. Then a man appeared at the water's edge, waving frantically. The tree line lit up. A shower of red tracers raced skyward followed by the staccato report of machine-gun fire. Miller ducked instinctively as a fighter roared by overhead, this one with afterburners spewing yellow flame.

The gunboats in front of the trawlers reversed course in a sweeping turn that sent a long, rounded swell rolling toward the beach. Meanwhile, Miller's fishing boat came to a stop, dropping anchor about a hundred yards from shore, beside a fishing boat already at anchor there. The trawler with the rest of the crew then tied up beside Miller's boat. A small dingy came out from the island and a few Khmers boarded it and headed for shore.

Miller watched the gunboats return to the ship. He wondered if the Khmer leader was heading back for the five thousand dollars Miller had left in the safe.

Long shadows began to slip across the water as both Captain Miller and Second Mate Myregard waited together. The fighters departed to the north and things settled into an eerie silence, with only the sound of surf lapping against the planks of the boat. Miller mulled over the situation, worried that things could easily get out of hand. Too many of the crew were mumbling about trying to disarm their captors and make a fight of it. So far the Cambodians had behaved reasonably, especially considering the amount of strafing that had gone on. Miller did not want a small renegade group starting something against the hijackers without his knowledge.

Myregard looked toward the island in the murky light. He'd heard the horror stories and complaints from the crew, too. "Captain, from what I hear the Khmer Rouge are great for taking people out and chopping their heads off."

"Let's just wait, Jerry. I don't want to get anyone in this crew shot and killed if we don't have to."

Myregard kept an edgy silence, but Miller began to wonder if his control was slipping away. He gazed skyward, but could only hear the steady droning of the propeller plane that had been circling the ship all day.

A few minutes later, the gunboats came motoring back from the *Mayaguez*. One slowed by Miller's craft and tied up. One of the crewmen from the gunboat spoke French and demanded to know what was inside the locked rooms up on the ship.

"Tell him nothing," Miller said to Crewman Pastrano, who spoke Cajun French. "No guns, no ammunition. Just a bunch of clothes and personal belongings."

Pastrano told the Cambodian crewman, but the man shook his head.

"Tell him," Miller said, "if he wants, we'll go back and unlock the doors. Then he can see for himself. But tell him the plant's dead. We have no electricity."

After a round of translations, the Cambodian decided to go back for a look.

Miller circulated among the crew, picking up all the locker keys and stuffing them in his pocket. Then the Cambodians made the rest of the crew move back onto the smaller fishing boat. Only Captain Miller and Myregard were left on the larger trawler with a group of Khmer Rouge.

The boat got under way, purring toward the darkened ship. In the moonless night, Miller could not even see the outline of the *Mayaguez* until she suddenly loomed out of the darkness, her white containers eerily outlining her deck, stark except for a fleeting shadow or two from the guards who were still aboard.

The fishing boat pulled alongside. Then Miller and Myregard climbed up the pilot's ladder behind the Cambodians. Miller stepped on deck just as a burst of brilliant light illuminated the darkened structure. The Cambodians ran for cover as each blast of light was followed by a loud popping sound. Miller watched as a plane spilled out a string of flares as it passed overhead. Miller surmised that the light was from a reconnaissance plane taking flash photos of the *Mayaguez*. The sea stayed lit for ninety seconds, bathing the ship in ghostly shadows. The Cambodians, however, had their own ideas. Panic-stricken, they began shouting as they hustled everyone back aboard the trawler and made speed back to the island cove.

7

BRING ON THE MARINES

These Marines have the swagger, confidence,
and hardness that must have been in Stonewall Jackson's
Army of the Shenandoah. . . . Upon this thin line of
reasoning, I cling to the hope of victory.

British dispatch from Miryang, Korea, 16 August 1950

Admiral Noel Gayler, commander in chief of all Pacific air, naval, and ground forces (CINCPAC), had been ingesting the reports coming in Tuesday morning. A sizeable rescue force was already on its way, and the rest of his western Pacific bases, ships, and surface and air units were on standby. The carrier USS *Coral Sea* was expected to arrive in the crisis area in two days, on Thursday the fifteenth, along with the frigate USS *Holt* and destroyer USS *Wilson*. But none of those ships carried ground troops. The attack carrier USS *Hancock* had a marine contingent aboard, but was nursing a steam valve failure and was not expected to arrive until the sixteenth. The helicopter carrier

USS *Okinawa* also had marines embarked but would not reach Koh Tang until the eighteenth at the earliest due to an out-of-commission boiler that cut her speed to eighteen knots. Gayler wanted an assault force there sooner. He sent a message alerting the 1st Battalion, 4th Marines stationed at Subic Bay to prepare for movement to Thailand.

By mid-afternoon on Tuesday the thirteenth, as confusing signals from air force and navy planes described the wandering circumstances of the *Mayaguez* and crew, Captain Walter J. Wood's D Company made ready to ship out. His seventy Marines at Subic had been through the routine repeatedly over the last month during the Vietnam and Cambodia evacuations. Each time they had eventually stood down. As the sun dipped in the west, they rested on their gear, assuming it would be the same this time. Then, at 6:30 P.M., they got orders to make ready for airlift. The ramp became a blur of adrenaline-pumped marines. Wood's men reconfigured their equipment by 9:00 P.M. Thirty minutes later, Wood and two of his platoon commanders were called to battalion headquarters. There they were told that Colonel John M. Johnson from the III Marine Assault Force (MAF) was designated as commander of Task Group 79.9, whose mission was to recover the *Mayaguez*. D Company had been chosen as the unit that would actually retake the ship. Major Raymond E. Porter, the battalion executive officer, assisted by Captain J. P. Feltner from the staff, would assume on-scene command of the seizure effort. Wood and his lieutenants exchanged glances. One of the last times U.S. Marines had retaken a ship was during the Civil War blockades. They did it then by going "over the side," ship to ship. D Company might be going into action, but none like they had ever imagined.

When General Burns, the theater commander at Nakhon Phanom in Thailand, looked over his inbound force list, he was not satisfied. Burns wanted some added muscle in addition to the troops from the Philippines. Orders went out to III Marine Division's amphibious force units in Okinawa. First Battalion, 9th Marine Regiment was on alert as primary air-contingency battalion.

Most of 1st Battalion, 9th Marines were nearing the end of their one-year tour on Okinawa and could not be extended except in case of an emergency. The III MAF sought authorization to extend the unit, but it was denied. Although a crisis was clearly looming, administrative issues took precedence at marine headquarters, so a fully trained unit stood down while an outfit just beginning its predeployment training cycle was chosen for the assignment. The question that begs to be answered is: What kind of logic has a unit sitting primary alert if that unit was not going to be used in a contingency?

The line troops of 2nd Battalion (BLT 2/9) were in the field and remained relatively unaware of the *Mayaguez* situation until orders came flooding in after dark on the thirteenth. Lieutenant Colonel Randall W. Austin had four rifle companies out in the Camp Schwab training area doing night maneuvers. Austin got word to bring his men back to base and get them ready "to go somewhere and do something."

Among the marines out on exercise that night were two E or "Echo" Company machine-gun crews comprised of three men each, the team leader, the gunner, and the ammo carrier. Each team had been positioned by the platoon leaders where the M-60 machine gun had good, open fields of fire. Each stayed in position until the unit advanced. With every repositioning, each machine-gun team dug in again because once the shooting starts, the simulated enemy would soon be able to locate their position, a fixed target. So, all members of the machine-gun teams had shovels and all worked to gouge U-shaped trenches for protection, with the two legs of the U facing the enemy. The gun was mounted on raised ground in the center. The ammo carriers normally positioned to the left and the spotters to the right, while the gunners squatted behind the M-60 at the back of the trench.

One of the machine-gun teams was headed by Corporal Joseph N. Hargrove. Hargrove was a lanky six-footer with a trim sandy crew cut from Mount Olive, North Carolina. His older brother, army private first class Lane K. Hargrove, had been killed in action in 1968 near Quang Ngai, South Vietnam. Despite family misgivings, Joseph decided to follow his older brother's footsteps, except he chose the marines over the army. By the time he finished training and was assigned to Okinawa, he had a change of heart in more ways than one. In February of 1975, Hargrove had married his hometown sweetheart, Gail. He tried to get the overseas assignment squashed, but to no avail. At Camp Schwab, he seemed a serious type to his peers, avoiding the temptations available in the downtown bars in Henoko, but to his supervisors he became a problem marine—an attitude case. A personnel record entry claims he had "a strong dislike for the Marine Corps since leaving boot camp."

Gail had a job in North Carolina, and the two remained separated geographically while he tried to wrestle an assignment back stateside, or preferably out of the Marine Corps. Hargrove exhibited "homesickness and a deep longing for his wife." His adjustment problems were serious enough to have him evaluated by medical personnel, but the medical officer, Lieutenant J. M. Hagen, found Hargrove "fit for duty."

Hargrove carried an M-16 rifle, an extra barrel for the M-60 machine gun, and the tripod upon which the gun would be mounted if dug into a defensive position. He also helped determine the best site for setting up the M-60 and spotted targets.

Under Hargrove's command was machine gunner private Gary L. Hall from Covington, Kentucky. At six feet two inches and 220 pounds, Hall presented a long-legged, gawky image. With a .45 pistol strapped to his waist, Hall slung the big M-60 to his back and in his free hand hefted an extra ammo can over all manner of terrain. Hall had found a home in the Marine Corps. Unlike the constant ribbing he had received at home, he was well liked by subordinates and superiors—a good Marine.

With Hargrove and Hall was blond-headed private Danny G. Marshall, at five feet three inches and all of 130 pounds. To Marshall fell the burden of hauling an M-16 and as many fully loaded M-60 ammo cans as he could carry into the field. Marshall had a lot on his mind that night. He had been "busted by four Japanese police and a Marine captain" ten days earlier in a drug sting off base in Henoko township. When apprehended, he had given a false ID number to the authorities. With a juvenile record at home hovering over him, he entertained thoughts of going "over the fence," since it was only a matter of time before the Marine Corps figured out who they had really arrested, dug up his past, and sent him to prison. Going AWOL was out of the question though, since there was no way he knew of to get off Okinawa.

So Danny was staying put for the time being, his mind going over options, wondering what possible chance he might have to escape the wrath of the law. But at the moment he was on maneuvers with two marine teammates, sharing something they all hated, the intimate familiarity with fatigue that is a machine gunner's lot.

Military units move often, especially on maneuvers. Digging trenches becomes tedious, repetitive work that soon takes the glamour out of a machine gunner's life. For Hargrove, Hall and Marshall, the night had been a long one of move-and-dig, then move-and-dig again.

At 10:30 P.M. Lieutenant Colonel Austin called a halt to the exercise and began bringing his companies back to camp. For the machine-gun team, it came as blessed relief, but for them and the other marines in their unit, the night had just begun.

Austin had orders to prepare a battalion landing team for departure by air at dawn on Wednesday the fourteenth. The exact mission remained a mystery, but rumors had reached Camp Schwab regarding the *Mayaguez* and it did not take much figuring to make the connection.

In addition to E Company, G "Golf" Company was also in the field that night. Commanded by Captain James H. Davis and Gunnery Sergeant Lester A. McNemar, it took two hours for them to assemble their troops and truck them back to camp. Davis was the only officer in the company with combat experience. McNemar and eight other noncommissioned officers had fought in Vietnam, but not a single man beneath them had ever been in action. When Davis arrived back in his office, a decision regarding one of their problem marines, Private K. O. Taylor, awaited him. Taylor, a nineteen-year-old raised in a Chicago ghetto, had clashed with the previous first sergeant and done two stints in the brig. With the end of the Vietnam era, the Corps was downsizing, and Taylor was a prime candidate for an undesirable discharge. The folder was sitting on Davis's desk. Davis studied the paperwork—an open-and-shut case—for a long moment. But Taylor had worked well recently, especially with the new first sergeant. So, for reasons he could not readily explain, Davis broke regulations, stuffing the papers in a drawer as he turned to other matters.

Over in Echo Company, Captain Mykle Stahl and his men sat in the parking lot removing their M-16 blank adapters. Hall removed the same from the barrel of his M-60. The adapters were needed to allow the weapons to fire blanks in training. The company had not even had time to complete the procedure for battle-sighting their weapons for combat, which required the firing of live rounds. They would deploy without knowing precisely where their weapons were shooting. E Company was so early in the training cycle that the platoon sergeant,

Staff Sergeant Clark H. Hale, did not yet know who all of his squad leaders were going to be.

Captain Stahl and Sergeant Hale had both seen combat in Vietnam, Stahl being highly decorated with a Navy Cross and five Purple Hearts. They knew the value of teamwork and the need to have confidence in the key men of the company. Though there were plenty of people with problems such as Hargrove and Marshall, no one was cut from the deployment roster.

At Camp Schwab, Okinawa, word spread like wildfire. "We're going to rescue the *Mayaguez*: a real mission." The idea that this time might really be it caused a frenzy. Even the clerk at the gym who issued sports equipment showed up for deployment with an M-16.

Hargrove, Hall, and Marshall grabbed their field packs and checked to make sure they had all they would need to deploy. Inside they had crammed a change of fatigue uniform, a few pairs of underwear and socks, soap, gas mask, mess kit, shovel, poncho, and two boxes of C rations. Hargrove stuffed a pocket Bible in his fatigue pocket. Then they gathered up their M-60 equipment, put on their helmets, and moved out to board the trucks that had rumbled into the parking lot. They were going off on a mission for God knew how long, and they had only one change of clothes. Welcome to the Marine Corps.

Throughout the early hours Wednesday morning, the camp and the big air base at Kadena were ablaze with activity as four-engine C-141 Starlifters descended from the sky onto a bustling tarmac.

As soon as the planes had cleared the runway and shut down, marines began the loading operation. Inside the big transport was a huge cargo space. The battalion's equipment pallets with ammunition were quickly loaded into the rear of the cargo area. Then marines boarded.

Hall had the M-60 strapped over his back, while Hargrove handled the extra barrel and Marshall lugged the bipod. The three men hefted their loads aboard and looked around.

There had been no time to reconfigure the forward cargo space for passengers, so no seats awaited the troops. The machine-gun team made their way into the cargo bay and once the C-141 was packed with standing marines, an NCO yelled, "Sit." Hargrove, Hall,

Marshall, and the other marines dropped onto the hard aluminum planking and sat without seat belts, using only their packs for back support. The floor of the plane was still cool from having cold-soaked at altitude on the way in. Sleep was going to be a problem once they were high in the sky and the floor again chilled down. The men got as comfortable as they could and tried to get some rest. No one had slept in over twenty-four hours.

At Subic Bay to the south, air force transports were already loaded and rolling down the runway with Major Porter and his ship-seizure team from Delta Company.

8

JOSEPH NELSON HARGROVE

They'd all seen Sands of Iwo Jima *and were totally pumped up by it. John Wayne recruited more dead kids than we'll ever know.*

Clancy Sigal, author

*H*e was a tall, slender man of twenty-four. His fine, sandy-blond hair accented a pale, drawn face sharpened by a new mustache. When he walked, he leaned forward as if he had just stumbled on a crack in the sidewalk. He was damn good with an M-60 machine gun, and he carried a pocket Bible into combat.

The road sign says CENTER, indulging neither the word "street" nor "avenue." Center in Mount Olive, North Carolina, stays hot and dusty most of the year. A single-line railroad track bisects the town separating its main drag. Angled parking places are aligned on both sides. In a faded color photo from the sixties, a scattering of pickups, an old Ford convertible, and a dust-covered bread truck all give the place an unwashed look. A ticket to see the movie at the Center Theater cost fifty cents then. Only now the Church of God-and-Deliverance holds services inside the old Center Theater building. Rose's Department Store, long since moved to a strip mall, was the biggest emporium in those days. In other photos, the local shops look small and dingy, their gray awnings hanging over a tired sidewalk where parking meters jut out of the pavement. The meters have since been ripped out like bad teeth to help lure penny-conscious customers back. They have not returned. As in a thousand towns across the country, one stares at images of downtown America withering into obsolescence.

The Duplin Senior High girls of the sixties used to show thin legs beneath short-shorts as they danced to their bugle call of liberation—rock 'n' roll—by the table jukes where Albert's Soda Grill used to be. Downtown "is where it was at." The barbershop up the block used to stay open till midnight on Saturday. Teen girls of the seventies wore granny gowns, beads, and flowers in their hair, and guys in jeans leaned on car fenders and flicked butts of spent Chesterfields onto the hot asphalt. The *Mount Olive Tribune* used to publish in town. It too has moved, but editor Steve Herring keeps all the old editions in an office he calls the "morgue." He allowed me access, and I began tediously poring over sometimes tattered pages. I was not sure what I was looking for other than to get a feel for the local life back in the sixties and seventies. Two hours later, on page eight of the January 3, 1969, issue I found an article headlined, "Beautancus Home Gutted by Fire." I read it, then headed for my car.

Two blocks off Center on the way to Beautancus, the back streets melt into the red-orange blush of cypress, dogwood, and tall oaks on shady lanes. Stately houses of old wood with white columns and slant-warped front porches sit in the sun sporting rusty swinging rockers and hanging plants. In another two blocks, the homes turn to one-story shotgun houses with matted grass lawns and chain-link fences. Neglected cars rust in backyards and a few black women still find time to sit on the porches and visit. Another quarter of a mile on is country. Mansions mix with house trailers. They dot rich-smelling acres of red clay that spew out tobacco, cotton, and corn. A few more miles east sits a junction called Beautancus, the place where Joseph Nelson

Hargrove, born on May 15, 1951, was raised on a half acre in a three-bedroom clapboard house surrounded by cotton fields.

Joseph was the sixth of nine children born to Charlotte and Rudolph Hargrove. Of the few things Rudolph Hargrove excelled at, fathering kids and hard drinking led the list.

Rudolph had been an army enlisted man, a cook. The family moved from post to post eighteen times in seventeen years. He even switched services to the air force and did a stint at Langley Air Force Base, up in Virginia. "Mr. Hargrove" is how neighbors referred to him after he left the military on disability. Rudolph tried to settle near Mount Olive, but kept moving from place to place within a few miles of the town. Booze, frequent relocations, and the certainty of a new baby every year or so made for hard living. Rudolph was heavily inebriated the evening he and Joseph's older brother Lelland Alvah got into it over a knife. Rudolph cut Lelland's wrist tendon, then stormed off.

Joseph, twelve at the time, and Lelland waited with a shotgun for the old man to return, but he did not come back that night. When he did show up a few days later, Rudolph turned his attention to his third offspring, Douglas Ray, threatening to kill him. Douglas took no guff from the old man. He tried to have his father arrested. The police said, "No, a man's home is his castle." So Douglas left town, but later learned from his mother that his father had been arrested for crashing his car into a cemetery wall after drinking too much moonshine. Soon, though, Rudolph was out of jail and back in the alcohol groove.

As the children grew older they split off, living with an aunt in Pennsylvania. The oldest daughter, Sandra Matilda, went first, followed by Steven Rudolph, Jr., who left when he was sixteen. Lane Kornegay, the fifth child, came north next, but got drafted into the army when he turned eighteen.

Joseph Nelson came of age and got his driver's license in 1967 when he was sixteen. He dropped out of high school that year, intending to head north, but the big moneymaker had always been "bacca" (tobacco), so nobody left town until the crop was in. After planting and caring for the plants all season, it was picked in early July, one leaf at a time from the bottom up as the leaves matured. Joseph and his brothers rode the harvester with the cart in back and they all reached out to pick the low leaves as they went by. The leaves were taken to the drying barn. By the end of the season, all that would be left were tobacco stalks with a crown of leaves still growing on top.

After the harvest, Joseph and some of the boys drove off to a Saturday night dance. The music and beer flowed, and Joseph rolled his mother's car on the way back. No one was seriously injured, but a DUI conviction cost him his license. Well on his way in his father's footsteps, he was sent north to his aunt and uncle's place, where his mother thought he might be able to right himself. He applied for a driver's license, but the Pennsylvania Department of Motor Vehicles already had the word on Joseph Nelson Hargrove.

On January 12, 1968, brother Lane Hargrove shipped out for Vietnam. Meanwhile Joseph worked up north for his uncle until he was able to get his license reissued. He started saving some money, preparing to head back to North Carolina.

On April 21, 1968, Charlotte Hargrove got a telegram from the army. Her twenty-year-old son, U.S. Army private first class Lane Kornegay Hargrove, had died of wounds suffered near Quang Ngai, Vietnam. He was buried in Mount Olive that spring and the army gave Charlotte and Rudolph an American flag and Lane's posthumous Purple Heart medal.

Returning to Beautancus after Lane's death, Joseph moved back in with his mother and the younger children. Charlotte had by then separated from her husband, and did "public work," as she called it, to support the family. But Rudolph wanted her back under his thumb. His stewed mind hatched a bizarre plan. On January 2, 1969, while Charlotte worked the graveyard shift at a textile plant, he waited until Joseph and his four other children, including grown son Lelland and his wife and children, were asleep. At the witching hour that cold night, he set a fire in a shed at the back of the house. Someone spotted the flames, and the fire department came to put the blaze out.

Rudolph lay watching from the nearby cotton field. After the fire trucks left, he slept. Hours later he woke shivering, then stumbled across the blacktop road to the house, remembering a can of gasoline kept in an outbuilding. He found it. Rudolph poured the contents over the porch and on around to the shed. Everyone was asleep inside. A match was tossed. Flames lit the night sky.

Joseph woke up first, smelling something burning. He raced through the house, rousing the rest of the family.

The fire department was called again, this time from the neighbors'. Charlotte came home and discovered her family outside, firemen dashing about, and pumper trucks idling with lights flashing and water spraying. The eight-thousand-dollar home was gutted. Consumed in the blaze were twenty-five hundred dollars in contents including all the family photos and the Purple Heart awarded posthumously to Lane Kornegay Hargrove. The clothing the family had on amounted to the only things salvaged. Neighbors took in the Hargroves.

Charlotte pressed charges. Deputy Sheriff Rodney Thigpen came out and collared Mr. Hargrove who admitted to committing arson.

"I thought that would be a good chance for me to get rid of the house," Mr. Hargrove claimed.

Thigpen took Rudolph to the county jail. "He told me that he figured if he could get rid of the house he'd get his family back."

On August 27, 1969, Rudolph Hargrove was sentenced to eight to ten years for unlawfully burning a dwelling.

By 1974, with his father still in prison, Joseph felt the need to launch out on his own. The Vietnam pullout had been completed over a year before, after the Peace Agreement was signed in Paris in January of 1973. No one in America was in any mood for more military adventures out of Washington. He enlisted in the Marine Corps, primarily because of steady pay and the big marine bases close to home at Cherry Point and Parris Island.

Joseph found the Marine Corps no walk in the park. All the drill instructors were Vietnam vets who were angry at the world. Joseph, however, came out of boot camp angry at the Marine Corps. Meanwhile, he met Gail, a hometown girl with a mind of her own. He got married right after receiving orders to report to Okinawa with the 2nd Batallion, 9th Marine Regiment. He tried to fight the assignment, but orders were orders, and marines follow orders.

Once on Okinawa, Joseph became moody, reclusive. He seldom went downtown to visit the bars like many of the other troops. He did go into the city on one occasion to buy a kimono for Gail. He was homesick, on a one-year unaccompanied tour, and he made an issue of trying to get back to the United States early. But for Joseph Hargrove there would be no early reassignment, there would only be the following of orders.

9

FIRST CASUALTIES

The end for which a soldier is recruited, clothed, armed,
and trained, the whole object of his sleeping, eating,
drinking, and marching is simply that he should fight at the
right place and the right time.

Clausewitz, *On War*

Two H-53 helicopter squadrons were stationed at Nakhon Phanom Royal Thai Air Base in northeastern Thailand. The 40th Air Rescue and Recovery Squadron had nine HH-53Cs, used for rescue of downed pilots. Their unit nickname, *Jolly Green Giants*, borrowed from the Libby company logo, stemmed from the huge size of the helicopter and its camouflage green paint scheme. The 21st Special Operations Squadron was equipped with ten *Knife* CH-53Cs, a helicopter version used for clandestine operations; insertion of road-watch teams into Laos being one. Although similar in appearance, the two versions of the aircraft had crucial differences. The Rescue HH-53s were air-to-air refuelable and carried extra fuel in two 450-gallon drop tanks. The Special Operations CH-53 could not air refuel but had larger, 650-gallon drop tanks. The HH-53 drop tanks were filled with fire-retardant foam, proven effective in stopping explosions from incendiary bullets. The larger tanks on the CH-53 were merely aluminum pods and thus quite vulnerable to fire or explosion. Both helicopter cockpits were heavily armor plated and the cargo area was fitted with 7.62-mm miniguns capable of firing four thousand rounds per minute. The CH-53 had guns located in the crew door and left forward cabin window. The Rescue HH-53s had those and a third gun mounted aft on the cargo ramp. Marksmanship was not a problem even though there were no longer any gunnery ranges to use in Thailand. The gunner merely squeezed the trigger and followed the tracer stream, moving the gun until bullets hit the target. The guns were prone to jam, however, unless gunners and maintenance workers had regular practice in dealing with their quirks.

The air force fleet of CH-53s and HH-53s was small, fewer than fifty aircraft, but four accidents had already happened, three of them fatal. Investigations were inconclusive, but the flight control servos, the hydraulic pistons that transfer control inputs to the main rotors, were suspected as flawed.

A contingency plan was hatched by General Burns and his staff at 7th Air Force in Nakhon Phanom, Thailand. The scheme involved using a force made up from the local 656th Air Force Security Police Squadron. The cops were to retake the *Mayaguez*. Even though neither the security policemen nor the helicopter pilots had been trained for anything like what General Burns envisioned, the men and aircraft were readied for an assault on the ship. The plan was to strike at first light the next morning, the fourteenth, landing the 656th element atop the containers on the *Mayaguez*. Seventy-five volunteers found themselves gathered on the ramp on the evening of the thirteenth. In addition, a staff element headed by Brigadier General Walter H. Baxter, III, from Udorn Air Base in northern Thailand was put together and readied for transport. Baxter's role was to be the 7th Air Force "senior facilitator in the planning process." He was not in charge of the operation, but instead was supposed to make sure things got coordinated properly between fighters, reconnaissance, and helicopters once the plan for the rescue was set.

General Burns elected to remain at Nakhon Phanom. There he had secure communication with higher headquarters in Hawaii, an HF radio link to the command and control aircraft over Koh Tang, a UHF radio link to all the fighters, and the availability of his own staff.

All operable 40th Rescue HH-53Cs and Special Operations CH-53C helicopters were loaded and ordered to U-Tapao for staging. They carried a staff element, security policemen, an assortment of maintenance stands, tow bars, servicing equipment, ammunition, and spare parts. As the night progressed, seven CH-53s launched toward U-Tapao along with five HH-53s.

One of the CH-53s, *Knife-13*, took off at 9:15 P.M. Thirty-six miles east of Nakhon Phanom, the rotor system failed and the helicopter nosed over, plummeting to a fiery impact.

Two of the special operations helicopters diverted and landed near the crash site. The inferno lit up the night sky. All five crew members and eighteen security policemen died in the crash. The *Mayaguez* Incident had claimed its first twenty-three victims.

Helicopters from the 40th Rescue Squadron were scrambled to the tragic scene as well, at the insistence of the squadron commander, even though the special operations aircraft had long been on the ground there and reported no survivors.

As a result of the detours, the first helicopter did not arrive at U-Tapao until 11:30 P.M. The rest dribbled in, most of them arriving before 3:00 A.M. on the fourteenth. Back at Nakhon Phanom, a special operations maintenance crew worked feverishly to get additional aircraft ready for flight. First Lieutenant Richard C. Brims, a 1971 U.S. Air Force Academy graduate, worked with maintenance as one of the test pilots who checked out each aircraft before it was released to the squadron for regular duty. Brims had distinguished himself during the evacuations in Saigon two weeks earlier. He was a highly respected pilot assigned to test flights on helicopters that had undergone maintenance, a task that usually fell to more experienced pilots. Brims had been at work all day, helping ready aircraft for the deployment. When the last possible aircraft was brought up to flight status, Brims was asked to perform a safety no-no: a night check-flight, and a quick one at that. He got the job done, then reboarded the aircraft and took off for U-Tapao, arriving just before dawn. At that point, Brims and most of the helicopter crews had been awake for more than twenty-four hours.

The latest developments were relayed by the various senior officers up the chain of command. While the accident took priority in message traffic, the P-3 headquarters at Cubi Point was also active. They relayed the Orion crew's report about the fishing boats with Caucasians aboard leaving the *Mayaguez* and heading for Koh Tang. The pilot had radioed back that he had seen a small group of people leaving the boats for shore. In all probability some of the crew were disembarked on the island. Also, just after sunset, a fishing boat had been spotted returning to the ship. Initial thoughts were that the Cambodians were about to move the *Mayaguez* under cover of darkness, but the periodic stream of flares revealed that whoever had gotten back aboard was now scurrying off the ship. What was certain was that the island was well defended. Every time a plane made a low pass, streams of tracers arced up from the island in pursuit.

The staffs dutifully forwarded their information to Admiral Gayler, commander of all Pacific forces, in Honolulu, and from there it was meshed with other intelligence before making its way to the White House.

At 2:11 A.M. on May 13, General Brent Scowcroft awakened President Ford with bad news. The *Mayaguez* was under way, headed for the mainland.

At 6:22 A.M. Washington time, Secretary of Defense Schlesinger phoned President Ford. The president took the call as he read the morning edition of the *Washington Post* with its front-page story about the *Mayaguez* seizure. Schlesinger made no mention of the helicopter crash, but did report that the ship was anchored off Koh Tang, a jungle island some thirty miles west of Kompong Som. Reconnaissance planes had drawn heavy antiaircraft fire, but only one P-3 was slightly damaged.

Although buoyed by the fact that at least for the time being the ship had not moved into port, Ford took note of the amount of resistance the Cambodians were putting up.

A little over an hour later, the president sat in his black leather swivel chair in the Oval Office. His first appointment was with General

Scowcroft, sitting in for Henry Kissinger who was still in Missouri. Scowcroft had been catching naps all night in his office while monitoring radio reports coming in from overhead the *Mayaguez*. He repeated what Schlesinger had said, adding information about the helicopter loss. To Ford, the message now was that twenty-three men were dead, and so far nothing substantive had been accomplished. Scowcroft was told to convene a second meeting of the National Security Council.

The NSC gathered at 10:22 A.M. With Kissinger still not back from Missouri, Undersecretary of State for Political Affairs Joseph Sisco sat in for him. Colby stated that the ship was not in Kompong Som Harbor as thought, but just off the island of Koh Tang, one anchor up and one down. General Jones added that people who appeared to be Caucasians were seen on the island, with their heads between their knees. What had been seen from above Koh Tang as a small group of people leaving the boats for shore had mysteriously become a more ominous description by the time it reached the president.

This bungled report, which would become the genesis for crucial decisions later on, was barely off General Jones's lips when Ford made a comment about the intelligence summaries. "Overnight, Brent gave me a series of different reports that we were getting about the ship's location and about what was happening. We have to be more factual or at least more precise in pointing out our degree of knowledge."

Undeterred, Colby reaffirmed the current information. Ford was then told by Schlesinger that the navy ships were still too far from the scene for a rescue attempt, but helicopters were available from U.S. bases in Thailand. Schlesinger thought it better to wait. Rockefeller was not swayed. "The issue is how we respond. Many are watching us, in Korea and elsewhere. The big question is whether or not we look silly. I think we need to respond quickly."

Also discussed was the security police option. The idea that the helicopters could land on top of the ship's containers had already been ruled out when a container expert explained that the boxes would "crumble like a cardboard box" from the weight of the helicopters. A proposal to hover the helos while troops descended rope ladders onto the containers was also quickly drubbed when one of the civilians present asked, "While the Cambodians spray them with Russian burp guns as they climb down?"

Schlesinger passed on a report from an A-7 pilot who had seen two small fishing boats move away from the darkened hull of the ship. The pilot thought he saw Caucasians on one of the boats, and observed people disembark on the beach. He dropped lower for a closer look, but heavy ground fire came blazing up from the beach.

Ford also learned from Schlesinger that the P-3 reconnaissance plane overhead at the scene was now joined by an AC-130H *Spectre* gunship from the 388th Tactical Fighter Wing out of Korat Royal Thai Air Base in Thailand. This four-engined turboprop was packed with night-vision devices, and projecting from left side-ports were 7.62-mm miniguns, 20- and 40-mm cannons, and a big recoilless 105-mm tube. Schlesinger reported that the *Spectre* crew used their infrared scope to watch as people moved from small boats into the island's heavily forested interior. At this point, the NSC members were convinced that at least some members of the crew were on the island.

For the time being, Ford was given no immediate solution other than to wait for navy ships to arrive off Koh Tang and the marines to fully assemble in Thailand. Only then, the reasoning went, could a proper assault on the ship and/or island be contemplated. Once again, Ford was mindful of the protracted negotiations surrounding the release of the USS *Pueblo* crew back in '68, caused by allowing that ship to reach port. He ordered the air force to stop any Cambodian boats from moving either to or from Koh Tang and the mainland.

Obvious to Ford was the fact that if he was to make the decisive choice in this matter, he had to have accurate information to base it on. "I am very concerned about the delay in reports. We must have the information immediately. There must be the quickest possible communication to me."

The meeting ended at 11:17 A.M. In order to keep the scope of the incident under control, Ford resumed his regular appointment schedule including a meeting to listen to Governor Hugh Carey and Mayor Abraham Beame plead for federal money to save New York City from bankruptcy.

At 12:46 P.M., the president phoned Henry Kissinger in Missouri. Although still wishing to appear firmly at the helm during the crisis, he seemed willing to discuss options with Kissinger as long as Henry stayed in the background. When the idea of an ultimatum to release the crew was raised by Ford, Kissinger was not in favor. Kissinger later confided, "The risks were greater than the benefits and the benefits were really domestic." The use of B-52s was also discussed. Henry was all for readying the bombers stationed in Guam. Schlesinger had argued against the use of the big bombers, which were so widely tied by antiwar groups to the unpopular cause in Vietnam.

Kissinger meanwhile was receiving continuous updates from the State Department and from Scowcroft. One of them later that day was an ultimatum from Thailand. Recently elected prime minister Kukrit Pramoj expressed outrage over the arrival of marines from the Philippines. He gave but twenty-four hours for the United States to remove them. Kissinger knew of course that the Thai military—the real power brokers in the country—had already given their concurrence before any U.S. troop carrier touched down on Thai soil.

To the press corps traveling with the secretary, Kissinger seemed lively, even animated, particularly in light of his recent morose state, witnessed during the Saigon and Phnom Penh evacuations. In Kansas City, Kissinger pounded the podium with unabashed enthusiasm proclaiming, "The United States will not accept harassment of its ships in international sea-lanes." When asked by *Time* correspondent Strobe Talbott if he could predict a time of resolution for the incident, Kissinger drew a confident smile and said, "I know your magazine's deadline. I think we can meet it."

10

GARY LEE HALL

Every bit of our training was to do one thing. To make us finely honed killing machines. And let me tell you something, pal. When I went to Parris Island I was a 145-pound sissy. When I left boot camp I was 175 pounds and a solid rock who could spit nails and love it.

Koh Tang veteran Lance Corporal Larry Barnett, USMC

A month before his nineteenth birthday, six-foot-two-inch Gary Lee Hall still showed peach fuzz on his chin, but had added back the forty pounds he initially lost at Parris Island boot camp. Those new pounds were muscle and sinew, the stuff needed to heft the M-60 machine gun that he strapped to his back and carried into battle.

My Toyota tires hummed over slotted metal on the drive across the Covington/Cincinnati Suspension Bridge. Skyscrapers and Cinergy Field filled the rearview mirror and the muddy Ohio River drifted by underneath. On the south bank, a big convention center loomed on the right with its adjacent Embassy Suites hotel and TGI Fridays waterfront bar and grill. A paddle-wheel steamer was docked to the left, all gentrified and ready for business. Then, as if a veil had been lowered, a mere block later I found myself in small-town America. Most of the streets are one-way, and many others dead-end at the river. I turned south onto Madison, passed the White Castle burger stand on Twelfth, went right on Fifteenth, then left on Banklick to the fourplex with the number 1618 on it. Born in 1956, Gary Lee Hall grew up there, just six minutes from downtown Cincinnati, yet some forty years away in time. Little has changed. The mortar has eroded from between many of the bricks on the facade of the place, but you can still hear tractor-trailers in the distance downshifting their diesels as they roll through the "cut in the hill" on Interstate 75, headed down the grade toward Cincinnati. The Southern Pacific trains still rumble through town every half hour just east of Banklick. Many of the same residents still live on the street, the next generation having taken over the property when parents passed away, or perhaps never having moved out at all.

Gary Hall was raised in the top apartment, a two-bedroom flat with a living room at the front and kitchen in the back. He had an older brother, David, younger brother, Michael, and two sisters, Jane and Janet.

Gary did not grow right. He was not disfigured or crippled, but not a pair of limbs on his body sprouted evenly. Mother Nature tried, but things never quite caught up the way they should: his legs always seemed too long for his torso. A curly tuft of hair flopped over his forehead, dominating his moody face.

Older brother David started the teasing early on and kept it up, a verbal assault that was relentless in its ego-crushing momentum. The goading continued through grade school, with Gary's lack of coordination adding fuel to the never-ending needling.

Gary had playmates though. He often teamed with David Sammons, but even among his age group, "Gary was a tall, clumsy kid who was the target for most of our jokes and put-downs." "Mad Scientist" Emerson and "Country Boy" Hass filled out their foursome. The same ages, the boys would gather behind the fourplex for war games. They set up front lines beside the big maple tree that threw shade across the yard, rendering it mostly dirt amid scattered patches of sod. The toy soldiers that fought in their wars were plastic action figures who clung to safety behind clumps of grass or in tiny trenches scraped out of the sand by dirty hands. The infantry rifleman's steady aim was forever frozen in time. The bazooka man stood tall, his weapon shouldered, ever ready to fire. The boys broke out their Blackcat firecrackers collected from the streets after the Fourth of July celebrations. They'd pull out the stubs of burned-out fuses a tad, then light and drop fireworks from the air, like bombs raining down on troops. A prone machine gunner, feet spread wide for control, would fly a few inches from the explosion. Some of the soldiers got buried in sand, their bodies recovered along with the others after the battle and placed safely inside a King Edwards cigar box until the next campaign. In these backyard wars, there were no real casualties.

Gary's father, Sheldon, was a hard-shell Baptist who took no lip from youngsters. A self-employed carpenter, he supported the family in fits and starts, making the monthly rent a chancy affair, not to mention putting food on the table. He had a legendary temper and the locals gave him a wide swath. "Strict is what he was. You knew exactly what the man had in mind when he spoke."

Gary lived in fear of his father, yet somehow made it to senior year at Holmes High School with all his teeth and no broken bones. He never attended a high school dance, never had a girlfriend. As far as anyone knows, he never even was allowed to go to the movies. Much of the time, he was dressed in a collared shirt while the rest of the boys ran around in T-shirts. Much of the time, he was on his way to or from the Baptist church.

During his last semester, the Marine Corps recruiter, a gunnery sergeant, made his annual visit. The gunny looked so John Wayne, so tough, so worthy. He wore chevrons on his sleeve and ribbons on a blouse of immaculately pressed khaki. A Vietnam veteran, he talked of the honor of being in the Marine Corps, of it being only for a few good men.

High school ended, and with a diploma in hand, Gary got a job at the White Castle on Twelfth. For two months he worked there, dishing out the small hamburgers they sold, until one night he got chased all the way home from the restaurant by a group of toughs. Arriving breathless and in tears, the episode seemed to have an effect beyond the other taunts he had endured. He told his mother, Norma Hall, that he was going to join the marines. She said, "No, I'm not signin' no papers while you're still under eighteen." Two months later, he no longer needed a parent's permission. America had pulled out of Vietnam, and the country had no stomach for more body counts. What the heck, the Marine Corps offered a steady job, but more important, it offered an escape from the thundering reproaches of his father and the biting taunts of his siblings. "I gotta get out of this town and make something of myself," he told twenty-one-year-old neighbor David Jones.

Before he joined the marines, he wrote a note in the high school yearbook to his schoolmate:

> David,
> So what can I say to you that I can't say to you
> during the day or week, so by[e].
> Friend—Hall '74

In July, Hall rode the green military bus filled with new recruits out of Beaufort, South Carolina, then across the causeway and bridge over Archer's Creek and on past an expanse of gloomy wetlands. Heat and humidity seemed to boil out of the marsh and get sucked inside the open windows. What happened next is described by Larry Barnett, a Koh Tang veteran and one of Hall's marine buddies.

"When we got to Parris Island, the bus stopped and the driver took up a clipboard while a drill instructor got aboard. The DI wore an impeccable khaki uniform, spit shined shoes, and a trooper hat cocked a bit on one side. The DI didn't do anything at first except to look at that clipboard. Some talking started on the bus. He said, 'Be quiet,' in a growly but low tone.

"Somebody in the back started laughing and hooting. That pissed him off. At the top of his lungs he bellowed, 'I said shut your goddamn mouth.' Man, you could have heard a pin drop on that bus. Me, I liked to piss my pants. Then he told us, 'You got fifteen seconds to get your asses off this bus and your feet in the yellow footprints outside.' To make sure we got our feet in a timely manner into footprints painted on the asphalt, there were two other DIs waiting. They went up and down the rows of men screamin' at us, daring us to move. If you blinked and he saw you, he would get right in your face, put the brim of that hat right on the bridge of your nose, and roar, 'What is your problem, numb-nuts? Can't you hear me? Do I need to clean the shit out of your ears for you?' By then sweat was pouring off me. Mosquitoes were eating me alive. That was the first time I heard the term, 'Don't touch them mosquitoes. They got a right to eat too!'"

Welcome to the Marine Corps, Gary Lee Hall.

Four months later, a Marine Corps private quick-stepped up Banklick Street toward fourplex number 1618, and not a soul recognized him. His friend David Jones gaped dumbstruck when he finally realized who the marine was. "Gary Hall had always been tall, but now he was forty pounds leaner and straight, appearing much stronger. He looked you right in the eye when he spoke, and there was none of the clumsiness in his moves that he had when he left for boot camp."

What Gary Hall's appearance said during his short furlough was that the marines had made a man of him. Four months later he finished infantry school and found himself on Okinawa.

11

WEDNESDAY OF THE *MAYAGUEZ*
INCIDENT

*Although prepared for martyrdom, I preferred that
it be postponed.*

Sir Winston Churchill

The night was long and uncomfortable for the crew of the *Mayaguez* spread aboard the two fishing trawlers that were tied together near the beach. Burton Coombes, who had sighted the first gunboat, got fleeting amounts of sleep curled up on a fishing net. The net reeked of dead fish, and its rough twine ripped into his back. He awoke with a start each time he moved, then listened to the undulating drone of the reconnaissance plane. He could not see it, but at least it was reassuring to know Uncle Sam was still there watching over them. He thought about Delores. He had just come off five months ashore, "playing golf, fishing, and fighting with my wife." A sailor's life was tough on a wife and marriage. For Delores, his long periods of absence generally followed a too-long period of presence. He wondered if she was in for a really extended period of his "absence."

Then there was the likes of former marine English to worry about. Coombes had heard the talk, mostly bravado, about grabbing grenade launchers and "sending these gooks overboard." But Coombes had heard lots of sea stories from World War II veterans who had lived through Japanese prison camps. These Cambodian kids came off as a little nervous to him, not like the ferocious look the Japanese were famous for. He decided he'd rather take his chances in a stockade and await release than be a dead hero.

Second Engineer Juan Sanchez could not sleep either. The few times he briefly drifted off, he began snoring, to the consternation of the others. Discomfort over snoring did not last for long. A burst of gunfire jerked everyone awake. Orange tracers rose above the island and crisscrossed the sky. Sanchez rolled on his back to watch. Wide awake now, he worried about how he was going to start up the power plant on the *Mayaguez* in the morning. Captain Miller had told him they were going back to the ship at dawn, so Sanchez went over in his mind all the things he would need to do to get the sometimes-cranky machinery running.

Dave English had spread his 250 pounds over the same fish net with Coombes. He never closed his eyes. He, too, listened to the plane grinding away the hours, a few thousand feet above. He wondered about the men up there. Navy men. He knew the P-3 was navy and the guys overhead were probably drinking coffee and talking about getting laid in Olongapo City when they get back to the Philippines or to Pattaya Beach in Thailand, wherever they were from. But down where English was, survival was the topic. English guessed that there were eighty or ninety Cambodians and at least four gunboats close by. Doing something "physical" to get free was beginning to seem more risky. He would need to wait until the Cambodians were thinned out a bit before trying anything.

Captain Charlie Miller had tried to get some shut-eye on top of a hatch cover. Considering the amount of gunfire going on, he decided things had gone pretty well for his crew. The worst was a bruise or two. But both English and Second Mate Jerry Myregard kept him on edge. English was a hothead and might act without thinking.

Myregard, on the other hand, had mentioned he might try slipping over the side and evading capture on the island. Either action could put the rest of the crew in for some hard times. *Pull something like that, and we all may get our heads chopped off*, thought Miller. He hoped they'd all be taken back to the ship in the morning as promised and could get some food and maybe figure a peaceful way out of this mess. He looked up. A lot of stars were out. The air was cool. He drifted off to sleep.

At six o'clock, Miller awoke to find the two fishing boats still lashed together. The sky glowed pink, and the white sand fifty yards away was bathed in early morning light, looking for all the world like something out of Robinson Crusoe . . . except for the tree line and its dark barrels that jutted above the gun pits. He saw only three Swift boats now, bobbing at anchor nearby. The Cambodian leader, Sa Mean, was nowhere to be seen.

For two hours, Miller and the crew waited while the sun rose in the sky, searing hot. Then the guards became active, herding all the crew onto the bigger fishing boat. It was untied from the smaller vessel, then got under way out of the inlet.

Miller took stock. Four or five guards, one with a radio pack, were squirreled away in the pilothouse. Two guards each with AK-47s stood in the bow and stern. Two of the gunboats ranged ahead, carving a brisk wake in the shimmering water. The trawler was headed straight for the *Mayaguez* as promised. It had been eighteen hours since Miller had eaten and his nerves were raw from tension and lack of food and sleep. He looked forward to getting back aboard.

Suddenly the trawler veered starboard. Miller hung on, wondering if the wheel had been turned loose. Then the boat rolled out of its turn and steadied on a new course, northeast toward the mainland.

"They're giving us a line of bullshit," Dave English bellowed, his red hair seeming to punctuate his mood. English was standing in the bow, close by the two guards with the guns. "Hey Skipper, looks like we're headed for Kompong Som."

English had barely gotten the words out of his mouth when two swept-wing jets swooped over the fishing boat. These were F-111 Ardvarks whose wings sweep to seventy degrees at high speed. The roar of their engines drowned out all other noise as their afterburners carved a climbing red gash across the sky. Then four fighters, A-7D Corsairs and F-4E Phantoms like the ones he had seen in Vietnam, flashed by two at a time. The planes arced upward in an aerial ballet, then the swept-wing planes descended again, this time to the northeast near the two Swift boats. Seconds later the dull sounds of explosions drifted back to the fishing boat. English saw the gunboats separate, one turning back to the island and the other barreling ahead. Down roared a second pair of fighters and another series of muted thuds was heard. This time, though, English saw a dirty puff of smoke on the horizon. The gunboat had been hit. He was sure of that. Otherwise there would only be a plume of water thrown up by the explosion. Then a four-engine turboprop joined the fighters. The turboprop was an AC-130 *Spectre* gunship, painted black for night operations, its usual environment. Flashes of cannon fire spit from its side ports above where the lone patrol boat still headed northeast. The air force might have been trying to turn the flotilla around with the first series of passes, but now they were shooting for effect. English wondered how the Cambodians on the trawler would react and whether their boat would be the next bombing target. He did not have to wait long to find out. The jets wheeled, and their noses were pointed right at the trawler.

"Here they come!"

The Cambodians in the bow crouched low behind the gunwale, using it as a shield against the incoming planes as the fighters came down one at a time, banking in front and behind the trawler. The next two meant business, each of them dropping bombs well in front of the boat.

English looked up and waved. Maybe they'd be watching, see him, and slow down for a closer look. Meanwhile, the trawler held a steady course. English looked north as another fighter rolled in. The others saw it, too. A group of men clustered by the gasoline drums in front of the pilothouse moved instinctively away, but there was no real protection anywhere.

Two more plumes of water gushed up a hundred yards in front of the boat, followed by the ear-splitting crack of the detonations. Still the boat plowed ahead. Another pair of jets spread wide and came roaring in. This time a quick succession of shell bursts erupted barely fifty feet in front of the bow. English knew the sound well: 20-mm cannons, every other shell either armor-piercing incendiary or high-explosive. A geyser of water sprayed the deck as English and the others huddled for cover.

"Jesus Christ, they're coming close!"

A piece of shrapnel dropped onto the nape of English's neck. The fiery-hot shard slid down the back of his shirt. English rolled on the deck, trying to dislodge it. His hand brushed another red-hot piece, the size of a dime. He heard his flesh sizzle and caught a glimpse of Second Mate Myregard crouched against the gunwale, blood streaming from his right arm.

"You okay?" English asked.

Myregard looked down at the wound but said nothing. English grabbed Myregard's arm and started squeezing it, trying to pop the piece of steel out. The shrapnel was too deeply imbedded, and English did not have a knife to open the wound to clean it out. He pulled out his handkerchief and tied it around the arm.

English glanced forward. The two Cambodian guards had abandoned their post and dived into the fish well to escape the gunfire. Their AK-47s were sliding around on deck, ready for the taking. English edged toward the guns, noting Captain Miller's look of approval as he made his way forward. Then the Khmers burst open the hatch cover and scampered out of the well, grabbing their rifles as they made their way forward. Another opportunity to turn things around had slipped away. When all was said and done, it was going to take decisive action the moment a good chance presented itself. Under the circumstances, a "good chance" was hard to recognize. Some of the men were praying. A lot of men were bleeding. No one onboard, it seemed, was willing to risk everything in a bold attempt to free themselves.

Captain Miller saw blood staining Third Engineer Rappenecker's leg. He moved to Rappenecker's side and tried to stem the flow of blood with his handkerchief. Nearby, Juan Sanchez had his hand cupped over his left ear. Blood oozed between his fingers.

Then another fighter came streaking in low and fast. The cannon rounds ripped the water's surface behind the trawler. Fragments of flying steel rattled through the pilothouse. The boat heeled hard port.

For a moment, Miller thought the helmsman had been hit. Then he saw one of the Khmer guards jump up and point his weapon inside the pilothouse at the helmsman. The boat righted itself and resumed its northeastern course. Miller wondered why the Khmer had to point his gun at the helmsman.

Captain Miller looked around at his battered crew. They had a lot more than bruises now. He glanced skyward. The planes were circling. He figured they had been trying to scare the boat driver into turning around. Now they were talking it over. Would they come in for the finish? He doubted they had any idea the *Mayaguez* crew was aboard.

12

"PILOT TO PRESIDENT, OVER"

Even the right decision is wrong if it's made too late.

Lee Iacocca

The first phone call to President Ford came at 8:10 P.M. Tuesday night. He was at the White House and had just finished dinner with his wife, Betty. Scowcroft was on the line. A Thai freighter had been seized by Cambodians and detained for two hours some forty miles east of where the *Mayaguez* had been boarded. A Swedish ship, the *Hirado*, had been fired upon near the same spot but was able to outrun her attackers. Last, the *Mayaguez* was still at anchor near Koh Tang.

By now, communications personnel at 7th Air Force Headquarters at Nakhon Phanom in Thailand had established a communications link that provided continuous contact between aircraft overhead the

Mayaguez and the National Military Command Center in Washington. The link passed information back and forth using satellites and a U-2 at high altitude as a radio-relay aircraft. Thus General Burns at Nakhon Phanom; the Pacific commander, Admiral Gayler, in Honolulu; the secretary of defense and the Joint Chiefs of Staff (JCS) generals and admirals; and those in the Situation Room in the White House were all directly connected to real-time events, or at least they believed they were.

Everyone at listening posts from Thailand to Hawaii to Washington knew that a P-3 Orion pilot above Koh Tang had reported a small flotilla departing the cove and heading toward Kompong Som. Instructions from the Situation Room in Washington were passed back to General Burns's headquarters in Thailand. "Halt any boat movement to the mainland." Standing by to carry out the orders were the pilots and crews orbiting in the AC-130 *Spectre* gunship, and F-111 Ardvarks, F-4 Phantoms, and A-7 Corsair fighter-bombers.

At first the F-111s had tried to turn the boats around with low passes. Then the Ardvarks got serious and dropped two sticks of two-thousand-pound bombs well in front of the gunboats. One turned back, but the other continued ahead along with a nondescript fishing trawler following behind. Discussions ensued between pilots and on up through the command centers. The AC-130 *Spectre* made a try, using its 20-mm cannon to ripple the water in front of the gunboat. Still no change of course, but the gunboat fired back. Another request to Washington produced an okay to take direct action against the persistent Swift boat. Lieutenant Colonel Don Robotoy from the 388th Tactical Fighter Wing at Korat, Thailand, swung his A-7D Corsair down to strafe. His wingman followed. Robotoy hoped to simply knock the boat out of action, but his gatling gun sprayed a hundred rounds a second and literally sawed off the end of the boat. It sank so fast that an inbound RF-4C reconnaissance plane could only photograph an ominous slick in the water.

The fighters turned their attention to the trawler. First in were the A-7s, flying as slow as they dared for a visual inspection, at not more than 450 miles an hour. They reported that the boat looked unarmed. Then the Ardvarks dropped more bombs in front of the boat. Next, F-4s fired 2.75-inch rocket pods to no avail. Finally, the A-7s took to strafing mere yards in front of the bow. When that did not dissuade the craft, they held high for another discussion. New information was passed to 7th Air Force. "Thirty to forty possible Caucasians are huddled in the bow."

A second call to Ford came from Scowcroft at 9:51 P.M. He told the president that air force jets had come under fire while trying to prevent several gunboats from reaching the mainland. The gunboats were being attacked. Things were heating up. The president decided to convene another National Security Council meeting.

At 10:30 P.M. the council members joined Ford in the Cabinet Room for the third NSC session in two days. Henry Kissinger was present, having returned from Missouri an hour earlier.

Just as the meeting started, a message came up from the Situation Room in the basement. Ford was told by Scowcroft that several gunboats had been engaged and sunk or turned around, but a fishing boat was still proceeding toward the mainland. One pilot saw an unusual gathering of passengers near the bow. He radioed, "I believe I see Caucasian faces." He was willing to try to shoot the rudder off rather than sink it, and was literally asking the president to call the next shot. Scowcroft was poised to relay the president's order to the pilot.

Ford asked Scowcroft for details. When told the boat was six miles from Kompong Som with the pilot overhead awaiting instructions, Ford found himself trapped into coming up with a decision he was not ready or eager to make.

Ford assumed that if the fishing boat with those crew members got ashore, the odds were against getting them back unharmed. But the president was torn with the other possibility. If he told the pilot to strafe the boat or sink it, he might kill them all.

Schlesinger urged caution, arguing that the United States should not be "in a position where the Cambodians can say that the F-4s killed our own men."

Ford looked around the room, a perplexed expression on his face. "What do we do? Do we let them go into port?"

Ford looked directly at the secretary of defense for a response.

Schlesinger thought a moment, then said, "Let's continue to try to stop them with riot-control agents."

That had already failed to turn the boat around, so Ford turned to Kissinger.

Kissinger was not eager to be pinned down. He chose the stall approach. "I have just come back into this problem, having been out of town all day. My instinct would [be] as follows: We have two problems: first, the problem of the crew and the ship and of how we win their release. Second, our general posture, which goes beyond the crew and the ship."

Even Kissinger realized his academic analysis was going over badly, an obvious attempt to gather his own thoughts.

"But that sort of thing comes later," he acknowledged. Then he launched into a lengthy "if we do this" or "if you are willing to do that" monologue. Meanwhile Scowcroft stewed. Eventually, Kissinger nudged closer to the point: "We will take a beating if we kill Americans," seguing into "We cannot negotiate for them once they are on the mainland." Then to keep his position firmly ambiguous, he ended with a comment about the crew: "We should not let them become bargaining chips."

None of that was any help to Ford. With an immediate decision required, he instead chose to avoid it by shifting the discussion to why the boat had been allowed to leave the island in the first place. "I gave the order at the meeting to stop all boats. I cannot understand what happened on that order."

Of course, had the pilots followed the president's order to the letter and attacked the trawler, the result also would have been catastrophic and everyone would have been scrambling to place the blame.

Acting JCS chairman General Jones stated that the "stop" order went out as directed, but offered no reason why it was not followed. Jones went on to say, "Our communications are so good that we can get all the information back here immediately to Washington in order to make the decisions from here." The arrangement was set up in response to the president's criticism about quick relay of information, made at the previous NSC meeting. Now, with the mechanism greased, Ford was finding it had boxed him into a corner. There would be no passing the buck and no excuse if his were the wrong call.

Schlesinger shifted the discussion to whether the patrol boats still at the island should be sunk. Meanwhile, the boat with Caucasians aboard was slipping away.

Another side issue came up, namely how fast the *Holt* was steaming to the scene. Scowcroft could stand this filibustering no longer.

"I have to get the word out," Scowcroft interrupted. "What should I tell them?"

A long, dramatic silence descended. All eyes fixed on the president as he pondered what to do.

Finally Ford spoke. "Tell them to sink the boats near the island. On the other boat, use riot-control agents or other methods, but do not attack it."

As Scowcroft put the word out, White House staffer John Marsh spoke up. "Supposing the boats near the island have Americans on it. Should we send some order to use only riot-control agents there?"

"I think the pilot should sink them," Kissinger said, following that opinion with a statement showing incredible callousness. "He should destroy the boats and not send situation reports."

Scowcroft sent word while discussions centered on what overall course to pursue.

Ford wanted to know about the timing of ship arrivals at Koh Tang. He immediately got into a touchy exchange with General Jones over how fast the *Coral Sea* could move.

"It is making twenty-five knots," Jones said.

"That is not flank speed," Ford noted.

Jones came back with, "That is the best time that they can do."

Ford, with his naval background, knew something the air force general did not, and the president wanted him to know it. "Flank speed is thirty-three knots."

Jones was not about to concede. "The navy says that that is the best time they can make."

The conversation continued on about timing of ships, marines, and aircraft, and eventually shifted to efforts to solve the crisis diplomatically. The Chinese in Beijing had returned the American note intended for Phnom Penh. In diplomatic terms, this meant they were refusing to pass it on. The Chinese had read it, though, according to George H. W. Bush, head of the U.S. Liaison Office in Beijing, and it may well have been relayed to the Cambodians. One Chinese official did hint that China would take no action in the event that the United States undertook military measures.

Henry Kissinger still called for tough action, but for reasons of international image. "I am thinking not of Cambodia, but of Korea, and of the Soviet Union and of others."

The plight of the *Pueblo* crew back in 1968 came up again. Nobody wanted a repeat of that. Ford felt he needed to move forcefully and fast, so he turned to General Jones for options.

Jones presented five. The first scenario was to seize the *Mayaguez* at the earliest opportunity, on the morning of May 14 or after arrival of the USS *Holt*. The main disadvantage was that it "put our initial effort on the *Mayaguez*, which we could probably obtain at any time, rather than on the crew." The second alternative was to attack Koh Tang. It produced a similar disadvantage: "There is some possibility that some American crewmen are on the *Mayaguez* and the attack of the island might incite reprisals against them." The third scenario was for a coordinated attack on the ship and island set for May 16 at first light. The fourth scenario involved bombing Cambodian warships participating in the *Mayaguez* operation, the idea being to use force to convince the Cambodian government to acquiesce. The fifth alternative was really a second part of option four and was to bomb additional mainland targets twenty-four hours after attacking Cambodian shipping. The ones that offered the best hope of having enough on-scene forces also involved the most risk of being too late. Based on the belief that crew members were on both the ship and the island, based on the bogus intelligence report to that effect received on the thirteenth, Ford combined options three and four, a simultaneous attack by marines on the *Mayaguez* and on Koh Tang, coupled with an aerial bombardment of selected shipping and mainland targets. The debate over timing centered on the arrival of the aircraft carrier *Coral Sea*. It was a thousand miles from the island at that point. As a former naval officer, Ford was well aware of the flexibility the carrier offered both in terms of close-in striking power and rescue capability. A twenty-four-hour hold was put on the effort to allow time for the big ship to close the distance.

Then Rumsfeld, a former naval aviator, brought up the fact that aircraft could launch from the carrier while still hours away. Up to that point in the crisis, no one in the room had even thought of that.

Ford squelched that notion by pointing out that the ship would have to turn into the wind to launch and recover aircraft and that would delay things too much if the winds were not favorable, a shaky claim.

With four catapults, a strike package of thirty or more aircraft could be airborne from the carrier in twelve minutes. The carrier recovers planes with as little as thirty seconds' spacing in daylight, but twenty minutes would normally be required to recover those thirty jets. Ocean winds tend to be light in that region so turning in and out of the wind might not even be required. If they had to reverse course every time, a maximum four-hour delay would be required to launch and recover the entire planned strike packages. The carrier nominally tries to provide a thirty-knot wind across the deck for launches and recoveries. This reduces the relative speed between aircraft and carrier as the planes engage the arresting gear, but planes can be recovered well below the thirty-knot head-wind condition. As Ford claimed, the *Coral Sea* could achieve thirty-three knots, so it could remain on course for launches and recoveries even with a sizeable tail wind. In combat, the navy can make adjustments within its established limitations depending on the priorities. No one pointed this out to the president. The enhanced communications had allowed data to be sent up the chain quickly and in prodigious amounts, but the information had to be filtered by people with varying degrees of expertise, then converted to word of mouth for delivery to the president.

In spite of the no-fire decision regarding the trawler, the National Security Council participants relished not only making big strategic decisions but, because of enhanced communications, were becoming enamored with making small tactical ones as well. Gerald Ford was a president whose military experience dated to World War II. His senior military man, General Jones, had a career in heavy bombers, and the rest of the National Security Council had little exposure in the trenches. General Jones, for example, did not advise the president about the accuracy of the A-7 gatling gun, which uses a computer-controlled sight, because as a bomber pilot he had no feel for it. Reliable A-7 information might have caused the president to change his mind about shooting off the tail of the trawler. But the real question is, should the president have been making that kind of decision in the first place?

Every squadron keeps tabs on their best strafers. Top guns are no secret in the macho world of fighter aviation. If a decision to try stopping the trawler was to be made, it should have come from no higher than the controlling team in *Cricket,* the orbiting EC-130, after considering the availability of helicopters for rescue, the qualifications and accuracy of the pilots and planes flying above the boat, risk to the captives, and the size and defenses of the target. With only small arms aboard the trawler, the fighters could get in very close for the shot. A talented A-7 strafer can routinely get off a very tight quarter-second burst, sending twenty or so rounds within a two-square-yard area. Rescue helicopters were less than two hours away at U-Tapao. The staff inside *Cricket* may have come to the same conclusion as did President Ford, but instead of dealing with the issue themselves, the controllers spent their time sending requests for guidance back to distant headquarters.

In any event, the National Security Council in Washington went on to discuss the attack time. Although Kissinger suggested going in at "first light," H-hour wound up being set by the Pentagon for just before sunrise May 15, Cambodia time. In fact, the JCS planners intended for the assault to begin right at sunrise, but got the time wrong by four minutes. Their thinking was to have the helicopters skim into the east beach and be hard to see by defenders who would be looking into a rising sun. That tactic may be appropriate for fighters coming out of the sun in a one-on-one dogfight, but to think the sun would be of much benefit to a helicopter attacking along a wide expanse of defended beach was wishful thinking at best. Since the captives were thought to be held in the buildings just behind the beach, it was hoped that the element of surprise would allow the marines to quickly envelop the compound and free the crew. Daylight was deemed necessary in order to keep from shooting *Mayaguez* crew members by mistake, a valid consideration. However, the decision makers either did not account for or ignored the fact that daybreak would actually begin twenty-six minutes before sunrise during the period of "first nautical twilight." The designated H-hour they set was well after good lighting was available.

Should the exact timing of the attack have been left to the marine commander involved in the assault? Events would soon answer that question.

13

"GAS!"

I accepted the realization that if any help was still contemplated by our Seventh Fleet or Fifth Air Force, its objective could no longer be rescue, only retaliation.

Commander Lloyd Bucher, USN, as the USS *Pueblo* approached
Wonsan Harbor, North Korea, 1968

While the battle around the fishing trawler was in full swing, events began coming together at the sprawling Thai naval base at U-Tapao.

The *Jolly Green* and *Knife* helicopters had delivered the remnants of the security police volunteers from Nakhon Phanom and by dawn the rescue force was ready to launch. However, General Burns at 7th Air Force was advised by his staff that the marines from D Company were much better suited than the policemen for the *Mayaguez* insertion effort. Burns delayed until the marines, who had just arrived from the Philippines, could be briefed and loaded aboard the choppers. He estimated the mission could be airborne by 7:50 A.M. that Wednesday morning.

Major Porter's D Company marines were told upon landing to be ready to launch in one hour. Besides his own men, Porter had six civilian mariners from the USNS *Greenville Victory* and six sailors from USS *Duluth* who were expected to start the power plant and operate the ship. He also had two air force Explosive Ordnance Disposal (EOD bomb squad) sergeants and an army officer who spoke Cambodian. Porter sent his men to the mess hall for a quick meal while he, Captain Feltner, and D Company commander Captain Wood proceeded to a building near the runway to receive 7th Air Force instructions. The briefing turned out to be more like a quiz session. Porter found himself "questioned as to the feasibility of a helo assault directly onto the deck of the *Mayaguez*." What Porter did not know was that General Burns wanted to have his ducks in order when he went forward to Hawaii and Washington.

With an estimated thirty Khmer soldiers aboard and in all likelihood the *Mayaguez* crewmen *off* the ship, Porter was not at all sanguine about a vertical assault. As the merits of the proposed plan were argued, time ticked away. The 7:50 departure came and went without orders. A new H-hour of 9:10 A.M. was set, but still no decision about how to retake the ship had been made.

When that deadline passed without a decision, Porter did some figuring. He estimated that it would take over two hours to fly to the scene, then at least three hours to secure the ship and get her under way. Since the ship was reported to be "cold," meaning it had no electricity, the nearly six-hour procedure would have to be completed in daylight. Porter calculated the revised launch time of 2:15 P.M. He learned that eleven hundred marines from Okinawa were due to land around 12:30 P.M. That would leave precious little time to agree on a plan, brief all the participants, and load out. Porter and his men continued struggling to piece together something that made sense.

One hundred and ninety nautical miles to the south, Third Mate Dave English watched as the fighters continued orbiting. He was certain a decision was being batted around up there. To live or die, that was what they were considering. The precision in putting their weapons so close to the trawler without a direct hit made him feel the pilots were only trying to scare the helmsman into turning around.

That had not worked. What would they do next? English decided to move away from the bow to a spot near the pilothouse. If the pilots decided to sink the boat, he wanted to be positioned where he could dive behind some cover, get his hands on a weapon and take action. He looked aft. Streaking low above the water were two fighters, line abreast, heading for the boat. With their jet engines roaring like great cats, the planes flew right over the trawler. Suddenly the air was filled with tumbling, burning, sizzling objects. Small gray cartridges, the size of flashlight batteries, rained down on the deck, spewing clouds of white tear gas.

English tried to get a lung full of clean air. Too late. The vapor singed his lungs. Searing pain shot up his mouth and nose. He could hear men around him gasping, retching, and coughing. His eyes smarted as he blinked while groping around in a ghostly gray-white cloud, convinced the pilots were swooping in for the kill.

The boat's heading began to waver.

Back in the pilothouse, a Khmer guard got to his feet and jammed his rifle against the helmsman's head. The trawler steadied out, on course.

Then the smoke cleared. The two guards in the bow had abandoned their weapons again and were nowhere to be seen—probably down the fish hole. The guards near the pilothouse had their arms wrapped tight around their faces, trying to ward off the burning chemical.

Now's the time, thought English. Just then Chief Engineer Cliff Harrington nudged him, giving English a knowing look. Harrington had seen the guns laying there, too. Between them and the guns was Second Engineer Juan Sanchez, unconscious on the deck.

"Are you okay, Juan?" Harrington called out. He moved forward, then bent at Sanchez's side. "You okay?"

Sanchez opened his eyes and took a breath of air as Harrington and English eyed the AK-47s a few yards away. English had handled AK-47s before, but would he know if the safety was on? The markings were probably in Chinese or Russian. What if he grabbed the weapon and pointed it at a Cambodian and it did not go off. Then he would have to lower the gun and flip the safety the other way. By then things would have started happening. Even if he guessed right about the safety, he would have to get all the Cambodians before they returned fire or dove for cover.

The guns might as well have been on the moon, because with their feet rooted in place, neither Harrington nor English was yet willing to make the irrevocable lunge that might either free them or get them all killed. For them it was the most common of human reactions in time of fear. The certainty of the next breath in captivity outweighed the uncertainty of a free breath a minute later.

When the smoke finally drifted away, English looked around. Just ahead was a black channel buoy. The low hills above Kompong Som Harbor loomed not far off. He had waited too long.

Captain Charlie Miller's lungs burned from the gas attack, but the planes had stopped coming and he could breathe easier. Now if only his head would clear. His eyes were still tearing as the trawler wound its way up the channel and curled toward the wharf. Off to his right, two Chinese freighters were berthed end to end. Sacks of rice were being off-loaded onto a long concrete pier.

Miller suddenly found himself looking dead ahead at a dock looming twenty feet above the deck of the fishing boat. A crowd of Cambodians stood shoulder to shoulder staring back with grim, unflinching faces as the trawler swung alongside.

Men, women, and children, most of them armed, most of them dressed in black garb, glared down at the Caucasians huddled together in the bow. Miller felt as though his crew was being looked upon as the daily catch, about to be gaffed and hauled to the dock for filleting.

Then the trawler backed away from the bulkhead and tied up next to another fishing boat, which was flying a Viet Cong flag.

"Welcome to Wharf Number Two," Miller said to himself. The Cambodian commander had wanted him to bring the *Mayaguez* there.

Dave English took one look at the crowd and all the guns and realized there would be no more chances to make an escape. People were pouring onto the dock, all of them eager to get a look at the new arrivals.

About a dozen new Khmer Rouge made their way from the Vietnamese boat onto the trawler. These arrivals began a gruff exchange with the guards who had brought the *Mayaguez* crew from the island. Miller tried to figure out who was in charge, his thought being that he might single him out, find out if he spoke English or French, and, if so, demand to speak with a government official. Before he could discern who was the leader, a Cambodian gunboat with the number 133 on its side swung into the harbor, pulling up beside the trawler. The gunboat crew began conversing with the trawler guards.

Unknown to Miller, the gist of the Khmer conversation was that the ground commander at Kompong Som wanted no part of handling the captured crew. He feared retaliation by the American forces, which had already demonstrated their willingness to bomb and shoot. His message was that this was a navy problem that should be dealt with on navy territory.

A minute later, the trawler's lines were cast off, and she was under way again, headed alone out of the harbor. The boat turned left, followed the coast for about fifteen minutes, turned left once more, and anchored a hundred yards off a white, sandy beach. Just behind the shore stood two austere cement buildings that faced an assembly area and helipad. Iron bars covered many of the windows. The entrance was wreathed in barbed wire. *Some type of military installation or a stockade*, thought Miller.

Miller gave the shoreline a good scan. The strand ran for a mile or more to the southeast. Two small islands stood offshore well to the south. Other than that, there was little to see. He noticed two men hauling a boat into the surf. They boarded and rowed awkwardly, zigzagging out past the light breakers as they aimed for the trawler. Miller assumed they were going to be ferried a few at a time to the beach and into the prison or garrison.

The fishing trawler helmsman, the one who had the gun put to his head during the gas attack, appeared from inside the pilothouse. He began handing out bowls of food. Then he made a motion, crossing his hands as though handcuffed. Miller turned to Harrington. "He's trying to tell me to eat before they cuff us and haul us away."

Seaman Gerald Bayless, standing near Miller, saw what was going on, too. He had spent a lot of time in Thailand, even had liberty money stashed in the Asia Trust Bank in Pattaya Beach where he liked to lay low after a trip. He took a long look at the helmsman. "This guy don't look Cambodian to me. I think he's Thai."

Miller did not quite know what to make of it, except that the Cambodian guards did not touch the helmsman's food. It looked tame enough, steamed rice with spinach-green shoots that looked like thick grass with pale buds on top and covered with a brown sauce. The guards only ate rice wrapped in leaves, brought to them by the gunboat crews.

When the rowboat with the Cambodians came abreast of the trawler, the two men just sat there unarmed, looking over the crew until gunboat 133 reappeared. Then they bobbed and weaved, oars flailing, back to shore.

The gunboat pulled alongside and another animated discussion began. After a few minutes, the trawler hauled anchor and began following the gunboat, which headed out to sea. It seemed they would neither be going back to the port nor landing at the garrison, though Miller was not sure what the new destination could be. He looked overhead. High off to the south, he saw two black specks combing the coastline. He hoped the jets were reconnaissance planes and that the pilots were keeping tabs on the crew's wanderings. Unfortunately, the two were A-7 attack fighters that were circling about, having lost track of the trawler after it entered the port at Kompong Som. While the A-7s were trying to locate the trawler, an RF-4 flew along the coast taking photographs of the installations. As the camera shutter operated, one frame captured the fishing trawler at anchor just off the coast. The pilot had no idea of the significance of what his camera had achieved, nor did anyone in the film-analysis room back at Udorn Royal Thai Air Base in Thailand when the film was developed an hour and a half later. Meanwhile, the A-7 report stating the trawler was last seen entering the harbor was forwarded up the chain of command and would set the stage for more errors in the reporting of events to Washington.

Chatter erupted among the *Mayaguez* hands. "We're going back to the ship" was one opinion. "We're headed for the Thai border" was another. The truth was, Miller thought, no one had a clue where they were going. It did not even seem that the Cambodians had any idea either.

The boats ran west for an hour and a half toward an island Miller remembered from his chart, Rong Sam Lem. On the day of the capture, a long, long two days earlier, he had not wanted to move the *Mayaguez* toward Kompong Som because of this island and unlit hazards that might be nearby.

The gunboat headed for a half-moon bay on the east side of the island while the trawler held steady in the gunboat's wake. As they eased into the inlet, Miller saw lush green hills sloping down to a glistening band of white sand. The idyllic scene was interrupted by a group of buildings, on stilts, at the northern edge of the bay. Two more gunboats were tied up against a wooden dock that projected out from one of the buildings. The boats had shrimp nets haphazardly tossed over the pilothouses to camouflage the craft. Next to the gunboats was a fishing trawler, like the one Miller was on. The captive-laden trawler made straight for the dock.

A lone man dressed in black pajamas and a red bandanna tied around his head came out of the building and stood on the wooden platform, waiting.

The tide was in, making an easy step from the gunwale to the dock. Miller was first off, and as his feet hit solid footing, the Cambodian stuck out his hand and smiled.

"Welcome to Cambodia," he said.

14

THE DIE IS CAST

I hope none of you gentlemen is so foolish as to think that aeroplanes will be usefully employed for reconnaissance from the air. There is only one way for a commander to get information by reconnaissance, and that is by the use of cavalry.

British general Sir Douglas Haig, summer 1914

At U-Tapao Air Base, Thailand, Major Porter's D Company marines from the Philippines had been on, off, and back on alert since 6:10 A.M. Wednesday morning. Except for the hasty breakfast upon arrival, they had been kept aboard helicopters or stretched out on the tarmac waiting for orders to launch. At noon, they boarded the choppers once again and two hours later were still sitting on the ramp, sweat-soaked in the stifling heat.

Shortly after 2:00 P.M., word reached General Burns at 7th Air Force that two A-7s flying above the Cambodian coast had seen the fishing trawler with Caucasians aboard dock at the port of Kompong Som.

Burns got on the radio and spoke directly to the A-7 pilot. "The pilot wasn't sure about the number of Caucasians on the boat." Burns understood from information received the previous evening that some crew members had been off-loaded onto Koh Tang. With the current news that crewmen were also on the Cambodian mainland, Burns decided the idea of a direct helicopter assault onto the *Mayaguez* was pointless. He aborted the current rescue plan, so Porter's men stood down. The first of the marines from Okinawa began arriving just as Major Porter's men left the helicopters for cooler respite inside a hangar.

Eleven hundred tired, hungry marines descended upon U-Tapao. They assembled in hangars and went through a chow line, machine gunners Hargrove, Hall, and Marshall among them. The food servers were Thai women who seemed friendlier, less reserved than the Japanese girls they encountered on Okinawa. The Thais had attractive tan skin and eyes that seemed more round than the Japanese. The marines thought the deployment might turn into a pleasant stay except for the lack of civilian clothes and any idea whether there would be any time off for the troops during the stay. Most of the men were operating on caffeine and the general excitement surrounding the quick deployment. Fatigue had not yet made its mark felt on performance.

For Danny Marshall, thoughts must have entered his mind about how indeed he had managed to get off Okinawa. Not that his situation had improved any. With no money to speak of, and no idea what he might do if he simply walked away from the ramp area, he was still in a fix over the drug bust. Maybe if the deployment lasted long enough, the authorities in Okinawa would lose interest in trying to track him down. Things could be worse.

At about the same time, General Burns got word of the decision in Washington to proceed with option four of the proposed plans, a simultaneous assault on Koh Tang and the ship, timed to begin at 5:42 A.M., four minutes before official sunrise on Thursday, May 15, the next morning. As noted, the JCS planners in Washington wanted the marines to have the element of surprise in their favor, but did not want the assault to begin at night. Firing at the enemy in darkness when there were hostages involved was out of the question. Still not yet considered by anyone in the chain of command was the fact that the break of day began some thirty minutes before sunrise.

By now, every echelon of command had "their guy" in place to keep each headquarters informed. General Burns had sent Brigadier General Baxter to work fighter issues. He also dispatched Colonel Lloyd J. Anders, the 56th Special Operations Wing deputy, to orchestrate the helicopter tasking, even though Anders had no helicopter combat experience. Colonel Robert R. Reed, the 7th Air Force plans chief, was also sent to coordinate the battle plan although he had no helicopter experience either. The overall marine task force was placed under Colonel John M. Johnson, USMC. He had arrived from the III Marine Amphibious Force Headquarters on Okinawa. Although Colonel Johnson was supposed to be in charge, General Burns told him that the mission commander in the airborne command and control aircraft "will coordinate the strike activities and receive directions from [me]." Meanwhile Admiral Gayler in Hawaii advised Burns that *he* was retaining control of the marines, acting under direction from the JCS in Washington. For the moment, everyone in the chain of command thought he was playing chief, except the commander in chief, President Ford.

Throughout the afternoon and evening of the fourteenth, Colonel Johnson and the other senior officers were continually being called away from vital planning sessions to take incoming calls over the secure net. The phone was located across the field, a five- to ten-minute drive from where the crews were doing the planning. The physical separation of Colonel Johnson from General Burns's headquarters at Nakhon Phanom was a source of particular irritation to Johnson. Due to the sophistication of the communications network, General Burns, Admiral Gayler, the Joint Chiefs of Staff in Washington, even the president would be able to talk to the troops on the battlefield via the ABCCC radio linkup while he, Colonel Johnson, supposedly in charge and only two hundred miles from the fight, could not.

The assault force was to be comprised of two elements. D Company from the Philippines led by Major Porter would drop onto the *Mayaguez*, while marines from Okinawa under the command of Colonel Johnson would attack the island. Due to the scarcity of helicopters, Colonel Johnson opted to go in with the second wave, effectively relinquishing his on-scene control to Lieutenant Colonel

Randall W. Austin, his second in charge. This awkward arrangement was certain to last a minimum of four hours given the round-trip timing. Colonel Johnson should have realized the operation would likely be over before he arrived on the scene if, as expected, only light resistance was encountered from the Cambodians. In any event, Johnson decided to lead from the rear, and Austin selected G Company, headed by Captain Davis, to hit the beach first.

Davis was ordered to prepare an assault plan. He held his first meeting inside one of the hangars at U-Tapao shortly after arrival. When Davis asked for photographs of the island, his request was met with silence. There was none. With the use of only a sketchy drawing on a map, planning an island attack seemed out of the question. Then Davis learned that a U-21, a Beech twin turboprop, was available at U-Tapao. The U-21 had eight VIP seats in the cabin but carried no cameras. Captain Davis had brought his 35-mm Minolta along, so he volunteered its use.

Lieutenant Colonel Austin, Captain Davis, and Colonel Johnson, along with five other officers, boarded the U-21 at 3:00 P.M. An hour later they approached the island. Koh Tang was shaped like an inverted crucifix at the southern end and a pork chop at the north, joined in the middle by a narrow neck of land. Four beaches were visible. The two on the southeast side were of little concern to the men peering from the windows of the U-21. The two northern beaches straddling the pork chop were of considerable interest, because it was here between the beaches that some of the *Mayaguez* crew were thought to be held. Though specifically restricted to no lower than six thousand feet, the plane descended to forty-five hundred feet to get a better look. Captain Davis took out his Minolta and snapped some photographs. No ground fire came rushing up to greet them, primarily because the U-21 stayed well clear, too far away in fact for Davis and the others to get a good view of the defenses. They did see a path running between the two beaches at the northern tip of the island. One small boat was seen maneuvering toward the eastern beach. The *Mayaguez* was visible one mile to the north, looking dead in the water.

After arriving at the dock on Rong Sam Lem, Captain Charlie Miller was led by the English-speaking Khmer into an airy one-room building. Cliff Harrington followed Miller inside. Chickens and pigs wandered in and out, nosing around with alacrity on the dirt floor. In the center of the room was a large table with benches able to seat ten or more. Alongside the walls were oversized cots. Thin mattresses lay scattered on the floor near some coconuts and a machete. Vern Greenlin came in, saw the mattresses, stretched out on one of them, and closed his eyes.

The Khmer had Miller and Harrington take seats on one side of the table. Then he offered some hot tea, which Miller accepted. The Khmer poured a pale steaming liquid into three glasses, stirred in some sugar, and placed the tea in front of his *guests*. Then he took out a notepad and got right to the point.

"Do any members of your crew work for the CIA?"

Charlie Miller glanced at the members of his crew that had wandered into the room. Sereno was trying to hack the top off a coconut with the machete that he had picked up. Two others stood by watching. Miller wanted to toss the question back at the Cambodian—*those guys CIA?*—but he decided against that.

"No," Miller said, "we have no CIA men on the *Mayaguez*."

The Cambodian then continued with a long list of prepared questions, asking about whether the ship had FBI men in the crew, what kind of cargo was loaded on the ship, what type of electronic equipment was aboard, and so forth. The quiz session lasted an hour. Toward the end, the Cambodian asked, "From your ship, can you talk to the American planes?"

Miller thought for a moment about the SOS he had Sparks send, but Sparks had not talked to any planes, so Miller answered, "No, we can only talk to commercial radio stations or to other ships."

"Then why did so many planes come? Three of our boats have been sunk and one hundred friendly Cambodian people have been hurt."

This news came as a surprise. Miller wondered if the Cambodians would extract revenge, but the English-speaking Khmer had related the situation without emotion. The fact that the Cambodian declined to admit fatalities and spoke with an almost "oh, by-the-way" casualness gave Miller a glimmer of hope. Maybe the Cambodians had realized they had overstepped their bounds and wanted a graceful end to the situation.

"The *Mayaguez*," Miller said, "was scheduled to reach Thailand at nine o'clock yesterday morning. When the ship failed to arrive, naturally they sent planes out to look for it."

The Cambodian considered Miller's answer for a moment. "Do you have a way to contact the American planes?"

"If we go back to the ship," Charlie explained, "get steam up, and start the generators so we have electricity, then we can call our office in Bangkok. The office can contact the American authorities."

The Cambodian made some notes. Then he wanted to know how many men it would take to get steam up, how long it would take, when he could contact Bangkok, and the big one, how quickly he could get the planes to stop coming.

Miller answered as best he could. Then the Cambodian wanted to know the names and jobs of all the crew. Miller began writing them down in the Cambodian's notebook.

Any casualness the Cambodian may have shown earlier was gone now. He seemed eager to find a way to stop the planes. As Miller wrote, the Khmer went on to explain that he was twenty-eight years old and merely the interpreter. His boss, the compound commander, was second in command of the Kompong Som region. From the tone of the conversation, someone well above the local commander wanted the shooting stopped, and quickly.

When Miller finished his list, the Cambodian stood. "Now, I will show you where you sleep."

They went out onto an elevated bamboo walkway, the Cambodian in the lead, followed by Miller and the crew. The parade stopped at the first building they came to, a wood-frame house or "hootch" on stilts. The Cambodian motioned for everyone to go inside.

The structure was of good size, with a deck extending fifteen feet out over the water. Inside, a pair of hammocks swung in the light breeze that came in through the open windows and from between the floor slats. A few more oversized cots were by one wall along with several roll-up mattresses. Miller was satisfied there was enough room to bed down the crew, although some of them would be consigned to the floor.

Off in the corner was a small office. The Cambodian ushered Miller into the space, explaining that he shared the office with his boss.

Inside were two more cots, a table, but no chairs. As Miller entered, he spotted a U.S. Army field radio on the table along with some spare batteries. The Cambodians must have captured the radio during the recent collapse of Phnom Penh, he thought.

"Sit down," the Cambodian said, motioning to one of the two cots. Miller sat and proceeded to wait while, outside, other Cambodians prepared some food. A few minutes later, bowls of rice and shredded chicken were handed out. Miller got his last, just as another Cambodian came into the room.

The English-speaker told Miller that the new arrival was the compound commander. To Miller, the commander looked a little older than the English-speaker and a lot less friendly. He did not speak English, but wanted to know if Miller could contact the planes to stop the bombing. Miller gave the same answer he had given earlier.

The English-speaker picked up the radio and began transmitting. Then the commander got on the microphone and the two took turns talking. When the radio exchange ended, the English-speaker told Miller that he and three of his crew would return to the ship, get the power plant going, and call off the bombing.

"Three men are not enough," Miller said.

The Cambodian used the radio again. Then with an air of finality, he said, "All right, you can take seven men."

Miller found Chief Harrington. He asked him how many men he would need to get up steam. Harrington thought about how hot it would be with the air-conditioning shut down. He wanted two shifts. "Seven, Captain," he said.

Miller wanted Second Mate Jerry Myregard to help and Sparks to operate the radio, plus Harrington's seven men. "I'll need nine men plus myself."

"All right," the English-speaker agreed.

Harrington led the way down the dock. He made straight for the fishing trawler, but the helmsman indicated he could not go. "Thailand," the helmsman said. Then he crossed his wrists. "Prisoner," he continued. "Me prisoner." He held up five fingers. "Five months."

"Jesus Christ," Harrington said. "Five months!" Harrington shook his head in disbelief. Now he understood what the ballyhoo was all about on the trawler when the Cambodian guard held his AK-47 to the helmsman's head. More important, they probably only give the helmsman enough fuel to get around the islands and he must be nearly out of gas. *Did he have enough to make it back to the ship?*

A gunboat pulled up to the dock as they gathered by the fishing trawler. The English-speaker indicated that Miller and his men should get on it.

Myregard would have none of that. "I'm not going by gunboat. Our own planes will blow that thing out of the water."

"You wait," the English-speaker said. "Another boat come in half an hour."

Miller checked his watch: 6:30 P.M. "It'll be dark long before we get to the ship."

"Wait until morning," the Cambodian said. "Then you can all go."

Miller was not sure he understood the Cambodian, but if waiting until morning would get his entire crew to the ship, he was all for that.

Back at U-Tapao, the helicopter crews had set up shop in a rear office of the Base Operations building next to the flight line. Manned by officers and NCOs from both squadrons, it became the hub for scheduling and maintenance. The men had a portable high-frequency radio, for contacting 7th Air Force Headquarters, and telephones. They also had a few short-range radios, called *bricks* due to their size and shape, for use on the flight line. By sundown, it looked as though no more than twelve helicopters would be available for the mission. Given the range–to–target, the HH-53 helicopters could carry twenty-seven troops while each CH-53 could only haul twenty.

The assault phase of the plan was being organized at U-Tapao while logistic planning was done at General Burns's 7th Air Force Headquarters at Nakhon Phanom. Since the fighter pilots were stationed at Korat, Udorn, and Takhli Air Bases, none of the pilots who had engaged in combat with the gunboats/defenders on Koh Tang was present during any of the planning sessions at either U-Tapao or Nakhon Phanom. Due to the post-Vietnam drawdown, those units were undermanned and all the pilots were needed at their bases. Given the amount of time involved, no one even considered sending fighter pilots who had sunk the gunboats to give briefings to the U-Tapao crews. It was assumed they could read the after-action reports. That, however, did not happen.

The tasks at 7th Air Force included: scheduling of the EC-130 airborne control and AC-130 gunships; providing the aerial tankers, of which two different types would be needed to refuel the Thailand-based fighters and helicopters; selecting mainland targets for the carrier strike force to attack; selecting targets for the B-52s that were on alert at Guam; assigning bomb and tear gas dispensers for each aircraft plus their weapon delivery times-on-target; and detailing the myriad items necessary to support the operation.

At U-Tapao, the planning meeting of the ground and sea forces was held at 7:00 P.M. in an office at Base Operations. A crude map was tacked to the wall. There were no chairs, so the planners stood as they briefed. Eleven, not twelve, helicopters were ready to go: six HH-53 *Jolly Greens* and five CH-53 *Knives*. None of the helicopter pilots was present. Regulations mandated crew rest for those expected to fly early on the morning of the fifteenth. Only Captain Vernon Sheffield, an experienced rescue pilot, was awake the evening of the fourteenth. Assigned the task of coordinating the helicopter effort but unaware of the planning meeting, Sheffield found himself immersed in maintenance details in the helicopter office in Base Operations. Also absent were the EC-130 representatives, the airborne command, control, and communication (ABCCC) staff, so critical to the management of the battle resources. Colonel James M. Shankles, ABCCC commander, and his battle staff were on the ground at U-Tapao during the critical planning period, but no one from his staff was brought to the meeting. Part of the reason for these absences was the fact that at the planning meeting, the junior officers did not fully comprehend what was available. There were senior officers present, including air force brigadier general Walter H. Baxter, III, from General Burns's staff at Nakhon Phanom, as well as marine colonel Johnson and Lieutenant Colonel Austin, who *did* know what the mission coordination would entail, but they elected to press ahead with the meeting without representation from all the participating units.

Still, no one at the Pentagon or at U-Tapao realized that dawn's early light would begin twenty-six minutes before sunrise and good ground visibility would exist long before the sun actually appeared.

The helicopters needed to be airborne no later than 3:04 A.M., to touch down at actual "first light," and 3:30 A.M. if they were to make the designated H-hour. In either case, the launch from U-Tapao was less than eight hours away, and there was still no approved plan of attack.

Colonel Johnson decided that Major Porter's marines would go on three of the more heavily armored HH-53s and be lowered by rope ladders directly onto the deck of the *Mayaguez*. Porter's group totaled sixty-eight men including marines, the Military Sealift Command volunteers needed to start the ship, an explosive ordnance disposal team, and a Cambodian linguist. The other eight helicopters, three *Jolly Greens* and five of the more vulnerable CH-53 *Knives*, would deliver marines onto the beachheads.

The marine plan was to have the assault on the *Mayaguez* and the island occur simultaneously. For the first island landing, a diversion employing two helicopters into the westernmost beach was chosen. The strategy relied on the Cambodians' attention being lured west while the main striking force (six helicopters) hit the wider, east beach. The east force would make a rapid assault on the nearby compound that was thought to hold the captives, then use the open area and path between the beaches to link up with the west group.

Since the survival of the hostages took precedence, there would be no preparatory naval gunfire, and, initially, close air support was limited to a flight of A-7s from Korat, Thailand, that would dispense riot-control gas over the *Mayaguez* during the boarding.

Once the ship and her crew were safe, air and naval bombardment, including a new fifteen-thousand-pound blockbuster bomb designed to clear landing sites, could be used to neutralize Cambodian forces north and south of the marine positions.

In the first wave, hitting the west beach, would be Captain Davis and his company aboard two helicopters. Lieutenant Colonel Austin and the rest of the marines from Okinawa would strike the east beach. Two more cycles would be needed to get all the marines on the island. The plan seemed simple and workable, but no one, certainly not Colonel Johnson, knew whether the landings would be unopposed.

Marine gunnery sergeant McGowan briefed the intelligence, estimating that only twenty to thirty Khmer Rouge irregulars defended the island. This information was gleaned from a former Cambodian naval officer who had fled the country in April and was contacted that afternoon in a refugee camp in Thailand. The fact that the naval officer had served under the pro-American Lon Nol regime, not the Khmer Rouge, was lost on the planners. Although a handful of written reports from the pilots who had been fired upon were available, none was used and, as noted, none of those pilots was available for briefings. The amount of anti-aircraft artillery gunfire and the number of gunboats in the area clearly suggested that the island was well defended, but this information never made it to the marine planners who had just arrived in Thailand. Regardless, there were those above the level of the planning group at U-Tapao who did know these details, from 7th Air Force at Nakhon Phanom in Thailand to the Pacific commander, Admiral Gayler, in Hawaii, to the president himself. These echelons knew the basic option that had been ordered by the president, but did not as yet know what the marine attack plan entailed.

Additional intelligence was available from Admiral Gayler's staff as well as from the Defense Intelligence Agency in Washington. Colonel Alfred Merrill, the 307th Strategic Wing intelligence chief at U-Tapao, had read those estimates and was aware of the heavy resistance put up by the defenders of Koh Tang. Before the U-Tapao planning meeting, he approached General Burns's senior man, Brigadier General Baxter, with his concerns. Baxter, preoccupied with the problems confronting him and struck by Merrill's negative attitude, dismissed him.

With the plan finalized, Captain Davis and Gunnery Sergeant McNemar checked the helicopter loads against the number of men in the company. Some G Company marines would not be able to go with the first group. Davis gathered his men, then called a small group aside. These men had committed infractions, mostly involving drinking and fighting in Kadena's Tenderloin District. Davis explained why they were not going on the first wave, but that they were still valuable members of the unit. Although Private K.O. Taylor had earned top billing as a problem marine, Davis did not include him in the session. Taylor's discharge was still in a desk drawer at Camp Schwab where Davis, following his gut feeling about Taylor, had left it. Private Taylor would go in with Davis on the first wave.

Davis and McNemar then made the helicopter assignments, keeping platoons, squads, and machine-gun teams together as much as possible. Then Davis opened the ammo container that had been shipped in with their gear. He and McNemar began passing out hand grenades "like popcorn." For the two veteran marines, it was like old, heart-thumping times in Vietnam.

At 11:00 P.M., the scheme was relayed by secure phone to General Burns at Nakhon Phanom. He approved the plan and called it in to Admiral Gayler in Hawaii. Gayler had just learned of a favorable change in the *Holt*'s ETA. Instead of arriving off Koh Tang as previously estimated, the ship would now be on-station at sunrise. Gayler had also been in touch with General Jones in Washington and had received feedback regarding the president's earlier opinion about a vertical assault on the *Mayaguez*. When the security-police option had been briefed, Ford had decided that the attack should be made from U.S. destroyers with sufficient gunfire to cover a boarding party. Ford was not at all sanguine about having men climb down swaying rope ladders onto the tops of shipping containers while a determined enemy opened fire. So Gayler trumped the idea of a simultaneous ship and island assault. Instead, he ordered the D Company marines from the Philippines to be airlifted to the deck of the *Holt*, and from there to proceed alongside the *Mayaguez* about an hour after the main attack on the island. Major Porter's men would "go over the side," retaking the ship in legendary Marine Corps fashion.

Back came Admiral Gayler's modification to General Burns at 7th Air Force. Burns called the change down to U-Tapao. At the execution end, using the *Holt* meant that the three *Jolly Green* helicopters would have to land one at a time to off-load troops onto the small landing pad aboard the ship. That would take time. How that would affect the element of surprise did not come up for discussion. Everyone was eager to get on with the action. After all, there were only supposed to be twenty or thirty ragtag militia on the island. The plan was set, the timing determined, and the forces assembled.

As the marines and helicopter pilots made ready for the planned operation, President Ford convened his fourth and final NSC session regarding the *Mayaguez*. Present were Vice President Rockefeller, Secretary of Defense Schlesinger, Secretary of State Kissinger, acting JCS chairman General Jones, Military Assistant Scowcroft, Press Secretary Nessen, and official photographer David Kennerly.

Ford opened the meeting at 3:52 P.M. in Washington (2:52 A.M. on the fifteenth in Thailand, three hours before H-hour). He was then informed that the UN message to Cambodia had not even been acknowledged by the Khmer Rouge. The ship was still anchored off Koh Tang, and the crew was believed to be split between the island and the mainland. Ford turned to General Jones for the military situation.

The aircraft carrier *Coral Sea* was within striking distance of the mainland. Eleven hundred marines were in place in Thailand awaiting orders. The *Holt* and the *Wilson* were approaching Koh Tang. Thailand-based fighters were loaded and ready, as were the B-52s on Guam. Jones explained how options three and four were to be carried out, detailing the island assault and the ship-seizure operation as modified by Admiral Gayler. Jones then stressed that the men were awake in Thailand and were preparing to launch. If a green light was to be given, it needed to be sent within the hour to allow a dawn attack. Still, no one in the Pentagon yet realized that the H-hour set by Washington was actually at sunrise, occurring some twenty-six minutes after the break of dawn.

In any event, the planned island/ship campaign gained quick approval from Ford, but the air bombardment portion—the attacks on the mainland—created controversy. General Jones offered that the air strikes on the port facilities at Kompong Som and Ream Naval Base might be construed as "punishing" Cambodia.

Henry Kissinger led the argument for use of the B-52s and the carrier strikes. "My recommendation is to do it ferociously. We should not just hit mobile targets, but others as well."

Secretary of Defense Schlesinger agreed. "We will destroy whatever targets there are."

Ford added, "And they should not stop until we tell them."

Meanwhile, twenty-eight-year-old official photographer David Kennerly moved quietly about the room taking photographs. Though a civilian and not part of the NSC, Kennerly did not lack for courage or common sense. He had reported on the war in Asia for several years before coming to the White House and had won a Pulitzer Prize for photographs taken in Cambodia. In fact, he had been in Phnom Penh in the previous month when, at his request, the president had allowed him a leave of absence to go back to Phnom Penh. Now in the

Situation Room, Kennerly snapped a photo of General Jones in front of what Kennerly called Jones's "Doomsday chart" showing the B-52 targets in Cambodia. To Kennerly, they were acting like they were going to blast the country back to the Stone Age over this provocation.

"Has anyone considered," Kennerly asked, breaking protocol, "that this might be the act of a local Cambodian commander who has just taken it into his own hands to halt any ship that comes by? Has anyone stopped to think that he might not have gotten his orders from Phnom Penh?"

Ford, Kissinger, Schlesinger, Jones, and the others sat in silence.

Encouraged by the lack of chastisement for deigning to speak up even though his presence was as part of the hired help, Kennerly continued. "Everyone here has been talking about Cambodia as if it were a traditional government, like France. We have trouble with France, we just pick up the phone and call. We know who to talk to. But I was in Cambodia just two weeks ago, and it's not that kind of government at all. We don't even know who the leadership is. Has anyone considered that?"

Another pause.

Finally Ford spoke up. "Massive strikes would constitute overkill."

Kennerly's comment had found its mark.

The president limited the bombing to four carrier-based attacks, beginning at 7:45 A.M. Cambodian time, designed to happen just after the estimated recovery of the *Mayaguez*. To hedge his bets, Ford kept the B-52s on alert at Guam. With the B-52 aspect resolved, Ford gave instructions regarding notifying the congressional leadership about his decision on the overall operation, which was . . .

Go!

15

DANNY G. MARSHALL

You never know what's inside a boy until the boy gets hit.

F.X. Toole, *Rope Burns, Stories from the Corner*

Wiry and hardened by a life spent settling his differences with his fists, Danny Marshall at five-feet two was one tough customer. His pack, M-16, and the ammo cans he carried into battle weighed half as much as he did, but size never mattered a lick to Danny.

The folks that lived in Waverly, West Virginia, still call it the "blockhouse." Made of gray cinder-blocks, the tiny bedrooms-and-a-kitchen structure on the corner of Second Street looked out of place in its smallness even in that unincorporated town of 250. The three Marshall girls, Barbara, Dorothy, and Susan, slept downstairs in two closet-size bedrooms across from their parents, Eugene Glen and Faye Marie Marshall. The four boys, Robert, Joe, Danny, and Rex, slept in the attic. When they were small, the boys could stand up there, but even little Danny, born in 1957, had to hunch over by the time he was eleven. The attic had a two-foot square window at each end for cross ventilation and a tin roof above their heads. In summer, the ceiling radiated heat like an open furnace, cooled only in late afternoon by the shade of the big maple tree behind the house. In winter, the room was an icebox, getting what little heat drifted up along with the cursing and turmoil from below.

Eugene Marshall had no job that anyone could remember. The neighbors did remember that "Gene sure could drink a bit, though." He was not around a lot and the neighborhood kids knew to steer clear of the house when he was. One of those kids was Teleah Cross, a sprite with brown hair and freckles on her face. Blond-headed Danny was her hero, her best friend. Together in the mornings they would balance on a still-cool track of the B & O railroad's single line that ran not fifty feet from the Marshall blockhouse. Danny, barefoot, shirtless, and wearing only tattered shorts, was surefooted and fast. He kept his skinny arms splayed out for balance as he sped along a gleaming rail, dipping low at times to snatch a chunk of West Virginia coal that the wind had blown from a freight car, rescued from an otherwise fiery end in a steel furnace up Pittsburgh way. Teleah tried to keep up, an inner tube angled over one shoulder and across her chest to her waist.

By the R. L. Howard & Son General Merchandise store, they turned right, then skipped fifty yards down a gravel road onto a knoll. The dew on the grass felt cold under their feet. They made their way to the wooden steps used by the men from the packet boat that delivered goods to the general store every week.

At the river's edge, they dove into brown water. Teleah pushed the inner tube ahead as she kicked, trying vainly to keep up. Danny cut a wake in the slow current as he clawed his way across. The Ohio River was half a mile wide at that point, so it took a good while to reach the other side. On the Ohio bank, they sat on the grass, chewed straw, and talked until they were rested and ready to swim back. It was a Mark Twain setting, but Danny was no Tom Sawyer.

His bicycle was made and maintained with spare parts he "obtained" by one means or another and collected in a cardboard box. When confronted with the possibility that some of his possessions belonged to another, he was ready to defend his horde. "Meet me at the park at noon," was a common challenge issued by Danny. He lost few encounters there, no matter how big the other boy was.

Danny got into real trouble in the sixth grade. After being told by his teacher, Mr. Darrell Allen, to stay in line, he moved aside to tie his shoe. Mr. Allen grabbed him by the collar and yanked. Danny reacted like a polecat and sucker punched the man. Mr. Allen promptly hauled Danny to the principal's office where he got a paddling. But Danny had trouble letting things pass. A few weeks later, he scouted Mr. Allen's home, spying the outhouse sitting behind the place. He cut school, returning with his brothers, and tied a rope to the outhouse. They pulled the flimsy structure off the foundation, then draped the rope over the roof of the home.

With two boys pulling at one end and two shoving on the outhouse, they maneuvered it on top of Allen's roof. They undid the rope, then ran home, doubled up with laughter all the way.

In December the Marshall boys stole all their neighbors' Christmas decorations. According to a neighbor who still lives on the street, "They took every darn ornament off the tree I decorated in the front yard. Didn't leave a one." From the other homes, they disconnected the light strings and hauled them away.

Had they been more discreet, they might have gotten away with it, but the ruckus it caused made their mother, Faye Marshall, do a little checking. She found the goods and made the boys return what loot she could locate. Her husband, Eugene, was away most of the time and mostly drunk when he was around, so she had to work when she could and still raise seven children. It was a task to challenge even the most capable person.

That next spring, Danny's friend Teleah got into a fight with another girl. Teleah made out the best of it, and the other girl's boyfriend came looking for revenge. Waiting for him at Teleah's front porch was Danny. He stood legs spread, a lug wrench in one hand, blocking the bigger boy's path. "You get by me and my friend here," Danny nodded at the tool, "you can have her." The boy backed off, cursing and waving his arms, but never making a move toward Teleah.

Danny's first visit from the Sheriff's Department came after he was seen throwing a rock through Mr. McPherson's front window. No one knows why he did it except it happened right after Halloween. The Deputy came, took him to Parkersburg, and made out a report.

Fighting and moving fast had become his means of survival. He started high school five miles east of Waverly at St. Mary's, just past the power plant. Three months later, he transferred to Williamstown High, having been at St. Mary's long enough to cause trouble but not long enough to get any grades.

At sixteen, Danny somehow became the proud owner of an old blue-and-white Plymouth. He hiked up the rear end in a California-rake and "would drive the thing two days, then work on it for ten." Car parts now filled the cardboard box. It took no time for him to get arrested for speeding and driving without a license.

While this was going on, Danny's father came home. The boy hid, but no matter, Eugene was riled, so he went after whoever was in reach: the girls. That set Danny off. He took on his father who likely would have killed him, but Danny was too fast for a man staggering around in a stupor, so the boy slipped free and ran.

By June of 1974, he had managed to finish his sophomore year at Williamstown. A few nights later, police officers Don White and Denny Huggins showed up at the Marshall house. They were checking on a report of a motorcycle that had been stolen and seen being ridden by a Marshall boy. Joe Marshall was working on the machine by the side of the house. They took Joe, cuffed him, and placed him in the cruiser. When Danny heard the commotion, he stormed downstairs, grabbed a stubby two-by-four, and came charging outside. He clubbed Huggins up the side of the head, then shoved White to the ground.

"Run!" Danny shouted at Joe as he flung the cruiser door open and hauled Joe out.

"I can't. I'm handcuffed!"

"They didn't cuff your feet," Danny yelled.

By then, White and Huggins had regained their footing and wrestled the wiry-haired interloper to the fender, then obliged Danny with his own set of handcuffs.

Danny G. Marshall was booked for assaulting police officers and complicity in grand theft auto (motorcycle). At his probation hearing, he was given a choice: jail or the military.

Finally home, Danny crawled into bed. He stared into the darkness, smelling the fetid, damp scent of the riverbank. Mosquitoes swarmed. A freight train rumbled past, making the blockhouse quake. The shriek of the locomotive's whistle bored through the heat as the engine approached the crossing by the general store. Danny thought long and hard about jumping from his mattress, racing out the door, and climbing aboard that coal train. He had to get out of there, but had no money, no future, no choice.

The next day, he stopped by Teleah's to tell her his decision. She was sixteen and pregnant by another boy. She had already told him about it, said she was not going to marry the father. That was fine with Danny. "Look, I'm going into the marines. Don't you worry. When I get back, I'm gonna spoil that kid rotten."

In August of 1974, Danny G. Marshall reported for boot camp at Parris Island Marine Corps Base, North Carolina. According to freckle-faced Teleah, Danny's hometown was rid of "the orneriest little white boy the Waverlians ever seen."

16

THE CAMBODIAN ALAMO

*I am besieged with a thousand or more of the Mexicans under
Santa Anna. I have sustained a continual bombardment and
cannonade for 24 hours and have not lost a man.*

William Barret Travis, commandant at the Alamo, February
24, 1836

Em Son was twenty-three, though if the amount of death and
chaos marked a man's age, he was old indeed. In his five-year rise
from recruit to battalion commander, he had been seriously wounded
sixteen times.

Em Son lay on his cot trying to sleep, but the buzz of the orbiting
plane kept waking him. It was not much noisier than the insects that
hovered outside his mosquito net. Or maybe it was the hunger that
denied sleep. He could not remember a time when he had not been
hungry. Thoughts of food dogged him and the men he led. But Em Son
had a lot more on his mind right now.

He had received his assignment after the April 12 victory over the Lon Nol government. By early May, he commandeered a small boat and took 100 of his 450-man battalion to the island. Malaria began taking its toll. Many of the troops on the island were also ill with dysentery, infections of various sorts, and malnutrition. Duty on Koh Tang was not a choice assignment. The inhabitants of the fishing village had been evacuated to the mainland after the takeover in April. There remained no restaurants, no women, nothing but bamboo and palm-roofed hootches. The men brought few personal possessions with them other than clothes, weapons, and mosquito netting. Water was taken from wells scattered around the island. Though coconuts were plentiful, most staples were delivered to the island on a daily basis. Although ammunition was not yet a problem, food was scarce. Three soldiers assigned as fishermen were able to catch some fish and crabs. Another two took care of raising pigs and chickens, but rice was always running short, and the men were on edge.

Em Son had received a message from Phnom Penh on his short wave radio. A voice of America broadcast in Cambodian language had been heard which stated that American President Ford had threatened serious consequences if the ship was not released. Two Swift boats with seven to ten men each were sent as reinforcements the day the American ship anchored off shore, but nothing had come in since. No one below Em Son's level had any idea what was going on. Em Son knew simply that the American ship was being held by the naval authority. The two gunboats that brought reinforcements had gone back to sea with the other Swift boats yesterday. Most had not returned. One had run aground off the east beach. So far, none of his own men had been killed, but the increasing amount of American air traffic did not bode well for the future.

One of Em Son's units was a platoon commanded by Soeun. Reduced by malaria to thirty men, Soeun's troops defended the east beach. Two heavy machine guns were dug in at opposing ends of the beach and Soeun's men built rock-fortified fighting positions every twenty-five yards along the beach behind the first sand berm. Between the fighting positions, a shallow zig-zag trench was dug connecting each fortification. Two more light machine guns were set up between the heavy weapons. These were M-60 machine guns captured from the Lon Nol government.

Shrubbery was hacked away with machetes to provide wide, over-lapping fields of fire. Teams using Chinese-made B-40 rocket-propelled grenades were set up between the machine-gun pits. Two DK-82 grenade launchers, which could also be set up as mortars, were emplaced.

Munitions storage was located in two dug-in bunkers, one right behind the fishing compound on east beach and another behind the defenses on west beach. Both could be easily reached by troops who could then move into the trench line for protection while bringing ammu-nition to each fighting position. A third ammo dump was at the radio shack midway between the northern beaches and the center of the island.

Ki was a favorite of Em Son's, both having fought together for many years. Ki was platoon commander in charge of defense of the west beach. The most vulnerable area on that side was a small beach that Ki fortified with a heavy machine gun on the south side and one M-60 on the north edge. He also had B-40 and DK-82 teams plus a 75-mm recoilless rifle team that he spread out to cover the beach. A trench line connecting fighting positions was constructed similar to the one on the east beach. Ki was also responsible for patrols around the seven-mile island.

Heang was Em Son's mortar platoon commander. He sited one 60-mm mortar on the northernmost point of the cove surrounding the east beach. Another was set up to defend the west beach. His 81-mm mor-tar was positioned near the radio shack at the headquarters. Ranging shots were fired to calibrate settings used to support either the east or the west beach since the emplacements were blind to those areas.

The unit took their orders by radio from III Division Headquarters on the mainland at Ream, commanded by Meas Mut. Em Son had a field-pack radio at his headquarters for communication with the mainland and outer islands. He used walkie-talkie radios to contact his dispersed troops.

With all the air activity, Em Son had ordered the heavy machine guns adjusted so they could be used as antiaircraft guns or lowered to defend the beaches. These had seen plenty of action already. They had not shot any aircraft down, but the gun crews were disciplined and well drilled. Their fields of fire overlapped to cover the length of both beaches.

"If the Americans come by boat or helicopter, you must wait until they are very close," he told them. "Otherwise, they will bomb us from afar."

Each member of the machine-gun crew was shown how to operate the weapon should the prime gunner get wounded. Ammunition was not a problem for the moment. The gun pits were well stocked and ammunition bunkers were easily reached.

The gunboat crew had wanted to put the American seamen ashore. Sa Mean had even brought them all to the east beach. While they waited in two boats just offshore, Sa Mean came to Em Son's headquarters to discuss the problem. Sa Mean wanted to keep the crew separated from the ship in case the Americans attacked. Em Son would not allow the crew onto the island. There were too many Americans, no stockade, and no way to feed them. More important, bringing the Americans ashore would mean the fighters would drop bombs on his men. Em Son had seen how they dealt with the gunboats. In his mind, this was a navy problem, not an issue for ground troops. "Keep them in the fishing boat or take them to Kompong Som," Em Son told Sa Mean.

So, the seamen who had been captured were taken away without ever setting foot on Koh Tang, while their ship remained at anchor a mile offshore the island. The big question was what the American military would do. If they attacked the island in force, Em Son had little doubt that his defenses, though well prepared, would be overrun. He relished being back on the mainland where he had been fighting. There he had room for maneuver, for guerrilla attacks, for night ambushes, for escape. Here he would have to fight from fixed positions, with no choice as to timing and without supporting artillery. The American air and naval power could wipe out his force in minutes if they chose. His only recourse would be to melt away into the thick jungle with what might be left of his men. But then what? They would starve without supplies. But orders were orders, and the word received by radio from the naval headquarters at Ream was to hold fast. Questioning orders was the surest way to get "sent up." Those who had violated the dictums of the revolution had been dealt with swiftly. He himself was charged with ordering and carrying out executions. Failure to act promptly in these matters was another way to meet one's end.

Near dawn, a report came in from one of Ki's patrols. The sound of a large ship had been heard off the west beach.

Em Son rolled off his cot and went into the radio room to contact headquarters at Ream. He was told to send out a P-111 Swift boat to investigate. Minutes later, the patrol boat sped to within a few miles of the contact, where an American destroyer was seen steaming north with running lights on. Em Son radioed the information to Ream and waited for instructions. "As long as the ship stays far from the island, do nothing," came the reply. "Our naval force is not strong enough to counter it."

Em Son called Ki and Soeun on his walkie-talkie. He increased the number of patrols and ordered the other men to continue work on defensive positions. Then Em Son returned to his cot. He lay down, staring into the darkness, while the constant sound of the orbiting plane mixed with the shrill night clatter of crickets, monkeys, and lizards. He listened, but could not hear the ship.

17

EM SON

Bright red blood that covers towns and plains of
Kampuchea, our motherland
Sublime blood of workers and peasants
Sublime blood of revolutionary men and women fighters . . .

First stanza, Khmer Rouge national anthem

*R*ice paddies stretched in all directions, their flow broken only by
banana and coconut palms. He grew of age surrounded by a sea of
green. At eighteen, the Viet Cong and Khmer Rouge came to the farm.
The choice was simple. If you did not join, you were shot.

Em Son was born in 1952, the fourth of seven children. He grew up
on a two-hectare rice farm near Ta Phren Village in Srok Tra Kak
District, Takeo Province, Cambodia. Dark complected, he had soft
features that gave him a gentle, rice-farmer look. He stood tall and
straight, and had a long, well-defined nose and a long thin face. His

oval brown eyes darted left and right, missing little that happened about him.

The family lived in a two-room hootch built on wooden poles high above ground. The roof was covered with palm fronds and the sound of the rain on it was comforting, like a muted drum. Em Son slept on a thin mat in the front room along with his five sisters and brother. Em Sao, his older sister, took care of him, carrying him on her hip up and down the wooden ladder that led from the hootch to the ground. He was her favorite, the one with the big oval eyes so clear and brown, so full of mischief.

At age five, he was enrolled in the local school. Em Som would wake early, eat rice soup for breakfast, then follow his two older sisters and brother single file along the berms between rice paddies. At the main road, they turned east, walking another kilometer to Wat Champa, the temple school. There among the monks and other teachers, Em Son learned to read and write.

Life was pleasant for the family of medium wealth until both parents died early in 1970. That was just before the war caught hold all over the country, but the loss of their parents' guiding hands plunged the children into hard times.

On July 26, 1970, twelve soldiers stopped at the farm. Eleven were Viet Cong, in camouflage with banana leaves attached to their pith helmets. They looked fierce, armed with AK-47s, AR-15s captured from the Lon Nol government troops, and Chinese B-40 grenade launchers. Bandoliers of ammunition hung from their shoulders. One of Em Son's local friends was with them. The dozen men stayed under the house all day as aircraft flew overhead, trying to locate their position. The Vietnamese leader of the group spoke Cambodian and began a lecture on how the American puppet, Lon Nol, had taken the government by force. He had overthrown beloved King Norodom Sihanouk and it was up to patriotic Cambodians to join the Khmer Rouge faction and help the Vietnamese defeat the Americans and their cronies. What the Vietnamese really wanted was for the Khmer Rouge to open another front against the American effort in Southeast Asia in hopes of taking pressure off the Viet Cong.

Anyone eighteen years old and above was inducted into the armed forces. Younger children were taken as well, to be trained in proper ideology until they, too, were of military age. Only Em Son's great-aunt, Em Seng, and his sister Em Sao were allowed to remain to care for the property. Em Son marched off into the setting sun, heading toward the mountains to begin what for him would be eighteen years of nearly non-stop combat.

Once in the Khmer Rouge, changing your mind meant instant execution. His indoctrination began immediately with political discussions about socialism and the excesses of the current American-backed government. Em Son listened. Who was he to question their teachings? The Khmer Rouge had no palaces, no walled estates, no fancy cars. Em Son bought into the rhetoric.

With no local place to train, Em Son was assigned to a three-man unit, the standard fighting team, and issued an AK-47. He began his combat lessons on the battlefield as they moved along Route 3 toward Phnom Penh. Combat was incessant, a tough, brutal slugfest where his orders were simply to fight until winning.

Takeo Province was the scene of some of the heaviest fighting during the Khmer Rouge struggle against the Lon Nol government. Em Son was quick to learn that both sides fought brutally, rarely ever taking prisoners except for brief question-and-answer sessions that ended in executions.

In 1971, an 80-mm mortar landed in front of him. The explosion threw shrapnel through his left leg, his first wound. He was dragged from the field by women cadres and taken to an aid station where a medic stuck a needle full of pain killer in him while the women went back for the dead. No medals or promotions in rank were given out for wounds or valor. Courage in battle was rewarded with increased position within the unit.

A month later he was back in action, part of a new fire team. Sokha was also part of the team. She had long black hair and was full of cadre zeal. He liked her spirit and he caught her private looks that said all he needed to know. But a personal relationship in those times was out of the question. There were rules. No fraternization. If a recruit was caught having sex with a woman, called a "Code 204" offense, both would be sent to a reeducation camp. Everyone had heard stories about the camps, because offenders might return from them, though no one had any wish to go there.

In time, cadre leaders discovered Em Son was good at fighting and winning, so they put him in command of a fifty-man platoon. By now his threesome included not only Sokha but Ki, a male veteran who would fight alongside Em Son for years to come. Eventually, another woman, Son, became part of his threesome when Ki obtained more responsibility. Em Son had moved up as well and was considered cadre rank now. If cadre were caught in intimacy with women soldiers they would be hauled in front of an ad-hoc tribunal to determine guilt, then execution of the guilty participants would follow. Em Son remained chaste, and both Sokha and Son eventually disappeared into the maw of combat.*

Em Son's next major injury came from a 105-mm artillery round that also landed in front of him. It triggered a secondary explosion that sent flames roaring in his direction. He was blown back and knocked unconscious. In and out of a coma for the next three months, Em Son recalled only the searing heat of the explosion, then darkness. He returned to combat months later, his face, neck, and chest now marked with discolored pigment from the burns.

Back in action, he became competent using all the small arms employed by the Khmer Rouge. Em Son walked, slept, and ate to the sounds of warfare. He became so numb to the fighting that he did not at first recognize his old school, Wat Champa, when he came upon it during a push to the north. The school buildings and temple had been razed by his own side. He wandered among the charred walls and scorched grounds remembering his early carefree days, saying nothing to anyone about it.

By the end of 1973 he was in charge of a 150-man company. He was gaining the power to make things happen. Now considered "cadre," Em Son acquired the responsibility to indoctrinate new recruits and to maintain discipline. For disciplinary actions, he was issued a pistol. The pistol was not given as an ornamental trapping of command. Killing became a way of life. The distinction between a combat casualty and an execution became nonexistent. Prisoners were a burden. Once information was gleaned from a captive, there was little point in keeping the prisoner alive.

But power in the Khmer Rouge came at a price. *Fight until you win.* Each time he was wounded, he would awaken later and wonder what parts of his body were shattered or missing. His right collar bone was broken and never set properly. Then he was caught in a crowd when a claymore mine detonated. Twenty people were killed. He was par-

---

*In the Khmer Rouge, women rose to the rank of battlion commander along with the men: Sokha survived the war, married another Khmer, and lives in Cambodia with her husband and children. Son's status is unknown.

tially protected by the man in front of him, but his exposed right arm was sieved with shrapnel.

In 1974, he found himself leading a 450-man battalion of troops up Route 4 from the port at Sihanoukville to Phnom Penh. Em Son and the other commanders met secretly with Pol Pot once a month where the strategy for the next thirty days of activity was decided. Pol Pot, the commander in chief, was conducting a modern military campaign, yet only one major meeting a month was required to make it work.

There was bitter fighting all the way with everyone joining front-line units. On both sides, nearly every company commander ended up being killed or wounded. Towns were overrun. Most of those who stayed behind were executed. Soldiers from the Lon Nol forces gathered their families and fled in droves. Less of that was happening on the winning Khmer Rouge side. Short of men, many of the Khmer Rouge fire teams had a two-to-one ratio of women to men. The bloodletting went on until April 12. After having been wounded sixteen times, Em Son and the Khmer Rouge entered Phnom Penh as victors. By April 17, 1975 the Khmer Rouge had established full control.

Although the fighting may have been over, the killing was far from finished. Pol Pot ordered the city populations evacuated to the countryside, which for millions meant eventual starvation and death. Em Son was sent to the coast where he was placed in charge of the Kompong Som District. Along with his responsibilities on the mainland, he was given control of the island of Koh Tang, thirty miles off the coast. Another battalion commander, Sa Mean, was given similar responsibility farther south, including the island of Poulo Wai, some sixty miles out at sea. With Vietnam and Thailand claiming the islands, both men were ordered to secure the territory for Cambodia.

On the first of May, after spending several days establishing his headquarters at Kompong Som, Em Son heard about the collapse of the South Vietnamese government the day prior. He also learned that the Vietnamese were occupying islands to the south that both Cambodia and Vietnam claimed. Em Son went immediately to Koh Tang with about a hundred men divided into three smaller units. A fishing village comprising some twenty people was situated on the northeast beach. Em Son ordered the village evacuated to the mainland as he began preparations to defend the island from attack.

18

LOAD OUT

If I were not to come back,
Know that I have never left.
To travel
Was for me only staying here,
Where I've never been.

Giorgio Caproni

The helicopter crews at U-Tapao and the marine commanders assembled at 1:00 A.M. on Thursday morning, May 15, with their staffs in the same room used earlier for planning. The briefing staff stood by the map tacked crudely to the wall while the combatants sat on the floor. The mood was informal, an almost relaxed attitude among the participants. The crews had been through the process before. During the Phnom Penh and Saigon evacuations the month prior, things had come together in much the same chaotic way. In those cases the opposition was expected to be intense, but it turned out to be relatively light; in fact, no helicopter from Nakhon Phanom had been lost, even though confusion ruled the day.

As the crews continued to fill the room, aircraft assignments, based on the earlier planning, were handed out in an almost offhand manner. The HH-53s, call sign *Jolly Greens*, would carry the ship assault team. The CH-53s, call sign *Knives*, would hit the beaches. The Koh Tang mission would tax the helicopters' range to the limit, so all the helicopters carried full fuel loads. Because the CH-53 *Knives* could not air refuel, they carried 650-gallon external fuel tanks that allowed the round-trip to and from the island. Thus the CH-53s hauled twenty-six hundred pounds more fuel than the HH-53 *Jolly Greens* at takeoff, which meant the CH-53s could not lift as many troops. The CH-53 *Knives* carried a pilot, copilot, two gunners, and nineteen or twenty troops. The HH-53 *Jolly Greens* carried a pilot, copilot, two gunners, two pararescue men, and twenty-six troops. Three of the more heavily armored HH-53s had been originally tasked to descend on the *Mayaguez*, but Admiral Gayler in Hawaii had changed the tasking and these helicopters were now going to put troops on the frigate *Holt*. The three HH-53s would have little exposure to hostile fire, yet they were not switched with the less heavily armored CH-53s assigned to the hazardous beach operation. By not reassigning the three CH-53 helicopters, eighteen to twenty-one fewer marines would be available for the first beach landings.

At this point, the rush to action had resulted in a failure to account for daylight before sunrise, with its attendant loss of surprise, and the use of the wrong helicopters for the island insertion. The consequences of these oversights were soon to become grist for second-guessing and recriminations.

The crews received formation assignments, radio call-signs, landing zones (LZs), radio frequencies, weather information, and intelligence. The intelligence portion was given by Colonel Lloyd J. Anders, who was not an intelligence specialist but rather was the deputy commander for operations, 56th Special Operations Wing, out of Nakhon Phanom. He told the assault force that they could expect the opposition to consist of between eighteen and thirty irregulars. As noted, no intelligence personnel was present to brief the Commander-Intelligence-Pacific (IPAC) on the estimate of between one hundred and two hundred regular troops, or the Defense Intelligence Agency's (DIA) similar estimate from Washington, nor was any of the pilots who had witnessed the ferocity of the antiaircraft fire present to dispute the numbers presented by Colonel Anders. Not one of the EC-130 or P-3 Orion crew members was present to relate what he had seen of the defenses. The briefing was solely based on intelligence received from the Cambodian refugee in Thailand who had served on the island but had not been a member of the Khmer Rouge force.

Lieutenant Colonel John Denham, 21st Special Operations Squadron commander, was designated as the formation leader. His CH-53, call sign *Knife-21*, would make the first landing on the west beach with 1st Platoon, G Company, from Okinawa, followed by *Knife-22* flown by First Lieutenant Terry D. Ohlemeier. Aboard Ohlemeier's CH-53 were Captain Davis, Gunnery Sergeant McNemar, and more of G Company, including Private K. O. Taylor, the trouble-prone marine from Chicago.

Major Porter's boarding party would embark on *Jolly-11, Jolly-12,* and *Jolly-13* HH-53s. These helicopters would refuel en route to the drop-off point, where the marines from the Philippines would be put aboard the *Holt*. The *Jolly*s would then return to U-Tapao to load troops for the second wave.

The airborne command and control (ABCCC) EC-130, call sign *Cricket*, was assigned to control the air operation. It took off at 3:15 A.M. Onboard was a staff of officers, including Colonel Anders from Nakhon Phanom. The staff manned radio consoles used to coordinate battle movements. ABCCC received the plan by radio shortly after takeoff. For the next hour and a half the men worked with Anders, "feverishly" assembling the details into a workable structure. Once the mission aircraft started showing up over Koh Tang, the staff *had* to know flight assignments, weapons loads, times-on-target, and all the myriad details needed to control the ebb and flow.

The marines were roused from what little sleep they had managed on cots or stretched out on the floor of a big hangar. A military chaplain passed among them offering blessings and asking if any among them wanted to have their confessions heard. Ammunition was handed out by the NCOs and a cursory briefing was conducted, but most of the line troops had little idea what they were supposed to do since the plan had been put together while they slept. Private First Class Gale Rogers from E 2/9 Company was told by his company commander, "Rogers, you're a three-five team." His military specialty (MOS) was actually 0351, an anti-tank assaultman, but now he was being placed in charge of a 3.5-inch bazooka team. "When we get on the island," the officer told him, "you'll set up a defensive perimeter and you'll shoot any enemy assaulting down the beach and any gunboats that try to come around behind us." That was the extent of the briefing Rogers got.

By 3:30, most of the first-wave helicopters were loaded, but E Company's Captain Mykle Stahl had a problem. He was scheduled to go on the second wave, but because his load included a medic, an air force photographer, and an army linguist, he had to pull three of his own men off the chopper. He chose to move his second machine-gun crew, Hargrove, Hall, and Marshall, to another helo.

Captain Davis and Gunnery Sergeant McNemar had seen to the loading of their marines onto *Knife-22*. As they waited in the darkness to board the aircraft themselves, they were approached by an air force NCO. The man handed a stack of photos to Davis. With McNemar looking on beside him, Davis took out his flashlight and scanned the pictures. They were photo reconnaissance images of the island. Davis could see the east and west beaches clearly. Near the east beach, he made out a structure that looked like a barracks. They saw bunkers sited in defense of the beaches. That gave Davis a shiver. A narrow path could be discerned that ran through a cleared area from the east to west beach where more defenses were visible. That meant it would be easy for the Cambodians to reinforce either beach. Davis ran the beam of light back to the east beach. McNemar's stubby finger pointed out open gun pits, antiaircraft positions adjacent to the beach. That was the worst feature as far as Davis was concerned. "It was then," McNemar was to say years later, "that we knew we were going into shit."

Davis clicked off the light. Then he stood beside McNemar in the flickering red glow of the anticollision beacon rotating beneath the helicopter. There was no time to revise the plan. He thought about showing the photos to the troops onboard *Knife- 22*, but decided it would only make them more nervous. Davis stuffed the photos in the pocket of his flak vest, climbed aboard the helicopter with McNemar, and passed the word to his men that they were to expect enemy resistance.

The plan now called for the helicopters to lift off at 4:05 A.M. As that time arrived, the force was told to hold in position. In compliance with the War Powers Act of 1973, President Ford was preparing to brief congressional leaders on his decision to assault the *Mayaguez* and Koh Tang. Once confirmation was received that the briefing had begun, the helicopters would be cleared for takeoff. At 4:14 A.M., an hour and ten minutes before first light of dawn, word finally came.

"Go!"

19

LAST CHANCE TO AVOID "BLOWING THE HELL OUT OF 'EM"

A diplomat's words must have no relation to actions—otherwise what kind of diplomacy is it? Words are one thing, actions another. Good words are a concealment of bad deeds. Sincere diplomacy is no more possible than dry water on iron wood.

Communist ideology of Josef V. Stalin

At 6:10 P.M. in Washington (5:10 A.M. Cambodian time), the bipartisan leaders of Congress hurried in their escorted black limousines toward the White House as American marines headed south toward Koh Tang and their rendezvous with the *Holt*. The Washington motorcycle police swept aside the last of the rush-hour traffic, and thirty minutes later the congressmen were seated in the Cabinet Room as President Ford marched in. He brushed right past James Cannon of the Domestic Council, who was trying to get him to sign a letter to Mayor Beame denying financial aid to nearly bankrupt New York City. The assembly rose, giving Ford a standing ovation.

A map of the crisis area and a reconnaissance photo of Koh Tang were positioned on metal easels. Also present were State and Defense Department staffers ready with backup details should they be needed.

Ford began with a review of the crisis. He outlined the seizure of the *Mayaguez*, the fruitless diplomatic initiatives, and the lack of response. "We gave the Cambodians clear orders," President Ford said. "They disregarded them. They were not to try to take the ship from the island to the mainland." Ford went on to enumerate the sequence of events surrounding the attempts to prevent movement of the *Mayaguez* or its crew. Three gunboats had been sunk and four others damaged, but one boat was permitted to proceed to the mainland.

Ford was well aware that "Caucasians" had been reported aboard a fishing trawler, but he initially avoided mention of that fact. If the crew were known to be on the mainland, then an attack on Koh Tang would seem pointless. If only *some* of the crew were on the mainland and *some* were on the island, then a rescue effort that freed only part of the crew would also seem dubious. The Cambodian reaction to the attack might be to take horrendous steps—tortured confessions, public executions— against those they held on the mainland, creating another *Pueblo*-type situation. Clearly, President Ford knew these possibilities but chose to ignore them in favor of taking determined action. He did eventually mention that he was not certain where most of the crew were located. Some might still be aboard the *Mayaguez*, on the small island nearby, or in the "vicinity." Ford was careful with his words, not wanting to allude to what he suspected—that the crew was already on the mainland. Was he trying to limit the amount of second-guessing should the rescue attempt fail? Was merely recovering the ship enough to make his point? These questions had to weigh heavily upon the president.

After the briefing, Ford opened the session to questions. Senator Mike Mansfield asked why the bombing of Kompong Som was being ordered, particularly since he heard that some members of the crew were believed to be there. The president was forced to concede that some of the crew might have been on the boat that reached the mainland. He insisted, however, that the attacks were on eight large landing barges and seventeen planes at naval and air facilities. The bombing was designed to prevent the launch of a counterattack by some twenty-four hundred troops stationed around Kompong Som.

Not mentioned by Ford was the fact that the oil storage facility at Kompong Som was also targeted in each of the four planned raids.

"I am not going to risk the life of one marine," Ford said. "I'd never forgive myself."

House Speaker Carl Albert raised a point. "Couldn't we have waited a bit longer before using force?"

"We waited as long as we could," Ford replied.

"I thought we were going to use minimum force," argued blustery Senator John McClellan. "Do we have to do it all at once? Can't we wait to see if the Cambodians attack before we attack the mainland?"

A very good question.

Ford pondered a moment. "It's too great a risk" was all he could manage.

Senator Mike Mansfield was not convinced. "I want to express my deep concern, apprehension, and uneasiness at this near-invasion of the Indochina mainland. We have plenty of firepower there in the two destroyers. Frankly, I have grave doubts about this move."

McClellan and Mansfield were right, of course. In no way were loaded barges going to slip by the American sea and air blockade in broad daylight. Oil storage facilities would play no role in such a short-term operation. As for the Cambodian aircraft, they were a mishmash of cargo planes and a few T-28 light fighter-bombers left over from the evacuation. It was doubtful the Khmer Rouge even had a single pilot able to fly these, no less to mount a serious attack. Finally, with no runway on the island, the cargo planes were useless. Colby had briefed those details over the previous three days—one of the few things the CIA got right.

But time was slipping away. The island and ship assaults were under way. If Ford was to delay the mainland strikes, he had to do it soon. Navy planes were thirty minutes from takeoff. For Ford, and Kissinger as well, the whole episode had been transformed into a political exercise, one designed to demonstrate to the world that the United States would defend its interests. Part of that demonstration was making the point that a rogue country would be punished for committing piracy. That punishment included the loss of valuable military facilities beyond those in the immediate crisis area. There can be little doubt before, during, and after the bombing that all concerned knew that the primary purpose of the raids was punitive.

Ford let the argument grind on until shortly after 7:00 P.M. He had to prepare for a state dinner with the Dutch prime minister scheduled for 8:00 P.M.

Crusty old James Eastland, president pro tem of the Senate, had sat slouched in his chair listening to the discourse. Finally he stirred, summing up Ford's decision as he mumbled to himself, "Blow the hell out of 'em."

20

TOO SOON THE SUN

*The affairs of war, like the destiny of battles, as well as
empires, hang upon a spider's thread.*

Napoleon Bonaparte

T he first three *Jolly Green* HH-53s took off at 4:14 A.M., loaded with
marines bound for the deck of the *Holt*. The next element of four CH-
53 *Knives* departed at 4:20, their mission to assault both beaches at Koh
Tang. Five minutes later, the last of the CH-53 *Knives* and three more
Jolly Green helicopters lifted off for Koh Tang, a total of eleven in all.
The prelaunch delay, spaced-out departures, and the need to refuel the
six HH-53s put the operation twenty precious minutes behind schedule.

To provide cover for the helicopters, a phalanx of F-4 Phantoms, A-7
Corsairs, F-111 Ardvarks, and AC-130 gunships took to the air from
Thailand. These planes began marshalling in orbits north of Koh Tang

after contacting *Cricket*, the airborne command post EC-130 whose orbit was halfway between Koh Tang and U-Tapao.

Some 350 miles to the southeast, the carrier USS *Coral Sea* had just completed fueling her strike force for bombing attacks over the Cambodian mainland. As dawn broke, the pilots headed from their ready rooms onto the flight deck where they began strapping into their aircraft. Ten A-6A Intruders from Attack Squadron VA-95 were loaded wall to wall with Mark 82 (five hundred-pound) laser-guided bombs while twenty-four A-7E Corsairs from VA-22 and VA-94 squadrons were loaded with twelve standard five-hundred-pounders each. The attack planes planned to launch and divide into four waves. Protected from MiGs by F-4N Phantoms from squadrons VF-51 and VF-111, the dive-bombers were assigned targets at anchor in Kompong Som Harbor, runways and hangars at Ream airfield, ships at Ream Naval Base, and Kompong Som Harbor port facilities including oil storage. It would take almost four hours to complete the planned strikes.

On Rong Sam Lem island, Captain Charlie Miller spent a fitful night inside the big hootch where the Cambodians held the captive *Mayaguez* crew. Packed in like sardines, Miller shared a cot with Pastrano, the pantryman. Without mosquito nets, the constant buzzing of insects made a shambles of any attempt at restful sleep. The guards forbade anyone from going outside to urinate. Miller wound up relieving himself between bamboo slats on the floor.

As light filtered through the open windows, Miller felt as though the day of destiny was about to begin. He hoped the Cambodians would come through with their word that the whole crew would be going back to the ship. He sat up and spread his arms, hearing the creaking and cracking of cartilage and sore tendons as he stretched. Then he felt a tap on the shoulder. He turned. A guard was motioning for him to lie back down. He complied. Looking around, he noticed there were lots of guards now, softly padding up and down the board-walk and in groups over on the beach. *A firing squad?* He had heard the rumors about summary executions that took place just weeks ago in Phnom Penh right after the Khmer Rouge took control. All kinds of horrors flooded his mind. Well, he decided he'd had sixty-two years of decent living, and if it ended this morning, so be it. Miller waited a few minutes, noticing that some of the others were waking up. Whatever their fate, the next few hours would likely tell the tale. Miller was anxious, but ready to be done with it.

"Everybody up!" Miller shouted.

Once everyone started moving, Miller figured the guards would not try to stop them all.

"Come on, everybody. Get up!"

Miller led the grumbling, stumbling gaggle out onto the boardwalk. Earlier, he had spotted a barrel of water near the shore. He headed for it.

The liquid in the barrel looked rainwater-clear. Miller leaned over, dipped his hand in, and made a crude attempt to brush his teeth with his finger. When he straightened, the English-speaking Cambodian was beside him.

"Good morning, Captain Miller."

The island commander was with him, bare to the waist. The commander scooped a cup of water from the barrel. His muscles glistened in the early morning humidity. Miller had not previously noticed how solidly built the man was compared to the scraggly looking youths that had been guarding them.

"At six o'clock," the English-speaker began, "we will talk to the first commander in Kompong Som. We will ask him if the high commander in Phnom Penh has given approval for you and your crew to leave."

Miller looked over at his expectant crew. "Looks like we're going to have to wait, fellas," he told them.

Standing nearby was Dave English. "What'd I tell you, Captain," English said, shaking his disheveled head of red hair. "More goddamn lies." He turned and walked away.

Thirty minutes after leaving U-Tapao, the helicopter armada was proceeding south, just off the coast of Cambodia. Inside *Knife-22*, Davis and his marines sat on the few webbed seats available or on the floor facing each other along the sides of the cabin area. The last of them were crammed against a row of water barrels near the ramp. The water was meant to last the unit for three to four days on the island. Conversation was difficult with the engines roaring overhead. Silence settled over the men. Most of the marines were engrossed in their own thoughts, trying to catch a little shut-eye, or going through the motions, checking and rechecking their rifles, hand grenades, chin straps, and canteens.

Davis peered out a side window. The helicopter was clipping along just above a ragged scud layer. A pale light was breaking to the east, turning the clouds pink. *We should be hitting the beach now*! As he breathed, he felt the lump from the photographs tucked inside his flak vest. Bad intelligence, plus bad timing equals bad plan. *Here we go again*, he thought. It was unlikely the *Mayaguez* crew would be in the trenches used for defending the island. Captain Davis put on a crew headset so as to be able to listen to the chatter from the pilot and the control group in *Cricket*, the orbiting EC-130, but made no request for close air support. Without someone overhead to direct where to put the ordnance, there was little point in suggesting a preparatory air strike. If the fighter pilots had to circle while they figured out where to shoot, the Khmers would be alerted and surprise would be totally lost.

The airborne force divided about twelve miles northwest of Koh Tang where the already arrived USS *Holt* waited to pick up the inbound *Mayaguez* boarding force. A minute later, the lead helicopters nosed over and began a descent as the controllers aboard *Cricket* tried frantically to come up with the *Holt*'s radio frequency. The *Jolly Green* crews did not have the number either. Precious minutes were spent while the controller inside *Cricket* used his UHF radio on 243.0 *Guard* channel to make contact with the ship. *Guard*, the universal emergency frequency monitored throughout the world for distress signals, is anything but secure.

Nine miles northwest of Koh Tang, the *Holt* maneuvered at slow speed, awaiting the helicopters. Inside the *Holt*'s communication center, a radioman heard *Cricket*'s *Guard* transmission. The frequency problem was ironed out in short order, and the first of the three HH-53s eased into position behind the *Holt*. The sea was calm as Lieutenant Donald R. Backlund's *Jolly-11* came to a hover behind the vessel. Marine captain Walter Wood looked out at an "incredibly small helo pad." The big HH-53 swung around in its hover, with only its rear wheels touching down on the steel landing pad. The cargo ramp was lowered and marines deplaned onto the deck of the *Holt*.

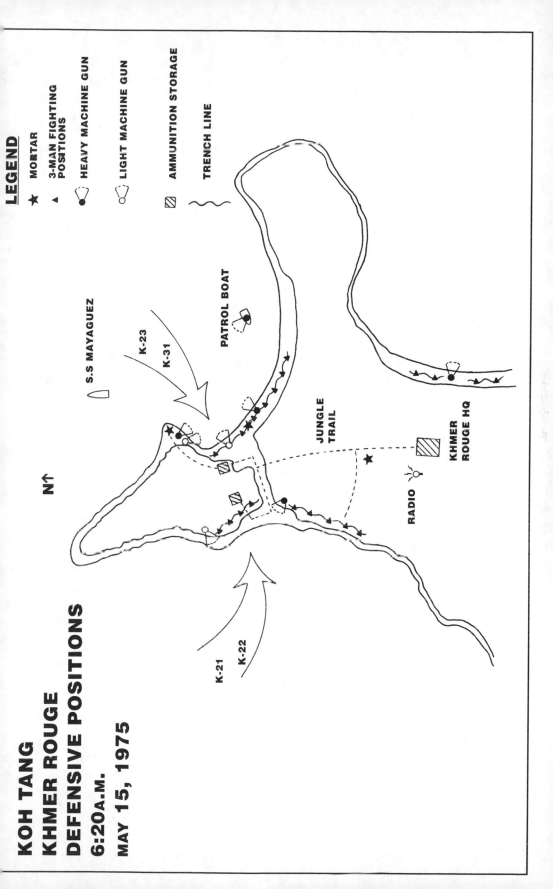

KOH TANG
KHMER ROUGE
DEFENSIVE POSITIONS
6:20 A.M.
MAY 15, 1975

N↑

S.S MAYAGUEZ

K-23
K-31

PATROL BOAT

JUNGLE
TRAIL

KHMER
ROUGE HQ

RADIO

K-21
K-22

LEGEND

★ MORTAR

▲ 3-MAN FIGHTING
    POSITIONS

🌢 HEAVY MACHINE GUN

🌢 LIGHT MACHINE GUN

▨ AMMUNITION STORAGE

〜 TRENCH LINE

Then the other two helicopters executed the same tricky maneuver. In the dim light of a breathless dawn, the sound traveled across the water far and wide.

At 6:12 A.M. Em Son, the Khmer Rouge battalion commander on Koh Tang, heard a faint but readily identifiable sound: the whoop, whoop of a helicopter. He leapt from his bunk. His worst nightmare was being realized. To the northwest, sentries were already sounding the alarm. Em Son grabbed his field-pack radio mike. He called the other islands to find out if they were experiencing any activity. None of the other units had heard a sound, not even at Poulo Wai. "Up, up, everyone up!" Em Son shouted as he grabbed his pistol belt and scrambled outside to rouse his men.

A hundred yards east on the island, company medics Bou Sorn and Rot Leng were sound asleep under mosquito nets inside a wood frame barracks. Rot Leng heard a shout. Rousing from sleep, he listened to a buzzing, rising crescendo for a moment. Then he shoved aside his net and staggered out.

The sun was not yet fully up. Rot Leng ran to a slight rise where visibility was better. Off to the northwest was a sight that brought him right out of his early-morning stupor.

He started counting the helicopters, but lost track as they maneuvered about. Some of them were taking off from a big ship. Then he heard more shouts. Men came tumbling out of barracks buildings and from inside makeshift tents.

Commander Em Son sighted a gaggle of helicopters crossing north of the island, moving east as though headed for the mainland. He looked west, scanning the sky in that direction. Two black dots appeared just above the horizon. They were a few miles out, but to Em Son there was no doubt where they were headed. He had been in literally hundreds of battles, badly wounded sixteen times, and had thought the fighting was over after the April 12 victory. It was not to be. He had long ago found a way to suppress fear, thinking only *Boudtho*, a Cambodian phrase that roughly translates: "Oh, my God, here we go again." It was not the type of term a Khmer Rouge cadre would say out loud. Em Son took a deep breath, set himself, then yelled for his men to get to their positions.

• • •

At 6:10 A.M., fifteen miles east on nearby Rong Sam Lem, the English-speaking Cambodian and his commander took Charlie Miller back to the room in the hootch where the U.S. Army field-pack radio was kept. The English-speaker got on the horn first to Kompong Som. After a reply, the island commander took the microphone. His neck pulsed with irritation as he spoke to the mainland. The English-speaker managed a weak smile as the proceedings went on. After a few more minutes, the commander turned off the radio.

"They are still waiting in Kompong Som," the English-speaker said. "The high commander in Phnom Penh has not given them permission to release the crew."

A molten sun boiled up out of the sea to the east of Koh Tang as *Knife-21*, flown by Lieutenant Colonel John Denham, and *Knife-22*, piloted by Lieutenanat Terry Ohlemeier, nosed their heavy helicopters over to begin the diversionary assault at the small beach on the west side of the island.

When Denham got a good look at the narrow beach, he radioed his wingman, "We'll go in one at a time."

Inside *Knife-21*, Second Lieutenant James McDaniel and half of 1st Platoon Company G from Okinawa waited, nerves stretched tight, much like leathernecks had so many times before in places like Guadalcanal, Tarawa, and Iwo Jima, only this time they were in helicopters instead of landing barges. They watched, every sense tuned razor sharp, as the flight mechanic, Staff Sergeant Elwood Rumbaugh, stood spread-legged at the cabin gun-port, his minigun sight swiveling onto the beach. This was it.

"Lock and load!" McDaniel shouted.

A flurry of nervous hands slapped ammo clips into M-16s and cycled the bolts, the sound of each click carrying to every ear.

Denham's helicopter came in low and fast. As he closed the distance, Denham scanned the beach for any indication of ground fire. Nothing moved. The surf was low, almost calm. *So far, so good.* He brought the helicopter to a hover, then to the surprise of the marines, swung around to present the rear exit ramp to shore. Normal marine procedure was for helicopters to go in nose first so the troops can use the fuselage for protection while they disembark, but the air force pilots were unaware of the procedure.

Suddenly, tracers whipped in front of Denham's eyes. He looked back, feeling impacts rock his aircraft. The green foliage behind the beach had come alive with flashing muzzle blasts.

Denham heard thud after thud as rounds pummeled the aircraft. Twenty marines shouted as they ran out the open ramp for cover. The helicopter was being torn apart in Denham's hands.

Lieutenant Ohlemeier in *Knife-22* came to a hover behind Denham. To him, the underbrush surrounding the landing zone (LZ) "looked like a string of Christmas lights."

"Hot LZ!" Ohlemeier radioed as his own helicopter began taking hits.

Denham had seen enough as more impacts rocked *Knife-21*. One of his engines was losing power. He tried to lift off, but his transmission indicators showed serious malfunctions. The helicopter banged back down onto the sand as pieces began shedding from its damaged engine. Bullets rattled like hail on a tin roof. Denham and his copilot, Lieutenant Karl Poulsen, jettisoned the external drop tanks and flipped on the fuel-dump switch. Then Denham laid on full-power and up-cyclical. *Knife-21* lifted off. With one engine out and the other pulling barely enough power, Denham eased his chopper out across the surf.

Then it was Lieutenant Ohlemeier's turn. Rounds thumped through the sides of his chopper as he came in close to shore. Ohlemeier pulled away. Inside the troop bay, Captain Davis thought the helicopter was aborting the run only to feel it reverse back toward the beach moments later.

Ohlemeier had decided to make a second pass, attempting to cover Denham's withdrawal. He came barreling in, guns blazing, as Denham in *Knife-21* passed underneath with fuel gushing from the aircraft dump mast.

Ohlemeier swung behind Denham's crippled machine. He could see rounds peppering the surface, waterspouts erupting all around Denham's damaged aircraft. Ohlemeier's miniguns sprayed the beachhead with fire. Then Ohlemeir's right door gunner fell back, clutching his stomach. The marine passengers watched, wide-eyed, as the gunner opened his hands, looking for blood. There was none. A round had penetrated the fuselage, then spent itself in the buckle of his harness.

Captain Davis stood in the center of the aircraft with the headset on, trying to find out what was happening. Another fragment ripped through the helicopter, catching Captain Davis in the face and also injuring his radioman, Lance Corporal Alan Wyatt. Davis reached up and felt blood oozing between his fingers. He felt around for the wound as the helicopter once again rolled away from the beach and the engines roared to full power. Then he noticed Wyatt, bleeding from his left ear. He went to Wyatt's aid, but Wyatt had no idea he was hurt. Davis looked around. Liquid was sloshing around on the floorboards, but he did not smell fuel. It was leakage from damaged water barrels.

Inside *Knife-21*, Denham had his hands full. His remaining engine was losing power, and vibrations from the damaged transmission shook the airframe. Every few seconds, the helicopter would slap back onto the surface. Each time, a fresh surge of seawater got scooped into the cockpit and cargo area through holes and open hatches. Spray flew up and got sucked into the screaming engine.

Finally, a mile from the beach, *Knife-21* settled into the water. The helicopter rolled on its side. Rotor blades plowed into the sea, then snapped off, sending pieces sailing across the waves. Water poured inside. Denham unstrapped while Lieutenant Poulsen lay unconscious in the copilot seat. Staff Sergeant Rumbaugh pulled Poulsen from the cockpit. Denham exited from a side door, inflated his life preserver, and looked around. Poulsen was floating nearby. Staff Sergeant Rumbaugh was nowhere in sight above the swirling, hissing surface.

Overhead, fuel began hemorrhaging from *Knife 22*'s tanks as Ohlemeier watched *Knife-21* disappear beneath churning waves. Ohlemeier looked north. *Knife-32* and *Jolly-41* were swinging around toward his location. They were supposed to be off-loading troops on the east beach. *Had they already finished their runs?* Ohlemeier did not have time to sort things out. He turned over the rescue effort to them and started back toward the beach.

In the troop bay, Captain Davis and his marines were shaken up, dizzy from the helicopter gyrations, and in no doubt about how things were going. To Davis, who had determined his wound was minor and cleaned himself up, anything would be better than sitting inside the machine taking hits without the ability to return fire.

Ohlemeier rolled out of his orbit and bored in for the beach. He jinked and bobbed, trying to avoid tracers that surged up from the tree line. Several 12.7-mm slugs ripped open *Knife-22*'s drop tanks. Captain Davis and his marines were tossed about as shrapnel and bits of the helicopter flew across the pitching cargo bay.

Another burst blew off part of the nose faring. The controls bucked in Ohlemeier's hands as he muscled the big helicopter toward the deadly spit of land. Fuel began streaming from the external tanks. Ohlemeier had seen enough. He added power, aborting the run, barely skimming over the thick jungle canopy as he swung the machine north.

Ohlemeier zoomed *Knife-22* away from the barrage and took up a heading for the Thai mainland. Then he called *Cricket* and radioed that he had wounded aboard.

On the east side of the island, machine gunner Phat Kheng heard the pop-pop-pop of machine-gun fire coming from the west beach. He tried to keep his balance as he stopped to pull on and tie his black trousers. Other men were running in their shorts, hell-bent in all directions toward both beaches. With his trousers cinched up, Kheng joined the rush. His bunker was a quarter of a mile around on the north side of the eastern beach. He sped past other gun pits, taking note as the nearest gunner swiveled his barrel from the antiaircraft position down to an aim point just above the surf. Phat Kheng sped past a reinforced fighting position where three men were readying a grenade launcher. Another crew was already set up and one man had hopped out of the pit to relieve himself behind the position.

Phat Kheng felt his heart hammering in his chest as the sound of approaching helicopters filled his ears. The increasing noise served to get his feet pounding even harder along the dark narrow path that ran beneath a canopy of green vegetation. Out of breath moments later, he leapt into his fortified bunker on the northern curve of the east beach, just in front of a 60-mm mortar position that was still unmanned. His two assistants were already in place. One of them had snatched the protective rag out of the barrel, opened the ammunition box, and was pulling an ammo belt free. The other was pointing in the direction of the approaching noise. Phat Kheng unlatched the breech as his assistant, with hands shaking, fed in the first round. Then Phat Kheng slammed the breech closed and cycled the bolt. Two helicopters were sliding in from the left toward the east beach. Phat Kheng took aim.

Knife-31, flown by Major Howard Corson, and *Knife-23*, piloted by First Lieutenant John Schramm, had heard the "Hot LZ" calls just as they swung in toward the eastern beach. Corson passed the word to the marines in back, then slowed to a hover just off the beach. Suddenly the tree line lit up with muzzle blasts. The left side-gunner, Sergeant Randy Hoffmaster, opened up with his minigun as a rocket-propelled grenade (RPG) round found its mark. The RPG penetrated the left side of the cabin area and exploded, immediately wounding the men seated there, including navy corpsmen HM1 Bernard Gause, who went down immediately, and HN Manning, who was also hit. Without foam fire-suppressant like that carried inside *Jolly Green* tanks, Corson's left tank burst into flames. The conflagration quickly spread inside the cargo bay.

With his helicopter on fire, RPGs exploding all over the aircraft, and machine-gun tracers tearing through the fuselage, Corson tried vainly to reverse course. As the chopper swung away to the right, Sergeant Randy Hoffmaster opened up with his minigun from inside the cabin inferno while copilot Second Lieutenant Richard Vandegeer fired an M-16 out his side window. An explosion from an RPG ripped away the nose of the aircraft. Dazed and wounded, with no instruments left in front of him, Major Corson rode the aircraft into the surf. He sat frozen in his seat, facing forty-five degrees away from the beach. What was once metal and Pexiglas in front of him was now nothing but a gaping hole.

Schramm in *Knife-23* had come in north of, and slightly behind Corson as he closed the distance to land. Schramm's eyes scanned ahead for signs of a firefight. He slowed to a hover, then swung his tail toward the beach. To the south, something flashed in his peripheral vision. It was Major Corson's helicopter, enveloped in a frightening ball of fire. Red hot tracers crisscrossed all around Corson's CH-53 as it plunged into the water.

Schramm had little time to sympathize as his aircraft was rocked as an RPG exploded against the tail section. Schramm heard a thunderous crack. The tail separated and swung away from the fuselage. The helicopter immediately lost yaw control and began to swing in a wild circle. Schramm had all he could do trying to keep it level. Seconds later it belly flopped into shallow surf, sending a shower of water flying outward. As the water settled, Schramm looked aft. The ramp was open to volleys from the beach. Marines were poking their M-16s out and firing in reply. Schramm undid his harness, grabbed an M-16, and moved into the cabin area.

Marine second lieutenant Michael A. Cicere was the senior marine aboard but had never been in combat. What to do now? That was the question. Cicere assumed no one had survived the fireball that was *Knife-31*. Should he remain inside the helicopter and fight from there or head out into the firestorm? With only a moment to consider the situation, Cicere motioned for the marines to move out onto the beach. Now that someone had taken charge, the men began to rush aft, jumping from the ramp into the surf and firing as they lunged toward land. Air force staff sergeant James M. Barschow chose to climb out the right minigun portal. Unknown to anyone else, he was immediately shot in the leg and arm. Schramm, his copilot, and the two gunners chose to follow the marines. With bullets churning the surf, the group dashed ashore. Cicere's glasses fell off as he fought his way ashore, but it would be some time before the nearsighted lieutenant would notice. The wounded sergeant was the last to reach safety as the helicopter disintegrated and explosions ripped the air.

Nearby, *Knife-31* was still receiving its share of Khmer Rouge attention. Heavy machine-gun rounds homed in on the stricken craft. Sergeant Hoffmaster and a few marines leapt through the forward entry hatch, just as it went underwater. Inside the troop bay, Lieutenant Terry Tonkin, the forward air controller (FAC), and the other marines were hopping around, dodging flames that swept in through the gun port while bullets cut through the fuselage "like green fire flies," and ammunition exploded in the intense heat.

Private First Class Timothy Trebil, stunned by the explosion, came to his senses at the very rear of the cabin area. Across from him machine-gun rounds bore through the fuselage, one slamming into the thigh bone of a marine. The man's leg buckled, shattered above the knee. He fell back against the flaming web seating.

Trebil and the remaining men, seeing no escape, tried to punch out windows with their rifle butts. One man got stuck in a gun-port opening, his legs protruding inside the helicopter and on fire. Trebil shoved on the man's boots until the legs slid through. "Thanks," he heard from outside the helicopter, but flames filled the void and Trebil did not want to risk getting stuck. Through the smoke, he could see light at the front of the helicopter.

Then Sergeant Jon D. Harston, shot in the leg, appeared from the half-submerged forward hatch. He grabbed an M-16 and shouted for the men to move through the hatch. Harston saw Vandegeer slumped over in the cockpit and Corson sitting motionless in his seat. He banged on the door, trying to open it. Corson came to as the door opened and, after waving Harston off, stepped through the open front of the aircraft and tumbled into the water. Sergeant Harston and a handful of marines ducked underwater and squeezed through the side opening. Once outside, nineteen-year-old Lance Corporal Gregory S. Copenhaver and two other marines charged the beach. As they shouted, with legs pounding through the shallows and M-16s blazing away at the beach, the Khmer Rouge gunners found their mark. Bullets riddled Copenhaver. Down he went. Then the second and third marine were hit. Their M-16s flew from their hands as they pitched forward into the foam, yards short of the beach.

Trebil was still trapped inside. He continued forward toward the light, found the cockpit door open, and squeezed through. The cockpit was on fire and the copilot, Lieutenant Vandegeer, was still strapped in his seat. The lieutenant was unconscious, a gaping wound in his chest. Trebil tried to release the fittings and in the process got second- and third-degree burns to his hands and arms. Finally he gave up and tumbled into the water, the last man to leave the helicopter alive.

The remaining survivors ducked behind the inferno that was consuming the helicopter. They made their way to the front of the wreckage in waist-deep water, shielded from the beach by smoke, flames, and the hulk of the helicopter. Khmer rounds kicked up water all around them. Ammunition exploded as trapped men screamed inside the helicopter.

With Corson, Hoffmaster, and Harston were ten marines including the forward air controller, Lieutenant Tonkin. They huddled at the front of the aircraft with only three life jackets between them. Wading ashore was sheer suicide. Corson rallied the wounded and shocked marines as Harston emptied his rifle and handgun at the beach.

Lieutenant Tonkin, who had not recovered his radio, shouted above the din at Corson, "Can I borrow your radio to call in an air strike?"

Corson pulled his small waterproof radio from his survival vest and gave it to the lieutenant. Then Tonkin started towing Corson away from the beach as they began shedding helmets, boots, and vests. The survivors dog-paddled seaward in small gaggles, hanging onto the three airmen with life vests. Seven marines, the two navy corpsmen, and Lieutenant Vandegeer never emerged from *Knife-31*.

Trebil, the last man out of the helicopter, headed seaward with a group of marines, including Private First Class James R. Maxwell, Corporal Gaston, and Sergeant Salinas. Salinas had facial burns and was swimming blind, assisted by the other marines. Trebil was working hard to stay afloat, still encumbered by his helmet and full combat gear. Bullets kicked up waterspouts around him, one knocking his helmet back and dunking him underwater. When he surfaced, he saw Maxwell, shot in the back of the head. Trebil swam to his aid, but Maxwell died in his arms. He released Maxwell and continued dog-paddling.

Down to his skivvies and Corson's radio, Lieutenant Tonkin kicked with his feet as he edged seaward on his back, still helping Corson swim. He pulled out the radio antenna and made a Mayday call. The defenders must have seen the sun-glint off the radio antenna, because the water around Tonkin erupted as rounds sought him out. He dove, then eased away from Corson and the group to avoid drawing fire on them while he continued to work the radio.

Overhead, three A7-D Corsairs from the 388th Tactical Fighter Wing at Korat Air Base in Thailand heard Tonkin's calls for help. Leading was air force captain Scott Ralston. He swooped in low to have a look, banking the aircraft as he passed the beach. He saw the northernmost helicopter minus its tail rotor. A huge black pillar of smoke rose from the other one. He could see men in the water, swimming seaward. Around the smoldering wreck, a massive crimson blot was spreading into the crystalline water. At first Ralston thought it was marker dye. Then he realized the stain was human blood. He fought down a twinge of nausea.

More Mayday calls came from Lieutenant Tonkin. It took a few minutes to begin sorting out where everyone was located. Then more minutes passed as the fighter pilots tried to make sure they were not going to hit friendly forces.

Inside the EC-130 airborne command post, *Cricket*, the scene had deteriorated into utter chaos. Numerous *Jolly* and *Knife* helicopters tried unsuccessfully to clarify instructions as to where they were to deposit their troops while radios blared out Mayday calls and air strikes were being urgently requested. The ABCCC battle staff aboard the EC-130 had no clear idea of the ground situation, let alone the air campaign. Colonel Anders from Nakhon Phanom aboard the ABCCC was clearly winging it. Compared with the eastern beach, the effort to the west seemed less murderous. Anders began diverting helicopters around to the western beach. Finally, he got a fair read on the situation. Three CH-53s were down and another heavily damaged one was struggling to reach the Thai coast. Two small clusters of marines were pinned down, one on each beach.

Speeding away, well to the north of Koh Tang, Lieutenant Ohlemeier was gamely trying to nurse his damaged CH-53 to the Thai coast. Gunny McNemar clung to his seat webbing inside the helicopter, wondering if they would make land before the shuddering machine came apart. McNemar had been almost right. His marines had indeed gone into shit, but he and Captain Davis were not with them.

21

THE BEACHES

Up to the very last moment it appeared as if the landing was to be unopposed. But a tornado of fire swept over the beach, the incoming boats, and the collier. The Dublin Fusiliers and the naval boats' crews suffered exceedingly heavy losses while still in the boats . . . and of these nearly half had been killed or wounded before they could reach the cover afforded by the steep, sandy bank at the top of the beach.

Sir Ian Hamilton, *Official Report of the Gallipoli Landings*, April 25, 1915

On the east beach, platoon leader Second Lieutenant Cicere and his men had deplaned through the open ramp of *Knife-23*, the wounded air force staff sergeant, Barschow, joining them last. All twenty-five men huddled behind scattered boulders along the shore while a navy medic began to work on Barschow's leg. Khmer Rouge heavy machine guns were firing at them from their left and right. Cambodian riflemen were shooting AK-47s and launching rocket-propelled grenades from along the length of the beach. A mortar battery was walking shells in from Cicere's right where the beach curved sharply behind their position. Cicere hastily established a perimeter with marines spread out to return fire.

First Lieutenant John Lucas, *Knife-23*'s copilot, found himself in very unfamiliar surroundings—ground combat. He hunkered low behind marines, a bit overwhelmed by the noise and tumult, but not inert. He took out his survival radio and requested air strikes on the UHF *Guard* emergency frequency, talking in a calm, deliberate voice. The airborne controller in *Cricket*, the orbiting EC-130 aircraft, was fooled by the composure in Lieutenant Lucas's voice. He told Lieutenant Lucas to stop transmitting—that he was attempting to maintain contact with survivors of a downed aircraft. Lucas halted his transmissions temporarily.

Floating off the coast nearby, Lieutenant Tonkin, the marine forward air controller who had been aboard *Knife-31*, was still trying to coordinate air strikes on the same frequency. The A-7s finally went to work as Tonkin settled down and began giving precise directions. The planes made multiple runs firing their 20-mm gatling guns and silencing one Khmer Rouge bunker after another. Tonkin continued to direct ordnance against heavy-weapons positions until his radio quit working. That left Lieutenant Lucas and his survival radio, tuned to the emergency frequency, as the only communications link between those on the eastern side of the island and the EC-130 control plane orbiting above.

Finally, Lieutenant Lucas cleared up the confusion with *Cricket* as to who he was and what he needed. He began controlling air strikes of his own just as *Knife-32*, piloted by First Lieutenant Michael B. Lackey, came roaring in overhead. The air filled with the sound of helicopter engines and rotors, mixed with an upsurge in machine-gun and RPG fire that rose to meet the aircraft. From the cockpit, Lackey saw nothing but heavy smoke and fire in the landing zone. He was unsure of what to do until an RPG slammed into the side of the helicopter and exploded, opening a gaping hole in its side. Lackey added power and sped over the treetops, aborting the run to the northwest.

Once clear of the island, Lackey saw the slick left by *Knife-21* after it had slid beneath the waves a mile off the west beach. From radio traffic, he knew that the crew was in the water needing rescue. He headed out over the spot and began looking for survivors but, fully loaded, his helicopter was too heavy to pick up anyone. Lackey began dumping fuel. He took a moment to scan the island as fuel sprayed beneath him into the sea. A thick, black column of smoke from *Knife-31* was boil-ing into the morning sky to the east. Closer in, the western beach was alive with gunfire. Things were going badly for the men on the island.

On the west beach, platoon commander Second Lieutenant James McDaniel and a scattered group of twenty marines from G Company hunkered down in the hot sand just beyond the first berm. Machine-gun fire was pouring in from a ridge on the north edge of the tiny beachhead. Mortar rounds sent up bursts of dirt, vegetation, and shrapnel as tracers whistled their fiery way through saw grass. McDaniel had a marine tactical radio, but trying to get anything coordinated was turning into a nightmarish undertaking. He made repeated attempts to contact Lieutenant Colonel Austin, his battalion commander, but the *Cricket* controller in the EC-130 answered and asked McDaniel to describe his position and what he needed. McDaniel replied that he was pinned down in an isolated area on the west beach and wanted air support. His men had managed to move inland a mere forty yards, he guessed, and had managed to overrun one 60-mm mortar position.

At this point, the tactical radio frequency being used aboard *Cricket* became a bedlam of overlapping transmissions. Among them were calls from Lieutenant Thomas Cooper, piloting *Jolly-41*, just back from refueling with an HC-130 airborne tanker, and another from Lieutenant Philip Pacini, piloting *Jolly-42*. Pacini radioed that he was part of a two-helicopter element, and they were ready to insert their troops. Meanwhile, Lieutenant Lackey's gunners in *Knife-32* had hauled Lieutenant Colonel Denham and two crew members from *Knife-21* from the water. Lackey had moved two miles north of Koh Tang with his fifteen marines and the *Knife-21* survivors aboard. He also asked *Cricket* for instructions.

Colonel Anders was on the radio inside the EC-130 trying to unravel the confusion. Anders cleared all four aircraft into their designated landing zones without fully understanding what had happened. Pacini in *Jolly-42*, his wingman, Captain Wayne Purser in *Jolly-43*, and Lackey in *Knife-32* began heading back toward the eastern beach, their original landing zone. Lackey took another look at the flaming wreckage of *Knife-31* and decided he wanted no part of repeating that scenario. He called Anders again.

"*Cricket*, do you want me to insert my marines in the same LZ where *Knife-Twenty-three* and *-Thirty-one* have gone down?"

Anders mulled his decision. After several moments of dramatic silence, he directed Lackey to the west beach. Hearing this exchange, Pacini asked for clarification regarding the *Jolly Green* landing zone. All the *Jolly*s were also diverted to the west beach.

Jolly-41 was nearest the western landing zone, so Cooper made the first try. As his helicopter neared shore at about 6:30 A.M., some ten to fifteen minutes after the first marines had landed there, he took hits in the right fuel tank and ramp area. Cooper pulled away.

Then *Jolly-42* began his run in. From the premission briefing, Pacini recalled that there were two separate landing zones, both north and south of the path that connected the east and west beaches. Pacini guided *Jolly-42* to what he thought was the southern landing zone. As he got in close, he saw neither marines nor signs of friendly activity around the landing zone. He decided he must be in the wrong place and he, too, pulled away. *Jolly Green 43*, piloted by Captain Wayne Purser and carrying the battalion landing team command group headed by Lieutenant Colonel Austin was next in the barrel. Purser aimed for the northernmost landing zone, but was met with intense small-arms fire, so he aborted and swung away. That left Lieutenant Lackey in his damaged *Knife-32*. He nosed his helicopter into the fray.

In the stifling-hot cabin area of *Knife-32*, marines were mostly in a state of shock. Of the fifteen troops aboard, two were wounded, including Lance Corporal Dale Clark. He had been hit in the face when fragments of the rocket-propelled grenade penetrated the fuselage. He was too stunned to even notice. All of the men just hung on, feeling more nauseous by the minute as the helicopter rocked and rolled to evade incoming fire. Sweat poured from their faces, soaking their uniforms. Some took swigs from their canteens, even though they did not know when they would next have a chance to refill them. The marines had seen *Knife-31* ablaze off the east beach, so every single man knew what might be in store. The worst part was not knowing or having any control over what was going to happen next. One minute they were about to off-load onto the east beach, then they were aborting as enemy rounds tore up the helicopter. The next minute they were helping pull drenched crew members from the water off the west beach. Now they were once again turning inbound toward a beach. But which beach? None of them had a clue.

From the way the helicopter picked up speed and began a descent, the marines all knew the pilot was going to risk another death run. Suddenly, the big helicopter came to a hover. Machine-gun bullets walked across the water and up the side of the fuselage. Mortar rounds exploded in the surf, sending up towering white geysers. Lieutenant Colonel Denham, soaking wet from his rescue, had taken enough from the Khmer Rouge. He grabbed an M-16 and began returning fire from the minigun portal. As he fired, a machine-gun round came through the opening, wounding the air force sergeant who manned the gatling gun. The sergeant fell back, bright arterial blood bubbling from his shattered chest.

Then the helicopter swung its tail toward the beach. These troops, too, were surprised that they were being asked to off-load right into the firestorm. Dale Clark heard his platoon sergeant shout for the men to move out. Clark and the other marines stood and began to make their way onto the deadly sand, but an army translator who was assigned the job of using a bullhorn to contact the Khmer Rouge refused to budge. The platoon sergeant grabbed him and tried to haul him off, but the man began yelling that he was not going. Clark, who was already wounded in the face, made his way aft to the ramp area. Bullets peppered the water near the helicopter. Clark dropped flat onto the ramp. Other marines stumbled their way past. Realizing that he was not going to do anyone much good where he was, Clark got up and staggered onto the beach. Over the din of the helicopter rotor he could hear sharp pops from small-arms fire out front and the sound of the army translator's panicky shouting still going on behind him. Sand from rotor wash was flying in all directions. Clark looked to his left and at the north end of the beach saw two armed men dressed in black pajamas running toward cover. He was shocked to see enemy combatants so close. Clark raised his M-16, firing off two rounds as marines ran past him. He could not tell if he hit either of the Khmer Rouge soldiers, but he saw friendlies moving up the beach. Fearing he might hit his own buddies or get shot himself, Clark stopped firing. With his boots pounding their way through gritty sand, he dashed toward the tree line. Cresting a small berm, Clark heard heavy-weapons fire off to his left, coming from the pesky machine gun Lieutenant McDaniel had been trying to silence earlier. Clark saw a shallow trench ahead. He dove into it. The trench ran parallel to the beach and had obviously been constructed by the Khmer Rouge, none of whom were in it at the time. Clark was alone and felt exposed. He rose to a crouch, then darted the last few yards to the tree line, hitting the ground in a heap. He took a moment to relish the fact that he was still alive, then called to find out who was to his left and right. Before anyone could answer, the air support that Lieutenant McDaniel had been coordinating showed up.

The first A-7 rolled in from the north. The underbelly of the Corsair sparkled as 20-mm rounds spewed from its gatling gun. For an instant, Clark thought he was directly in the line of fire. He curled up on the ground, trying to get smaller. Trees just overhead began shredding leaves as 20-mm ammunition bore through the branches, the rounds impacting with an earsplitting crescendo just yards in front of Clark's position.

Looking back toward the beach, Clark watched as another helicopter made an attempt to land troops. As the helicopter neared the beach, Khmer Rouge fire opened up all along the front, driving the helicopter away. The Khmer Rouge defenders were disciplined and accurate, allowing no more reinforcements to arrive for the moment.

Flying well south of the landing zone, Captain Purser maneuvered *Jolly-43* toward a more rugged location near a rocky outcropping. No opposing gunfire greeted the helicopter's arrival, so the command element off-loaded onto the rocks and bolted for cover. Lieutenant Colonel Austin gathered his troops and took stock. He had twenty-eight men including clerks, radio operators, staff officers, and an 81-mm mortar section. They were armed with .45-caliber pistols, grenades, and mortar rounds, but had only four M-16 rifles. Austin was far from the fighting and wanted to head north quickly before the Khmer Rouge discovered the vulnerability of his troops. He gave orders to move out, and the men began inching from one fighting position to another along the beach.

To the north, Lieutenant Pacini in *Jolly-42* decided to make one more try at inserting his troops. He came boring in to the primary landing zone where Lackey had managed to deliver his marines. Pacini came to a hover, swung the helicopter away from the beach, and waited as his gunner used the minigun mounted on the ramp to fire away at Khmer positions. Among the marines on the helicopter was Lieutenant Dick Keith, Golf Company's executive officer. As Keith jumped from the helicopter, the marine in front of him was hit. Keith helped him to cover, then found a medic for him.

Lieutenant Keith soon found McDaniel, who had set up his command center and aid station beneath an abandoned thatched hut. Keith was senior, so McDaniel briefed him on the mostly grim situation.

Keith wasted no time taking charge. Regarding the troublesome machine gun on the north end of the beach, Keith summoned Staff Sergeant Fofo Tutele, an assistant platoon sergeant. Tutele was a highly respected six-foot-two Samoan weighing some 250 pounds, all muscle. Tutele and Staff Sergeant Serferino Bernal were ordered to take out the Khmer machine gun.

While the two-man team moved off, the action shifted to the eastern beach. Lieutenant Cicere's platoon was still pinned down, but the Khmer Rouge had not made any attempt to overrun their position. Instead, the Cambodians seemed content to pour on the fire whenever a big target like a helicopter appeared.

A decision was made inside *Cricket* to withdraw Cicere's small enclave from the east beach by helicopter. *Cricket* ordered *Jolly-13*, piloted by First Lieutenant Charles Greer and copilot First Lieutenant Charles Brown, to attempt an extraction of the twenty-five men who were isolated at the north edge of the beach. As Greer maneuvered his helicopter for his run in, an AC-130 *Spectre* fired ten 40-mm rounds against Cambodian positions pointed out by Lieutenant Lucas. He was still directing strikes using his survival radio onshore.

Lieutenant Greer made his dash, bringing the helicopter to a hover as his gunners raked the beach with minigun fire, but Greer landed some seventy-five yards north of where Lieutenant Cicere and his group were pinned down. Greer expected Lieutenant Cicere and his men to run across the distance separating them and board the helicopter.

Looking from the cockpit, copilot Brown saw muzzle flashes to the north. Neither he nor Greer had been under fire before and as rounds impacted the helicopter, they initially mistook the thumping for the sound of marine boots on the ramp entry. Unknown to the cockpit crew, a burst of machine-gun fire damaged the fuel system. Another round penetrated the fuselage, striking a box of signal flares and setting it afire.

Lieutenant Cicere watched from the protection of his boulder enclave and decided the helicopter could not survive the pummeling it was taking. He and his men held their positions.

Then Plexiglas from *Jolly-13*'s canopy showered across the cockpit. Lieutenants Greer and Brown came to their senses as more rounds struck the fuselage. Greer added power and lifted off, aborting the rescue attempt. With his helicopter badly damaged, he swung left and away from the landing area while tracers continued to stalk the aircraft. The right external fuel tank caught fire. Inside the cabin, the flare case had become a roaring inferno. A pararescueman, Staff Sergeant Steven Lemminn, grabbed the flaming box and heaved it out the open ramp. The foam retardant material in the external fuel tank operated as advertised, keeping the flames from penetrating the tank and preventing an explosion. Billowing flames streaked along the side of the tank as the aircraft gained speed. The increase in airflow managed to snuff out the flames. Though the protective equipment had saved the aircraft from immediate disaster, *Jolly-13* was in serious trouble. With fuel a real problem now that the external tank was punctured, Greer requested a heading for the airborne tanker.

By 7:00 A.M., 109 marines and five air force crewmen were now on the island in three separate locations, all of them in dire straits.

Lieutenant Keith on the west beach was settled inside the thatched hut trying to determine where the other elements were positioned. Using the FM radio, he discovered that Lieutenant Colonel Austin was making his way along the shore from the south. Austin's 81-mm mortar crew had already blasted their way past a Khmer Rouge 60-mm mortar position, capturing the weapon along with a 57-mm recoilless rifle. Keith wanted to expedite the linkup he felt was critical to maintaining his position against continuing attacks. He noted that the machine gun to the north had quit firing—Tutele and Bernal must have succeeded—and the heaviest firing was coming from the south, between his position and that of the command element. Keith told Lieutenant McDaniel to send a squad south to silence the string of

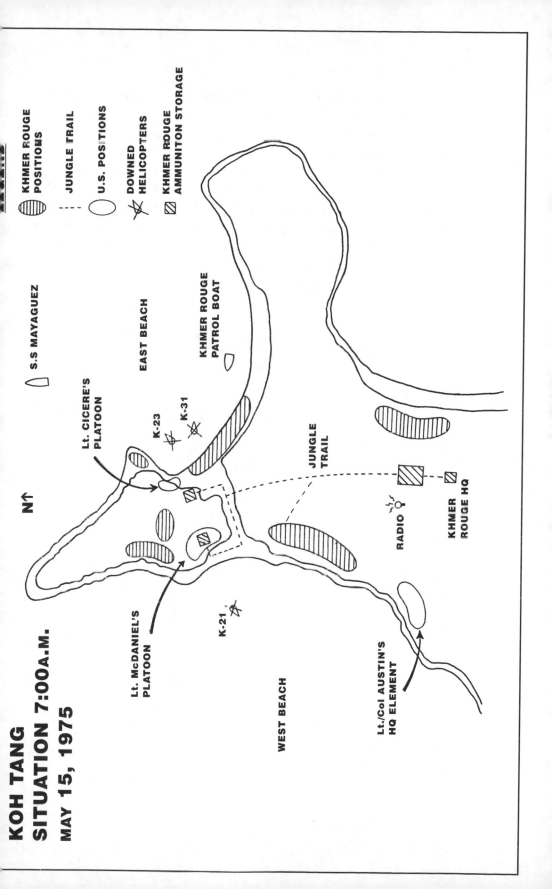

KOH TANG
SITUATION 7:00A.M.
MAY 15, 1975

N↑

KHMER ROUGE
POSITIONS

JUNGLE TRAIL

U.S. POSITIONS

DOWNED
HELICOPTERS

KHMER ROUGE
AMMUNITON STORAGE

S.S MAYAGUEZ

EAST BEACH

KHMER ROUGE
PATROL BOAT

Lt. CICERE'S
PLATOON

K-23

K-31

JUNGLE
TRAIL

RADIO

KHMER
ROUGE HQ

Lt. McDANIEL'S
PLATOON

K-21

WEST BEACH

Lt./Col AUSTIN'S
HQ ELEMENT

active Khmer weapons bunkers. McDaniel chose fourteen marines and moved out with Lance Corporal Ashton Loney on point. The small force made it just beyond the front lines and were moving up a rise when a machine gun opened up. Loney was hit and dropped. Grenades bounced down the hill, landed in the midst of the column, and exploded. Four other men including Lieutenant McDaniel were hit as the marines dove for cover. The two marines in front and directly behind McDaniel moaned in pain. Others were dazed, mumbling in prayer. Loney, a few yards ahead, lay motionless. McDaniel tried to gather his senses. He thought he was about to be overrun.

The SS Mayaguez. The commercial containers were too lightweight for landing rescue helicopters. **DEPARTMENT OF THE NAVY**

President Gerald R. Ford convenes the first of four National Security Council meetings during the *Mayaguez* Incident. William Colby, CIA director (r.), and David C. Jones, Air Force Chief of Staff (l.), face questions from the president, who is second from the left with his back to the camera. **WHITE HOUSE**

The crew of the *Mayaguez* aboard the *Henry B. Wilson*. Captain Charles T. Miller is fourth from the right; third mate Dave English is on the far right; first engineer Vernon Greenlin is standing third from left. **COURTESY: WAYNE STEWART**

Marines from Okinawa on the ramp at U-Tapao Air Base in Thailand await orders on May 14, 1975 to rescue the *Mayaguez* and crew. The marines departed before dawn on the 15th for what would be the last battle of the war. **COURTESY: GALE ROGERS**

A *Jolly Green* rescue helicopter approaches the USS *Holt* at dawn, May 15, 1975. Marines aboard the helicopter will later retake the *Mayaguez* from the deck of the *Holt*. **U.S. AIR FORCE**

Commander Robert A. Peterson (L) confers with a civilian mariner (back to camera) from the SS *Greenville Victory* prior to boarding the *Mayaguez*. The mariners were needed to restart the powerplant on the *Mayaguez*. **DEPARTMENT OF THE NAVY**

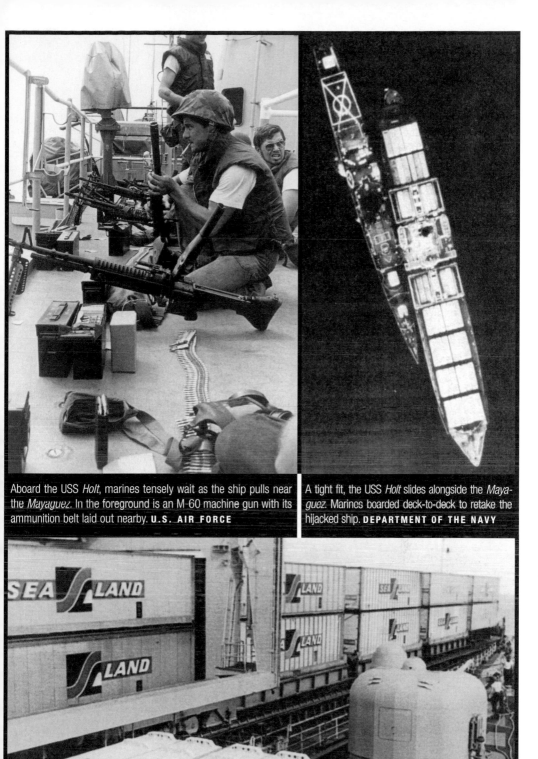

Aboard the USS *Holt*, marines tensely wait as the ship pulls near the *Mayaguez*. In the foreground is an M-60 machine gun with its ammunition belt laid out nearby. **U.S. AIR FORCE**

A tight fit, the USS *Holt* slides alongside the *Mayaguez*. Marines boarded deck-to-deck to retake the hijacked ship. **DEPARTMENT OF THE NAVY**

The crew of the USS *Holt* accomplished the dangerous task of coming alongside another vessel without damaging either ship. **DEPARTMENT OF THE NAVY**

Marines, wearing gas masks to protect them from tear gas, storm aboard the *Mayaguez*.
DEPARTMENT OF THE NAVY

Major Raymond E. Porter (l.) pulls the lanyard to raise the American flag as an unidentified marine assists aboard the newly recovered SS *Mayaguez*. **DEPARTMENT OF THE NAVY**

The Thai fishing trawler, *Sinvari*, approaches the USS *Wilson*. All forty crewmembers from the *Mayaguez* were safely recovered at sea while the battle raged on Koh Tang. **COURTESY: WAYNE STEWART**

A CH-53 rescue helicopter inbound to Koh Tang. The external fuel tanks located just above the main landing wheels in the above photo had no foam fire suppressant installed inside, making them vulnerable to anti-aircraft fire. **U.S. AIR FORCE**

The Mayaguez being towed to safety by the USS *Holt*. Steam begins to rise from the *Mayaguez* stack as its engine power is restored. **U.S. AIR FORCE**

Two marines struggle to stay afloat after surviving the shootdown of *Knife-31*. A life preserver has just been thrown to them by a crewman from the USS *Wilson*. **COURTESY: WAYNE STEWART**

Wounded marines and airmen, who had been swimming for hours without life preservers after being shot out of the sky in *Knife-31*, climb aboard the USS *Wilson*. **COURTESY: WAYNE STEWART**

A crewman (bottom) from the USS *Wilson* tries to assist PFC Tim Trebil who had been seriously burned while trying to rescue the mortally wounded co-pilot, 2/Lt. Richard Vandegeer. Trebil was the last man to exit alive from the burning hulk of *Knife-31*. **COURTESY: WAYNE STEWART**

Major Al Corson, pilot of *Knife-31*, lies on his stomach, exhausted from spending two hours in the water. Corson has just been hauled aboard the USS Wilson's gig, *Black Velvet-1*, and is being treated for his injuries. **COURTESY: WAYNE STEWART**

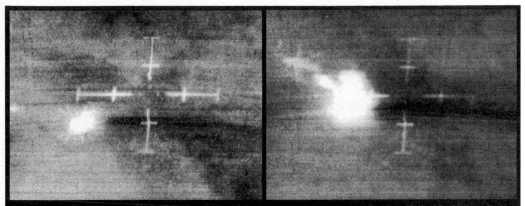

A sequence of photos taken by the Specter C-130 showing *Jolly-13* helicopter on fire and *Knife-23* with its tail shot off. **U.S. AIR FORCE**

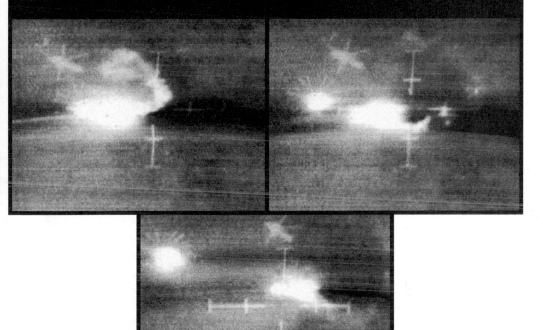

TOP LEFT: As viewed from a *Specter* AC-130 infrared camera, the bright spot (left of center) is from the fuel tank catching fire on *Jolly-13*. To *Jolly-13*'s left can be seen the image of *Knife-23*, which was shot down earlier.

TOP RIGHT: As flames spread on *Jolly-13*, a flare case inside the helicopter catches fire, adding to the bright infrared return. *Knife-23* is located to the upper left of the flames.

CENTER LEFT: Inside the burning helicopter, S/Sgt. Steven Lemminn hurls the ignited flare case out the rear ramp as *Jolly-13* maneuvers near the downed helicopter.

CENTER RIGHT: Burning flares separate from the helicopter and continue to blaze with great intensity as *Jolly-13* struggles to escape, passing abeam *Knife-23*.

BOTTOM CENTER: *Jolly-13* gathers speed, her fuel tank still in flames, while the jettisoned flares continue to burn near the wreck of *Knife-23*. Because *Jolly-23* had fire-retardant foam inside the fuel tank, those flames were soon snuffed out as her speed increased.

As darkness approaches, a 15,000 pound BLU-82 explodes south of the marine position near west beach. The explosion would level trees and leave a crater still visible after 26 years. The effect on the Khmer Rouge was negligible, since it landed too far from the fighting to be effective. **COURTESY: WAYNE STEWART**

Jolly-43 begins his run into the death zone on east beach, followed by *Jolly-11* who covers the approach. Tear gas dropped in advance by A-7s has blown off course as the helicopters near the beach. **COURTESY: WAYNE STEWART**

A Khmer Rouge RPG misses to the left of *Jolly-43* and impacts on the water's surface as the helicopter maneuvers through tear gas near the beach. White spots above the tree line are tracers. Khmer Rouge machine guns would soon find their mark and *Jolly-43* was forced to abort its rescue attempt. **COURTESY: WAYNE STEWART**

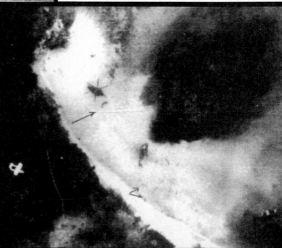

Overhead east beach. Maj. Undorf, flying the *OV-10* pictured above the jungle on the left, has just fired a marking rocket near the wreck of *Knife-23* (above upper arrow) in preparation for airstrikes. The upper arrow points to the severed tail of *Knife-23*. The men from Lt. Cicere's platoon have just been rescued, and the Khmer Rouge forces have moved into that vacated position. The two arrows near the wreck of *Knife-31*, center of photo, indicate where two bodies of fallen marines were still floating. **COURTESY: GREG WILSON**

USS *Wilson* steaming off Koh Tang as tear gas is spread near the east beach during an attempt to rescue Lt. Cicere's pinned-down platoon. **U.S. AIR FORCE**

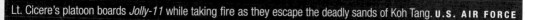

Lt. Cicere's platoon boards *Jolly-11* while taking fire as they escape the deadly sands of Koh Tang. **U.S. AIR FORCE**

President Ford celebrates with cigars and cheering along with his advisors Henry Kissinger, Donald Rumsfeld, and Brent Scowcroft in the oval office after announcing the rescue of the *Mayaguez* crew. Meanwhile servicemen were bleeding and dying on Koh Tang. **WHITE HOUSE**

Partially submerged patrol boat that continued to fire at U.S. forces throughout the last battle until silenced by A-7 fighter bombers and the USS *Wilson*'s guns. **U.S. AIR FORCE**

A crewmember stands beside one of the helicopters that made it back. Large caliber bullet holes are visible in the fuel tank and to the right of the crewman's head on the fuselage. COURTESY: C. BROWN

22

THE CAMBODIANS BLINK

We must, indeed, all hang together or, most assuredly, we shall all hang separately.

Benjamin Franklin

At 6:30 A.M. things were relatively calm on Rong Sam Lem island where the *Mayaguez* crew was held. Unknown to those on the island, the opening phase of the Koh Tang attack had just begun not twenty miles away.

The English-speaker, the compound commander, and Captain Miller stood in the small office inside the commander's hootch. The rest of the crew hovered around the open doorway, trying to listen in on the conversations. The English-speaker cranked up the radio again and contacted Kompong Som. Captain Miller tried to get a reading on what was going on by watching the Cambodian's expressions, but the conversation lasted only ten seconds.

"Yes," the Cambodian said, nodding and smiling at Miller. "The high commander says you and your men can go back to your ship."

Miller took in a deep breath, but was not ready to celebrate just yet. "Can we go now?"

"Yes," the English-speaker said, "but first we must prepare the manifests."

Manifests? The word confused Miller. His cargo manifests were still in the file cabinet on the ship. He had not succeeded in getting them two nights ago because flares were dropped as they boarded the ship. "What kind of manifests?"

"I will tell you what they are," the English-speaker said. "You write them down."

Miller needed something to write on. He had seen First Engineer Vern Greenlin writing in a spiral notebook the day before. As Miller fumbled to get his pen out, he had Chief Harrington get Greenlin. When Greenlin produced the notebook, Miller sat on the English-speaker's cot and opened the pad. He had no idea what was about to transpire, but he wanted names for the investigation that was sure to come. Miller took out his reading glasses, then looked at the English-speaker. "What is your name?"

The English-speaker nodded toward his well-built superior. "The compound commander, who is also the second commander in Kompong Som, is named Chhan." The English-speaker took Miller's pen and wrote on the pad: SECOND COMMANDER—CHHAN. "I am the speaker. My name is Samkol." He printed the words: SPEAKER—SAMKOL.

The Cambodian then began reciting his "manifest" or more properly, his *manifesto*. "Manifest number one." He suddenly got flustered, began stumbling with his English, a little apprehensive, possibly about how those names he had given could be used later.

"Four ships destroyed," he blurted. Then, "One hundred friendly people wounded."

Miller wrote it down.

"Manifest number two." The Cambodian was back in control of his English. "Cambodian people treat crew very good and no harm was done to the crew of forty people."

Except for the gas attack and the cuts and bruises from shrapnel, Miller thought, but he wrote it down as given.

"Manifest number three." Again the English-speaker got tongue tied. "The crew respect the country of Cambodia and the forty crew are responsible for the people and no more damage to the country— no bombs shooting, no airplanes fly over Cambodia."

Miller paused, trying to untangle the sentence. To Miller, it sounded like the Cambodians were holding his crew responsible for the damages that happened and any that might happen in the future. He wanted to take issue, but more important, he wanted to finish this and get back to his ship. Again, he wrote it down as spoken.

"Manifest number four. The Cambodian high commander has contacted the international and the forty crew about the numbers one, two, and three point same as written. The international know the situation very bad for country Cambodia."

Once more Miller was confused about what that had to do with his ship, but he wrote it all down.

"Manifest number five. Forty crew very friendly to people of Cambodia. Good friends." Miller thought the English-speaker was searching his mind at this point, trying to embellish the manifesto. He jotted the message as fast as he could, sensing things were coming to a close.

"Manifest number six. The people of Cambodia no like war and want peace and want many friend in the international and have forty friend in this crew." The Cambodian flashed a hesitant smile. "That is all, Captain Miller. Please sign."

Miller signed it.

The English-speaker picked up the notebook and wrote at the bottom: THE PEOPLE CAMBODIA GOOD FRIENDLY WITH 40 PEOPLES U.S. Then he gave the pad back to Miller. "You keep it."

Miller was confused again. "You want me to take it back to the ship with me?"

"It is for you," the Cambodian said. He looked insulted that Miller seemed reticent to take the document.

Whatever makes him happy, Miller decided. "Oh, fine, I'll bring this back to the ship. Can we go now?"

"After you vote," the English-speaker said.

"Vote?" Miller took off his reading glasses and held them in his hand.

"The forty crew must vote. Isn't that the way you do things in your democracy? The manifests must be unanimous."

Miller shrugged. "Okay, I'll take a vote." He stood, then moved into the center of the hootch and stood among the crew. "All right fellas, we're going to take a vote."

"Let's get the fuck outta here, Capt'n," Miller heard someone bellow. The crew looked haggard, unshaven, dirty, smelly, their faces covered with festering lumps from the mosquito bites. There was a good chance they'd all come down with malaria before this was over. Better hurry before the Cambodians change their minds, Miller thought. "Fellas, I'm going to read six points which the English-speaker here has asked me to write down. Then if you agree with these six points unanimously, we're going to go."

Miller put his tortoiseshell glasses back on. He stood in the center of the gathering looking like a school principal as he read the six items. When finished, he looked up. "All those in favor say aye."

A chorus of "ayes," "yeahs," and "yups" resounded.

As Miller glanced at the English-speaker and the commander for assurance they were satisfied, an angry announcement met his ears from somewhere behind him.

"You're not signing a confession for me. It's against my principles."

Miller whirled around toward whoever had spoken, thoroughly rankled that one of his crew was making a stink over this trifle of a statement. He knew the voice. He'd had trouble before with the owner of that voice. His eyes settled on Able Bodied Seaman Tom LaBue.

Cliff Harrington was angry, too. "The captain's not asking you to sign anything, LaBue. Where do you see the word confession?"

A stern, disappointed expression came over the English-speaker and the Cambodian commander.

Miller looked to see if anyone else was getting ready to back LaBue up. "Do you fellows think I'm signing a confession or do you think I'm signing the points this man wants, so the world will know the Cambodians were friendly to us?"

The crew started hollering, "Yeah, you're right, Capt'n."

"I got my rights," LaBue railed. "I've got the right to speak up."

Miller remembered that LaBue had written an anonymous but threatening note aboard ship some six weeks ago. "When I don't get overtime, I get mad," the note had read. "When I get mad, I get pissed. And when I get pissed, I get dangerous." Miller had compared the note with all the signatures on the log. LaBue's matched. When confronted, LaBue had admitted writing it.

Well, Miller had heard and read about enough from LaBue. "Just shut up and we'll all go back to the ship."

At that point, the other members of the crew chimed in. "Keep out of it, LaBue." "Shut up, LaBue." "Fuck you, LaBue."

Tom LaBue shut his mouth.

23

"MARINES, OVER THE SIDE!"

Sir: I have to state for the information of the Department that I have taken a valuable prize this morning, now called the Susan Jane, *of Nevis, West Indies. . . . I send Lieutenant Crosby in charge of the prise because he is the important witness of what occurred after we boarded.*

Report of U.S. Navy flag officer Stringham, commanding the Atlantic Blockading Squadron, September 10, 1861

During the night the USS *Holt*'s maintenance crew had finally managed to jury-rig a power supply for their 5-inch gun, which had been out of service since before the start of their race toward Koh Tang. As the ship came abeam the island with only her running lights on, Commander Robert A. Peterson, skipper of the *Holt*, slowed the ship to await the opening of hostilities. He had entered into harm's way, and he and his crew were ready.

As the sun rose in the east, Peterson saw the flight of helicopters approach and the first one set down on his helipad at 6:13 A.M.

Major Porter's D Company boarding party off-loaded and gathered around Commander Peterson and Lieutenant Commander John Todd, the *Holt*'s Executive officer. The men began discussing the plan for retaking the *Mayaguez*.

The volunteer civil service sailors recruited to start the *Mayaguez* power plant were next, led by USNS *Greenville Victory* first officer Clinton J. Harriman from their helicopter onto the deck of the *Holt* at 6:24 A.M.

Located west of Koh Tang, the navy ship maneuvered east, planning to swing past the *Mayaguez*, then hook back to the west for the boarding. Peterson intended to bring his ship against the side of the hijacked vessel that faced away from the island. The *Holt*, one hundred feet shorter than the *Mayaguez*, would use the hull of the cargo ship as a shield against hostile fire that might come from Koh Tang. Even though the *Holt* was smaller than the *Mayaguez*, Peterson thought that the O-1 deck just above the *Holt*'s main deck would be nearly level with the *Mayaguez* main deck. The marine boarding party set up on the higher deck and waited.

Air Force A7-D Corsairs were to swoop low and deliver tear gas over the *Mayaguez* ten minutes prior to the *Holt* coming alongside. Five minutes later, the A-7s would strafe near the ship, intending to have its Khmer Rouge defenders hunker down for safety while the *Holt* pulled alongside.

As the *Holt* maneuvered east, navy fire teams armed with machine guns and automatic weapons spread out along the deck. Once the ships were close together, Peterson's 5-inch gun would be useless so he wanted to be ready to return fire if need be. Marine captain Wood huddled with Corporal Carl R. Coker and his assault squad on the O-1 deck. The squad fitted their gas masks and went over last-minute details. Theirs would be the onerous task of boarding first and fighting their way to the bridge of the ship.

By 7:00 A.M., Peterson, back in the pilothouse, peered through binoculars at the *Mayaguez*. The ship lay silhouetted against Koh Tang, where an ominous black pall rose steadily into the morning sky. *Knife* and *Jolly* helicopters were buzzing around the north side of the island. He could see that the landing campaign was running into problems.

Peterson knew full well his task would not be a milk run either. On the deck of the *Mayaguez*, Peterson spotted six armed Cambodians. The container ship was swinging freely about its only anchor, suspended from the bow. Without line handlers, the boarding party would have mere seconds to transfer to the other ship since Peterson did not expect the *Holt* to remain side to side against the *Mayaguez* for more than a few moments. The *Holt* had rope fenders laid over the side to cushion the impact. Regardless, the maneuver would be dicey, and Peterson would probably have only one chance to succeed.

At 7:10 A.M., two A-7s streaked across the sky spewing gas canisters along a wide swath enveloping the *Mayaguez*. Peterson watched as the gas dispersed and a gray fog obscured the ship. He ordered his crew to don masks since the cloud mass began drifting in a light wind toward the *Holt*.

Hatches were battened down for combat as the morning sun streamed into the closed pilothouse. The *Holt*'s 5-inch gun was aimed directly at the *Mayaguez*. Antiaircraft *Sea Sparrow* missiles were trained on the container ship as well. Even the antisubmarine rocket launcher was primed for use if needed.

Sweat poured from around the seals of Peterson's mask as his helmsman slowed the ship and made ready to come alongside. He scanned the white superstructure of the *Mayaguez*, his eyes shifting from deck to deck looking for movement, a muzzle flash, a human figure, anything. Nothing stirred. At two hundred yards astern the cargo ship, Peterson made a radio call for the strafing run, then immediately canceled it. He was already too close. Peering through his mask's foggy lenses, Peterson watched the hulk of the *Mayaguez* loom larger, silent in the near-breathless dawn, wreathed in ghostly wisps of lingering tear gas.

Peterson glanced down upon the marines, spaced out along the decks. Thirty-caliber machine guns were mounted and aimed at the *Mayaguez*. Captain Wood and his boarding party were positioned on the O-1 deck, all tense, crouching low, every M-16 pointed at the hijacked ship. Then Peterson, contrary to his original prediction, noticed that both main decks were on the same level. Captain Wood, who realized this at the same time, raced below with his squad, arriving near the bow on the main deck just as the *Holt* slid abeam.

On the port side, Lieutenant Commander Todd stood by as the *Holt* eased within a yard of the *Mayaguez*. Coker and Wood each lifted a shaky boot, placing it on the *Holt*'s gunwale. At 7:25 A.M., the hulls came together, squeezing the rope fenders flat with a hiss. Todd shouted the boarding order heard rarely since the Civil War blockades.

"Marines over the side!"

Corporal Coker and Captain Wood leapt across the gap, landing amidship on the *Mayaguez*. Coker immediately headed up an outside ladder for the bridge while Wood moved aft along the deck to cover the rear. Wood went only a few paces before turning to see how the rest of the squad was doing. To his surprise no one else had boarded. The backwash created by the *Holt* coming alongside the *Mayaguez* had pushed the two ships apart. Some twenty-five feet separated the two. Wood and Coker found themselves alone on a vessel thought to be held by armed defenders. Unable to be heard clearly, Wood lifted his mask and shouted for Coker to come back. Tense moments followed as the two of them caught lines thrown across by sailors on the *Holt*. "Motivated partially out of loneliness," Wood remembered, "Corporal Coker and I worked feverishly at the lines and the two ships were made fast." The rest of the squad then clambered aboard and Coker again took off for the bridge. His squad followed this time, as Coker took the steps two at a time.

A second squad led by marine sergeant William J. Owens jumped over the side next. This squad, using flashlights, moved deliberately but quickly deep into the darkened bowels of the ship toward the engine room. Two air force sergeants checked for booby traps, but none was discovered. Open food cans were found but the marines were greeted with silence. Whoever had been aboard moments before had abandoned ship. The vessel was deserted.

24

TIMING IS EVERYTHING

The commander in the field is always right and the rear echelon is wrong, unless proved otherwise.

Colin Powell

A Cambodian-language radio broadcast, beginning at 6:07 A.M. on May 15 (7:07 P.M. May 14, Washington time), by Khmer Rouge information and propaganda minister Hu Nim was picked up by the CIA's Foreign Broadcast Information Service in Bangkok. After nineteen minutes of diatribe, Hu Nim got to the point. "Wishing to provoke no one or to make trouble, adhering to the stand of peace and neutrality, we will release the ship, but we will not allow the U.S. imperialists to violate our territorial waters, conduct espionage in our territorial waters, provoke incidents in our territorial waters, or force us to release their ships whenever they want by applying threats." The

CIA's translators delivered a copy by teletype to the White House forty minutes later, which, according to Press Secretary Ron Nessen, was "an impressive demonstration of the intelligence agency's abilities."

Kissinger was monitoring the operation in his spacious, art-filled NSC office in the White House when word of the Cambodian dispatch reached him some minutes later, at around 8:15 P.M. He took a few moments to mull over the situation. Operations were already under way. The United States could not stop the military action on Koh Tang without risking the lives of over one hundred marines pinned down there. By checking the time, Kissinger also knew the *Mayaguez* was likely to have been retaken within minutes of the receipt of the Cambodian broadcast.

A decision had to be made whether to follow through with the air strikes against the mainland. The planes from the *Coral Sea* were airborne but would not reach their targets for another fifteen to thirty minutes.

First Kissinger phoned his assistant, Lieutenant General Brent Scowcroft. He told Scowcroft to inform the National Military Command Center that the planes from the *Coral Sea* should proceed on course but drop no ordnance until notified by the president.

Kissinger then called the president at 8:29 P.M. Ford, delayed some thirty minutes by the dragged-on congressional briefing, had just received Dutch prime minister Johannes den Uyl and was trying to enjoy his first martini on the rocks with den Uyl in the Red Room prior to the state dinner. He had already been interrupted once to be informed of the Phnom Penh radio overture. When Kissinger got him on the line, "Ford proved skeptical." No mention in the broadcast was made regarding the *Mayaguez* crew, so Ford wanted clarification. He ordered a message be sent to the Cambodians acknowledging their announcement and promising to call off military operations as soon as the crew members were freed. The president had no intention of altering any of his directives until he was sure of the crew's release.

Kissinger, by his recommendation to the NMCC, had already altered the bombing directive, but either forgot or chose not to inform the president of that fact.

At 8:41 P.M., at *the* critical moment in the crisis, the working dinner for den Uyl began.

The party moved from the Red Room to the scheduled meal beneath the enormous chandeliers in the state dining room. Guests began popping in and out, not in itself unusual, but the amount of chair-hopping was inordinate. The affair was black-tie, which created a farcical scene as intense White House participants darted about in tuxedos in the midst of an international imbroglio. Scowcroft and Rumsfeld made only token appearances, and many guest seats remained empty.

Kissinger was still in his office wrestling with the problem of how to contact Phnom Penh in a timely manner regarding their radio broadcast. Since the United States had no direct line to the authorities there, he felt the best way to overcome the difficulty was to use the media wire services. For that he would need help. He dialed Nessen's number.

Nessen took the call in his office. "Come down here right away," Kissinger ordered in an agitated voice, then hung up.

Nessen, no fan of Kissinger, did not appreciate being ordered around by someone he did not consider his superior, so he ignored the command and kept working on his own problems. While egos parried, the clock ticked on.

Kissinger marked time for a few minutes, meanwhile learning that U.S. forces had successfully recovered the *Mayaguez*. Still, the press secretary had not shown up, so Kissinger sent Scowcroft after him.

Scowcroft, dressed in his tuxedo, burst into Nessen's office, grabbed Nessen by the arm, and literally pulled him to Kissinger's office.

"We have got to get a message through to Cambodia," Kissinger announced excitedly. "They've got to read it on the AP." Nessen, at last aware of the urgency involved, helped Kissinger put the finishing touches on a communiqué that read:

> We have heard a radio broadcast that you are prepared to release the SS *Mayaguez*. We welcome this development, if true.
>
> As you know, we have seized the ship. As soon as you issue a statement that you are prepared to release the crew members you hold unconditionally and immediately, we will promptly cease military operations.

Kissinger sent Nessen to the pressroom to make the announcement. Then the secretary of state proceeded to the dinner.

Prime Minister den Uyl, from the pacifist wing of the Dutch Labor Party, was decidedly an unsympathetic guest when it came to U.S. military adventures in Asia. He had apparently been briefed to refrain from being provocative, a result he didn't quite manage to achieve. His statement during the exchange of toasts contained small jibes, including a comment about the contribution of the Dutch to New York City, and that the name New York "should still be New Amsterdam." Then followed, "Relations between the Western democracies and the countries of the Third World have, as I see it, been strained in recent years by an apparent lack of confidence in our willingness to share their burdens and to help them solve their immense problems." The prime minister made clear during dinner conversation that he did not consider military force the appropriate way to solve political problems.

Ford proved unreceptive to den Uyl's pontificating lectures, especially coming from a representative of a country the United States had helped liberate in World War II and whose defense America still largely supported through NATO.

The president was up and down repeatedly, excusing himself to receive reports from the military operations in the usher's office adjoining the state dining room. Abbreviated news was streaming in via three different channels: from beleaguered marines on Koh Tang, from the air force pilots overhead the scene, and from the navy about to attack Kompong Som. By this time, Ford knew that the ship had been retaken and the marines were running into serious resistance on Koh Tang.

Eleven thousand miles away, planes from the *Coral Sea* were circling in a holding pattern off the coast, just minutes from their scheduled 7:45 A.M. first strike on the Kompong Som oil storage complex and Ream airfield.

In the jumble of messages emanating from Washington over the Cambodian radio transmission, Kissinger had essentially put the navy on hold awaiting the president's decision. The planes continued circling for several minutes. Finally, with fuel running low, an order from the Pentagon was received rescinding the attack. The strike force jettisoned their bombs into the sea and headed back to the carrier. Ford's order regarding the urgent need to ensure that no troops or planes from the mainland endanger the marines on Koh Tang had been trumped without his knowledge. No bombs were dropped on the mainland until the initial cancellation was reversed by yet another message from the Pentagon. The planned second and third strikes against the same targets began an hour later, at 9:05 A.M. Cambodia time, and were carried out. The fourth strike, due to begin at 11:30 A.M., was diverted from their mainland targets to Koh Tang where they were to provide close air support for the marines. When word of the diversion reached the navy, the new tasking was rejected because the carrier-based attack aircraft had not been briefed and were not equipped with the proper radios to communicate with the men on the ground. As a result, the fourth mission was scrubbed. Clearly, if tactical decisions were going to be made at the top, then the person at the top—the president—needed to be in the Situation Room in the thick of things, not getting light-headed making toasts. Ford had wanted all four strikes to go in, but in the confusion half the sorties never even reached their targets.

A little before 9:00 P.M. in Washington, what surely was a most perplexed secretary of defense finally arrived at the den Uyl dinner and took his seat. Schlesinger stayed through an awkward serving of dessert, then left.

At 9:15 P.M., Nessen found himself climbing onto the small platform in the press briefing room. In Nessen's opinion, "There are no bigger stories than international military confrontations." To him, the packed room that late at night was clear evidence of that. He began reading the statement at a brisk pace. "In further pursuit of our efforts to obtain the release—"

"Would you read it slow, please?" came a chorus of requests from the audience. The press wanted to get the statement accurately while Nessen was energized to get word to the Cambodians quickly.

"Look!" Nessen shouted. "What I have to say . . . there is some urgency about it."

The reporters picked up on the fact that there was more here than just the recording of a press release. The room grew quiet. Nessen resumed reading the message. When he finished Nessen ordered the cameras turned off. Then he told the press corps why he had read so fast. "We believe the news channels may be the fastest way for this message to get through. Go file!"

The newsmen rushed to their phones or to their spots in front of television cameras.

25

"THEY'RE (NOT) ALL SAFE!"

How many deaths will it take till he knows
That too many people have died?

Bob Dylan, *Blowin' in the Wind*, (song) 1962

Commander J. Michael Rodgers, at the helm of the guided missile destroyer USS *Wilson*, arrived on the scene about forty-five minutes after the first marines hit the deadly beaches of Koh Tang. He navigated his ship in from the southeast with all four boilers up and running, his general-quarters horn blaring, and his 5-inch guns trained on the beach.

He spotted the *Holt* moving into position near the *Mayaguez*, which was partially obscured by tear gas. From the radio traffic, Rodgers knew that things were not going well.

Rodgers scanned the crescent-shaped beach, which curved gently around from the northeast. The jungle terrain behind the shore rose to a small, dense knoll at the southern end. Further west, a mesalike promontory jutted two hundred feet into the air.

Black smoke was billowing near the beach. Jet fighters swooped low over the island, raking the area with cannon fire. Helicopters swarmed around the north end of Koh Tang. As the *Wilson* pulled to within a mile, Rodgers could see red tracers ricocheting into the morning sky. The buzzlike sound of an A-7's gatling gun reached his ears followed by the crackle of explosions as hundreds of 20-mm rounds ripped through thick vegetation. The answering tattoo of heavy machine guns from the island mixed with dull whoomps as mortar rounds threw up dirty clouds of sand and smoke all along the beach. Rodgers peered through binoculars at the hulks of two helicopters in the shallows near shore. One was barely visible, its top and rotor head jutting from the water. The other blazed fiercely, a towering column of black smoke marking its location. South of the burning helicopter, he spotted a gunboat, partially submerged in the cove.

Then as Rodgers was trying to locate weapon emplacements on the beach for his 5-inch guns to attack, one of his lookouts called out that he saw a head in the water off the port bow. Rodgers focused his attention closer to his ship and saw red smoke spewing into the air. Underneath the ballooning cloud bobbed another head, this one frantically waving a smoldering marker flare. Rodgers brought his ship to a stop, ignoring machine-gun fire that began peppering the water nearby. He had two motor-driven boats used for ship-to-shore transportation. He ordered his personal gig to be lowered over the side. This boat, manned by Petty Officers First Class Alvin Ellis and Thomas Noble, had a forward deck where two M-60 machine guns were hastily set up. The other craft, an unarmed whaleboat, stayed aboard the ship for the moment.

While the *Wilson* remained a sitting duck, Rodgers stopped the ship near the swimmers. He counted three of them now.

The marines, Privates First Class Timothy Trebil and Gaston were helping Sergeant V. G. Salinas, who was temporarily blinded. The trio had been in the water for nearly two hours. They started waving and screaming. Marine guards onboard came forward and pointed their rifles at the three men. Trebil thought they were mistaking them for Cambodian sappers. The marines started firing, but not at the three swimmers. They were shooting at sharks.

A line with a loop at the end was lowered over the side. When it was Trebil's turn, he shoved a leg through the loop, grabbed the line with his hands, and held on as he was hauled up. Two of the *Wilson's* crew grabbed Trebil's arms to pull him aboard. That's when he felt real pain for the first time. His arms had been burned and loose flesh tore off as strong hands grasped him. "My ass hit the deck and the medic was right on top of me giving me morphine. Boy, did that feel good."

Meanwhile, the gig pulled away and began plucking other survivors out of the water as Ellis and Noble used their machine guns to return fire from the beach.

At 7:29 A.M., at the same moment President Ford and Secretary of State Kissinger were discussing the Phnom Penh radio broadcast, Captain Miller and his crew boarded a fishing boat, the *Sinvari*, the one they had ridden the day before through strafing and gas attacks. Miller had learned that the five-man crew of the trawler were Thais who had been held captive for the last five months. As the boat left the dock, Miller looked around. There were only four Cambodian guards aboard. A second trawler pulled out with seven guards and Sa Mean onboard, the same Khmer commander who had hijacked the *Mayaguez* three days earlier. The second boat slid in trail.

Miller did not like the looks of things. *Why were there more guards on the second boat when there weren't any Americans onboard?* He had visions of the guards mowing down his crew and throwing them all over the side once they were at sea. Miller did not have much time to consider the matter before Sa Mean signaled for the Thai boat to turn around. Back to the dock they went, where four more guards climbed aboard the *Sinvari*. Then the two-boat armada headed out once again.

Back on shore, the English-speaker stood on the deck of the bamboo hootch that squatted on spindly teakwood pilings at the water's edge. Dressed in black, the Cambodian waved a solemn good-bye, his tiny figure receding as the boats made their way out of the harbor. To the west, where they would soon be headed, jets were diving at the sea, then pulling up in wide swooping turns.

They were still too far away to hear the combat taking place on Koh Tang, but the Khmer Rouge engaged in the fighting had radioed to the mainland and the other islands at dawn regarding the situation, so the Khmer Rouge on Rong Sam Len probably knew what was happening. Before the trawlers had pulled out, the English-speaker told Miller, "You will contact the American government when you get on your ship. Tell them to stop the jets." With that order echoing in his head, Miller wondered if it was not already too late.

"We're off and running now," Miller shouted to his engineer, Cliff Harrington. The two of them glanced skyward, looking for signs that the fighter planes had noticed them, both of them wondering if the jets would fire on the trawler once they were spotted. If the guards on the boats fired at the planes, Miller knew their fishing boat would be headed for the bottom. But the sky directly above was undisturbed, the only nearby movement being the ocean swells they were plowing through.

Minutes later, Miller saw Sa Mean take his walkie-talkie into the escort boat's wheelhouse. When Sa Mean came out, he had his trawler pull alongside the *Sinvari* and began waving excitedly for the Thai fishing boat to stop.

"He must have gotten a call on his walkie-talkie," Miller said to crew members standing nearby. He wondered if the jets were already in action out by the island. If so, that radio call could spell trouble. To the west, he could see the northern part of the island peeking above the sea. Planes were circling.

When the two boats were bobbing gunwale to gunwale, Sa Mean jumped aboard Miller's trawler. He went up to the Thai captain and spoke. Suddenly the captain began jumping up and down. "We free," he yelled. "We free." He started prancing around, and the other four Thais began whooping it up, too.

The Khmer commander then ordered all the Cambodian guards out of the Thai boat. Before Sa Mean stepped back across to the other trawler, he reached over and shook Miller's hand.

"Good-bye," Sa Mean said.

"Good-bye," Miller answered.

The Khmer jumped into the other vessel, and it peeled away, making a beeline back toward the dock.

The *Sinvari* had motored beyond the rocky outcropping that sheltered the cove, its bow now pointed westward toward the *Mayaguez* and the chaos unfolding on the distant horizon.

Meanwhile the Thai captain was still doing an Asian version of the Scottish jig. Then he began to peel off his sarong. Underneath he wore a *pacama*, a loincloth wound around his midsection. He unwrapped the *pacama*; strapped to the Thai's scrotum was a gold watch. He held the wristwatch aloft for all to see, then reached down and pulled five U.S. twenty-dollar bills from the folds of the undergarment.

Harrington shook his head. "Must have been kind of uncomfortable for five months!"

Not everyone was elated. Former marine Dave English came forward, concerned about what might lay ahead on the *Mayaguez*. "What if Cambodians are still on the ship, Captain? We'd be right back in captivity."

As far as Miller was concerned, English always expected the worst. There were enough things to worry about right here without conjuring up future woes. The first concern was how to keep from getting shot out of the water. Miller made the crew take off their white shirts and undershirts; he even had Omer doff his white mess jacket. They began attaching these to bamboo poles that they had wisely placed aboard before casting off.

Miller looked west. A lot of activity was going on out by Koh Tang. He wondered if the Khmer Rouge had decided to head back to safety before the shooting started.

Aboard the *Wilson*, medic petty officer first class Donald Pourman was having all he could do to deal with the burns and wounds of the thirteen men who had been plucked from the sea near the burning wreck of *Knife-31*. Some of those men had been in shark-infested water almost four hours with only three life preservers between them before the *Wilson*'s gig could fight its way close enough to pull them aboard.

Now that all the wounded were safely on the *Wilson*, Commander Mike Rodgers maneuvered his ship closer to the *Mayaguez*. He saw a dozen or so marines positioned along her deck. The men seemed almost at ease, a stark contrast to what he had witnessed near the island, where the battle continued to rage. At the bow of the *Mayaguez*, men were trying to rig a bridle to attach to the *Holt* for towing. As he watched, Rogers got a call from his executive officer, Jim Hall.

"Captain, there's a gunboat coming out from the mainland!"

Hall had received a radio call from the orbiting P-3 Orion, which had spotted a boat approaching Koh Tang from the east. The task force commander aboard the *Holt* heard the transmission, too. With the *Holt* engaged in taking the *Mayaguez* under tow, he ordered Rodgers to intercept the gunboat.

Rodgers ordered his engines all-ahead full, and the *Wilson* swung her bow eastward to engage. Within seconds, the *Wilson*'s radar picked up the target, a single blip heading straight toward Roger's ship. The radar locked on and the *Wilson*'s missiles were armed, her gun barrels aimed and ready. Rodgers held the collision course and stood by to fire once a positive identification was made or the target opened fire.

A second call came in from the P-3. "Looks more like a pleasure craft."

Rodgers held his fire.

The P-3 Orion was above the target now. The sighting had been so sudden, the pilot had not even had time to start the engine he had earlier shut down and feathered to save on fuel. The Orion swung low, three engines running, as it circled the boat. Then the pilot got all excited. He saw twenty to thirty men standing on the open foredeck, waving white flags. Six or more were standing atop the pilothouse.

"They're Caucasians!" the pilot radioed. "Must be thirty of them waving white flags!"

Mike Rodgers locked his guns to the centerline safe position and reached for the microphone to his external loudspeakers.

"Are you the crew of the *Mayaguez*?"

The question boomed out across the open sea. Rodgers brought his binoculars up to his eyes. On the trawler, people were waving white flags like mad, jumping up and down, and hollering.

As the Wilson drew abeam, Rodgers saw one of the men on the trawler cup his hands and appear to ask for permission to come alongside. That was fine with Rodgers.

"Permission to come alongside," boomed the *Wilson*'s loudspeaker in response.

The trawler pulled abeam the *Wilson*, which lowered a steel boarding ladder. Captain Miller was first to climb onto the destroyer deck. He was taken to the bridge, where he met Commander Rodgers. Miller immediately relayed the agreement he had made with his Cambodian captors, to have all overflights and bombing halted.

"Captain," Commander Rodgers said, "you're just about an hour late. They've already started bombing Kompong Som."

Miller was then escorted to the communications section, where he met Executive Officer Jim Hall, who was on the radiophone to Washington. Miller told Hall that all of the *Mayaguez* crew had been rescued. Hall began relaying the information over the phone.

At the White House, the time was 11:10 P.M., just minutes after the conclusion of what Kissinger later described as "the den Uyl fiasco." The president, Press Secretary Ron Nessen, Henry Kissinger, Brent Scowcroft, Robert T. Hartmann, and White House Chief of Staff Donald Rumsfeld were gathered in the Oval Office. Still in their tuxedos, the group settled into chairs around the president, who sat at his desk. Ford began taking calls on the white phone connected directly to Schlesinger, who was monitoring the operation from the Pentagon. Kissinger grabbed an extension so he could overhear the reports. The first call was all bad news. Marines were under heavy fire from Cambodian troops entrenched on Tang Island. The *Mayaguez* had been retaken, but no crewmen were aboard. Then came word that a fishing vessel had been spotted with people on deck waving white flags. The mood shifted from glum to hopeful. A few minutes before midnight, the white phone on Ford's desk buzzed softly. Ford picked up the receiver. There came a hushed moment as Ford listened. Then the president settled the phone back in its desktop cradle.

White House photographer David Kennerly had been lurking unobtrusively on the left side of the Oval Office. Sensing the drama, he readied his camera. Ford came half out of his chair as Kennerly caught the moment on film.

"They're all safe," Ford whooped, breaking the hush. "We got them all out, thank God. It went perfectly."

26

"PERFECTLY" AWFUL

Politics is war without bloodshed while war is politics with
bloodshed.

Mao Zedong

Lieutenant McDaniel lay prone on the ground, still reeling from the
attack on his squad. McDaniel could hear foreign voices not far off. The
shouting sounded as though they were taunting him. He glanced around.
His marines were scattered in the brush. Every time one of his men fired
an M-16, the Khmer Rouge countered with a volley. A machine gun
chattered away to the south. Bullets clipped overhead branches.

McDaniel felt the pressure of a hand grenade he had stowed in his
vest. He carefully eased it and another out of his pockets, then pulled
the pin on the first one. Rolling onto his side, McDaniel looked ahead
to ensure his intended trajectory was clear of vines or branches. Satisfied

the grenade would not carom back, he hurled the weapon. Moments later, he threw the second grenade. Two muffled explosions followed.

McDaniel craned his head, looking forward. Nothing moved. His ears, ringing a moment ago, were greeted with an eerie silence. Loney was lying motionless yards ahead. Blood was oozing from where his chin had been. A red stain covered his chest. McDaniel passed the word to withdraw, and the squad began to pull back, dragging their wounded, including Loney.

The patrol crawled inside the perimeter line, and the result of the probe that attempted to link with Lieutenant Colonel Austin's group was passed to Lieutenant Keith back at the thatched hooch. Thoughts of linking with Austin's group were abandoned. Keith figured the Khmer Rouge would try to press their counterattack, and he was right. The entire southern flank came alive with gunfire. Shouts were heard as the Khmer Rouge maneuvered forward. The marines yelled orders of their own as the two forces converged to within fifteen yards of each other. Hand grenades came flying at the beleaguered marines. They grabbed them as fast as they came in and tossed them back along with some of their own. Then as quickly as it had begun, the Khmer Rouge ceased firing and withdrew.

In the EC-130 command ship circling fifty miles to the north, Colonel Anders had finally gotten a reasonably accurate grip on the situation. Of the eleven helicopters that flew in the first wave, two were smoking wreckages near the east beach, one had sunk off the west beach, and a fourth, *Knife-22*, was on the ground somewhere near the Thai/Cambodian border. Two others, *Knife-32* and *Jolly-42*, were battling all manner of cockpit emergencies while trying to make it back to Thailand. The three helicopters that had dropped troops on the *Holt* were undamaged and were assisting in rescue attempts or escorting shot-up helicopters. *Jolly-41* was orbiting near the KC-130 tanker, still waiting for instructions on inserting its marines. The *Mayaguez* crew had been released by the Cambodians and were in friendly hands on the *Wilson*.

The question on everyone's mind in the chain of command now was what to do about the island assault.

Back in Washington, the president was jubilant over the news of the crew release and the securing of the *Mayaguez*. Cigars were passed around and handshakes exchanged in congratulations. Ford wanted the successful resolution of the crisis to be announced from the White House.

Ron Nessen returned to his office to make the arrangements. He was about to call Joe Laitin, Department of Defense spokesman at the Pentagon, to forestall any premature announcements. Laitin had been leaking information to reporters throughout the crisis. Before Nessen could dial the number, his secretary dropped a wire-service bulletin on his desk. Laitin had done it again, scooping the president with news that the crew was safe.

Nessen rushed back to the Oval Office. "That goddamn Laitin has already leaked the news!"

Curses were directed at the Pentagon spokesman by the aides around Ford. But Nessen wanted his boss to get the attention he deserved after the apparent success of this, his first military test.

"Look, we have one thing that Laitin doesn't have," Nessen argued. "We have the president. Why doesn't the president go out and announce the recovery of the *Mayaguez* and the crew on live television, in the middle of the *Johnny Carson Show*?"

"That's a good idea," Ford allowed. Rumsfeld, Kissinger, and the other aides thought so, too.

Ford went to his residence to change out of his tuxedo. Meanwhile, the announcement was written in the NSC office while Nessen notified the networks to stand by for a Ford statement. The president returned to the pressroom wearing a suit, but before he could get on camera, there was a hitch. Rumsfeld was not at all sanguine about the accuracy of reports coming from the Pentagon. He insisted on calling Schlesinger one more time. Ford took the phone once the secretary of defense was on the line.

"I'm sure you can understand, Jim," Ford cautioned. "Under the circumstances I need to be absolutely assured that all the crew members are out."

Schlesinger answered that it had been confirmed from three different sources. When asked about casualties, Schlesinger stalled. Things were still so chaotic that he did not really have a clear idea.

Before the president could declare the incident over, though, the withdrawal of U.S. military forces had to be resolved.

"Is there any reason for the Pentagon not to disengage?" Scowcroft asked. By now, they were all aware that no hostages had been on Koh Tang, making the assault there and its resulting casualties unnecessary.

"No," Kissinger interrupted, "but tell them to bomb the mainland. Let's look ferocious. Otherwise they'll attack us as the ship leaves." Kissinger still wanted to be in charge, wanted to give orders, and he certainly knew the Cambodians had no viable means with which to mount a counterattack from the coast.

None of them considered the more important issue. Should the president engage in punitive strikes against port facilities and woefully armed Cambodian air and naval facilities, or should all available U.S. forces be harnessed in getting the marines safely off the island?

Ford sided with Kissinger, probably because no one raised the issue of what might be needed to get the marines out. Once again, the filtering of details negatively affected decision making. The president ordered the mainland air strikes, then headed for the pressroom still wearing the black patten pumps he had been wearing with the tuxedo earlier, though they were now mismatched with a brown suit. He looked tired and edgy and when he finally got on camera he muffled some of the words. His carefully crafted statement did not reveal how the crew was actually recovered.

> At my direction, the United States forces tonight boarded the American merchant ship SS *Mayaguez* and landed at the Island of Koh Tang for the purpose of rescuing the crew and the ship, which had been illegally seized by Cambodian forces. They also conducted supporting strikes against nearby military installations.
>
> I have now received information that the vessel has been recovered intact and the entire crew has been rescued. The forces that have successfully accomplished this mission are still under hostile fire but are preparing to disengage.

> I wish to express my deep appreciation
> and that of the entire nation to the units
> and the men who participated in these oper-
> ations for their valor and for their sacri-
> fice.

No mention was made that the Cambodians released the crew voluntarily, a fact of which Ford was well aware.

At the conclusion of the TV bulletin, Ford and his aides trooped
back to the Oval Office. The president took another round of congratulations. Then, with the strain of the past three days clearly showing, he announced, "I'm going home and going to bed."

Ford walked through the portico by the Rose Garden and over to
the elevator to his residence. Following along in silence with him were
aides Robert T. Hartmann and army major Bob Barrett, who kept
close behind with the ever-present "doomsday" briefcase containing
the nuclear launch codes.

As they waited for the elevator, Ford turned to the major. "Say, Bob,
how did Baltimore do tonight?"*

*The Orioles won in a nail-biter, beating the White Sox 3-2 in the bottom of the ninth
inning.

27

THE SECOND WAVE

You do not fire a machine gun burst for Democracy's sake,
but to destroy somebody who is trying to destroy you. You
fight for survival, not for apple pie and next year's prom.

Andrew Tully, *Pacific Stars and Stripes*, July 13, 1975

*K*nife-22, hit during the first attempt at landing on the western beach, was still struggling to stay airborne. Inside were half a dozen wounded from Captain Davis's company. Up in the cockpit, Lieutenant Ohlemeier had a caution light telling him his transmission was damaged, but the shaking of the machine already told him that. If the transmission failed and the rotor locked, the helicopter would fall like a stone. It had only been two days since the fiery death of twenty-three men aboard the CH-53 that had been en route to U-Tapao with the security police detachment, so Ohlemeier aimed for the closest point of land, escorted by *Jolly-11* and *Jolly-12*. Ohlemeier's helicopter had trouble holding altitude.

Gunny McNemar began ordering men to toss excess weight overboard. About thirty minutes later, when one of Ohlemeier's engines began to lose power, he looked for a landing site. To the right was the mountain range that from their map looked like the one that separated Cambodia from Thailand. The coast curved around to the west. Ohlemeier spotted a clearing that looked hospitable and aimed for it. The arrival was more a controlled crash than a landing. Both *Jolly* helicopters set down near the stricken aircraft in Trat Province, Thailand.

Most of the men inside *Knife-22* erroneously assumed they were in Cambodia because of the short time they were in the air after being hit. As they got off *Knife-22*, Davis's wounded radioman, Lance Corporal Alan Wyatt, looked around. A cluster of thatched hootches were visible about half a mile away. Although he could see villagers looking his way, none of them made any move toward the helicopters. Captain Davis and Gunnery Sergeant McNemar had the men set up a defensive perimeter around the landing zone. A squad spread out, belly flopping to the ground with rifles at the ready but with orders not to shoot unless told to do so. If the local inhabitants attacked, they were going to have to cover a lot of open ground to get to the helicopter. Then Davis organized a group to haul equipment and ammunition from *Knife-22* onto *Jolly-12* while *Jolly-11* headed back to U-Tapao. Once the off-load was completed, some forty to sixty minutes later, McNemar returned to the downed helicopter and shot up the instrument panel, rendering the machine unflyable. The marines along with the flight crew from *Knife-22* boarded *Jolly-12* for the return to U-Tapao.

Minutes after *Knife-22*'s landing in Trat, Lieutenant Greer was having his own problems piloting *Jolly-13* away from Koh Tang. His helicopter was the one that had been on fire after attempting to rescue Lieutenant Cicere's group off the east beach. Lieutenant Greer rendezvoused with a KC-130 tanker and made his hookup. As fuel started to transfer, it began pouring inside from ruptured lines overhead in the cabin area. The crew elected to cancel refueling and instead to try to reach the coast. Escorted by an A-7 Corsair from Korat Air Base, Greer made it to within twenty-five miles of U-Tapao before setting down in Rayong Province in Thailand. *Jolly-13* was out of action with some thirty-five gaping holes punched through the fuselage and its last few gallons of fuel and hydraulic fluid leaking onto the ground.

Back at U-Tapao three helicopters were landing and off-loading wounded. The scene became an item of great interest to the marines waiting to go in with the second wave. To Hargrove, Hall, and Marshall, the sight of their blood-covered buddies and the helicopter battle damage told them and the rest of the troops all they needed to know about what was in store. Eleven helicopters had departed before dawn. Only three had returned so far, and of those, one had a football-size hole in its side, while the others had numerous smaller holes. Maintenance men were scrambling around the aircraft, evaluating the damage and continued flyability of the machines as ambulances rushed the wounded to the base hospital.

Amid the bustle, two new helicopters, *Knife-51* and *Knife-52*, arrived after being brought to flight status at Nakhon Phanom. *Knife-51* was loaded and launched immediately toward Koh Tang, only to be recalled after getting three quarters of the way there. A total of eight aircraft were scattered on the ramp or still inbound, but after all had landed only five were found to be airworthy. Two were lightly armored CH-53s and three were the more heavily armored HH-53 *Jolly Greens*.

Inside the helicopter operations section, pilots and maintenance personnel were busy working with Colonel Johnson, the senior marine from the battalion staff, III Marine Amphibious Force. They were engaged in assigning the proper infantry units to the remaining helicopters. Although there was talk of disengagement, Colonel Johnson was vehement about reinforcing the men on the island before any thought of pulling out would be entertained. E Company had been scheduled in on the second wave, so Captain Mykle Stahl and his men were mustered aboard two of the aircraft. Among E Company's troops were two three-man machine-gun teams, including the one led by Lance Corporal Joseph N. Hargrove and included Private First Class Gary L. Hall and Private Danny G. Marshall. They had received word of the switch in helicopter assignments dictated by Captain Stahl when the linguist, medic, and photographer were put aboard Stahl's helicopter. The three men headed for their assigned aircraft and were attached to a squad led by Lance Corporal John S. Standfast.

Captain Davis and members of G Company, including his command element, had returned from their aborted landing and side trip to the Cambodian mainland. Half of Davis's company was on the west beach. He wasted no time letting the operations staff know he intended to return to the island. The wounded from G Company were given medical attention while the rest of the men stood by to reboard helicopters. Included in the injured group was Lance Corporal Wyatt, who had taken shrapnel in the face and ear. A medic stitched his ear and bandaged his face. A white tag on a string was placed around his neck, signifying evacuation status. But Wyatt was Captain Davis's radio operator, a key position in the unit. Gunnery Sergeant McNemar was aware that the loss of Wyatt would create a critical absence. He approached Wyatt. "You want to go back in with us?" McNemar asked.

"No," Wyatt replied.

McNemar stared hard at him for a moment, then said, "Yes, you do."

Wyatt took off his evacuation tag, grabbed his radio gear, and rejoined his helicopter team as they boarded the remaining choppers.

None of the five helicopters carried any water for resupply of the men on the island. The marines had landed with one or two canteens each, and the lack of fresh water was just one more issue the staff at U-Tapao did not address.

The second wave began launching without any attempt to organize it into a single formation. The priority was to get more troops on the island before the three isolated pockets of marines were wiped out. *Knife-52* and *Jolly-43* were first off, departing U-Tapao at about 9:30 A.M., followed by *Jolly-11* and *Jolly-12* half an hour later. At 10:10 A.M., *Knife-51* departed. Although the initial plan called for 250 marines to be inserted in the second wave, only 127 men could be squeezed into the limited number of available helicopters. As they headed south on the two-hour trip, the *Specter* AC-130 gunship passed by overhead, returning to U-Tapao to refuel. Thus the helicopters would have no orbiting close air support. Only fast-moving fighters would be available to help with the insertion.

In Washington, the National Military Command Center gears were still turning while President Ford slept. His last directions were to continue navy strikes against the Cambodian mainland while terminating the marine engagement on Koh Tang. Orders went out from the

Pentagon, stopping first at Admiral Gayler's headquarters in Hawaii. There remained, however, a huge impediment in properly responding to these presidential orders. Both at Gayler's headquarters in Hawaii and further down at 7th Air Force in Nakhon Phanom, an information bottleneck had developed as reports and requests for details were being processed inside *Cricket*, the EC-130 command ship.

Aboard *Cricket*, the battle staff was trying to control a war that was going badly. The EC-130 was circling some fifty miles north of the island, so the staff could not simply look out of window ports to see what was happening. The constantly changing situation kept Colonel Anders and his men in a fog as they tried to make sense out of data that arrived simultaneously through various HF, VHF, and UHF radios.

Helicopters were headed in numerous directions with each pilot trying to find out what he was supposed to be doing. Marines were pinned down in three places. Airborne tankers were standing by for orders while air force fighters were trying to put ordnance on island targets. Marines were calling for close-air support, but the normal tactical radio used by the forward air controller on the east beach had been lost so he was working on the emergency rescue frequency.

On top of this chatter came queries from higher headquarters on the secure net. Staffers at every level were flooding the channels with information requests as these officers tried to update their commanders with tail numbers, sortie counts, battle damage reports, and other minutiae. The number of people trying to manage the battle far exceeded the number of soldiers, sailors, airmen, and marines involved in the actual fighting.

The situation was still in disarray as the first three helicopters of the second wave were about to insert troops onto the eastern beach, in spite of the fact that the most intense defenses had been encountered there all morning.

Lieutenant Robert Rakitis lowered the nose of *Knife-52*, swung around the northern edge of the cove, and came boring in at high speed toward the deadly strip of sand. First Lieutenant Richard Brims, flying *Knife-51*, and Captain Wayne Purser in *Jolly-43* followed right behind him.

Tracers rose to greet Rakitis's arrival before he could even come to a hover. Bullets pierced his fuel tanks. He continued straight ahead, flying right over the beach from east to west, aborting the insertion. Without the ability to refuel in the air, Rakitis was concerned he might not be able to reach Thailand on the return trip. He took up a heading for U-Tapao.

The other two helicopter pilots, Lieutenant Brims and Captain Purser, made their attempt. Captain Stahl inside *Knife-51* could see the beach looming in front of the cockpit windscreen. Then the helicopter abruptly pulled up and away.

Both Lieutenant Brims and Captain Purser aborted their runs, zooming above the narrow neck of the island that separated the two beaches. They cleared the island and gathered their wits while watching Rakitis leave the area with fuel streaming behind his aircraft.

Then came word to *Cricket* from Admiral Gayler's staff in Hawaii ordering "all concerned to immediately cease all offensive operations against the Khmer Republic . . . [and to] disengage and withdraw all forces from operating areas as soon as possible." To someone sitting in the relative safety of a command and control aircraft, the words "as soon as possible" coming from the admiral meant now!

Brims in *Knife-51* was holding north, and from the cockpit he spotted the *Mayaguez* being towed away from Koh Tang by the USS *Holt*. He radioed that information to *Cricket* and from there it went to 7th Air Force.

That cinched the decision on what to do. Word came from *Cricket* to return to Thailand. The helicopters began heading back, but Captain Stahl in *Knife-51* leaned into the cockpit and registered his opinion regarding the decision to return. "Bullshit, there are marines down there. Who's going to take them off?" First Lieutenant Richard C. Brims, piloting *Knife-51*, relayed that question to *Cricket*.

On Koh Tang, Lieutenant Colonel Austin was becoming concerned about his reinforcements. He called *Cricket* and asked about the delay. When told that the second wave had been canceled, he insisted he still needed them to help consolidate his position.

Back at U-Tapao, Colonel Johnson got word of the decision to cancel the second wave and had similar reservations. No one above that level had any idea that the situation on Koh Tang required that more troops be landed.*

---

*Admiral George P. Steele, 7th Fleet commander, recounted his view on command and control. "This complicated, jury-rigged arrangement and detailed management from the Joint Chiefs of staff level endangered and nearly destroyed the forces on the island."

The marine protests were passed to 7th Air Force, and within fifteen minutes the order was rescinded. The second wave once again took up a heading for Koh Tang. The two pilots who had aborted the east beach were joined by *Jolly-11* and *Jolly-12*. Together they argued for inserting their troops onto the west beach. *Cricket* agreed. Nobody went above that level to find out if it was okay.

Knife-51 and *Jolly-43* swung around and made the first approach. Lieutenant Brims led, with Captain Stahl and elements of E Company aboard. Brims brought the aircraft to a hover, then swung the tail around to face the beach as a crewman lowered the ramp.

Inside, Captain Stahl and his men waited for the aircraft to stabilize, all the while hearing the ping and thud of rounds that peppered the fuselage. The helicopter miniguns at the side ports returned fire as the helicopter swayed above the surf, trying to maneuver backward to a safe landing.

Captain Stahl was poised on the ramp, rifle in hand, a loaded pack on his back, mortar rounds and hand grenades in his pockets. He waited as more hits stung the aircraft. *Knife-51* made two attempts to set down, then stabilized for a moment. Just as the aircraft began to lift again, Captain Stahl jumped. The surf was shallow at that point, but underneath was a slab of black volcanic rock and coral. Stahl hit hard, twisted his knee, and fell. He struggled to his feet and watched as the helicopter began moving away. For a moment he thought he might be left alone on a beach he knew nothing about. Then the helo slid back in and settled at the edge of the water. Stahl scampered out of its way, falling again before reaching the sand. The rest of the company rushed ashore. Captain Stahl merged with them as they charged toward the tree line. Meanwhile marines from Davis's G Company were coming toward them carrying five wounded men to the helicopter. As soon as the wounded were loaded, Brims took off.

Jolly-43 was next in, followed by *Jolly-11* and finally *Jolly-12*. Landing with this group was navy medic HM3 Steven Poore. He rushed ashore with his medical kit, a .45-caliber pistol, and two canteens of water, and was sent directly to the aid station.

By this time, Lieutenant Colonel Austin and his group managed to work their way north from their drop-off location and joined E and G Company marines on the western beach. All three elements were intermingled at that point, with both E and G Company troops pushing deeper beyond the tree line toward the east beach. Scattered firing was coming from Khmer positions and men in black attire were seen running south. Overhead, fighters were still putting 20-mm rounds close to the front lines, so the marines dug in.

At the aid station, navy medic Poore had hypodermic needles in his mouth and one hand, and his .45 pistol within grasp of the other, working feverishly to get morphine into the screaming wounded. He started work on a second lieutenant who had been shot in the ankle. As he began dressing the wound, the marine saw that Poore had two canteens. He asked for one of them, then drained it in one long guzzle.

The last three insertions had gone relatively smoothly and within thirty minutes, a total of 100 of the 127 who had started out in the second wave were on the island, all inserted on the western beach. Captain Davis and Gunny McNemar were finally in the thick of things.

Lieutenant Colonel Austin tried to bring some semblance of order to his command. Together with Captains Davis and Stahl, he divided the beach into two areas. The left, or north, side became the responsibility of Captain Davis and G Company.

The right side became the position that E Company was to control. Word was passed up the line and E Company's men began pulling back from dug-in positions along the tree line in front of the aid station/command hootch.

Captain Stahl and his men assembled near the aid station. If there were any doubts in the minds of machine gunners Hargrove, Hall, or Marshall about the seriousness of their situation, they were erased by the cries of the wounded and the sight of Ashton Loney's body wrapped in a poncho. With those images keeping them alert, E Company began to move south into unsecured territory. Included were two M-60 teams, the second one led by Lance Corporal J. E. Taylor plus Private First Class D. A. Ramirez and Private P. G. Mehzof.

Hall had his M-60 strapped to his back, steadying it with one hand as he humped across the loose sand. In his free hand he carried an ammo can. Hargrove lugged the tripod, extra M-60 barrel, and an M-16 with an attached M-79 grenade launcher. Marshall hefted ammo cans and an M-16 rifle. As the group plodded around a rocky point at the end of the landing zone, a mortar round landed twenty yards away. Captain Stahl slipped as the men scurried along the rocky shore, trying to reach cover. Down Stahl went, falling on his shoulder. Stunned, he tried to get to his feet. His knee, still shaky from the earlier fall, buckled under him. Finally a marine grabbed Stahl by his injured arm and pulled him upright. From that point on he ceased to be fully effective as a commander. His subordinates, Lieutenant James W. Davis, Staff Sergeant Clark H. Hale, and Sergeant Carl C. Anderson took up the slack. They went about defining the southern perimeter. Two machine-gun positions were set up, one to the east of the rocky point that now separated E from G Company, and another 150 yards farther south at the extreme edge of the perimeter.

Two arrows in Sergeant Anderson's notebook point to where the unit's machine guns were positioned. Hargrove, Hall and Marshall dug in at the top-most position on the extreme right flank of the perimeter. After it began collapsing, they set up at or near the other position which had been vacated earlier.

E Company's Lance Corporal J. E. Taylor headed the northernmost machine-gun emplacement along with Private First Class D. A. Ramirez and Private P. G. Mehzof. Both teams began to dig trenches for their assigned gun position. Lance Corporal Hargrove, Private First Class Hall, and Private Marshall occupied the southern site. Of the two positions, Hargrove's team's was the more critical. With a broad field of fire, it commanded a view for eight hundred yards south along the beach and well up into the jungle. If an attempt to flank the marines came from this direction, it would have the difficult task of crossing open ground in front of Private First Class Hall's machine-gun barrel. Taylor's machine gun had a field of fire across a narrow open area that ended at a tree line, but this position had control of neither the flank nor the beach. Interspersed between the two locations were pockets of marines who dug foxholes and waited for instructions to move or fire. Captain Stahl set up his base beneath a poncho that was slung between two trees near the rocky point on the beach close to G Company's lines. He now had his injured arm in a sling.

To the north around the landing zone, Captain Davis and Gunnery Sergeant McNemar spread their men, but due to the proximity of the tree line, there were no good positions to set up a machine-gun team, so they set two up with limited fields of fire. Davis was operating out of the thatched hootch that Lieutenants McDaniel and Keith had been using. Lieutenant Colonel Austin set up his staff and radio inside the hootch as well. They had captured some water in plastic bottles, but no one knew if it was potable. No fresh water had come in with the second wave except what men carried in their canteens.

With the lines set, the marines solidified their position all along the front, penetrating about a hundred yards into the island. The two M-60 machine guns were dug in and Austin could hear the periodic chatter of the light machine guns to his south.

The amount of Khmer resistance began to drop markedly by 2:30 P.M.

The Khmer Rouge battalion commander, Em Son, and his men had been in a brutal fight on the west beach. One American helicopter had been shot down and many had been driven off, but too many had managed to land their troops. Soeun's platoon on the east beach had a better time of it, but the eastern approach was easier to defend and Soeun had heavier weapons than the platoon defending the west beach. Soeun reported five of his men killed during the first few minutes and an unknown number thereafter.

Two helicopters had been downed on the east side, and smoke still rose in the air from one of them. No more helicopters had successfully landed on that side, so only a few Americans were fighting there. Not so on the west beach.

Although the Americans were contained on both fronts, the cost had been high to the island defenders. Em Son had lost a recoilless rifle team and several mortars, and his machine gun on the north side of the Americans' landing zone had quit firing. A number of troops had been wounded by the cannon fire that came from the jet fighters and the big black plane that orbited overhead.

In the first hour, Em Son thought his men might prevail, but now too many Americans had landed. He had tried to flank their position, but that too had cost him men. It was noon, and another group of helicopters had tried to reinforce the Americans on the east beach only to be driven off by Soeun's defenders. These helicopters flew to the other side of the island and managed to put troops ashore in spite of the furious attempt to drive them away. Until help arrived from the mainland, Em Son decided his best course of action was to withdraw and wait for nightfall. He passed the order and his men began moving out of their bunkers and into the low trenches, taking them south and away from the fight. When he gathered the men at his headquarters a quarter mile from the American position, he counted roughly forty. He had begun the day with eighty-five. All together, they had three rocket-propelled-grenade rounds, about 300 AK-47 rounds, a handful of mortar rounds, and some hand grenades. He had moved ammo north all morning into his primary ammunition store near the east beach, which now lay abandoned between the two American positions. When it got dark, he might be able to launch a counterattack, recover his cache, and rearm his men. Em Son posted guards and sent out three-man patrols to keep some pressure on the Americans. He still had a mortar unit, and he told Heang to fire periodically at both beaches to keep pressure on the Americans.

Water was pulled from a well near his headquarters and coconuts were hacked open with machetes and passed around. Em Son took a coconut, found some shade, and sat. If the Americans pressed their assault, he and his men would have to retreat further into the jungle. If the Americans did not attack, then what would he do?

Incoming fire had dropped off considerably around the west beach, and some of the marines there took to removing their helmets and moving about in other than the standard battlefield crouch. Three men assigned to a mortar battery lay on the sandy beach in the open, trying to stay cool despite the relentless heat, mere yards from the cool but undrinkable gulf waters.

To the south, E Company's Sergeant Carl C. Anderson moved along the newly established perimeter checking on his men. When he had worked his way to the extreme right flank, he discovered Lance Corporal Hargrove, Private First Class Hall, and Private Marshall occupying an M-60 machine-gun position. Because of the change in helicopter loading assignment for the M-60 team back at U-Tapao, the men had been attached to a squad led by Lance Corporal John S. Standfast. He had positioned the M-60 crew, without Anderson's knowledge. The location had a good field of fire, but because it was on the edge of the perimeter, the position was vulnerable. With things relatively quiet, Anderson thought chances were they might spend the night on the island. That would make things even more precarious for the M-60 team. The machine gun fires a tracer every fifth round, so the gunner can see where he is placing fire. At night, tracers can at times be more of a help to the opposition since the visible tracer acts like a beacon highlighting the machine gun's position. Anderson moved some twenty-five yards beyond the lines and set up three trip flares to warn the men should the Khmer Rouge decide to try infiltrating in the dark. Then he and Private First Class Rios, manning an M-79 grenade launcher, dug foxholes behind the machine-gun pit and waited.

To the north where G Company had its positions, Gunnery Sergeant McNemar took stock of their situation. Khmer return fire had diminished. Only sporadic firing was heard from the area where Lieutenant Cicere and his men were dug in on the east beach. McNemar and Sergeant Tutele, the man who had silenced the machine-gun position earlier in the day, moved out toward the east beach. They proceeded a hundred yards along the cleared path, tossing grenades in front as they moved. There was no opposition. Convinced that the way was clear to the other beach, McNemar pulled back and approached his company commander. "Captain, let's take this damn island."

Captain Davis considered the matter. Although his men had done well, they were still green, had not slept in a couple of days, were out of water, and their stock of ammunition was not likely to be increased anytime soon. If he stretched his force across the island, he could be in for a rough time if the Khmers chose to counterattack. A decision on how to withdraw from the island was being considered by Lieutenant Colonel Austin. If that process was begun, it would be even more difficult to pull his men back and get them to the helicopters.

The weapons cache the Khmer Rouge had abandoned between the beaches lay in the direct route between the marine lines and Lieutenant Cicere's group, but Davis did not know that.

Finally, Davis made up his mind. "Gunny, this is my decision, and I'm gonna have to live with it, but we're not going to take this island."

McNemar was disappointed but knew how to follow orders.

The afternoon wore on in relative quiet. How long would it be before Captain Davis and Khmer Rouge commander Em Son realized they were taking a breather during the deceptive calm within the eye of the storm?

III Marine Amphibious Force Battalion Landing Team Attack on Koh Tang, May 15, 1975

	Planned	*Actual*
First Wave		
H-hour	5:42 A.M.	6:07 A.M.*
Insertion:	2 helicopters to west beach 1st platoon, G-Company	4 helicopters to west beach G-Company (part)
Insertion:	6 helicopters to east beach G-Company (part)	1 helicopter to east beach 3rd Platoon (part)
	81-mm Mortar Section BLT Command Group	1 helicopter south of west beach BLT Command Group 81-mm Mortar Section
Total:	180 marines	131 marines
Second Wave		
Time-on-Target:	10:00 A.M.	11:30 A.M.
Insertion:	12 helicopters to east beach 3-Companys	4 helicopters to west beach E-Company (part)
Total:	250 marines	100 marines
Grand Total	450 marines	225 marines**

*Marines didn't actually attack the beach until approximately 6:20 A.M. The offload of troops onto the USS *Holt* was the first action, which began at 6:07 A.M.
**Six wounded marines were withdrawn during the second wave landings.

28

PULLOUT FROM THE EAST BEACH

*When great causes are on the move in the world . . . we learn
that we are spirits, not animals, and that something is going
on in space and time and beyond space and time, which
whether we like it or not, spells duty.*

Winston Churchill, Rochester, New York, 1941

Word of the debacle on Koh Tang began to work its way up the communication links. By mid-morning on the fifteenth, at Nakhom Phanom, Colonel Harry Goodall, commander of the 56th Special Operations Wing, guessed correctly that the situation had gone from one involving a quick overrun of a poorly defended fishing village to one consisting of heavy combat requiring well-orchestrated close air support. He picked four pilots and had maintenance prepare that number of his OV-10 aircraft for launch.

The OV-10 was a lightly armed aircraft with good low-altitude endurance and excellent visibility, making it well suited for its designed mission: calling in air strikes to support ground troops.

Armed with pods of spotting rockets and four internally mounted 7.62-mm machine guns, it has twin turboprops and seats for two, a pilot in front and an observer in tandem. Given the nature of the Koh Tang operation, it was an enormous oversight by those in command not to have these aircraft in place at the outset.

Not until 10:47 A.M. did the first two OV-10 aircraft take off from Nakhon Phanom, followed shortly by two more. Flying solo in the lead aircraft was Major Robert W. Undorf, call sign *Nail-68*, an experienced forward air controller (FAC) and former fighter pilot. He landed at U-Tapao around 1:00 P.M., refueled, and waited for instructions. Those instructions were slow to materialize. Finally, at 2:40 P.M., orders arrived from 7th Air Force to launch the OV-10s "ASAP." *Nail-68* and *Nail-47* were airborne minutes later.

The orbiting AC-130 *Specter-61* aircraft was acting as a quasi-control agency for attacks by the A-7 and F-4 fighters. These air strikes were being conducted under difficult circumstances utilizing two different radio channels and constantly rotating fighter support. The marines on the ground were using smoke grenades to mark their boundaries. The marine forward air controller might call for a strafing run offset fifty yards east of his smoke mark, but smoke moved with the wind and the speed of the fighters made it impossible for pilots to maintain constant eye contact with friendly positions and nearby targets. Strafing runs had come close to friendly lines all day, which kept the marines hunkered down, deterring them from aggressively pushing forward to link up with the men on the east beach.

By mid-afternoon, the marine position on the west side was considered secure. Things were relatively quiet with only occasional firing along the front, so Lieutenant Colonel Austin asked *Cricket* whether he should attempt to rescue Lieutenant Cicere's element, pinned down all day on the east beach. The word came back to wait; an attempt to pull out Cicere's twenty-five-man unit by helicopter would be tried first.

Two helicopters that had refueled after the second wave had gone in were immediately available, *Jolly-11* and *Jolly-43*. A plan was quickly hatched by *Cricket* and *Specter* overhead and by Lieutenant Lucas, the ground FAC.

After *Specter* laid down supporting gunfire along the east beach, A-7s came in to dispense tear gas, intending for its cloud to shield the helicopters. *Jolly-43*, flown by Captain Wayne Purser, got the nod to go in first for the pickup of the eastern enclave. The plan might have worked, but the execution was flawed. The A-7s dropped their gas canisters cross-wind or perpendicular to the helicopter approach rather than upwind and parallel. Captain Purser and his crew donned gas masks as *Jolly-43* plunged into the drifting cloud. When it appeared on the other side, the helicopter was silhouetted against a white background.

The Khmer Rouge took full advantage, lining up their sights as Captain Purser brought the machine to a hover fifty yards from Cicere's position. Not one marine moved toward the helicopter as heavy machine-gun fire engulfed it. A round severed a fuel line on the side of the fuselage, causing the left engine to lose power as its fuel pressure dropped. The left door gunner tried to return fire, but his minigun jammed. Raw fuel sprayed inside the cabin while the cockpit crew tried to deal with the failing engine. Impacts from mortar rounds walked up to the rear of the helicopter, and shrapnel from the last one felled Sergeant Thomas Bateson as he tried to return fire from the ramp minigun, the only one still operating.

Captain Purser had taken enough. He added power on the good engine and swung away from the island as the crew in *Jolly-11* swept overhead to provide cover fire with its miniguns.

Pressurized fuel continued to spray from *Jolly-43*'s ruptured line and was sucked inside the cabin area. It mixed with airflow blowing in through the door and gun ports, creating a volatile mixture that streamed behind the fleeing helicopter for 150 yards. Had her mini-guns still been firing, the helicopter would have likely exploded.

Once clear of the island, Captain Purser relayed his status to *Cricket* and was advised that the *Coral Sea* was the closest possibility for safe recovery, some seventy miles south. Purser set course for the aircraft carrier; for the time being, that ended the attempt to rescue the men from the east beach. Another botched plan had taken a much-needed helicopter out of action.

Shortly thereafter, Lieutenant Lucas radioed that a Khmer Swift boat, partially submerged on a reef across the cove from his position, had been seen firing at *Jolly-43* when it tried to come in. This was the gunboat that had been run aground by *Specter* the previous day. When the fighters approached, Lieutenant Lucas saw men disappear inside the pilothouse on the boat. They emerged to operate the twin 7.62-mm machine gun on the forward deck when the helicopter intruded. With its field of fire and proximity to the eastern landing zone, this machine gun was likely responsible for much of the deadly fire that had been taken all day.

An A-7 flight engaged the gunboat. Twenty-millimeter rounds from the A-7's gatling guns raked the Swift boat. Although chewed up, the boat remained intact.

As that action was in progress, *Specter-61* headed home to refuel at about four in the afternoon while another AC-130 was still en route to the area. The job of overseeing air support fell, and rightfully so, to OV-10 pilot, Major Undorf, and his wingman, who had finally arrived at 4:20 P.M.

He assumed on-scene command from the flight of A-7 Corsairs that had strafed the gunboat. Undorf focused his attention on the east beach while he had Captain Roehrkasse set up his OV-10 in an orbit supporting the west-beach contingent.

An event now occurred on the east beach that would have considerable impact later. Cicere's men were running out of steam. Perched in foxholes just yards from the surf, the men were suffering in the heat without fresh water. Their canteens had long been emptied. Some were so fatigued from lack of sleep and the drain from the constant adrenaline rush that they took to momentary dozing, hunched over their rifles. They twitched to alertness at the slightest sound.

A Khmer Rouge clothed in black came trotting out of the jungle toward the wreckage of *Knife-31*, about a hundred yards away from Cicere's platoon. The Khmer lifted the head of one of the men floating in the surf near the fuselage, looked at the dead man's face, then let the head drop. Cicere's platoon sergeant grabbed an M-16, but none of the rifles had been properly battle sighted because, as mentioned, the Okinawa training cycle had been interrupted by this deployment. The marine took aim and fired. The Khmer heard the noise, so he began hurrying back toward the tree line. The platoon sergeant got off two more rounds, also missing the Khmer who disappeared before anyone else could take a bead. The platoon sergeant stood watching, livid, while the other members of the platoon wondered why the Khmer went out there in the first place. Had the

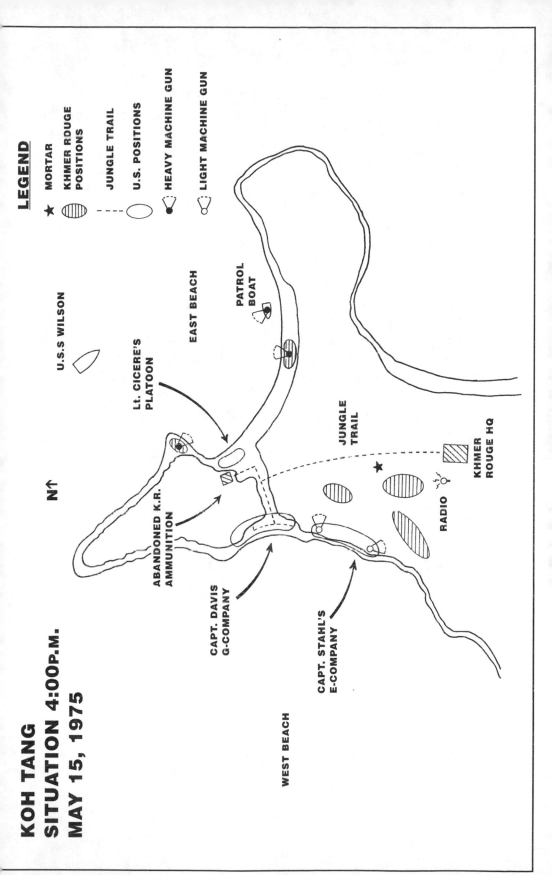

KOH TANG
SITUATION 4:00P.M.
MAY 15, 1975

N↑

U.S.S WILSON

EAST BEACH

PATROL BOAT

Lt. CICERE'S PLATOON

JUNGLE TRAIL

ABANDONED K.R. AMMUNITION

KHMER ROUGE HQ

RADIO

CAPT. DAVIS G-COMPANY

CAPT. STAHL'S E-COMPANY

WEST BEACH

LEGEND

★ MORTAR

🌐 KHMER ROUGE POSITIONS

- - - JUNGLE TRAIL

◯ U.S. POSITIONS

⚲ HEAVY MACHINE GUN

⚲ LIGHT MACHINE GUN

Cambodian seen someone moving in or near the helicopter? A communication mix-up about this event and a rumor involving *Knife-23* later on would lead Undorf to believe an American might be hiding in the fuselage of one of the downed helicopters.

Meanwhile, Undorf circled overhead, considering options for extracting the men from the east beach. Then he noticed the Swift boat that had run aground on the coral, now laying with its deck battered and awash. He discussed the gunboat situation with Lieutenant Lucas, the ground FAC. On the *Wilson*, Captain Rogers heard the exchange and volunteered use of his 5-inch guns. Undorf gave the okay, and at 4:33 P.M. the *Wilson* shot her first round at the Swift boat. Undorf made corrections as the *Wilson*'s gun crew zeroed in. After twenty-one more rounds were fired, the gunboat was consumed by secondary explosions, her machine guns silenced for good.

Undorf, flying in a tight circle above the beaches, soon had a solid grasp of who was where on the island and what the marines needed from him. Using his smoke rockets, Undorf began bringing in F-4 and A-7 strikes, which kept the Khmer Rouge from moving back in force into the positions they had vacated after the second wave landed. Khmer casualties up to that point had been inflicted primarily by 20-mm aircraft cannons, so the Cambodians now had a healthy respect for the planes. By mid-afternoon, except for a few well-dug-in mortar and machine-gun positions on the north end of the island, most of the able-bodied Khmer troops had gathered well south of the two beaches.

After the air strikes, Undorf began a dialogue with *Cricket*, Lieutenant Colonel Austin, and Lieutenant Lucas about what to do next. Whether the force on Koh Tang would stay overnight or be extracted that afternoon by helicopter and/or naval craft was the dilemma. Lieutenant Colonel Austin felt that his position was defendable overnight, and except for the lack of water, his men were in good shape. The chances of Cicere's marines surviving the night on the east beach was another matter. With no heavy weapons and a tiny perimeter, the twenty-five-man force would be vulnerable to Khmer attacks under darkness. If a decision to pull out was to be made, these men would have to be extracted first. If that failed, pulling out the men on the west beach would mean writing off the marines who were trying to hold the eastern enclave.

At the time the decision was being mulled over, Undorf could only count on three armed helicopters, *Jolly-11*, *Jolly-12*, and *Knife-51*. Two unarmed SH 3 helicopters onboard the *Coral Sea* could also be used in a pinch. The *Wilson*'s two boats—the armed gig and the open whale-boat—could come near the shore to load troops, but had room for only about a dozen men without the risk of floundering. Bringing either of them through surf presented unacceptable risks, so if the boats were to be used, the marines would have to wade past the surf to board.

As Khmer Rouge soldiers continued to dribble in from the north, bringing the total to about sixty men, Em Son watched as artillery pounded the east-beach area from off shore. Jet fighters swooped low, laying down a continuous echo of exploding bombs and 20-mm cannon fire.

Em Son received word that "the American leader had been killed and the invaders were preparing to depart." Whether this word arrived from Kompong Som by radio—a Khmer radio facility was located on the island and had not been taken out by air strikes—or was derived from intercepted American radio transmissions overhead or simply originated from rumor is unknown. What Em Som did know was that casualties had been inflicted on all the American elements that had come ashore. How it was determined that the leader had been killed was not for him to question. If the Americans were pulling out because of their losses, he intended to make their exit memorable.

Em Son divided the remaining force into three sections. One element was ordered to attack up the middle of the island and the other two split left and right toward the beaches. Em Son moved out with Ki's platoon headed west. After moving 150 yards into the jungle, Em Son could hear voice chatter coming from the American position. He spread his men out, then gave the order to move forward. His men on the left flank reached the beach south of the American lines near where Lieutenant Colonel Austin's group had landed. The Khmer troops began to work their way north.

On the right flank of the marine west-beach position, Lance Corporal Joseph Hargrove had his machine gun dug in and ready.

Positioned next to Hargrove in the gun pit was Private First Class Hall, the M-60 stock tucked into his shoulder. An ammo can lay open next to Hargrove, and the 7.62-mm belt led to the gun's breech. Marshall was in a foxhole on the right side, M-16 at the ready, grenades close at hand. Hargrove's orders passed from Captain Stahl were clear: "Hold the flank." Behind their position, Sergeant Anderson was dug in next to Private First Class Rios, who manned an M-79 grenade launcher. The rest of the thirty-two-man contingent were dug in north of the machine gun.

Shouts were heard from foxholes. "Does anyone have any water?" But no fresh water came up the line. They had not slept for over forty-eight hours, apart from brief naps. Images seemed overexposed. Marines moved about as if in slow motion. Movement and noises in the jungle made them jumpy.

At 5:00 P.M., the first shots were heard—small-arms fire—coming from the ridge and tree line to the south and east. Off in the distance, Cambodian voices were heard shouting. Men in black garb were spotted moving among the rocks along the shoreline to the south.

Hall squeezed the trigger, sending a burst in the direction of the sound of gunfire and another along the shore. The M-60 tracers ricocheted off rocks. Back came a fusillade of AK-47 fire, the rounds slashing through leaves above the marines. More yelling was heard.

With their position now known to the Cambodians, Hargrove chose to have Hall pour on the fire, hoping to keep the opposition from penetrating their sector. The back-and-forth exchange of fire lasted almost thirty minutes, and by the time the Cambodians quit responding, Hall was low on ammunition. He began shouting for ammo. At 5:30 P.M., Private First Class Robert K. Atkins brought belts of M-60 rounds to the team. None of the machine-gun crew was injured, and they had halted a determined Khmer Rouge offensive.

With little ammunition of his own, and a stubborn machine gun blocking his advance, Em Son decided it was "too dangerous for the moment to proceed with the flanking maneuver."

In the center between the beaches, the second Khmer Rouge unit had moved forward. Progress was good as they hedge-hopped under a canopy-covered trail while trying to avoid being seen by the small aircraft that circled above the island. They came to an open area where the intersecting trail connected east and west beaches. The point man slipped across the trail and crouched in the elephant grass beyond. No shots rang out. No hand grenade came bouncing in. He waved the squad forward. More men sped across the opening. They froze as an aircraft zoomed overhead, then moved off again. Fifty yards on, they came to what they sought. In front of them was a bunker, dug low and camouflaged with brush. The squad leader approached slowly and peeked carefully inside, looking for trip wires. He saw none. Satisfied, he motioned his men ahead. To his amazement, they had recovered their ammunition cache unscathed.

A Khmer squad from the center element appeared as the men in Em Son's unit waited to resume their flanking attempt on the west beach. The squad leader reported no opposition and the recovery of the munitions. The element that had started toward the east beach had already been rearmed. Now the west element was being resupplied. Things were about to heat up.

At the marine enclave on the east beach, Lieutenant Cicere got a call on the radio. *Cricket* was debating whether to use helicopters or one of the *Wilson*'s boats to try bringing the men out. If the gig or whaleboat came in, only a dozen would be ferried out at a time on each. The gig was armed with M-60s set up on its deck while the steep-sided and unarmed whaleboat was more vulnerable and more difficult to board, so its successful use in daylight was chancy. Only the gig would be used if at all.

Cicere pulled in the perimeter. Exhausted, thirsty men huddled, looking at him with dazed eyes as he passed the word. "If they send one boat, I'm staying," Cicere said. "So is the platoon sergeant. The wounded go out first." Cicere looked at his next in line, platoon guide Lance Corporal Larry Barnett. "You have to stay, too. Pick ten men."

Barnett opened his mouth to speak, but nothing came out. After all they had been through, no one wanted to be on the last boat. Barnett simply gave a thumbs-up. Then he turned to the other marines and found his voice. "Please don't make me pick." Lance Corporal A. L. Ybarra was the first man to raise his hand. Then each man down the line raised his, until every man had his hand up. For Barnett, seeing those hands in the air was the proudest moment in his Marine Corps career.

In addition to the three helicopters already available, Lieutenant Robert Blough arrived on scene in *Jolly-44*, the damaged aircraft having been brought back up to flyable status at Nakhon Phanom, Thailand, earlier in the day. That made four armed helicopters available.

Unable to get any clear guidance from *Cricket*, Major Undorf, in coordination with Lieutenant Colonel Austin on the west beach and Lieutenant Cicere on the east side, came to a decision. They would hold the *Wilson*'s boats in reserve and use whatever helicopters were available to begin the extraction on the east beach. Thus, with four H-53s, the gig, plus the whaleboat and two unarmed navy SH-3 helicopters as backup, Undorf began the operation as the sun hovered low on the western horizon at 6:00 P.M.

Piloted by Lieutenant Don Backlund, *Jolly-11* was chosen as the first helo to go in. Backlund and his crew had been airborne for fourteen hours, cycling back and forth from the tanker aircraft. He knew the score, especially from watching *Jolly-43* in its aborted earlier attempt. Undeterred, though, Backlund requested preparatory close air support—"hard stuff," as he put it—to neutralize the beach defenses or at least make them keep their heads down. Backlund then reminded Undorf in blunt terms that less than two hours of daylight remained. "It's time to get the action going." Undorf got the message.

An AC-130 gunship, *Specter-11*, arrived. Undorf had the big AC-130 lay in a barrage of cannon fire along the edge of the east beach. Then F-4 and A-7 fighters rolled in to deliver their weapons.

Within minutes, five C-130 cargo planes arrived over the island. One carried supplies and each of the others carried a fifteen-thousand-pound BLU-82 bomb, the largest in the U.S. inventory. Without the slightest coordination with marines on the ground, 7th Air Force ordered the dropping of the first of these weapons. Undorf had no idea what to do with the bomb, but orders were to drop it. He sent the plane well south of friendly positions. The first C-130 began to maneuver for its bomb run, using its radar as a rudimentary bombsight.

Satisfied that things were ready, Undorf cleared *Jolly-11* in for the pickup on the east beach. At 6:15 P.M., Backlund called the ground

FAC, Lieutenant Lucas, and asked for smoke. Seconds later, he saw a telltale orange cloud blossoming on the north end of the beach. Backlund roared in while his door gunners, Technical Sergeant Harry Cash and Master Sergeant John Eldridge, opened up with their miniguns. Muzzle flashes appeared all along the beach. *Jolly-11* bucked and rocked as Khmer rounds found their mark. Backlund pressed on, came to a hover just off shore, then swung his open stern toward the sand. It was a tight fit as he backed the helicopter right into the sandy niche where the marines were holed up.

At that point, the *Wilson*'s gig, *Black Velvet-1*, was just outside the cove. The crew asked for permission to fire. Undorf cleared them and the gig's machine gun sent rounds tearing into the jungle to the north of the marine position.

The newly rearmed Khmer Rouge squad on the east side responded. Moving along the trench line, Khmer riflemen increased their firing at the helicopter. To them, it became obvious that the Americans were pulling out. Encouraged, they surged ahead.

Second Lieutenant Cicere's contingent sloshed through the surf, emptying their M-16s as they clambered aboard *Jolly-11*. Staff Sergeant Barschow, wounded in the leg earlier, had to be helped aboard. By this time, Khmer troops were within hand-grenade range. Gunners Cash and Eldridge responded with bursts of minigun fire. With no time to call in air strikes, Undorf rolled in and opened up with his 7.62-mm machine guns.

Also just outside the cove, *Knife-51* joined the fray, adding her miniguns to the firefight. Inside her cabin, pararescuemen Technical Sergeant Wayne L. Fisk and Sergeant Ronald A. Cooper, Jr., used the butts of their GAU-5 rifles—short-barreled versions of the M-16—to knock out two cabin windows. Then they joined the barrage.

Three minutes after *Jolly-11*'s touchdown, Staff Sergeant Joseph S. Stanaland relayed to the cockpit that all the marines were aboard. Then gunner Staff Sergeant Cash saw a Khmer Rouge soldier racing toward the helicopter, a hand grenade held high. Cash swiveled his weapon and cut down the Cambodian as the man hurled the grenade. It exploded just beyond the whirling tail rotor.

Backlund added power and lifted from the surf. As the helicopter picked up speed, a Khmer machine gun located at the extreme north edge of the cove opened up. Its position was given away by a line of waterspouts that trailed from the beach toward the escaping helicopter. Undorf rolled his OV-10 in, placed his gunsight pipper where the waterspouts led, and squeezed the trigger. The pipper jittered as his guns spit a stream of bullets. Firing immediately ceased from the machine-gun bunker.

To the south, the first BLU-82 was pulled from the cargo bay of the C-130 aircraft by a small extraction parachute. Then the parachute assembly floated away after a larger chute opened. The huge bomb descended over the center of the island.

The marines on the west beach watched it drop way to the south, thinking it was an off-target resupply, most of them dreading the thought that they might be sent out to retrieve it. Then the ground shook.

As the bomb detonated, a shock wave arced through the humid tropical air, visible even from the bridge of the *Wilson*, half a mile off shore.

On the west beach, marines were knocked off their feet. Others crouched low in foxholes as debris rained down from the sky. Then a marine looked up. The extraction parachute and assembly were still airborne and floating toward their position. Not knowing what it was, but fearing it was another huge bomb, marines screamed for everyone to take cover. Moments later, the parachute disappeared into the tree line and nothing happened. Lieutenant Colonel Austin then got on the radio and passed his unambiguous opinion regarding the matter to *Cricket*. No more BLU-82s were dropped.

Now clear of the island, Captain Backlund headed *Jolly-11* directly for the *Coral Sea*. He had wounded aboard, a bone-tired crew, and his helicopter coming apart around him. Backlund nursed the machine onto the deck of the carrier. For Backlund, his crew, and for Lieutenant Cicere's platoon, their long hours in hell were over.

At this crucial juncture, tactical decisions continued to be made by agencies far removed from the battlefield. In support of Ford and Kissinger's desire to "be ferocious," actions were being taken without adequate regard for their local consequences. In the BLU-82 instance, a huge bomb was available, though its use in close proximity to friendly forces carried unacceptable risk. But Washington wanted it dropped. So it was released far from the front lines, a nuisance to everyone involved. Here again, the desire in Washington for punitive action against the Cambodians interfered with addressing the needs of the combatants and on-scene commanders. As is often the case with punitive actions, it may well have had the opposite impact.

The effect of the BLU-82, if any, was to induce the Cambodians to inch closer to the American lines. They knew the Americans would be unable to use these weapons near the front. In fact, the Khmer Rouge had already moved much of its remaining forces forward and, as Em Son remarked, "We heard it, but we had been getting shelled all day by ships and airplanes whose bombs and cannon fire came much closer to us, so we ignored it."

Sunlight was fading fast, and Major Undorf had completed the first part of his plan. The east coast was evacuated, but confusion still reigned regarding whether everyone had been pulled out. A report from Lieutenant Lucas aboard the fleeing *Jolly-11* still indicated that a marine may have taken refuge inside the shattered fuselage of one of the downed helicopters.

Undorf cleared *Specter* back overhead followed by a flight of A-7s that pounded the beach with suppressive fire. Then he had Captain Barry Walls bring *Jolly-12* in to search for the possible survivor Lucas had mentioned. Walls flew his helicopter to a hover directly over the hulk of *Knife-23*, the helicopter that had had its tail shot off. By cable, a crewman lowered a jungle penetrator, a teardrop-shaped apparatus that could be opened to provide a seat for hoisting. The device dangled beside the open door on the partially submerged helicopter. No one emerged from the wreckage. Meanwhile the Cambodian defenders poured on the ground fire.

Walls pulled away after hovering for what seemed to him like hours, even though it was only a few minutes. His helicopter was sieved by bullet holes. Walls managed to get the aircraft to the *Coral Sea*, but actions taken on dubious information had put another helicopter out of action for the duration.

Aboard the *Coral Sea*, Technical Sergeant Billy D. Willingham, the flight mechanic from *Jolly-43*, was not sitting idly by while the battle raged. His aircraft had sustained the massive fuel leak while attempting the unsuccessful rescue off the east beach. Willingham got together with navy maintenance men to see if the helicopter could be repaired. A chief petty officer took a hacksaw and cut away the ruptured section of fuel line. Then a piece of rubber tubing was inserted over the two open pipe ends and secured with radiator clamps. It certainly was not by the book, but when they put pressure on the line, it held.

With numerous holes in the aircraft and fuel and hydraulic fluid still dripping onto the deck, the crew climbed aboard. Minutes later, Captain Purser and his men were back in the fray.

Undorf in his OV-10 had by now turned his attention to the west beach. He contacted Lieutenant Colonel Austin. The sun had set, and twilight was melting into a moonless night. At his disposal were *Knife-51*, *Jolly-44*, plus the newly repaired *Jolly-43*. Off shore, he had the *Wilson*'s boats positioned to provide support with their machine guns. Undorf felt he could orchestrate his forces to bring in reinforcements for Austin, or use the helicopters to extract the remaining 195 marines. One thing was certain: if an extraction was begun, it would have to be continued until everyone was off the island. Otherwise, the Khmer Rouge, who were obviously familiar with the terrain, could encircle a small remaining detachment of marines in the night and wipe them out. Undorf felt he could keep fighters overhead throughout the process of reinforcing or extracting. At this point, both Undorf and Austin were entertaining no inputs from higher headquarters. Austin considered his options, then chose extraction.

29

THE EXTRACTION—WEST BEACH

I knew wherever I was that you thought of me, and if I got in a tight place you would come—if alive.

William Tecumseh Sherman, letter to Gen. Ulysses S. Grant, May 11, 1864, *Memoirs of General W. T. Sherman*

Major Undorf wasted no time once the decision to pull out the west-beach marines was made. The plan, quickly worked out, included a phased withdrawal on the ground. The perimeter would be collapsed as the size of the marine force was reduced.

Inside the command hootch, Lieutenant Colonel Austin went over the scheme with Captains Davis and Stahl. Upon hearing three whistle blasts from Captain Stahl, E Company was to begin withdrawing north, the men shifting toward the landing zone located in front of Captain Davis's foxhole. Most of the incoming fire was concentrated to the south, so as the helicopters came in, marines to the left (north) of the foxhole would board first. The marines to the right in the southern sector would go last. Loney's body, still wrapped in a poncho, had been moved to the shore, the intent being to load it aboard the first chopper to come in. Supplies and other gear were also piled on the beach for loading if there were time and room.

After the planning session broke up, Captain Davis approached Austin, who was the only one of the three who had landed on the first wave. "You got the day shift," Davis said. "I'll take the night." Captain Stahl, with his arm in a sling, was in no shape to be staying to the end. Austin thought the offer over, then agreed to let Davis bring the last marines out.

Coordination complete, Undorf, circling overhead in his OV-10, began the west-beach extraction not ten minutes after the futile search by *Jolly-12* for the lone survivor on the east side.

Knife-51 was low on fuel so Undorf ordered it in first. First Lieutenant Richard C. Brims brought the big CH-53 boring in toward the center of the beach. The aircraft outline silhouetted against the fading blue of twilight's end.

The quick appearance of the helicopter caught the marines unprepared. It did not surprise the Khmers, however, as firing erupted from the southern and eastern zones. Major Hendricks, from Lieutenant Colonel Austin's command group, watched as "tracers streamed into the perimeter and bounced around like flaming popcorn."

On the flank, Private First Class Hall opened up with his M-60, laying down a curtain of fire along the tree line well out in front of his position. Marshall to his right and Hargrove on his left joined in with their M-16s.

Knife-51 by now had come to a hover in the shallow surf. As men from the left of Captain Davis's foxhole approached the helicopter, they emptied their M-16s in all directions just before scrambling toward the boarding ramp. In clusters they surged, bumping into each other, dragging their wounded, tripping over equipment and the body of Lance Corporal Loney as they stumbled in the flickering light from the helicopter, with wind and sand from rotor wash swirling about them. Pararescueman Technical Sergeant Wayne Fisk assisted the marines in boarding. Then he went outside and moved along the beach, sending short bursts from his GAU-5 into the tree line where he heard gunfire. As he made his way back, he noticed a body up on the beach, near a stack of ammunition boxes. Fisk returned to the helicopter as the last of forty-one men clambered aboard. Before he could do anything about the dead body, Lieutenant Brims poured on the power and lifted off into the night. He took up a heading for the *Coral Sea*. A Khmer rocket-propelled grenade streaked across the blackness only to explode on the inky sea beyond the helicopter.

Captain Stahl watched the helicopter depart and heard the noise from the increase in gunfire. He blew three whistle blasts, indicating that his marines were to pull back to new positions closer to the landing zone. Sergeant Anderson, ordered the men on the extreme flank to move out. With Hall's M-60 ammunition nearly depleted, Hargrove and Marshall helped him strap the machine gun to his back. Hargrove and Marshall then led the way toward the landing zone, with Hall, Sergeant Anderson, and Private First Class Rios following. Above them illumination flares arced into the night sky, creating spooky shadows that danced among the brush, sand, and trees as the marines withdrew. When the machine-gun team got close to G Company's lines, Anderson, sent them ahead since they were low on ammunition. The men moved off into the night and, upon reaching the beach, they set up the M-60 on the flank, either per orders or on their own initiative. Private Mario Gutierrez saw them after they had dug in again with the M-60 and heard Hall yelling for more ammunition. Neither Captain Davis nor Gunnery Sergeant McNemar ever saw the three men. In fact, machine-gun positions on the northern portion of the west beach were so poor in terms of field of fire that McNemar had already sent his M-60 teams off the island. Had Hargrove reported in, the team would have been put on the next chopper out.

Marines to the right of Captain Davis's foxhole shifted into positions to his left to reestablish the perimeter on that side. In the process, the machine-gun team became isolated on the flank.

Overhead, Undorf would have liked to use close air support, but it was too dark to determine where the front lines were, so he elected to bring in the second helicopter without any suppressive fire.

Jolly-43, flown by Captain Purser, was next in the chute. He brought his HH-53 into shore without using any lights. As marines were surging up *Jolly-43*'s ramp, Lieutenant Blough, confused by the chaotic radio traffic, began his approach to the landing zone in *Jolly-44*. He, too, approached without lights since they had been shot out earlier in the day. Inside the hovering cockpit of *Jolly-43,* the copilot, First Lieutenant Robert Gradle, overheard Blough on the radio. He looked west and saw the murky shadow of a helicopter looming out of the night. Gradle turned on his helicopter's searchlight. The brilliant beam highlighted the position of Blough's helicopter. *Jolly-44* veered away, narrowly avoiding a collision. The landing zone was too small for more than one helicopter, so Lieutenant Blough swung away into an orbit while *Jolly-43* continued loading marines.

Doubtless, the Khmer Rouge saw the lights of *Jolly-44.* Mortar rounds began thumping through the jungle, walking their way toward the landing zone. A mortar flare lit up the night sky.

As marines scrambled to board, Hall returned to the beach area, asking for more ammunition. Hargrove and Marshall remained in their foxholes, defending their position since they had the two M-16s. Private First Class David M. Wagner gave Hall all the M-60 ammunition he had just prior to boarding a helicopter.

On the beach, Captain Stahl thought he had all his men accounted for. Stahl checked with his platoon commander, Lieutenant Davis, and was told that all the men were in, so Stahl told McNemar and Captain Davis that all his men were inside the perimeter. Stahl waded out toward the helicopter and helped his wounded radioman aboard. More men surged inside, pinning Stahl inside. Confused and thinking everyone including G Company was getting aboard, he stayed put. Marines continued to scramble up the ramp. The body of Lance Corporal Loney was brought off shore, but there was no room for it inside the helicopter. Then rounds began striking the helicopter and the water. The marines could not squeeze Loney's body aboard. At that point, navy medic HM3 Steven Poore waded through the surf assisting a wounded marine. Bullets were hitting all around the two men. Loney's body got dropped, then was pulled toward shore, still wrapped in the poncho. One round wounded another marine right behind Poore. The injured marine fell back on the sand and called for a medic. Poore wanted no part of going back on the island, but he handed his wounded man to other troops inside the chopper, then started wading ashore to aid the new casualty. As he did so, a round struck coral nearby and fragments slammed into his knee. Bloodied, Poore limped to shore and began putting a battle dressing on the freshly wounded marine.

Moments later, Captain Purser added full power and began to lift off. Inside were fifty-four marines, twice the normal combat load, jammed on top of each other. The helicopter clawed its way into the air as a Khmer Rouge 7.62-mm machine gun opened up. A round tore a hole in the main rotor spar, but the assembly held together as Purser headed for the *Coral Sea*. With the departure of *Jolly-43*, E Company's commander was no longer on the beach.

On the Khmer side of the battle, ammunition was again running low. Em Son had brought all his extra men up from the south and had swung Soeun's men from east beach to support the west beach effort. Most of the men had been fighting all day. They were exhausted and in the dark, no longer functioning effectively. Em Son radioed his units to cease any advancing maneuvers, dig in, and fire only at helicopters if a clear shot presented itself. He radioed the mainland for reinforcements, but a patrol craft that had been sent out was driven off by American gunfire. He could expect no resupply.

Lieutenant Blough was then cleared by Major Undorf for his second approach. As he began his run, Cambodian rounds began thumping into the fuselage. He aborted the pass. After the marines on the beach put out five minutes of suppressive fire, Undorf cleared *Jolly-44* for another try. By now it was pitch black with no visible horizon. With no lights on, Lieutenant Blough started in once again, taking instructions from crew members hanging outside the helicopter doors. He eased the helicopter into the landing zone, fighting vertigo all the way as he tried using his instruments and outside references to stay oriented. Finally Blough touched down on the beach and marines began running for the ramp. E Company platoon sergeant Clark Hale went among the men still on the line, prodding and kicking at legs in order to get the exhausted men up and moving toward the helicopter. Less than three minutes later, Blough pulled off the beach with forty-four marines loaded inside. Seventy-nine marines remained on the west beach.

Above the island, Undorf got word from the marines that all their forces were within fifty yards of the landing zone. Undorf rolled in to bring his machine guns to bear on the firing positions he had noted to the south. Meanwhile *Wilson*'s gig, *Black Velvet-1*, opened up with her M-60, spraying bullets in the same area.

As Blough cleared the landing zone, he noted that the *Holt* had returned to the area, having been released from escort duty once the *Mayaguez* was out of Cambodian waters. Blough listened as Undorf tried vainly to reestablish radio contact with the marines still on the beach. With the situation sounding grave, Undorf asked Blough to try landing aboard the *Holt* in order to save precious minutes in returning to the island instead of flying thirty miles south to the *Coral Sea*.

Hovering over the tiny helo pad on the *Holt* had been tricky for the *Jolly Green* pilots in daylight. Now it was dark and Blough did not have the advantage of having tried it that morning.

With both his landing light and searchlight shot out, Blough made his first pass at the tiny landing area unaided by lighting. Illumination from the superstructure near the pad was useless in helping orient Blough. He aborted the attempt. Staff Sergeant Bobby Bounds leaned outside the door and helped guide his pilot in for another attempt. Blough pulled away once again. A third try also ended in an abort. Finally, Blough came in at an angle, avoiding the protruding super-structure. It was a tight fit, but Blough steadied the aircraft over the deck and touched down. Forty-four marines hustled off the helicopter before Blough lifted off at 7:08 P.M., heading once again for Koh Tang.

Overhead the island, *Specter-11* was running low on fuel and ammunition, so with another AC-130 gunship inbound, *Specter-11* departed for U-Tapao. Major Undorf was precariously low on fuel as well. He began briefing two recently arrived OV-10s, *Nail-69* and *Nail-51*, piloted by Captain Greg Wilson and First Lieutenant Will Carroll, respectively.

For several minutes, the OV-10 FACs were unable to raise the marines on the radio. Fearing the perimeter had been overrun, Undorf dove low, then turned on his landing light to illuminate the landing zone. The island lit up with small-arms fire directed at the OV-10, but Undorf could see the marines were still in position. Moments later, Captain Davis came back on the air, and Undorf, relieved in more ways than one, set course for home. For the major, his mission was complete, but during his watch he had established a level of control in the air that would continue, one that the operation had not experienced up to his arrival.

Greg Wilson now took charge, giving his wingman Carroll the role of controlling fire support while he, Wilson, ran the helicopter program. Wilson also briefed the inbound *Specter-21* crew on what he needed after they arrived. Once over the island, the AC-130 crew began a ten-minute process sighting in its guns. Off shore, the crew on *Black Velvet-1* radioed that they were down to a thousand rounds. Time, helicopters, and ammunition were running out.

Captain Davis radioed that he had set up a strobe light on the beach to help guide the helicopters in. Wilson spotted it, then cleared *Jolly-44* in for his second pickup. Using the strobe as a reference, Lieutenant Blough took up a heading for the landing zone. Both he and his copilot, First Lieutenant Henry Mason, were quickly disoriented, suffering from vertigo induced by the lack of a visual horizon. Staff Sergeant Bounds once again leaned out the cabin door to give directions as Blough struggled to keep the helicopter level. *Jolly-44* landed under fire at 7:15 P.M. as *Specter-21* circled overhead, her crew using its infrared system to locate Cambodian gun emplacements. Twenty- and 40-mm cannon fire from her side mounts rained down on the Khmer units.

Thirty-four marines surged inside *Jolly-44* as Blough held the aircraft steady over the landing zone. In this group were navy corpsman Poore and the wounded marine for whom he had gone back to render aid.

Two minutes later, Blough was given the word to go. He added throttle but could not get full power. The helicopter cleared the landing zone and began to climb, but another attempt at hovering over the *Holt* was out of the question. With less than full power available and unknown damage to his other systems, Blough made for the *Coral Sea* and set down on the carrier deck twelve minutes later. He, his crew, and the helicopter were out of action.

There were now thirty-two marines still on Koh Tang. Captain Davis came back up on the radio and said that they were in danger of being overrun. "They're all around us," Davis radioed. "What can you do for us? Over?"

"We're coming! We're coming!" Wilson replied. "How many people you gonna have left?"

"I just don't know," Davis answered. "It's dark out here and I don't know who's gone and who's here. I'm just going to have to do the best I can."

The marines had no flotation gear, and many of the marines were not swimmers. Overhead, Greg Wilson heard the exchange, but he had no helicopters inbound at the moment. Wilson also had another problem. The oil pressure on his right engine gauge started to flicker. He wondered if his engine had suffered battle damage.

At this point, the Khmer attacks slackened and a period of relative quiet began. A lot of troops had been firing their M-16s at shadows and noises. If they ran out of ammunition, they could be overrun easily. The order was passed to hold fire unless an obvious attack was under way. An eerie silence settled around the tight perimeter.

Thirty miles south, *Knife-51* had been refueled and her 7.62-mm miniguns rearmed while on deck the *Coral Sea*. Lieutenant Brims lifted the helicopter into the darkness at 7:46 P.M. The moonless night had combined with smoke and haze brought on by the constant shelling to make visibility nightmarish near the island. *Specter-23* tried to improve the situation by dropping parachute flares over the landing zone. The flares oscillated under small canopies that slowed their descent. When they hit the ground or water, they cast shadows or bobbed in the surf, giving the appearance of starlight. Into that visual clutter, *Knife-51* was cleared for the next run to the beach.

Lieutenant Brims extinguished all his external lights and aimed for the strobe Davis had put on the beach. As Brims made his move, Captain Wilson flew his OV-10 to a thousand feet over the beach, then periodically turned on his landing light to guide the CH-53 in. Each time Wilson flicked on his light, muzzle flashes lit up the island beneath him.

Specter-21 kept close watch overhead and returned fire as fast as her crew could locate the Cambodian positions.

On the beach, Captain Davis had reduced his front line once again, but unknown to Davis the three-man machine-gun crew of Hargrove, Hall, and Marshall was still in position on the flank, out of sight beyond the rocky point to the south. Two marines, Privates First Class Willy J. Overton and Emelio Trevino, who had been positioned as "tail-end charlie" on the north flank, also remained in their foxholes, overlooked by Davis.

Brims came to a hover over the landing zone, then swung the helicopter around, bringing his open ramp to face the beach. As he steadied the aircraft, the scene in front spun as sea and sky merged in a black void. Disoriented, he instinctively pulled the nose up. Warning shouts came over the intercom, as the cabin crew screamed for an abort of the landing attempt. The helicopter began drifting backward toward the tree line and above dug-in marines. Brims added power. Sand and vegetation flew in all directions as nearby marines rolled to safety away from the aircraft. In the cockpit, Brims locked his eyes on the attitude indicator and began an instrument takeoff out over the open sea.

Once everyone had calmed down inside the helicopter, Brims turned back toward the island. Again, he became disoriented in the shimmering flare light, smoke, and haze. He pulled up and away, trying to gather his senses and overcome the maddening vertigo he was experiencing. He was not about to give up.

On his third attempt, as he neared the coast, Brims felt a sickening bump. To his horror, he realized he had just flown into the water. Once again, Brims reacted to urgent calls from his crew and was able to lift off.

Though Brims had no intention of abandoning the marines, it was time to talk things over with his crew. He listened to input from his experienced pararescuemen and flight mechanics. Then he suggested they turn on their lights to illuminate the landing zone. The crew agreed.

On his fourth try, Brims came boring in with his landing, hoist, hover, and spotlights on, a veritable "shoot at me" notice for the Cambodians. They responded.

Overhead, *Specter-21* answered the Khmer ground fire with a fusillade of 20-mm and 40-mm rounds that streamed from the AC-130 in a curtain of fire.

As Brims neared the beach, his gunners added their minigun fire to the barrage. Then Brims slowed to a hover, stabilized over the shore, and swung around just above the surf. The ramp was lowered and kept in the neutral position, allowing its end to move freely and maintain contact with the sand as the helicopter rose and settled above the easy swells that lapped ashore.

On the ground Captain Davis knew it was now or never. He had twenty-six men strung out in a horseshoe perimeter within fifteen yards of the landing zone. Beyond the perimeter to the left were Privates Trevino and Overton who had not heard the call to close in, while outside the lines on the right were Hargrove, Hall, and Marshall, whose original instructions had been to hold the flank at all cost and wait for a whistle from Captain Stahl to pull back. Stahl was gone. So was the whistle.

Captain Davis and Gunnery Sergeant McNemar began urging their troops out of dug-in positions and onto the helicopter. The men were exhausted from the heat, lack of water, and constant pressure from the Khmer Rouge. They were dug in, staying low, trying to keep from getting hit by all the lead that was flying above them from all directions, friendly and otherwise. Captain Davis and Gunny McNemar moved around the perimeter, kicking at men's legs and grabbing them by the shirttails. Up they stood, one by one, then staggered toward the roaring noise, lights, and blowing sand near the helicopter.

Inside *Knife-51*'s cabin, Technical Sergeant Wayne L. Fisk saw the difficulty Davis and McNemar were having. Fisk's intercom had gotten wet and shorted out, so he used hand signals to the senior flight mechanic, Staff Sergeant Marion Riley, indicating he wanted to go ashore and assist. Riley relayed the request to the cockpit. Brims' gloved hand appeared from the cockpit in a thumbs-up position. Fisk ran down the ramp and began urging marines inside. As the marines boarded, each one emptied his M-16 toward the tree line to the north and also south, where the machine-gun crew was positioned. The right minigun blazed away to the north. Anyone trying to come through either area was almost certain to be hit. Sergeant Fisk saw muzzle flashes coming from the north side, so he sent short bursts from his GAU-5 in response. Then *Spectre* opened up from above, sending a stream of 20-mm rounds tearing through the jungle just a few yards beyond the tree line. *Knife-51*'s miniguns added to the din as sixty rounds per second were hurled beyond the perimeter.

On the left flank, Privates First Class Trevino and Overton were still dug in. They had watched from a mortar hole as the helicopter landed. When the aircraft's side minigun began firing in their direction, Trevino and Overton stayed low, then opened fire on the tree line where the minigun rounds were clipping branches. Minutes passed. After a number of repeats of the firing, and the firepower display from the orbiting *Spectre* aircraft, Trevino looked to his right and saw no one in any of the fighting positions. He grabbed Overton by the shirt and yelled above the din, "Let's get out of here."

When all in sight were aboard, Fisk followed Davis and McNemar up the ramp. Then Fisk remembered the body he had seen wrapped in a poncho near the ammo boxes during the last pickup. As he turned around, intent on going back out to check on it, someone slammed into his right shoulder. He brought his GAU-5 rifle to bear, then held his fire. Sprawled in front of him were Trevino and Overton, trying to claw their way aboard in the blackness.

Fisk was concerned there might be more men outside, so he looked for a marine officer. He spotted a pair of captain's bars in the dim red glow of the interior lighting. Fisk approached the officer and shouted above the noise of the engine and gunfire, "Are all your men aboard?"

Davis yelled back that they were. The fatigue in Davis's eyes revealed more than his words. Fisk again relayed a request to the cockpit for another sweep of the beach. Once more, Brims momentarily swung his gloved hand into sight. Another thumbs-up. Fisk ran down the ramp and crouched low just beyond the tail rotor.

Knife-51 had been on the ground for ten minutes, the landing zone fully illuminated by her lights. With the thought that no more marines were in defensive positions on the beach, Brims and his copilot, Second Lieutenant Dennis Danielson, waited nervously for the word to launch.

Fisk stayed low, looking up and down the beach to see if any more marines were firing into the tree line. He waited about fifteen seconds, when a green mortar flare arced above the jungle. With the thought that it might be a signal for the Khmer Rouge to charge, Fisk hurriedly returned to the helicopter and started up the ramp.

Brims heard the "go" signal and added power. As the helicopter rose, the ramp whose operating switch was still in the neutral position started to drop, maintaining contact with the sand.

Davis saw the look of astonishment on Fisk's face as he fell over backward onto the slippery ramp. Fisk reached out a hand as the helicopter began accelerating and he started sliding down and out. Closest to him was Gunnery Sergeant McNemar. Flailing in the wind was Fisk's microphone cord. McNemar snatched it and pulled. The cable came loose, so McNemar grabbed hold of one of Fisk's legs. Fisk got a hand on McNemar and wound up pulling him off his feet. Now two men were sliding out. Meanwhile, Davis grabbed McNemar's flak vest and hung on. Fisk threw his other arm backward and was rewarded with the feel of a "viselike grip" that grabbed onto his extended hand. In the cabin area, other marines realized the impending disaster. They formed a human chain just as the ramp went full down. Pulling and heaving, the group managed to get Fisk far enough inside to reach the ramp control. Fisk cycled the switch, and the ramp swung level. No longer fighting gravity, the human chain catapulted Davis, McNemar, and Fisk safely inside. Fisk landed on top of Davis, and the two men wrapped arms in an embrace.

Fisk then looked forward toward the cockpit and watched while a man he would later describe in three simple but emotional words as "that magnificent pilot," Lieutenant Richard C. Brims, flew them to safety.

Above the beach, Captain Wilson banked his OV-10 and watched the helicopter leave the landing zone. He had two more helicopters standing by, *Jolly-11* and *-44*. A discussion began.

Brims radioed, "some of the marines on board say there are still marines on the island at this time."

"OK there [are] still marines on the island, in the LZ? Is that affirmative," Wilson asked.

"That's affirmative," Brims replied. "That's what was passed on to us by the Marines on the chopper at this time."

"OK," Wilson said, "Find out if they were in the LZ or whether they were maintaining a perimeter defense position."

"Sir," Brims said, "We are told by the people in here that there are more marines on the beach."

Wilson's right engine oil pressure was bouncing off zero, but he had no intention of leaving until the marines were safe.

Moments later, word from Captain Davis was passed over the radio from the helicopter by Brims, "Captain Davis advises that all Marines are off the island."

"Outstanding," Wilson said. "That's exactly what we're looking for."

Wilson scanned the island one last time. Fires in the Cambodian compound near the east beach blazed on as the flashes of gunfire came to a halt.

Cricket released the helicopters to return to U-Tapao at 8:10 P.M., along with *Specter-21*. The *Wilson's* gig headed toward her ship.

As Captain Greg Wilson turned for home with the ailing engine running in idle, he could still see the strobe light blinking on the shore.

On the beach, three marines waited. They had done their duty, beaten back the last Khmer assault, defended the right flank with everything they had, but none of them had heard any signal to come further in. For Hargrove, as the minutes, then hours, ticked by without another helicopter returning, it had indeed been one hell of a day. May 15, 1975, was his twenty-fourth birthday. He had saved his siblings on a horrible night back in 1969 when his father torched their home. Now he waited on a rocky shore, having done it once again, except this time he had saved his marine buddies. Thoughts of his dead brother may have crossed his mind as he came upon the poncho-wrapped body of Ashton Loney. With that loss in his family, Hargrove did not even have to be in the military, not to mention combat. For Hall, who joined the marines as an eighteen-year-old boy, he had attained his manhood through the Corps and proved it better than his idol John Wayne ever could, humping the heavy machine gun up and down the beach and holding off the Khmer Rouge to the very end. And for Danny Marshall, the "orneriest little white boy the Waverlians ever saw," as his friend Teleah had dubbed him, he redeemed himself as he had always done, defending those he cared about no matter the consequences.

PART III

THE AFTERMATH

30

POSTMORTEM

*I think it is to our interest to punish the first insult; because
an insult unpunished is the parent of many others.*

Thomas Jefferson to John Jay, 1785

The Koh Tang marines were scattered among three navy ships and at
U-Tapao. A quick count was made of those who had been recovered. Within
two hours, an initial tally was complete. Eighteen were missing, one of
whom, Private First Class Loney, was certain to have been killed. Fourteen
others were thought to have died aboard the helicopters that went down, but
three men who were on the west beach were still unaccounted for.

Aboard the *Coral Sea,* Captain Stahl could not find Hargrove, Hall
and Marshall. After rechecking the ships and U-Tapao, Stahl inspected
all returned equipment to see if any of the serial numbers matched
those from weapons issued to the missing men. None was found.

Volunteers were sought, the intent to go back to the island before dawn to try to recover the missing. Only three armed helicopters were available. Marines and airmen were exhausted, and heavy resistance was likely if the Khmers had retaken the west beach. Captain Stahl volunteered and was given the use of a stateroom assigned to a naval pilot who was not aboard the carrier. Stahl fell asleep believing he would be awakened in a few hours, once the means to return to the island had been determined.

Meanwhile, the commander of Task Force 73, Rear Admiral R. T. Coogan, was told of the missing men, so he convened a meeting. Invited to the session were Lieutenant Colonel Austin, Captain Davis, and Gunny McNemar from G Company, and Lieutenant Junior Grade R. T. Coulter from Subic Bay, who had been flown aboard the carrier on a small transport aircraft while the battle was in progress. He brought with him a fourteen-man SEAL team. By the time Coulter was escorted to the Admiral's cabin, he had been well briefed about the fighting on Koh Tang. Admiral Coogan asked the lieutenant to go ashore aboard the *Wilson*'s gig in daylight, unarmed and under a white flag of truce, to retrieve the bodies of American dead on both beaches and determine the status of the three missing men if possible. Leaflets would be dropped in advance and the *Wilson*'s loudspeakers would broadcast intentions. Lieutenant Coulter was not inclined to partake of a plan that relied on Cambodian literacy and hearing. He offered to take his team in at night for a reconnaissance, but that was rejected. The lieutenant refused to approach the island in daylight. The admiral said "Okay." Davis did not like the way the conversation was going so he volunteered himself and McNemar to ride in on the gig to try to retrieve the three men. That was rejected by the admiral, too. Davis and Lieutenant Colonel Austin then began a heated exchange with the admiral over the prospect of abandoning the men. The admiral halted the meeting and asked all the others except Davis and Austin to leave the room. Admiral Coogan had to weigh the order received from Admiral Gayler in Hawaii to cease all offensive operations in Cambodia versus the idea of reengaging the Khmer Rouge on Koh Tang without any clear idea that the three missing marines were still alive.

A short while later, Captain Stahl was awakened in his stateroom and told the plan to go back to Koh Tang was off. Coogan's decision was to wait for some confirmation that the men were alive before committing forces.

Aboard the *Wilson*, Commander Rodgers was apprised regarding the need to determine if any live marines were still on the island. He canvassed the crew for French- and Cambodian-speaking personnel. He had several French-speakers in the crew, and one or two marines who could speak some Khmer. They worked up some phrases to be broadcast over the *Wilson*'s topside speakers to the effect that American forces meant no (additional) harm and only desired to retrieve any U.S. personnel left on the island, living or dead. Furthermore, the announcement would indicate readiness to send in an unarmed boat carrying a flag of truce if the Cambodians showed some sign that they were interested in a parley. With his plan in the works, Rodgers waited for daylight.

After the sun was up, the *Wilson* rounded the northern point of Koh Tang and steamed slowly into the east beach cove. Several Khmer Rouge were seen in black pajamas. Some were bathing while others squatted, washing clothes at the waterline. The *Wilson* moved to within a few hundred yards. Captain Rodgers was on the bridge. "A steam-driven destroyer is very quiet," he recalled, "yet very big at that range. One of the Khmer bathers looked up, pointed at the ship, and screamed. The rest took notice, then ran pell-mell into the trees." Rodgers could hear their shouts so he assumed that the Khmer Rouge could easily hear his loudspeakers as they blared out the messages in English, French, and Khmai.

The *Wilson* spent three hours slowly cruising back and forth around the northern tip of the island, especially in the area of the two coves where the fighting had occurred. There were some fires burning in the jungle, and a few buildings were still standing among the trees. Once the people on east beach disappeared, not another soul appeared, nor was there any indication of a response to the loudspeaker messages. Half the crew and almost all the air force and marines were topside, looking for any sign at all from the shore. Rodgers handed out every pair of binoculars on the ship. "The men were highly motivated to search," Rodgers observed, but no one was seen to make a break for the beach or to signal. No hostility was shown by those hidden ashore. The *Wilson* then departed the area as ordered by Admiral Gayler's staff in Hawaii.

A decision to go back to the island really centered around whether more men would be lost trying another assault versus the possibility that the three marines were still alive. Since no hostility had been seen since the pullout the night before, the Khmer Rouge had plenty of time to reoccupy its fighting positions. It seemed certain that another attack with fewer helicopters and marines would be opposed as strongly as on the day prior. Before committing to another assault, there needed to be some visual or radio signal from the missing men proving they were still alive, but there was none.

So, as quietly as the *Wilson* had steamed back into east beach cove, it was decided by Admiral Coogan and the military chain of command that the three marines could not have survived and the matter of returning to Koh Tang was dropped.

By dawn in Bangkok, the word was out. Thailand had already lodged a protest over the use of its sovereign territory for the operation. By noon, rioting was occurring outside the U.S. embassy, where American flags were burned. The Thai government had ordered the cessation of the use of its bases for military operations and immediate removal of U.S. forces from U-Tapao. Aboard the *Wilson* and *Holt,* the marines had been ordered to throw their grenades and ammunition overboard, since the ships did not have handling procedures or storage space for those explosives. The ships, jammed with marines, were headed for Subic Bay in the Philippines. At U-Tapao, only three helicopters were flyable.

Throughout the free world, headlines touted Ford's victory. The May 16 *New York Times* headline read, "Copters Evacuate U.S. Marines and Ship-Rescue Mission Ends; Toll Includes One Known Dead." Below it, a caption incorrectly stated that the marines in the accompanying photograph were moving out on Koh Tang. In actual fact, they were abandoning their downed chopper on the Thai mainland. In spite of a host of inaccuracies, nearly every news outlet reported Ford's action as a diplomatic and political triumph. Praise came gushing in. Even the democrats in Congress termed his actions right and accorded him high marks for leadership. The naysayers kept relatively quiet for the moment. Favorable letters came pouring in at the ratio of fourteen to one. By week's end more than fifteen thousand letters, telegrams, and phone messages had been received at the White House.

The crew had been saved, the *Mayaguez* recovered. Captain Miller attributed their release to the jet strikes against Cambodian patrol boats and the marine assault on Koh Tang.

Showing U.S. resolve in the wake of the Vietnam disaster had been accomplished. No one in the chain of command was going to rain on that parade. Even though the accounting had been completed and verified within twenty-four hours of the cessation of hostilities, the numbers were withheld from the White House. There can be little doubt that the information on the missing and the dead made it as far as the Pentagon and hence to the secretary of defense. For five days following the conclusion of the incident, the Pentagon doggedly stuck to its original story that only one marine had been killed, a few were missing, and seventy to eighty had been wounded. With communications so good that a pilot could be ordered via radio contact from the White House not to shoot at a trawler, how was it possible to require nine days to get a final casualty tally through to that same White House contact? Yet that is how long it took. By then, *Time, Newsweek,* and all the major weekly news magazines were out with cover stories hailing the incident as a victory for Ford.

While the president bathed in accolades, how was it going to look if word came out that forty-one had given their lives (twenty-three in the helicopter crash in Thailand and eighteen on Koh Tang) to free forty? How was it going to be taken if it were learned that bad intelligence given to Ford had caused him to attack the wrong island, where the crew had never set foot? If those stories hit the papers so soon after the "victory," wouldn't the pundits claim the president's actions were tantamount to hitting yet another errant golf ball that somehow smacked a bystander in the head, then bounded onto the green and into the hole for a birdie?

A solid case can be made that the administration deliberately withheld the true casualty figures to foster a maximum amount of enthusiasm for the president and the military's handling of the affair. Both the White House and the Pentagon knew of the twenty-three airmen killed in the helicopter crash in Thailand on the thirteenth, yet this information was kept secret from the press for over a week. When it was finally released, the Pentagon claimed that the men were not part of the operation, when they clearly were involved.

There can be little doubt that the use of military force was the key ingredient that prompted the release of the crew, but the military force Phnom Penh responded to occurred the day prior to the island assault. Notwithstanding, the assault on Koh Tang had its effect locally. As the fishing trawler carrying the U.S. crew, along with its escort boat, were heading from Rong Sam Lem island toward the *Mayaguez*, Cambodian hijacker Sa Mean had taken his walkie-talkie into the escort boat's wheelhouse. When Sa Mean came out, he had his craft pull alongside the *Sinvari* and began waving excitedly for the Thai fishing boat to stop. There can be little doubt that he had heard that Koh Tang was under attack, which it was. Island commander Em Son had already passed word to the mainland and the other islands regarding that information. The only reasonable rationale for the Cambodians to change plans and abandon the Thai trawler at that point was due to fear that they, the Khmer Rouge, would be attacked if they continued to the island. Would they have been? Yes. Had the marines not attacked Koh Tang, would the crew and ship have been released anyway? Probably, but military action made it happen sooner.

Immediately after the rescue, the Cambodians clearly showed that force had made itself felt. They announced over Phnom Penh radio, "Our weak country cannot afford to have a confrontation with the U.S.A." Without Ford's strong response, the crew would have likely languished in a Cambodian jail until confessions were obtained. Judging from their treatment of other foreign nationals, executions would have probably followed. Information Minister Hu Nim, the same official who the prior evening had announced the release of the ship, asserted that the *Mayaguez* was "only one of several spy ships seized in the gulf of Siam. These crews admitted that they were agents of the CIA who had to establish contact with other agents in hiding on Cambodian soil."

That statement also gives strong evidence that Phnom Penh was indeed well aware of and involved in the seizures. What photographer David Kennerly had postulated—that the whole incident was undertaken by rogue elements—appears partially correct, however. In September, some four months after the incident, the deputy premier of

Cambodia stated that the seizure of the *Mayaguez* was initiated by a local commander and that authorities in Phnom Penh learned of it many hours later. Specific seizures probably were not ordered by Phnom Penh, but the policy of halting maritime movement in the region had been promulgated. The Khmer Rouge wanted to move quickly in bringing the islands off the coast under their control before the Vietnamese or Thais moved in. Regardless, the use of B-52s in a punitive raid would have been unnecessary and were rightly rejected as overkill. Later, Ford would take Kennerly aside and tell him that while his intrusion was proper, he was not to make a habit of it.

As far as how other hostile nations viewed the incident, one can never be sure about Kim Il Sung's feelings in North Korea, but history shows he made no overt move to unify Korea. China's vice premier, Li Xiannian, claimed at a reception that the U.S. attacks had amounted to "acts of piracy," but he went no further. Nations outside the Communist bloc handled the issue with relief or indifference.

Beneath the domestic surface, however, egos continued to simmer. At the postmortem NSC meeting Ford found out that the mainland strikes had not come off as planned. When General Jones began the navy portion of the briefing, he did not mention the hold in the execution order that Kissinger had instigated. Jones stated, "The first (strike) was armed reconnaissance. They did not expend ordnance."

Ford's face reddened.

Kissinger asked Jones, "How many aircraft were used all together?"

"About thirty-two to forty," came the answer.

Schlesinger added, "Not the eighty-one that had been on the carrier."

With the outcome so positive—the ship and crew being rescued—one might think the president would be somewhat pleased that less force was required, but no, Ford was interested in two things. He had wanted his orders followed, and he had wanted the Cambodians punished.

Ford interrupted the meeting and had Henry Kissinger step outside the Cabinet Room with him. He asked Henry to summarize what he thought the presidential orders were. Kissinger did so, but neglected to mention that he, Henry, had instructed Scowcroft to put the attacks on hold until the president had a chance to review the Cambodian radio announcement. By the time the strikes were ordered back on by Ford, the planes were too low on gas to continue to target. They were definitely not on a reconnaissance mission, but since the pilots had obviously taken a look around, reconnaissance is what it wound up being called by General Jones.

Ford went back into the meeting only to then learn that the fourth strike never took place, either. He ordered Schlesinger to prepare "a full factual report." Schlesinger prepared one, but never gave the president the data with which to make a satisfactory determination as to how the orders got mishandled.

Among all the aftershocks, no one questioned whether a president should be deciding how many aircraft and strikes should be used to carry out a presidential order in the first place. Should not a president instead simply tell the navy to destroy mainland targets that might affect the Koh Tang operation and let the navy determine how and with what force to do the job?

The navy performance, or lack of it in Ford's mind, was added to the list of sins committed by Schlesinger and led to his dismissal from office six months later, on November 19, 1975.

As days passed immediately following the *Mayaguez* Incident, it became impossible to keep the lid on all the errors that had occurred. Questions were raised about whether Ford had overreacted. Had he made judgments on the basis of an excessive concern about boosting his own reputation? Why didn't the president cancel the air strikes against the mainland immediately upon learning the Cambodians were going to release the ship? In spite of Ford's statements to the contrary, the mainland attacks were clearly punitive, not tactical. Had they not been intended as punishment, their execution might have been halted.

Ford heard and read all about the criticism, but dismissed it as Monday-morning quarterbacking by those who never had to make life-and-death decisions under pressure of time and incomplete information. A question arises: if the situation is indeed life-and-death, is it appropriate to be distracted by a formal dinner party while these decisions are being contemplated?

As more and more mistakes came to light Congress initiated an investigation to be conducted by the General Accounting Office (GAO), whose intended purpose was to look into "the processes and procedures for handling the crisis." Its recommendations focused on the need to improve warnings to help mariners avoid hostile areas.

Intelligence shortfalls and the role of Congress in crisis management were also considered in the GAO review. Unfortunately, it was hampered at every turn by its inability to gain access to executive branch records and by extensive delays in obtaining access to other records and to key personnel involved in the crisis.

The GAO researchers did learn that five thousand to six thousand reconnaissance photographs were taken during the crisis. One of them was a picture of the Thai fishing trawler, anchored offshore Kompong Som. This was taken by the RF-4 that unknowingly overflew the trawler just prior to the boat heading to sea again, bound for Rong Sam Len. The GAO staff poured over the stack of photos and knew only that they were looking for a fishing trawler with people on deck. The correct image was discovered after an hour-long search of not more than a thousand of the pictures. Twenty-nine persons could be counted crammed on the forward deck.

All the higher-ups in the chain of command had heard about "Caucasians" being sighted on a trawler, but no one took the time to tell the photo analysts at Udorn to look for that.

No picture was found that showed the Thai boat anchored at Rong Sam Len. But a photograph taken anywhere in the Kompong Som area showing twenty-nine personnel on a fishing boat should have raised eyebrows if the viewer was aware of the pilot's report. One would almost have to deduce that it included a major part of the *Mayaguez* crew, since a trawler had been seen departing Koh Tang with "possible Caucasians" aboard. If the president had known a large number of the crew were likely still floating around somewhere off the coast, what would he have decided regarded the timing and location of the marine assault? Would attacking Koh Tang still have made sense, or would orders have gone out to locate the trawler first?

In any event, the GAO report focused attention on the intelligence shortfalls that were addressed by the military and maritime commands. According to the report, Admiral Gayler's headquarters in Hawaii established a feedback system to ensure acknowledgment of critical intelligence by all concerned commands in the future. Another investigation conducted by the Department of Defense delved into the intelligence failure regarding the strength of the Cambodian force on Koh Tang. The result mirrored the GAO report in that its conclusion was that there had been no failure in intelligence gathering. Instead, it was stated that the proper word never got to the crews because of a number of bureaucratic errors.

The GAO in its report also took a swipe at the congressional notification process. The summary suggested that the Congressional Subcommittee on International Affairs "may want to explore ways of keeping the Congress informed during crises, such as implementation of the Congressional watch center proposal or requiring a senior administration official to observe executive branch deliberations during crises, and provid[e] Congress with full information on ongoing matters." With Congress's known propensity for leaking sensitive information, as far as the author can determine, these steps were never implemented.

But, had these postmortems really missed the most important lesson to be learned? In many ways, the *Mayaquez* Incident could have focused attention on the real problem of the entire Southeast Asian War. Washington and the Pentagon had over the years improved communication links and computer systems needed to automate battlefield actions. As a result, tactical decisions kept moving higher and higher up the chain of command, the domain where the larger, strategic decisions are customarily made. They had not yet gotten to the point where the president was telling every soldier when to fire each bullet, but they were getting darn close. And if a commander in chief found himself in a war, who wouldn't want to run it in detail from the comfort of his office in Washington if he could?

A few years earlier during the Vietnam War, the air campaign was controlled by the daily fragmentation or "frag" order that rolled out of the computer at 7th Air Force when it was located in Saigon. The number of strikes, planes, sorties, bomb loads, times-on-target, refueling details—all of it came spewing forth daily to each of the combat flying units. Although there were some notable exceptions, commanders were seldom ever simply given a direction to destroy certain targets and use whatever means was thought appropriate. As a result, commanders flew sorties, dropped bombs, and sent back glowing reports. The measure of merit was not whether targets got leveled, but rather whether a given commander had launched more sorties than the outfit down the road. Those data were something a computer program could tabulate easily. Trying to figure out if a bridge had been knocked out and who had actually destroyed it took a whole lot more subjective and objective analysis than tabulations of sortie totals. No time was devoted to damage assessment beyond seeing if the target still stood. There was no way to quickly determine which unit had been successful in destroying each target.

By 1975, the battle management system had become so streamlined that the president was now able to generate the frag order, designate the number of sorties, and indicate precisely what to strike. That is exactly what Ford had tried to do. And later, was he interested in whether the targets were destroyed? No, he wanted to know what happened to the number of sorties and strikes he had ordered. It should be noted, the navy had indeed destroyed the targets.

On May 17, the *Mayaguez* sailed into Singapore none the worse for wear, except for the $5,000 that was noted missing from Captain Miller's safe when the crew had reboarded off Koh Tang. As the ship docked, a gaggle of journalists descended on the *Mayaguez*. During the news conference held at the pier, it quickly became apparent that Captain Miller and the crew were not going to bend to the script preferred by some of the journalists. In reply to leading questions of the negative variety, Miller instead praised President Ford and the marines for rescuing ship and crew. We "would be in prison or dead now," Miller declared. Miller was visibly moved as he described how he went below on the USS *Wilson* and saw the wounds and suffering the marines were going through for him and his men. Able-bodied seaman Earl Gilbert said, "After the marines came, God I felt good. Damn good. Those marines are great. Ford did a damn good job, but I just want to thank those marines."

By eight days after the battle, the troops from Marine Amphibious Force III were back on Okinawa. A memorial ceremony was conducted the next day using the marine casualty figures President Ford had not yet seen.

Regarding the key questions of whether President Ford was ever told of the possibility that three marines were left behind alive, I wrote and asked him. President Ford replied, "Not to my best recollection." The troops were assembled for the ceremony and told not to discuss the missing-in-action with the media, under pain of court-martial. The memorial program distributed by Chaplin R. Fenton Wicker, Jr., listed only thirteen marine and navy casualties. Ignored were the two air force losses on Koh Tang and the twenty-three lost in the helicopter crash in Thailand, but these were likely omitted as an oversight. The other three missing names, Hargrove, Hall, and Marshall, were intentionally left out. The three-man machine-gun crew that the Marine Corps leadership felt could not have survived the last battle of America's Southeast Asia War apparently were not worthy of remembrance, either. That same day the local Camp Schwab newspaper, *Okinawa Marine,* came out with a front-page *Mayaguez* story. No mention was made of the missing-in-action. Hargrove, Hall, and Marshall had not only vanished on Koh Tang; one week later they had vanished from the military's public acknowledgments.

As much as the Marine Corps wanted to bask in the glory of Ford's victory, the leadership knew better. Marines had been left behind, a traditional no-no. A closed-door investigation was quietly begun. Interviews were arranged with those who had seen or had knowledge of the movements of the machine-gun team. Sworn testimony was taken. In June, a report was forwarded to Admiral Gayler's office in Hawaii and on to the commandant of the Marine Corps. In it were several "statements of fact," one of which said, "Hall, Hargrove and Marshall did not report to Captain Davis" as ordered by Sergeant Anderson. In the opinion section, the three were accused of disobeying that order to report. Incredibly, the blame for being left behind was being placed on the missing-in-action. Another opinion referred to Hargrove's mental state as a contributing factor, yet indicated he was "fit for duty." Finally, "If Hall, Hargrove and Marshall had been in the general vicinity of a helicopter landing site area, they would have attempted to board either the 5th or 6th helicopter unless they were unconscious, incapacitated because of wounds or dead." This statement came even though testimony revealed that two more marines, Privates First Class Willy J. Overton and Emelio Trevino, were nearly left behind. Had it not been for a momentary delay by an air force crewman, Technical Sergeant Fisk, five, not three would have been abandoned.

A careful reading of the testimony, however, revealed quite a different story from the one recounted in the "Facts and Opinions" section of the report. The team had been seen alive and functioning well as a machine-gun crew up to the very last moments of the extraction. Private First Class Jeffery M. Kern recognized "Hall as one of [at least] two people" he saw in a machine-gun "hole." On two separate occasions ammunition was delivered to the men in the late afternoon and in the waning minutes of the engagement, first by Private First Class Robert K. Atkins who stated, "I brought some M-60 ammunition to them. They were not wounded and their mental condition seemed average." Later, well after the perimeter had been pulled back and darkness had descended, Private First Class David M. Wagner saw "PFC Hall on the beach with his machine-gun. He was supposed to provide cover for us. I heard Hall yell for ammo, so I gave him mine." Every account had the machine-gun team positioned on the "extreme" right flank as the perimeter collapsed.

Before E Company commander Captain Stahl left the island, he gave the machine-gun team an order "to defend the flank with your M-16s if necessary." Not interviewed on Okinawa for the marine report was Private First Class William J. Thornton. He recalled about the machine-gun crew: "They were crucial as rear security and were ordered to hold their position if necessary using the M-16 rifles and grenades they had." Although there is only Thornton's years-later recollection on the matter, he told me that the crew was informed, "The last helicopter would swing around to their position and pick them up." If true, Captain Stahl's premature departure would explain why that word never got passed to Captain Davis, the senior man in the last load of marines flown off the island.

After compiling the testimony (except the last items from Captain Stahl and Private First Class Thornton), the investigative officer, Major Peter C. Brown, sent forward the startling recommendation "that the status of Hall, Hargrove and Marshall be changed from missing-in-action to killed-in-action (body not recovered)."

General John N. McLaughlin, the commanding general, Fleet Marine Force, Pacific, in his attached comments disapproved the opinion regarding the three marines' disobedience of an order and Hargrove's mental condition as a factor. He did, however, concur in the recommendation. The report went forward to Admiral Gayler in Hawaii and from there to the desk of the Commandant of the Marine

Corps where it was read but not released to the public. Then, on July 21, 1976, little more than a year after the incident, the Marine Corps declared a presumptive finding of death for these men. Determinations were not based on the acquisition of new information, but rather the absence of information that the three marines had survived and the lapse of time without any indication of survival. During the Vietnam War, numerous missing-in-action servicemen who were thought to have died wound up years later being mentioned by North Vietnamese propaganda as being in captivity. Many, but not all, were eventually released in 1973. Still, the Marine Corps declared Hargrove, Hall, and Marshall dead only fourteen months after they went missing. The families were notified, but not given access to the investigation testimony.

It would take twenty more years before the events of the night of May 15, 1975, and the fates of Lance Corporal Joseph N. Hargrove, Private First Class Gary L. Hall, and Private First Class Danny G. Marshall would begin to emerge.

31

RETURN VISITS TO KOH TANG, 1996-2001

*. . . that, from these honored dead we take increased devotion
to that cause for which they here gave the last full measure of
devotion — that we here highly resolve these dead shall not
have died in vain . . .*

Abraham Lincoln, "Gettysburg Address," November 18, 1863

Upon returning from Cambodia after my first trip there in 1995, I submitted two magazine articles. One was about the recovery operation and the other about the battle. A third assignment, with *Popular Science* was about the DNA process, but that one would take time for me to finish since the results of the bone tests would take many months. I put the assignments behind me, but subconsciously the likelihood that Hargrove, Hall, and Marshall had been left on Koh Tang—and forgotten—kept gnawing at me. The fact that the story continued to be kept from the public eye added to my interest and that of my magazine editors. In talking with the officers involved, the unspoken message was that the three men *had* to be dead before the pullout. It was too horrible to think otherwise. "We'd have had to go back," Captain Davis said. Captain Stahl, the missing men's company commander, wrote to Hargrove's wife and indicated he was "on the last helicopter" to leave the island when in fact he left well before the last helicopter. Consequently his explanation that the men did not survive had no firsthand confirmation in fact.

I contacted the Marine Corps and learned the men received no medals for bravery and were posthumously awarded only Purple Hearts, an automatic honor received by all casualties. Then I learned that although twenty years had passed, Joseph Hargrove's Purple Heart had not yet been presented to his next of kin. That oversight was eventually corrected three years later, in 1999.

In an attempt to obtain photos of the machine-gun team, I contacted the Marine Corps via a Freedom of Information Request. The Navy department responsible (the marines officially come under the Department of the Navy) denied there were any photos available. Photos of recruits are maintained at the training centers, so I knew they had them.

Finally, late in 1996, the U.S. ambassador to Cambodia, Kenneth Quinn, read one of my articles. Quinn had been a White House staffer during the *Mayaguez* Incident and had maintained an avid interest in the subject ever since. Used to surprises by this time, it was still startling to read from him, "I was stunned to learn that three men had been left alive on the island and had held out . . . against impossible odds and no chance of rescue." Quinn may have never heard about the three missing marines, but he was tuned in now. I had finally found someone highly placed who offered to help.

My next return to Cambodia was in November 1996, at Ambassador Quinn's invitation. Former POW, Senator John McCain, was invited as the guest speaker at the establishing of a memorial in honor of servicemen who had died in Cambodia. I donated some artifacts that the Joint Task Force had allowed me to keep from the 1995 expedition. Quinn added those to what had already been assembled. After the ceremony, the decision was made to not return to the island because the rainy season had continued unabated—most of the island was a swamp at the moment. Each of these trips was costing between three thousand and five thousand dollars, and although my wife, Carol, was supportive of my continued interest, I had added financial responsibilities that were not going to disappear. On my military service retirement check, I could not justify continuing these trips without some financial help. I queried the *Washington Post, New York Times, Chicago Tribune, Los Angeles Times, Navy Times, Esquire, Harper's, Parade, Life,* and on and on. However, as soon as each publication understood the travel expenses involved, they bailed. The *Washington Post* editor said I could try it on-spec, no expenses provided, adding, "We always stand ready to read completed manuscripts." They read a draft after one of my visits, but passed on it. The others flat out rejected the proposal, except for the *New York Times,* which did not respond at all, even after a follow-up.

I was driving a 1984 Volvo I had bought at a repo auction. That was our "new" car. My wife, a former Peace Corps volunteer who had worked for years with refugees in Asia, understood well the trauma families go through in wartime. She applied for a substitute teaching position, got hired, and drove her '78 Toyota to the schools. "Go find out what happened to those three marines," she told me.

I was back on the hunt.

In February of 1997, I found myself again in Cambodia, this time to finish the assignment with *Popular Science* about the mitochondria DNA process used to identify remains. No additional travel expenses were provided by the magazine since I had already exceeded the budget estimate on other research.

Ambassador Quinn had cleared the way for me to return to the island and also to sit in on an interview of a Cambodian, identified as a veteran of the battle. Before I departed my home in California, I reviewed numerous interview reports made by Khmer Rouge witnesses, compiled and finally released by the Joint Task Force, plus anything else I could get my hands on. I found in many but not all cases that the lower the level of contact, the more help I was getting.

Among the reports, at least seven different witnesses related information pertaining to the capture of one or more American soldiers after the battle for Koh Tang. Similarities in the descriptions kept cropping up, but the number of captured Americans ranged from one to five. Many of the reports were hearsay, but there were eyewitness accounts from Cambodians whose knowledge indicated they were probably on the island at the time of the battle or shortly thereafter when prisoners were taken. Reports from the participants claiming firsthand knowledge showed the most consistency.

After arriving at the airport in Phnom Penh, I was invited to ride in a Joint Task Force vehicle to Kompong Som for the interview. The plan was to take the witness statement, then proceed to the island itself with a JTF team to conduct another search for remains. Before we departed, it was discovered there was no seat belt for me in the vehicle. JTF regulations prohibit travel without seat belts—for valid reasons.

I was ushered to the rear door of a Cambodian government Mitsubishi Pajero 4WD. The Cambodians had no such regulations. Also climbing aboard were Lieutenant General Noun Sareth, police colonel Chum Soyath, a bodyguard, and a driver.

General Sareth was a member of Hun Sen's Cambodian Peoples Party (CPP), the coalition government's pro-socialist, pro-Vietnam faction. At five-feet-one in height, Sareth did not overwhelm me with brawn. His jaw protruded slightly, and his lower lip shoved against the upper, giving his features a stern, angry look. As we were introduced, he stuck out his hand and jutted that jaw, offering a penetrating image laced with smoldering dare. But it was when he spoke that he sent a chill down my spine. His tone stabbed the eardrums and made the driver jump to action. Away we roared.

Sareth had a colorful history. As district commander back in 1975, he marched into Phnom Penh at the head of his Khmer Rouge troops the day they took control of the city. Then began the purges. Pol Pot started culling units. Sareth's peer commanders began disappearing into the torture chambers at Toul Sleng and eventually to the mass graves twelve miles south of the capital at Choeng Ek, the infamous Killing Fields. Sareth envisioned a grim future, so he took some of his troops with him and fled to Vietnam. In 1979 he returned to Phnom Penh once again, this time leading a Vietnamese/Cambodian force to help recapture the city from his old masters, the Khmer Rouge. Ever since, he had avoided death through all the upheavals, purges, and assassination attempts that had plagued the country. Lieutenant General Noun Sareth was a very careful, calculating man. He communicated with me from the onset through his English-speaking subordinate, police colonel Chum Soyath, never referring to me by name, merely as "the newspaper man."

As I rode in the seat behind the driver, I noticed Sareth in the front passenger seat staring straight ahead. Slung loosely over the seat back behind the general was a webbed belt containing a holster and .22-caliber pistol—a weapon meant more for administering summary verdicts than for a firefight.

Sitting beside me was Colonel Soyath. Behind us, sitting sideways in the jump seat, was the bodyguard.

We moved at a steady pace through the city of Phnom Penh, past blue CPP banners and out into the verdant countryside. The chords of *Take My Breath Away* drifted from the rear speaker with an ache. Twenty minutes later the driver turned the radio off as we approached the foothills. The police colonel took *my* breath away as he drew a Russian-made submachine gun from the floor, checked it, then handed it to the soldier in back. Sareth took his pistol belt and hooked it over a handhold mounted on the dash. The weapon's grip poked from the holster and was now instantly available. Holding steady a hundred yards behind was the JTF vehicle with their team. They had no guns. Of that I was certain.

I discerned no reason for the sudden increase in attention to security, but conversation came to a halt as everyone began rubbernecking the activity ahead and to the side. The road stayed straight; our speed held at 55 mph. Traffic, though sparse, was continuous, but the CPP banners disappeared. Here, I guessed, the villagers were in favor of whatever politics the latest armed visitor happened to embrace.

The police colonel spoke English and explained that we were on Route 4, passing through disputed territory. The threat was from hit-and-run roadblocks where Khmer Rouge troops would suddenly appear, block vehicle traffic for ten minutes or so, and rob and often shoot some of the occupants. With Sareth's background, he could not afford to be passive if we got stopped.

Tension held high, especially during periods where the traffic slowed. Two edgy hours later we neared the coast. The Cambodians seemed to relax as Sareth took a hand radio and began a one-sided chat with someone. Following five minutes of this, he put the radio away, rolled down his window, checked his appearance in the side mirror, then took a comb and had a go at his unruly hair—to absolutely no avail.

Ten minutes later, we pulled into a compound to make a courtesy call on the district police chief, a short, chubby Cambodian. That protocol completed, we finally rolled into Kompong Som, none the worse for wear.

The next morning at 9:00 A.M. sharp the interview began with the witness, Rot Leng. He was a former Khmer Rouge medic born in 1946 who had spent his whole life ministering to the ill and wounded. He claimed he was on the island during and after the battle. The man seemed loose and eager to talk. He stated that twenty days after the liberation of Phnom Penh, he was assigned to Koh Tang and Ream Naval Base, moving back and forth to work at both places. At the time of the *Mayaguez* capture, he was part of the 450th Battalion on the island. A patrol-boat squadron constituted the other military force defending the place. The ground unit had about a hundred men to start with and the naval force had five boats, crewed by about half a dozen men each. By May 12, when the *Mayaguez* was hijacked, each platoon had already been reduced by 15 percent due to malaria and other maladies, leaving about eighty-five troops, plus the patrol-boat crews.

On the day of the battle, the sun was not all the way up at around 6 A.M., but Rot Leng estimated thirty helicopters were sighted. He saw them taking off from a "big ship." In actuality, only eleven attack helos participated in the first assault. With all the maneuvering around the *Holt* and between beaches, it might have seemed like thirty to someone being fired upon. Rot Leng saw the helicopters approach the northern part of the island, but by then the Khmer Rouge were up and ready. "Had the Americans arrived earlier, things might have been different," Rot Leng stated. After two days of tension, shooting at planes and a long work period the previous night, "the men were tired and most were still asleep." The witness then pointed to the precise place on the map that the battle took place and filled in many of the details later confirmed by other veterans.

Rot Leng then related a new story about captured Americans. His description differed from previous reports, but contained many elements consistent with the accounts of other witnesses. Even though the witness was known to have firsthand information on the missing marines, regrettably no photographs of the men were available to show him: the JTF-FA personnel came unprepared.

At 7:00 A.M. the following morning, General Sareth, the JTF team, Rot Leng, and I boarded the *Singha Gold '97* and began a two-hour speedboat ride through choppy, pounding swells before arriving on the island. Rot Leng walked directly to the area where the ammunition cache had been located. It had been recovered by Soeun's men prior to the renewed fighting that accompanied the pullout from the east beach. Nothing remained of the site; however, the location was later confirmed by Em Son. Rot Leng pointed out precisely where the two helicopters had been shot down off the east beach. Then he went to where Phat Kheng had been positioned with his 12.7-mm machine gun on the north side of the east beach. From there it was a clear, easy shot to where *Knife-31* had actually been downed. Rock fortifications were still visible. By digging around the loose sand nearby, 12.7-mm machine-gun casings were uncovered.

Then began the search for remains. The witness pointed to an area on the west beach where he thought the leg and boot of one American had been buried, but no one made any effort to dig. The team had brought shovels, but the ground was thick with roots and vegetation. Digging, had it begun, would have been an arduous undertaking. I could sympathize. The heat was all-consuming, and I already had a welt on my face where I was stung by some jungle critter. But I could not excuse the U.S. Army soldier who had brought a metal detector all the way from Alaska. It was not my place to give orders, but I asked him if the device would detect the metal-lined lace holes on combat boots. He claimed it would but made no move to take his device out of its canvas cover. The other members of the team stood by leaning on shovels and offering no inducement for the man to begin a search. None was made. Not one sweep of the detector occurred, not one shovelful of dirt was moved.

This group's job was not to do the excavation, but to determine whether the site was a good candidate for further exploration. Still, they did have shovels and I found it disconcerting that not even a metal detector sweep was made.

Back on the east beach, I mentioned to the team leader that there might be evidence in the jungle to the south. The Cambodian witness stated that he thought the MIAs had hidden there. I wanted time to do a ground search, possibly using the Cambodian security troops to assist. I asked the local Cambodians whether they had ever found any helmets or M-16s in the jungle. One man replied that he had heard that an M-16 was found in the jungle south of the beaches about a year after the battle. The JTF team leader suddenly advanced the return time to the mainland by two hours, allowing me only half an hour to look. It would take nearly that amount of time to get to the location and return. He was adamant, and I must assume he was concerned I might encounter unexploded ordnance, but I went anyway without any Cambodians to help, and found nothing. The message seemed clear: it would be preferable that I not find anything that might prove marines had been left behind. The team leader, though a civil service employee at the time, had been a marine in years past. I could understand his desire not to tarnish the marine tradition of never leaving their dead or wounded behind, but it had happened before[*] and would likely happen again, particularly if the facts were covered up. I also was aware that certain marine officers and NCOs felt a responsibility for having left men behind and their peace of mind needed to be considered. In contemplating the effect on others, I had only to look in the mirror.

Digressing for a moment, I should mention an incident that once happened to me. On February 6, 1967, I took off in an F-4 Phantom from Ubon Royal Thai Air Base for my end-of-tour hundredth mission. There had been a time when I thought that attaining that vaunted number of combat sorties was beyond reach, but now I was nearly finished.

As I did my aircraft preflight, I remembered sitting in the officer's mess having dinner a few weeks earlier with Lieutenant Robert Gilchrist. At that time, "Gilly" was engaged to be married in ten days and was about to head to the flight line for his ninety-eighth mission. He already had his orders to Europe and a ticket to Hawaii for his wedding. He was flying only night sorties for his last few missions because they were deemed safer. Commanders do not like the morale impact if someone dies near the end of his tour. And yet Gilchrist shook my hand after dinner, walked out the door that night, took off, and was never seen again.

My last flight was to be armed reconnaissance, scheduled to occur in what we called the *Easy Packs,* the zone well south of the heavily

---

[*]For example, during the Makin Island attack in 1942, Marine Raiders left nineteen dead along with nine missing on the island. The nine were captured by the Japanese and executed. Remains of the nineteen were recovered by CIL-HI in 2000.

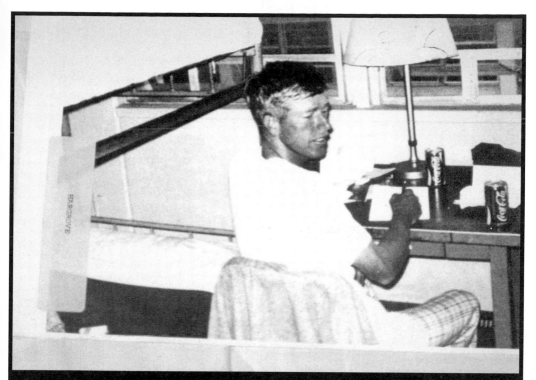

L/CPL Joseph N. Hargrove seen writing a letter home while stationed on Okinawa. He was in charge of the machine gun team that guarded the right flank of the marine position on the night of May 15, 1975. **JOINT TASK FORCE ON FULL ACCOUNTING**

L/CPL Joseph N. Hargrove as he looked at the completion of boot camp. **JTF-FA**

PFC Gary Hall from Covington, Kentucky, carried the M-60 machine gun into the last battle. **JTF-FA**

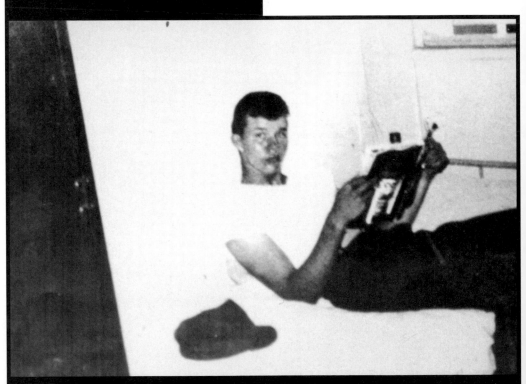

PFC Gary Hall reading on his bunk at Camp Schwab, Okinawa. This photo is the one that Khmer Rouge battalion commander Em Son used to identify one of the marines captured after the last battle. **JTF-FA**

PVT Danny G. Marshall, the 130-pound marine from Waverly, West Virginia. He was the ammunition carrier defending the right flank of the marine position. **JTF-FA**

The tiny "blockhouse" where PVT Danny G. Marshall grew up. Danny slept upstairs with three brothers. His parents and the three Marshall girls had rooms downstairs. **JTF-FA**

Location of the machine gun position on the right flank of the collapsed marine perimeter. This is the area where Hargrove, Hall and Marshall repositioned during the withdrawal the night of May 15, 1975. **RALPH WETTERHAHN**

Former Khmer Rouge battalion commander Em Son standing beside the house he was raised in. Originally a two room structure, Pol Pot allowed families to have only one room per dwelling, so the back room was torn down and never restored. **RALPH WETTERHAHN**

The late Lt. Gen. Noun Sareth, former Khmer Rouge commander who defected to Vietnam after Pol Pot's excesses threatened his life. He joined the Hun Sen faction and returned to fight against the Khmer Rouge. Working in the late 90's with the Joint Task Force recovery teams, the general's pistol was always close at hand. After surviving twenty-seven years of conflict, Sareth died of cancer in 1999. **RALPH WETTERHAHN**

Koh Tang as seen today. Lighter shaded circle to the left of center is where the 15,000 pound BLU-82 bomb detonated unannounced, close to the marine position. The white strip seen above the impact circle is the west beach. Across the narrow isthmus is the east beach. **RALPH WETTERHAHN**

A dead palm tree located near the compound area on the east beach gives testimony to the violence of the combat that took place during the last battle. **RALPH WETTERHAHN**

The barge used in 1995 by personnel from the Joint Task Force to recover remains of casualties from downed helicopter *Knife-31*. Sand was pumped from wreckage beneath the surface, and debris was sifted through screening tables set up on the barge. **RALPH WETTERHAHN**

The burned and battered rotor head of *Knife-31* beneath the surf off Koh Tang. **COURTESY: ALAN WYATT**

Marine Gunnery Sergeant Wayne Westt from the Central Identification Laboratory in Hawaii sorts through coral and sand at a screening table near Koh Tang in search of remains of casualties from the last battle. **RALPH WETTERHAHN**

Personal items brought up from the wreckage of *Knife-31*. Kevlar armor shows damage caused by the intense heat of the fire inside the helicopter. Part of a T-shirt and an equipment clip were also recovered. **RALPH WETTERHAHN**

A pilot's checklist, recovered from inside the downed helicopter. The cockpit procedures could still be read after having remained in salt water for over 20 years. **RALPH WETTERHAHN**

This mess kit belonged to a marine who did not survive the last battle. **RALPH WETTERHAHN**

Marine helmet recovered from inside the wreckage of *Knife-31*. Ten helmets and liners were discovered inside the helicopter. **RALPH WETTERHAHN**

Side panel (R) and tail ramp sections (L) from *Knife-31*. After exposure to sunlight, phosphorus from a grenade ignited after 20 years under water. Main landing gear tire shows extensive battle damage incurred during the last battle. **RALPH WETTERHAHN**

Marine sgt. Bryant Malone from the Central Identification Laboratory painstakingly removes sand from helicopter wreckage. The sand is then sifted for remains at screening tables set up on the beach. **RALPH WETTERHAHN**

Ti Nean Pagoda located above Sihanoukville, Cambodia, where two marine captives were taken and eventually executed. The facility was used by the Khmer Rouge to exterminate Buddist monks and other "reactionaries." **RALPH WETTERHAHN**

Army major Ronald Stafford looking down on the marker where former Khmer Rouge commander Em Son said "the big one" was buried. A burial pit was later uncovered beneath the marker, but because the area had been bulldozed in 1985, only small bone fragments were recovered. **RALPH WETTERHAHN**

Army sergeant Al Vincent (L) and Sergeant First Class Mason Fail (R) from the Central Identification laboratory use trowels to scrape away the top layer of dirt where Khmer Rouge witness Em Son indicated a marine was buried. The remnants of a burial pit were discovered here in 1999. **RALPH WETTERHAHN**

Heavy manacles made of wire cable were found at the site where one of the marines was buried. **RALPH WETTERHAHN**

Army major Ronald Stafford inspects the sandy alcove the Joint Task Force team dubbed, "the grotto." This is the area where Khmer Rouge commander Em Son left the body of PVT Danny G. Marshall. **RALPH WETTERHAHN**

Em Son was the Khmer Rouge battalion commander on Koh Tang during the *Mayaguez* Incident. By 1975, he had been seriously wounded sixteen times. Em Son came face-to-face with marines Hargrove, Hall, and Marshall and was involved in all of their deaths. **RALPH WETTERHAHN**

Em Son (L) points out where he buried a marine who was left for dead on the west beach. To his right is Central Identification Laboratory Anthropologist Richard Wills and interpreter, air force Master Sergeant Joseph Fraley. On the far right is an unidentified U.S. embassy staff officer. The excavation team reached this site on the last day of the mission in January, 2001, and unearthed human remains, thought to be that of L/CPL Ashton Loney. DNA results are pending. **RALPH WETTERHAHN**

Em Son, who lost his leg in 1988 to a Vietnamese land mine, stands beside a taped-off area near the stump of a mango tree. This is where a marine was executed and buried, the day after the *Mayaguez* crew was rescued. The JTF-FA team was unable to excavate this area during the January, 2001 mission and will return next year for the recovery. **RALPH WETTERHAHN**

An honor guard made up of US Embassy personnel escorts what is thought to be the remains of Lance Corporal Ashton Loney onto a C-130 aircraft for repatriation back to America in January, 2001. Loney's body was abandoned under fire during the nighttime helicopter extraction off Koh Tang. **COURTESY: RICHARD LANE**

defended Hanoi area. Safer. We found no moving targets, so I had my wingmen drop their bombs on a "suspected" truck park. Before I had a chance to drop mine, I heard on the radio a beeper signal, the chirping tone a survival radio puts out after a pilot bails out. The sound had always sent a chill up my spine.

I reported the beeper to *Cricket,* the very same EC-130 controlling aircraft used in the *Mayaguez* operation. The radio operator aboard *Cricket* relayed that a single-engine Cessna, an O-1 Bird Dog used for directing air strikes by fast-moving jets, had gone down the day before. The forward air controller aboard it had not been heard from since. I tuned my direction-finder radio to pinpoint the origin of the signal and tracked the bearing needle until it swung. Then I circled and made contact with the forward air controller who switched his radio to voice mode and relayed that he had parachuted into the jungle where he was still evading capture. Nearby I spotted an antiaircraft installation. Knowing that this gunner would present a hazard to any attempt at rescue, I rolled in to try knocking out the battery. Now, mind you, when dive-bombing a gun pit, the man aiming the weapon has no tracking problem to solve since the plane is coming right at the site. The gunner merely points and shoots. However, halfway into this bomb run, my mind fastened onto one thought: not getting shot down on my last mission. My tracking of the gun pit was abysmal and my bombs missed the target.

We were low on fuel at that point, so we headed home while *Cricket* brought in the helicopter force. I landed, asked how the rescue went, and was told it was still in progress. I thought nothing more of the matter until six months later stateside, when I was notified that someone had put me in for a decoration, an Air Medal for that final mission. Upon checking how this could be, I discovered that after I had departed the scene, the rescue helicopter had come in, picked up the pilot, and then was knocked out of the sky by the gun battery, the one I had failed to silence. The forward air controller and all but one member of the crew were killed. The lone survivor, a pararescueman, had fallen out of the aircraft and landed in trees. For his actions, the rescueman was awarded the Air Force Cross. Other servicemen who came in to rescue him were awarded medals as well. The officer who did the paperwork for the medals did not know I had missed my intended target that day. He simply put me in for the award since I had located the downed pilot while getting fired upon. I was stunned. I felt the distraction over saving my own skin had resulted in the loss of a helicopter full of people. I have learned to live with that mistake and would never have wanted to deny the other participants their honors in order to save myself some anguish. I decided that those who had a hand in leaving behind Hargrove, Hall, and Marshall would probably feel the same way.

Following that third visit to Cambodia in 1997, I began my research in earnest. I contacted marines, navy, and air force men who had participated in the *Mayaguez* Incident. I went to the hometowns of each of the missing marines and interviewed parents, siblings, friends, and classmates. I devoured everything written I could find, reviewing a number of additional reports from JTF-FA that cited similar circumstances regarding the capture and fate of the three missing marines on Koh Tang. My wife, Carol, continued to work so that my trips could proceed.

I managed to place some articles and had begun to get noticed outside military circles. My August 1998 feature about MIAs and mitochondria DNA in *Popular Science* was nominated for an American Society of Magazine Editors Award in investigative journalism. It did not win, but reporter Vince Gonzales from CBS News in Los Angeles saw the piece and called me about a documentary they were contemplating on the subject. I was later contacted by William Howard, a director with Henninger Productions, who also wanted to do a documentary on the *Mayaguez*.

I made twelve more trips on this story, four of them to Cambodia. The first of those was in March of 1999, when a team from JTF-FA returned to Koh Tang and the coastal area at Kompong Som. Additional Khmer Rouge veterans were interviewed. Each related similar-sounding stories. Archaeological "digs" were made at five sites on Koh Tang and two on the mainland.

While snorkeling off the east beach, I found a Kevlar panel from the vest of one of the marines who had been aboard *Knife-31*. Over on the west side, I brought a copy of the E Company platoon sergeant's notebook that I had obtained from Sergeant Freddy Lungren who worked for JTF-FA at the embassy in Phnom Penh. I used the notebook to try locating the site of the machine-gun pit defended by the three missing marines. USAF major Joe Davis, the new public affairs officer from JTF-FA, accompanied me and was the first to spot the site, right where the notebook indicated it would be. A bush had grown up around the trench dug by the three men, but it was still clearly visible. Buried at that location on the extreme right flank were live M-16 rounds the men had apparently abandoned. I knew that the missing M-60 team also was armed with two M-16s and a .45-caliber pistol, but none of those was found. Evidence of the heavy fighting that had occurred there was plentiful, including 12.7-mm machine-gun rounds that had embedded in the sand berm the men had built around their position.

Then I met Em Son, the commander of the unit that defended Koh Tang in 1975. Here was the man who had been in charge. He had been wounded sixteen times prior to that particular battle, and twice more after that. His last injury, caused by stepping on a land mine, cost him his right leg. He was in the hands of the JTF interpreter, so I was allowed to do only a brief interview with him on Koh Tang. I was present, however, when he showed us burial sites on the mainland and got further information there. I asked the interpreter, Master Sergeant Fraley, where they had found him. "He just showed up in Phnom Penh. Came in at his own expense when he heard we were looking for information about Koh Tang." Later, I obtained Em Son's full debriefing report from JTF-FA upon my return to the States. In it, Em Son indicated how two of the Americans died.

The true details of what actually happened in May 1975 were beginning to come together. Although each Khmer Rouge account had discrepancies—much like those of the American participants I interviewed—enough congruity was present to construct a highly plausible account based on proven facts and circumstantial evidence. The missing Americans were dead, so they would never be able to tell their own story. The best I could hope for was to assemble the narrative as accurately as I could. To do that, I would need a full exchange with the man I felt was the key to the Khmer Rouge side of the story, Em Son. Before I met with him again, though, I wanted to get photos of the missing marines.

The *Popular Science* article was showing up all over the World Wide Web. Sites honoring the eighteen lost on Koh Tang were sprouting, some designed by high school students doing class projects, others by various POW/MIA groups. Finally, the Marine Corps realized that Lance Corporal Hargrove's Purple Heart had never been presented to his next of kin. Hargrove's widow was contacted and agreed to accept the medal in November of 1999. I called her to ask if I might attend. Though somewhat reserved over the phone, Gail Hargrove gave her permission.

The ceremony was held in the Marine Reserve Headquarters parking lot in Raleigh, North Carolina, on November 9, the day before the 224th birthday of the Marine Corps. Many from Joseph Hargrove's family attended, including his younger brother, Kochise, and sister Kathleen, but their mother was too frail to attend. Gail Hargrove was there to receive the medal. Kochise, bearded and all country-looking, and Kathleen were friendly to me, but Gail kept her distance. After the ceremony I attended the Marine Corps Anniversary Ball at the reserve center. I'm not particularly superstitious, but it was beginning to seem poignant that important turns of events were always occurring on the Corps' birthday. I considered that a positive sign and drove the next morning to Mount Olive, North Carolina. At the local newspaper office, I discovered the article about Rudolph Hargrove's 1969 arson.

I drove to Beautancus to get a feel for the place, blowing through the burg before I knew it. A general store and a few nearby houses were it, no town to speak of. I backtracked, asked a few questions, but got no answers about where the Hargroves had lived back in the sixties.

Back in my car, I decided to just drive around. Even though it was November, I rolled down the window of the rental car, put my arm on the sill, and breathed in the cool Carolina air. Half a mile later, I saw a road on the left. I took it for no other reason than because it was there. Half a mile on I saw a bearded man standing beside a small frame house. He was splitting wood, but looked up as I drove by. Kochise.

He recognized me and waved, so I stopped and got out. Minutes later, I was inside the house and met Charlotte Hargrove, Joseph's mother. She looked fragile, but the sure grip of her small hand passed to me the sense of a lifetime of hard work done with commitment. In her eyes there was still spirit, but a deep sense of sadness lurked there as well. She poured some tea and began to tell me about Joseph. Later,

I mentioned that I was going back to Cambodia and was trying to find good photographs of the three missing marines. Kochise found the family album, but all Joseph's mother had was one distant shot of Joseph sitting on a couch. It was as if Joseph never had a childhood. No photo of him existed before the age of seventeen. As for her son Lane, who had been killed in Vietnam in 1968, not a single photo existed. Everything had burned up in that fire.

I asked about the old house, and Kochise offered to go with me to the location. We drove there, and I stood in the field where Rudolph had waited for the fire trucks to leave, before he went back to finish the job of burning the house down. Then I dropped Kochise off at his mother's home and headed on my way.

In October 2000, I arranged to meet with Em Son once again. By this time, however, General Noun Sareth had died from cancer. His assistant, Police Colonel Chum Soyath, continued to assist me and arranged for Em Son to be brought to Phnom Penh for an unrestricted interview.

My interpreter, Noma Sarvong, Police Colonel Chum Soyath, and Khem Ngun, a high-ranking ex-Khmer Rouge, met privately with Em Son in Phnom Penh. We gathered on the Goldiana Hotel's fifth-floor patio roof at 1:00 P.M., immediately after my arrival from California. The air was hot and muggy, but at least there was a breeze at that height. I had room service bring up some water and ice. As we broke open the water bottles and poured the contents into ice filled glasses, I studied Em Son. I found myself looking at a one-legged, bullet-riddled, burned-up body of a warrior. This is a man who wakes up every morning, realizing, as he wanders off to empty his bladder, that his leg is gone. Certainly his initial thought every single day is about what war took from him and probably what he took from others. Maybe that is why he had come forward a year ago with his story. He was not getting paid anything for his trouble by JTF-FA, and all I was providing was some expense money for his travel on this occasion.

Before I began the questions, I showed Em Son copies of articles I had recently published about Russian pilots who had fought against Americans in the Korean War and the galleys of another article about North Vietnamese pilots who had shot down squadron mates of mine.

The photos showed Russian and Vietnamese veterans in pleasant poses (as opposed to being led off in chains). The idea was to allay any fear he might have about my purpose in speaking with him. The matter of retribution for Khmer Rouge atrocities is still a hot topic in Cambodia. Khem Ngun was here to protect Em Son's interests. He looked at the articles as well and spoke to Em Son. Whatever misgivings the two of them may have held about me, they accepted my intention to learn the truth. After the first hour of questions, Khem Ngun got bored and left.

I spent three days with the former Khmer Rouge battalion commander, visited the farm in Takeo Province where he grew up, met his sister, great-aunt, and extended family. We stopped by at his temple school, now rebuilt, where he attended classes before being recruited into the Khmer Rouge at age nineteen.

During the same October trip to Cambodia, I went to Koh Tang with four former marines who had fought in the battle. These were the first American veterans to return to the island. Lance Corporal Larry Barnett had been aboard *Knife-23* when its tail got blown off near the east beach. Staff Sergeant Clark H. Hale, Private First Class Curtis D. Myrick, and Private First Class Alfred G. Rogers were all from E Company and had been on the right flank of the west beach. They were able to locate their fighting positions and those of the machine-gun crews. Sergeant Hale, a Vietnam and Koh Tang combat veteran, was the 3rd Platoon sergeant responsible for the men on the right flank. His recollections supported the evidence I had already obtained.

Now I had the details I needed.

32

LAST FULL MEASURE

We have defeated the imperialist Americans and their dog Lon Nol.
Now we save our bullets to kill more. If you do something wrong we
will not shoot you. We have other ways of punishment.

Rhetoric of the Khmer Rouge *Angha*

On the morning following the end of the battle, Em Son had waited until daybreak before mustering his men out of their fighting positions. Everyone was groggy, but in the several hours of quiet since the helicopters quit landing and taking off, a few of his men had gotten some rest. He wondered if the Americans were coming back. He had been in radio contact with the mainland, so he knew the bombing had stopped there and none of the other islands were undergoing any attacks. His brigade commander at Kompong Som instructed Em Son to attempt to capture alive any Americans still on Koh Tang.

He knew of no Americans on the island and doubted there were any left because not a single helicopter had come in for ten hours, and no jet fighters had bombed or strafed since. The Americans appeared to have withdrawn, but to the northeast he saw the big ship, still maneuvering offshore. If they planned to come back, they would do it soon.

Em Son had fewer than sixty men left and not all were able-bodied. Four had been killed by a direct hit on one of his heavy-weapons pits during the first few minutes of the attack, one more was killed a few minutes later, and at least another eight died during the afternoon and evening. These last were found at night and as dawn broke. His medics were treating the wounded, some fifteen men. Most had shrapnel wounds from the strafing. A few were in serious condition and were not expected to live.

Em Son had the east beach covered with what was left of Soeun's company. They had never lost control of that area. The west beach was another matter. As the last of the helicopters were coming in during the night, Heang had lobbed mortar shells in that direction. Then Ki's men advanced. They ran into trip flares, which slowed them down, but only distant counterfire erupted. Most of the shooting came from the planes orbiting overhead. The Khmers waited, lobbed more mortars, then pushed on to several points along the coast, but they ran into heavy counterfire and halted when their ammunition ran low.

Now as it got lighter, Em Son assembled Ki's platoon, spread them out, and had them push off toward the west. Em Son remained at the radio shack while his mortar section laid a round about a hundred yards in front of Ki's line. The Cambodians plodded forward, then hit the dirt as the next round went in closer to the beach.

The troops listened for a response. The rustling of leaves in the trees above was all they heard. Ki's men staggered to their feet and shuffled ahead, moving in their infantrymen's crouch, rifles at the ready, eyes scanning the ground for mines or trip wires.

About 100 meters from the beach shots rang out. Everyone dropped flat. From the sound of it, the firing had been from an M-16, but some of the Khmers carried those. Won, one of the point men, was hit. They returned fire with their AK-47s. Moments later a grenade exploded nearby.

Another of the lead troops had seen the muzzle blast from a single location firing at them from near the beach. Ki used his walkie-talkie and relayed the information back to Em Son.

Em Son passed the word to try to take the American alive. He had Ki deploy his men left and right to encircle the position while Heang lay in some more mortar rounds. Then Ki ordered his men forward to surround the American position. He and Em Son had done the maneuver many times before when they had isolated small pockets of enemy troops on the mainland. According to Em Son, "When I order them what to do, that's exactly what they do."

Ki's men made their way within twenty yards of the American. Word came back that only one man was laying low in a foxhole. On command, the Khmers stood, rifles aimed at the lone American. They shouted orders in Cambodian for the man to surrender. The American seemed dazed. He put his hands up. The closest Khmer used the muzzle of his rifle to indicate that the man should stand, but the American was unable to get to his feet. He lay there hands raised, saying nothing.

One of the Khmers grabbed the weapon the American had, an M-16 with an attached grenade launcher. The launcher was empty. The captive's right leg was bloody just above the knee. The amount and color of dried blood on his trouser leg indicated to the Cambodians that the American had been wounded prior to the recent exchange of fire. The Khmers searched him. Then two men helped carry him toward Em Son's headquarters while Em Son, who had arrived on the scene, and another Khmer went along to guard him.

Ki continued to push north with the rest of the platoon, looking for more Americans. He had not gone far when one of his men came running up. He had found an American M-60 machine-gun a few yards from where the captive American had been taken. He radioed back to Em Son who was still with the prisoner.

After making sure he had his rear protected, Ki continued north and west. The platoon moved through saw grass and Ki found himself peering at what looked like a deserted beach. Equipment was scattered everywhere. Then Ki saw the boots. The soles were sticking from beneath a poncho. Was the man asleep or dead? A Khmer was sent forward. With his AK-47 pointed at the man's torso, the soldier kicked the boots. The body did not move. Another Khmer grabbed the poncho and rolled it open. The body came tumbling out. As the dead man's arm flopped free, Ki noticed the American was black. Another Khmer reached down and tried to remove a watch. He had difficulty because the watchband was stretched tight around the dead man's swollen wrist, but he finally managed to free it.

Em Son returned to the beach. His man searched the pockets of the dead marine, removing their contents. Then Em Son ordered the men to bury the body. One Khmer took hold of the boots and began dragging the body up past the dune into a slight depression. They threw some sand to cover the body. Then Em Son headed back to the headquarters.

Ki pushed north and half an hour later saw the big ship coming around from the north. The Khmers dispersed into the tree line. The crewmen on the *Wilson* were using French, Thai, and rudimentary Khmer, broadcasting over loudspeakers, but the Cambodians on the island could not understand what was being said, or if they did they were unwilling to relay the information. To do so might expose their education and lead to execution.

Ki watched as the *Wilson* moved past. Then it reversed and headed around the point toward the east beach. He radioed Em Son again, telling him about the ship's movement.

Back near headquarters, Em Son got Ki's message. It made him wonder, *Were the Americans preparing to come back?* They had left at least one man on the island, and the big ship did not seem intent on going away, so he guessed they would return. On the other hand, the ship had quit firing at the beach and the planes had not reappeared. Slowly the possibility began to set in. He had nearly been overrun, had lost a lot of men, but his troops had held. As he mulled over the situation, one of his troops came in to report that Won had died from his wounds.

Outside, Khmer troops were gathered around staring at the American who stood silently, leaning on his good leg while peering back at his captors. The prisoner was tall and thin, and had light-colored hair and stubble on his chin. The description by Em Son closely resembled that of Lance Corporal Joseph N. Hargrove (blond hair, six feet tall, 148 pounds). The marine's trouser leg was stained with dried blood. This would indicate the man was wounded during the night. Many possibilities exist to explain how he might have gotten shot, but one can be ruled out. He was *not* wounded prior to the arrival of the last helicopter. If he had, one of the members of the machine-gun team would have made that fact known to Captain Davis or Gunnery Sergeant McNemar during the period of quiet known to have occurred prior to the arrival of that final helicopter. The injured man would have been brought in and loaded aboard a helicopter. What likely *did* happen was that the men were cut off by the heavy volume of friendly fire that occurred as the last helicopter was loading. Since the team was positioned outside Captain Davis's perimeter without his knowledge, neither Davis nor anyone else had any reason to suspect they were there. The shooting would have forced the team to take cover while waiting for the firing to cease, but it may not have stopped soon enough for them to emerge and be recognized as friendlies.

The helicopter engines were roaring close by and sand was being whipped by the rotor blades as air force technical sergeant Fisk made one last exit onto the sand. He saw no more marines. Then a green flare arced overhead. With the thought that it might be a signal for the Khmer Rouge to charge, Fisk hurriedly returned to the helicopter and it departed.

There is a chance that the tall captured marine, possibly Hargrove, was hit by friendly fire during those last chaotic minutes. He would have ducked for cover, and the other two teammates would probably have been unable to bring him to the beach in time. Another possibility is that the Khmer Rouge were attacking at that time, as evidenced by the igniting of the trip flares on the ground and those fired from the 60-mm mortar that Heang was using. Em Son claims that no attack took place at that time since he ordered his men to dig in and fire only at helicopters, due to the shortage of ammunition. Although the Khmer Rouge were dug in, the machine-gun crew probably responded with M-60 and/or M-16 fire. By the time they looked around, the helicopter had lifted off. Hargrove could have been wounded by the Khmers during this exchange.

After Em Son received word that his Khmer Rouge comrade, Won had died from American gunfire, he stood staring at the prisoner.

Another Khmer Rouge soldier described for the JTF-FA interpreter what happened next. "The American did not attempt to run or resist because he was badly wounded in one leg. The cadre [either Em Son or Soeun, but excised from the report] aimed a pistol at the American

[who] held his hands over his head and yelled out '*too she!*' [possibly, 'Don't shoot']. The cadre fired at the American but missed because he was very nervous and trembling. The cadre then called to another Khmer who was armed with an AK-47 rifle and this man shot the American in the thigh. The round to the thigh did not kill the American, and so he shot him again in the chest and the American died."

Em Son's own description of the incident matched the soldier's except he omitted the portion about the errant pistol shot. Later under a different line of questioning, Em Son confirmed that only two members of his unit had pistols, he and Platoon Commander Soeun.

After the execution, Em Son ordered his men to dispose of the body. The American was "dragged beside a mango tree nearby and buried." The location was about two hundred yards from where the JTF-FA had searched in 1995, four years before Em Son had come forward. Em Son's October 2000 admission indicated where the "fruit tree" mentioned in the other reports was really located. The other details from Em Son were as the soldier and other corroborating reports had described.

The question arises as to where the other two, Hall, most likely, and Marshall, were during this period. It is unlikely they would have abandoned Hargrove, if he was indeed the wounded marine, unless ordered to do so. They may have been sent north to try to make contact with the *Wilson,* since they could have heard the loudspeakers blaring over in that direction. If they did go north, then Ki's men would have cut them off from Hargrove when the shooting started. Hall and Marshall would have likely gone into hiding. When the *Wilson* came around to the west beach, Ki's men had already moved in and any attempt by Hall or Marshall to show themselves would have likely been fatal. Em Son was certain that no other Americans were sighted by his men during that time frame.

For a week after the battle, aircraft overflew Koh Tang but stayed high, circling as though doing reconnaissance. Em Son wondered what they were up to, so he had Ki and Soeun continue a heavy schedule of patrols around the island. Each night, the outgoing patrol ate at the main headquarters area near the mango tree, where they had a kitchen. The guard shift would set off from there on the night circuit along the beaches.

On one occasion, upon their return the next morning, a patrol member noticed that their leftovers—crusts of rice and fish remnants—had been disturbed. They paid little heed until it happened a second time. Then they began a systematic search. Within minutes, one of the Cambodians shouted that he had found a footprint. The Cambodians gathered around to look. There in the mud were two sets of prints, one showing the cleatlike tread of an American combat boot. The footprint was huge in size compared to any Cambodian's foot, never mind that the Khmers did not even wear boots. The other set of prints was made by a barefoot man, the size of which could have been Cambodian or otherwise.

An initial search proved fruitless, but for the next several evenings the Khmers set a trap. They positioned armed men in the brush around the compound area and waited. Around midnight, on the second or third night, the moon was bright. The guards heard movement in the jungle. Moments later two men emerged from the trail and made their way toward the food preparation area. The Cambodians jumped from hiding to surround the men. One was tall with dark hair, a big man over six feet and brawny. The other was blond, much shorter and skinny. These matched the features of Private First Class Gary L. Hall (brown hair, six-foot-two, and 220 pounds) and Private Danny G. Marshall (sandy blond hair, five-foot-three, and 130 pounds). The skinny one had an M-16 but did not fire.

Again Em Son was summoned. This time emotions did not get the best of anyone. He radioed Kompong Som and was ordered to deliver the captives to the mainland in the morning.

At dawn the two Americans were loaded aboard a gunboat and headed for Kompong Som. Em Son boarded his own smaller craft and followed.

Once on the mainland, the Cambodians put the prisoners in a car for the short ride up the winding road, past deserted bullet-riddled homes, to the Ti Nean Pagoda overlooking Sihanoukville. A long wall topped with razor wire and broken glass surrounded the temple grounds. A sculptured stone portal manned by sentries barred entry.

The truck ground to a halt at the main entrance while a guard checked identities. Once inside the gate, the two foreigners could certainly smell the incense. It still permeated the wood, the trees, and the stone slabs underfoot even though no Buddhist ceremony had taken place there in many months. What was left of the temple stood in the center of the compound. Its dormered spire, blackened by fire, jutted from the top. Its gold paint lay faded and peeling on partially demolished walls. For Khmer Rouge purposes, it was the perfect place for their needs, high above the town, out of earshot.

The two new arrivals were taken outside monks' cells on the ground floor of the priory.

A cadre leader named Ieng barked an order. A soldier signaled each of the new prisoners to remove their outer clothing and boots. The two men sat and undid their laces, then slipped off their combat boots. Then they removed their trousers and uniform shirts. They stood, dressed only in skivvies and green T-shirts as another Khmer slapped irons around the big one's ankles. The two irons were connected by a chain and locked. The small one was shackled in like manner and placed inside an adjacent cell where a fetid odor confronted them as they stumbled into the dark, humid spaces. The windowless rooms had drawn and locked shutters on the doors.

An empty ammunition can sat in the corner of each room. It was the source of the foul aroma. No doubt they had just smelled their toilets.

Two men, boys really, guarded the cell block, and while the new prisoners waited, other captives were brought into different cells and removed at various times during the day and night. Screams were heard. The two Americans probably tried to talk to the guards, but low-ranking troops who showed any inclination to speak a word of English would be marked as reactionary and executed for bourgeois appearances.

More than a week later, a final decision was made in Phnom Penh. The two Americans had their hands tied behind them with heavy wire and were brought to the temple one at a time. The big one was led in first. The temple was barren of any religious symbols. He must have smelled the fear, the vomit, must have seen the bloodstains, the AK-47s leaning against the wall, the grenade launchers. They pulled him forward and bound him to a chair. There was no need to worry about security regulations, no need for questions. They had all the answers they cared about. They had their orders. The cadre reached for the barrel of a B-40 grenade launcher. He raised the launcher, readying it for the first blow, in the approved Pol Pot manner, not wasting ammunition. The impact landed with a bone-jarring *thwack*. Then the Khmer struck again. Blood seeped out the victim's ears, nose, and mouth.

They took the ankle chains off the big one, dragged him outside by the feet, then loaded him into the trunk of the car. The cadre rode in the cab as they drove slowly north along the beach road in the dark. The vehicle's headlights swept the deserted pavement ahead until they approached the shore at its closest point, where the leader ordered a stop. They muscled the body out of the trunk and began dragging it through saw grass toward the beach. As they struggled with their load, a guard went ahead, only to return moments later to report that there was a cliff. They'd be unable to dump the remains into the water. The Khmer leader decided to bury the body, so one of them got a shovel from a nearby hootch. A shallow grave was dug. They dumped the big one in face up. After the dirt was shoveled over him, both feet still protruded from the soil. The men threw dirt and rocks over the feet.

Then they went back for the small one. He was led to the temple. The cadre raised the weapon's barrel in front of the man. The small one with the yellow hair lifted his shoulder to protect his head. Down came the barrel, glancing off the small one's upper arm. Again and again, blows rained down until the small one lay slumped in the chair. Blood and mucus streamed from his nose.

This time they took a different route, turning south to avoid the cliff. They stopped near the beach and hauled the body through thick brush to shore. The Khmers pushed it into the surf near where the battalion commander kept his boat.

The next day, the body of the small one washed up on shore. They pushed it seaward again but it continued to come in with the tide. By the third day, it was bloated, and the smell carried for half a mile. Em Son noticed the odor, saw the body of the small one, now naked, beached at the south edge of the shoreline. He took a length of rope, tied it to the small one's legs, and towed the body along the shallow surf, until he passed a rocky outcropping. He dragged the body onto the sand between two large volcanic boulders, up to where the rocks parted and formed an alcove. There he tied the end of the rope to vines that overhung the rocks and left.

A month later, he checked the grotto. Bones, still held to the vines by the rope, were bleaching in the sun.

33

END OF THE *MAYAGUEZ* INCIDENT

We had entered Indochina to save a country, and ended by rescuing a ship.

Henry Kissinger

The fate and resting place of the last American servicemen who gave full measure for their country during the Vietnam War might have remained unknown outside Cambodia had it not been for the pursuit of information regarding missing-in-action by members of the Joint Task Force for Full Accounting (JTF-FA), the American embassy in Phnom Penh, and the voluntary contribution of information made by numerous Cambodians.

On March 9, 1999, the tenth mission seeking remains from the *Mayaguez* Incident got under way. Nine men and one woman took part, and everyone wielded axe, shovel, and trowel in addition to doing their primary tasks. On this, my fourth, assignment to Cambodia, we lived mostly out of backpacks, dining on tins of tuna fish and sardines spread on saltine crackers. The temperature was 104 degrees in the shade, 126 degrees in the sun, and most of the work was in the sun. I lost seven pounds the first week, even though I was drinking two to three gallons of water a day—and not doing heavy manual labor. The team members lost even more weight. Archaeologic digs were completed at five locations on Koh Tang, and all had proven devoid of human remains. Everyone had hands and arms covered with raised blisters and open sores from red-ant bites. The team had two encounters with deadly snakes and a third with a green-striped variety whose lethality remained undetermined. The area was not only "hot" in terms of temperature and vipers, but unexploded ordnance was still scattered throughout the island. By the seventeenth day without a find, the team was running on empty.

We moved to the Cambodian mainland on March 26, 1999, and began excavating the sites where bodies of two of the captured marines bodies were left, described during the initial interview with Em Son a few days earlier.

This search began in a grassy field near a dilapidated building. A weathered sign above the oval structure read in English, VICTORY SIDE. Em Son walked into the field, got his bearings, and pointed at the ground, claiming "the big one" had been buried there. After the grass was cleared away, forensic anthropologist Dr. John Byrd tested the soil. He got a litmus reading of 5.5 acidic (a 7.0 litmus is neutral). "One of the most acidic soils I've encountered so far," Dr. Byrd said. "Not a good sign." Bones decay rapidly in acidic soil, he pointed out.

Dr. Byrd dropped to his knees and began carefully troweling the surface, exposing the earth beneath. Sweat stained his khakis as he scraped away layer after layer. A macabre outline, dark and shaped like a human silhouette, emerged on the excavation floor. "A burial pit," Dr. Byrd said.

The pit corresponded nearly exactly in terms of size, shape, and orientation to Em Son's description of the one that he had dug in 1975. After a little more scraping, the silhouette disappeared. What had been found was the bottom of the pit. The rest, with the bones, was no longer present. Dr. Byrd stood. "From what the witness said, we won't find much here." He wiped his brow, then pointed downslope. "That's where we'll find remains, probably leg bones, if we find anything." A road grader was known to have partially leveled the area some years before, and dirt had been shoved down the incline. Because the witness described the marine's feet as being very near the surface when buried, Dr. Byrd expected the leg bones to have been the first to be disturbed by the earthmover.

An hour later what was thought to be a human fibula (lower leg bone) was unearthed downslope. "The fibula is a uniquely human bone of the size we found here," noted Dr. Byrd. An ominous-looking set of hand manacles made from wire cable was found nearby. A few other small pieces of bone were found in the area, but none of them appeared to be large enough to provide a satisfactory mitochondria DNA sample. About an inch and a half is required, along with enough density to allow impurities to be removed from the surface. From all indications, we had found the remains of Private First Class Gary L. Hall, but JTF-FA might not be able to prove it scientifically.

The next morning, I went to the Ti Nean Pagoda, located high on a promontory above Sihanoukville, wondering if I would be able to verify the brutality of Em Son's testimony. The temple grounds, restored in recent years by local labor and both local and foreign contributions, included a new administration building. A Buddha statue was back inside the rebuilt temple now. The razor wire was gone, and monks of all ages dressed in saffron robes once again walked the paths, their amblings adding a mystical irony to the scene that had once been a human slaughterhouse.

When I tried my shaky Thai on a group of monks, an older one piped right up in fluent Thai. I asked him about the history of the place during the war, and he confirmed that the Khmer Rouge had used the temple grounds for interrogations and killings during the revolution. "They killed all the monks and countless other Cambodians here and buried them in a mass grave nearby," he told me. I asked about Americans, but he had no information. The only building still standing from before the Khmer Rouge period was the monks' quarters where Hall and Marshall were probably imprisoned. Even that structure had been given a makeover.

I left the temple at 10:30 A.M. and rode in a van along the second route the Khmer Rouge had taken the night of the executions. Then I got out, walked the path to the southern beach, passed a relatively new open-air restaurant, and some fifty yards farther across the sand, came to the alcove Em Son had mentioned.

Three men from JTF and a group of Cambodian workers were already at the site. Army major Ronald Stafford headed the operation. Stafford is a bull of a man, capable of strenuous physical work. I had seen him dig with a passion, fell trees, and fill buckets with sand when most officers of his rank might simply have stood by and supervised. In spite of his penchant for manual labor, he had never once lost an ounce of respect from the other team members. At one point, he had been digging with his gloved hand and broke through an underground lair of one of those aforementioned deadly snakes. Even the Cambodians recoiled when the animal came slithering out in a fury. Stafford killed the thing with his shovel, then dropped back into the hole as he said, "Wonder where its brother is?" He gave me an uncertain smile as he began searching for remains again.

With him now on the mainland this day were Army sergeant Scott Richardson, team photographer, and Marine gunnery sergeant Vincent P. Owsley, the explosive ordnance disposal (EOD) technician. Richardson had contracted malaria on a previous mission in Laos, but had recuperated enough for this trip. Owsley had recently recovered from a bout of skin cancer, so he kept himself well covered, even in the intense heat.

The Cambodians constituted the bucket brigade, hauling sand to the lone screening table that had been strung up by Gunny Owsley across a rock crevasse. The ever-present guard watched the activity from under the shade of a palm tree, his AK-47 slung by its web belt over his shoulder, a cigarette dangling from his lips.

As I worked my way atop a large, flat protrusion that jutted out to sea, I checked the screening table manned by the gunny. Nothing of significance had been brought up all morning.

Just then, Stafford called for a break. Built like a linebacker, the major clanged his shovel against the shear rock face and took off his gloves. He shoved his hat a little higher on his brow as he leaned against a massive boulder, tilted his head back, and stared off into space. Sweat ran in rivulets from his forehead onto his cheeks and neck, then onto his already soaked shirt. Huge dark stains circled his fatigue armpits. His expression betrayed the thought, *This is bullshit*!

I had the feeling he was getting close to packing it in. He was the senior man in the operation and also the hardest working, but he had not been onboard back when the *Brunswick* salvage ship had come to Cambodia. He had not seen what happened on the island. I approached Stafford, out of earshot of the others, and spoke. "In 1995, it wasn't until the team pulled the wreckage to the beach that the stuff started coming up. They had to suck sand from deep underneath the helicopter rubble. A hundred sixty-one bones: teeth, arms, leg bones, everything came out."

The major remained intent on whatever he was contemplating. A few moments passed; without looking down, he slowly started putting on his gloves. A huge sigh, almost a moan, slipped from his lips as he grabbed the shovel and began digging by himself around the base of a nearby rock. He dug, obviously boiling inside, until he had filled all the empty buckets nearby. He brought up nothing but sand. With no more empties, he called the men back onto the bucket brigade, then moved to another point where a large boulder had split, creating a wedge-shaped notch. He jammed the shovel in the small opening but the blade was too wide, so he flung it aside and dropped to his knees.

I peered over as he started pulling sand from between the rocks, using only his gloved hands. The tensing and uncoiling of his back muscles, visible through his taut shirt, betrayed the bitterness he felt for me, the meddler, the pain in the ass. He filled three buckets and handed them to Richardson, who passed them to the Cambodians. The major continued pulling sand from the hole, his torso almost totally disappearing as he clawed at the loose wet muck. Then he slowed. His head turned ever so slightly. "Wait," he muttered. "There's a niche in here." He reached down with only one hand now, his face still turned, his mind and body bent to the task. "Did you find any coral attached to the bones found at Koh Tang?" he asked.

"No," I answered, "but lots of loose coral came up *with* the bones."

He filled another bucket and shoved it toward Richardson, then started on the next. Up it went, but Richardson paused before passing this last one on. "Take a look at this, Major." Richardson reached into the bucket and lifted something. It was small, curved, and toned the color of stained glass. He set the bucket down and with a voice filled with release, tension, joy, and sorrow he shouted, "That's bone, Major, that's bone!"

The major stood, took the fragment, and turned it over in his hand, then reached for his cell phone. Five minutes later the anthropologist, Dr. John Byrd, arrived. "Definitely could be human," he said after closely examining it. Byrd touched his arm, near the shoulder. "Humerus, the upper arm bone, busted up pretty good."

"The orneriest little white boy the Waverlians ever seen" had fought his heart out to the very end. He had probably raised his arm and shoulder to fend off the blows. No matter how hard the Khmer Rouge tried to erase the evidence of what they had done to him, even in death he simply refused to let that happen. Danny Marshall's toughness showed one more time.

Back in Long Beach, I waited while the Central Identification Lab in Hawaii tried to make a determination from the pieces of bone that had been found on the Cambodian mainland. After a few months, I checked with Dr. Byrd. "The bones are too small for the DNA test. By the way, we found several more small pieces at the site by the monument. We're hanging on to all of them in case some new science comes along that allows us to get a sequence with less bone matter."

We had a burial pit, a credible eye witness, bones, and a stack of other witness testimony in support, but no way to positively identify which marine had been killed where.

I decided to try another approach. If I could get Em Son to identify the marines he claimed to have seen, maybe that would clear up any ambiguities about what happened. To get photos for this purpose, I decided to go to Covington, Kentucky, the hometown of Gary Hall, and also to Waverly, West Virginia, where Danny Marshall grew up. I had no addresses, so before leaving I tried the Internet white pages and came up with a phone number of Gary's mother, Norma Hall. When I called, a man answered and said the Halls had moved, location unknown. With such a common name, I knew it was not going to be easy finding her, but after an hour on the phone using the Internet directory, I finally got lucky. Gary's sister Jane answered, acknowledged her relationship, and told me the original number I had called for Norma Hall was accurate, but one of Gary's brothers lived there and protected his mother's privacy. I had a phone number and an address, but no one wanted to talk.

When I arrived in Covington, Kentucky, I went to Holmes High School, the only high school I could find listed in the phone book. There, in the school library, I went through the yearbooks from the early seventies until I found Gary's picture in the 1974 volume. The librarian helped me go over the list of Gary's classmates in the hope of locating one or two who still lived in the area. That is how I found one of Gary's friends, David Jones. He told me that the Halls used to live on Banklick and he knew their current address. He was certain Norma Hall would like to talk to me.

I drove to the street where Gary Hall's mother now resided. She lived next to a store, which was on the corner and had absolutely no sign outside to indicate what kind of business was conducted within. I stared at Norma Hall's two-story home for the longest time, then went into the shop. It was a convenience store run by an Iranian man. I bought a Snickers bar, went back outside and munched on it, trying to decide what to do.

My chocolate fix complete, I opened the gate to her house, walked up the steps, and knocked.

Norma Hall came to the door. She stood there, all small and delicate, as I struggled for words. I told her I was a writer who had gone to Cambodia in search of what happened to Gary and two other MIAs from the war. She peered through the screen, her eyes roaming over me, her expression unchanged for what seemed like an eternity. As a writer, I well understood inspection and rejection, but this was different. I was sure rejection would cut deep.

"Come on in," she finally said, almost in a whisper.

Seated in the tiny living room, Norma Hall showed me pictures of Gary, but none in uniform, none with a crew cut. She showed me a photo of Sheldon, Gary's father, who had died the past November. He did not look all that fearsome, but then I was not a little kid looking up at him. I listened as she thanked me for my interest in her son. Then I told her I had learned that he helped save his marine buddies that terrible night. I was quite certain how Gary had died, but thought it best the Marine Corps take care of delivering that news. She cried three times while I was there.

When I got to Waverly, West Virginia, I had even less to go on than with the Covington search. The town consisted of a gas stop, post office, and library scattered among houses built along the Ohio River. I stopped at the post office and asked if anyone knew where the Marshalls had lived in the seventies. No one knew. I had been lucky with high schools in Covington, so I asked where a teen back in the seventies might have attended school around here.

"St. Mary's is closest," came the answer. I drove east past the power plant and found the building five miles from Waverly. School records showed Danny had attended for three months, but he did not appear in any of the yearbooks. As I was about to leave, a clerk overheard me asking about Danny Marshall. She remembered the story about him dying during the war. She knew of a childhood friend, Teleah Cross. We found Teleah's number in the phone book, but no one picked up when we dialed, and no answering machine clicked on, even after seven or eight rings.

My next stop was Williamstown High, which was in the other direction. On the way, I decide to drop in at the public library in Waverly. The librarian there helped me find another of Danny's childhood playmates, Roger McPherson. I called and Roger agreed to talk to me later in the day.

At Williamstown High, I learned that Danny managed to finish his sophomore year in 1974, but that yearbook was missing. No photo. I went from there to my interview with McPherson and got my first glimpse of Danny's troubled childhood. I also found out where Danny lived in the block house on Second Street.

That night, I tried calling Teleah again from my motel near the highway. She answered with a raspy voice, sounding older than she should be. Teleah agreed to an interview and gave me her address. "Look for the red pickup," she said, then hung up.

When I got out of my rental car, a sturdy figure of a man approached from around the side of the house.

His chin shot forward. "What can I do fer you?" he said, without the slightest hint of friendliness.

I told him I had come to see Teleah.

He started walking toward the front door. "Wait right here. If she wants to see you, I'll send her out."

She wanted to.

I was led around the outside of the house. On the back porch, she sat me down and lit a cigarette. After my call, she told me she had gone tearing through the house looking for her scrapbook with Danny's picture in it, but could not find it. Then, as mosquitoes had a feast on my arms, legs, and neck, she told me all about Danny.

When she finished, she looked at me. "You'd think after twenty-five years I'd be over it . . . but I ain't." Teleah also cried three times.

The next morning I drove to Parkersburg, West Virginia, to try to get a photo of Danny. The county courthouse and jail were located there. According to the interviews with Teleah and Roger, Danny had spent time there. I figured they might have a decent mug shot. Could I get a copy? After a few dead ends encountered while poking my head in various offices at the county seat, I was directed to the detention center.

I entered the one-story brick building and looked around. The foyer had several chairs, all occupied by women. Each pair of eyes turned away as I scanned the group. To my right was a bulletproof window. On the other side stood shapely Captain Myers, a blond-headed cop who oozed authority, but was easy on the eyes, nonetheless.

"Can I help you?" she asked.

"I'm trying to get a mug shot of a resident who got in trouble in 1974. A juvenile."

"A juvenile?" Her eyebrows rose. "I can't give you that."

"He died in 1975."

Her words, spoken slowly, clearly expressed the idea that she was dealing with a journalistic bumpkin. "You'll need a court order."

"How do I get one?"

She smiled, pointed her finger out the door, and said, "Courthouse," as though any idiot would know you get a court order at a courthouse. I walked across the plaza toward the building Captain Myers had indicated, wondering if I was violating any privacy laws. I knew ignorance of the law was no legal defense, but if my quest was carried out strictly within the legal system, I assumed I would soon be told if my effort was leading into trouble.

Ten minutes later, I was seated in the chambers of Judge George W. Hall. I had no idea if the judge was a veteran or what his background might be, but he listened intently without saying a word until I finished explaining my purpose. Then he called out, "Linda!"

In popped his honor's steno. "Draw up a court order for this here feller, and I'll sign it."

Five minutes after that, with court order in hand, I was directed to the basement records section where the staff began showing the thing around like it was a winning lottery ticket. They searched for hours but found no photo. In the process, I did confirm that Danny had had a juvenile record.

I was scheduled to fly back to California the next afternoon, so I went back to Williamstown High hoping they might have found the 1974 yearbook, but they had not. I tried the local newspaper office, where I was directed to the town library. There I located an article on microfiche, but the accompanying photo was of such poor quality, it was not worth copying.

The next morning Teleah called at dawn. She had found the photo album. If I could stop by right then, she would let me have a look before she had to get to work.

The album contained the same photograph I had seen at the library, but to my delight, this one was in excellent condition. I took a snapshot of the newspaper clipping I had seen on fiche. While there, we also figured out where Danny's mother, Faye, who had remarried, now resided. Then I left for Faye Marshall's place.

Parking in front of the house where Danny's mother lived brought back memories of the session with Norma Hall. A late-model car was parked in the driveway, and since it was the weekend, I was pretty sure someone was inside the house. I waited a few minutes, staring at the front door, almost hoping it would open and someone would wave me inside. Finally, I went to the door and pressed the bell. It chimed inside, but no one came to the door. I walked around to the side of the house, passed the car, and looked to see if someone was in the backyard. No luck there. I tried one more time at the front door, but no one answered. I began to wonder if the local rumor mill had been efficient enough to alert the woman to my presence and purpose in town.

After hanging around for another twenty minutes, I drove off, relieved that I did not have to make another person cry.

Considering what these families have and continue to endure, whatever small stipend the government gives them, it is not nearly enough.

In October, 2000, I went back to Cambodia, where I reinterviewed Em Son. We went over details regarding the two American captives buried on the mainland. When I asked about the third marine, he took a long time before answering. Although I certainly did not understand Cambodian, Em Son, for the first time in our conversations, appeared more deliberate as he resumed speaking. His forehead began to glisten. The particulars were specific and matched the collected accounts from previous witnesses. The brutality of what happened and his involvement in it were clear. I felt unsettled, stomach churning, by the time he finished. I had gotten to know the missing marines' pasts and met some of their relatives; mentally I had adopted the three as my own. Discussions of their deaths had become personal to me. I felt anger, too, but Em Son was no headquarters hack. He was tip-of-the-spear personified, a grunt soldier who fought in the trenches. I had to give him credit for that. In the end, I was more overcome by a deep sense of sadness at hearing how human lives were destroyed for nothing. "Quiz 'em and kill 'em" was the Khmer Rouge method with prisoners, and since they were finished questioning the Americans or had not bothered, there was only one thing left to do.

I asked if he knew how valuable POWs were—remember, the *Mayaguez* Incident was in 1975, so the 1973 POW release from Vietnam and all its hoopla were common knowledge in most of the world—but Em Son knew nothing about that, nor had he any inkling about the political value of POWs. They took few prisoners during his whole military career. Too much hassle.

I showed him a collection of pictures I had made up, including the three missing marines. He paused for a long time only once, over Gary Hall's photo. From the way he delayed, staring long and hard at the photo but being careful not to betray a change of expression, I could tell his mind was contemplating a course of action. A moment later he looked at the next photo. I would have bet a month's pay a memory had been jarred loose.

Em Son went on to tell about the killing of the third Marine on the island, disclosing that this one was buried on the west side of Koh Tang by a mango tree near his island headquarters, an admission he had not previously made to the JTF. Upon my return to California, I relayed the new information to JTF headquarters in Hawaii. They sent a team to Cambodia to check on these details. From that interview, another mission was scheduled for January 2001.

In mid-December, I called the public affairs office in Hawaii and asked if I could accompany the team. I wanted to be on site if there was a chance that either Joseph Hargrove or Ashton Loney's remains might be recovered. Since I had provided the information being used to determine the dig sites, headquarters agreed to let me travel with the team.

On January 5, 2001, I joined forty-five personnel of the JTF-FA recovery team in Hawaii aboard an air force C-117 cargo aircraft. We launched for Guam, crossed the date line, refueled, then headed for U-Tapao in Thailand. We tried our best to sleep on the floor of the cargo bay, your basic aluminum mattress.

I had visited the Central Identification Lab in Hawaii the previous day. There, I had been told only one site was to be worked on the island, not two as I had thought, based on Em Son's October testimony. Try as I might, I could get no clear answers to my queries.

On the C-117, I continued discussions with interpreter Master Sergeant Joe Fraley and Mr. Joel Patterson, the JTF-FA people who had re-interviewed Em Son after my October session. Em Son had been uncooperative with them, so they talked with other witnesses and took several to the island. A former low-ranking Khmer Rouge soldier, Mao Run, pointed to where he had heard a marine was buried. That location was on the east beach. I had serious doubts about the success of the mission if the only site they were going to work was on the east beach, and was based on hearsay testimony. My mind was in turmoil as we hurtled along at 500 miles an hour, bound for a destination that I was fast realizing was hopelessly wrong.

We stayed overnight at Pattaya Beach, Thailand. The following morning, the public affairs officer from Hawaii, Lieutenant Colonel Franklin Childress, and I, plus four JTF members departed from U-Tapao—me to do an interview, and Childress to set up a VIP visit—ahead of the team in a C-130 turboprop bound for Phnom Penh. I had to convince someone that the current recovery concept was flawed, someone with the clout to change things. I began working out a plan.

Upon arrival, I contacted Noma Sarvong, my interpreter, to find out about a scheduled follow-up interview I had arranged with Em Son. "The rules have changed," he told me, "because of the tribunals Prime Minister Hun Sen is setting up to try Khmer Rouge leadership." International and internal pressure was being applied to Hun Sen, in part because the surviving Khmer Rouge leaders were now in Phnom Penh and Pailin, living in modern homes with servants and being driven around in fancy sedans.

For my October meeting with Em Son, Khem Ngun, a former high ranking Khmer Rouge, had escorted him to my hotel. Khem Ngun is one of my go-betweens for contacting witnesses. He is also used by the Hun Sen faction to negotiate with the Khmer Rouge leadership, including the notorious Khieu Samphan, Nuon Chea, Ieng Sary and his wife Thirith, and army commanders, Ta Mok and Ke Pauk. According to Noma Sarvong, ordinary Khmer Rouge have been ordered to keep quiet about the past. If our meeting was to take place at all, it must be held in private. Em Son's location was secret as he was being kept in a safe house. Arrangements were being made by Noma Sarvong using cell phones.

The next morning, I got word from Noma Sarvong that Em Son would talk to me. He would be brought to my hotel room at 6:30 P.M. I had intended to do the session in private, but decided to allow Lieutenant Colonel Childress to sit in on the interview. If I could get Em Son to relate what he had told me in October, Childress might be able to sway some opinions regarding where to dig. I called Childress at his hotel and invited him to attend, but not at the start of the interview, only after I had gotten Em Son "comfortable." I mentioned I would introduce him to Em Son as an Army officer interested in the battle. No mention of JTF-FA would be made. For Childress, it was his first visit to Cambodia and he got excited about meeting a former Khmer Rouge. Childress agreed to come to the hotel at around 7:30 P.M. and phone my room.

Em Son and Noma Sarvong arrived early, minus Khem Ngun. I had set up chairs and a table, put out glasses, Cokes, Ankhor and Heineken beers, plus chilled water. No tape recorder was in sight or used. Noma even asked about it, but I wanted Em Son totally relaxed. My notebook was not even open. Em Son poured a Coke. For an hour, I asked questions I had prepared to clarify aspects of Em Son's early life, about the role of women in the Khmer Rouge and such. Then I opened my notepad to where I had drawn a detailed map of Koh Tang. Right on time, Childress called. Quietly I told him to come up, but not to ask any questions until I gave the okay. He agreed.

Childress was introduced and pulled up a chair. We began talking about the combat on May 15th. Then I asked about the morning after the last battle. Em Son became more excited, louder. He related the incident involving the combat and death of the lone marine, but now claimed that the man died of wounds at the scene of the firefight. I asked about the mango tree burial. Em Son appeared flustered, his expression betraying that I had caught him in a lie. He waffled, coming back with, "Oh, yes, we carried the man to the mango tree, and he died *there* of wounds."

Confused, I rubbed my forehead. "What about the guy you said used the AK-47 to shoot the man?"

"No," said Em Son, his voice even more agitated, "he died of wounds." He took my pen and marked the burial site on my map, "Fifty meters or less from the mango tree, where the terrain is a bit rolling."

Then I asked Em Son the key question, "Did you tell this to the JTF-FA interviewer a few weeks ago?"

"No," he said, after some hesitation.

Childress leaned toward me and whispered, "This isn't my job. There'll be some bruised egos if I jump in with this info."

I shrugged. "The team is coming six thousand miles to dig in the wrong place?"

Now Childress held the hand grenade. Would he pull the pin and cause an explosion at JTF headquarters or just toss it away, unarmed?

The next morning, I left in a van for Kompong Som, part of a caravan to the coast, wondering what Childress would do with the information from the interview. He had to stay in Phnom Penh until the 13th, when he intended to escort the current Pacific commander in chief, Admiral Blair, to the island.

Security on Route 4 was tight, tighter than ever before. We had a truck full of troops with us. When we stopped to take a break along the highway, the soldiers dispersed along the road, weapons at the ready.

This was a no-nonsense operation, but quite unnecessary since the Khmer Rouge would not try anything against us in an armed caravan.

I had an uneasy feeling that Khem Ngun's Khmer Rouge cronies were trying to figure out a response to the government attempt to bring them to justice. If their warped thinking involved planning a kidnapping or worse, they could do it in Kompong Som. The Khmer Rouge knew which hotel we always stayed in.

At the Seaside Hotel in Kompong Som, for added safety, I asked for a second floor room in the middle of the hall. It would be harder to snatch me, and I could exit via the window to a ledge and then a short jump.

On Thursday, January 11, 2001, I traveled to Koh Tang aboard a Lao West Coast helicopter piloted by New Zealander Eric Thum. Once on the island, I followed the team to the site where Mao Run had told them the marine had fought, died, and was buried. It was located at the extreme southern edge of the east beach. The chance that one of the machine gun crew crossed the island, twice made his way through Khmer Rouge lines and wet marshlands to this point, was pure fantasy.

Anthropologist Richard Wills pointed at the site. "Does this agree with your research as being where we might find remains?"

"No," I said.

Wills looked west. "How could he have gotten all the way over here from the west beach?"

How indeed.

At 3:00 P.M., I arrived back at the hotel, napped, then went to Feuilles, a small French restaurant around the corner. When I returned to the hotel, Em Son was in the lobby talking through an interpreter with Richard Wills and Captain Angel Velez, the JTF team leader. Childress had come through, bless his heart, and forgive my designing mind.

Em Son looked tense. Then he saw me approach and his face brightened with a toothy grin as he extended his hand.

I joined them, and Em Son told about the fight on the island with the lone marine. This time he admitted that the marine killed one of his guys, Won, of whom he thought highly. Won had been point man on the squad that the marine had fired upon. His injuries were severe, and a short time later when Em Son learned that Won had succumbed to his wounds, the execution took place, or in the current version, the marine suddenly died of wounds sustained in battle. Now we had reasoning behind the execution that may have occurred near the mango tree. Next, Em Son described the discovery of Lance Corporal Ashton Loney's body on the beach.

Richard Wills took notes as he listened to the account. Wills decided he wanted Em Son to go to the island to show the locations. I mention I had a photo of Loney's body lying on the beach.

Wills's jaw dropped. "You have what?"

Later, back in my room, Wills looked at the 1975 photo I had obtained from marine veteran Gale Rogers. I had scanned it into my lap top. It showed Ashton Loney, lying prone on the west beach, his body wrapped in a poncho, his boots exposed.

"You've just become a source," Wills said. He now had indisputable evidence of where the body was left. I had provided the image to JTF a year ago, but it was probably sitting in a file back in Hawaii.

On Friday, 12 January 2001, Em Son arrived by helicopter on the island at 11:00 A.M. Master Sergeant Joe Fraley was with him. Joel Patterson landed forty minutes later on a following flight.

Patterson informed me that the information Childress had relayed forward had caused them to be pulled off their assigned mission. They had returned to Phnom Penh two days ago to interview Em Son once again. "He didn't want to talk about this incident [the killing on the west beach]. He's afraid of being picked up for trial during the tribunals. I told him, 'Look, we have always delivered on our promises in the past. Nothing is going to happen to you over this. We are only interested in remains.'" Em Son had finally agreed to talk to them about the incident, except, as mentioned, the execution had now become "died of wounds."

Em Son led the way from the west beach, where the engagement on May 16 took place. He pointed to the spot where Ashton Loney's body was found. It jibed with the Gale Rogers photo. Then he indicated where he remembered the body later being buried. Next, we shoved our way into the jungle along a narrow trail, heading toward the former Khmer Rouge headquarters. About half way there, we stopped at a site where Em Son claimed the marine died and was buried. He tapped a decaying stump with his crutch, saying that it was all that was left of the mango tree. The terrain was rolling, just like he had told me earlier.

Master Sergeant Joe Fraley listened as Em Son explained what happened. Fraley turned to me. "This is the fourth time I've interviewed this guy. First time I'm hearing this. It's getting a little embarrassing." Bruised egos to the forefront. Fraley continued, "When I told him that Mao Run described this incident as occuring on the east beach, he said, 'Mao Run only heard about this. I was here.'"

Richard Wills asked Fraley if showing pictures of the three missing marines might be helpful, but he warned that he had only photos of the three MIAs, so it may not be proper, based on rules of evidence. Fraley decided it could not hurt at this point, so the photo stack was produced. Em Son looked through the pictures and stopped at one of Hall, one I had not seen before. This photo showed Hall without a hat, sitting on a bunk. Em Son positively identified "the man with dark hair" as one of the three captives. Now, however, he thought Hall was the one who died on the west beach. In October, he had identified the American buried there as blond, medium height. The two marines that were taken to the mainland were described as "the big one, tanned [but not Negroid], dark hair, and the small, skinny blond one." My thinking was, if it were Marshall and Hargrove who were taken to the mainland, he would have described them as "tall" and "short, both with blond hair." Hargrove was slim. The fact that he used "big" instead of "tall" led me to believe he had switched them in his mind, placing Hall's death on the island. Hargrove had an M-16 as did the marine killed on Koh Tang. Only one M-16 was on the two marines who were later captured. Marshall had an M-16 while Hall had only a .45 caliber pistol. In spite of the possible confusion, Em Son on two occasions, in October and here in the jungle, showed interest in photos of Hall, so I had to give weight to his identification. If Em Son was telling the truth, a proper dig should clear up the issue, since there is a good chance a full set of remains, including dog tags, may be found.

The JTF team staked out both sites, took photos, then headed back to the east beach. As Patterson waited for the helicopter to lift him to the mainland, he walked over, cigarette in hand. I thought I was about to get a lecture.

"You know," he said, "you're a breath of fresh air around here."
I was struck speechless.

He continued, "If the team finds anything on the west beach, and there's a good chance of that, it will be because of you."

For five years we had maintained a sort of professional toleration, he doing the dangerous task of rooting through the countryside to interview Khmer Rouge in search of information about remains, and me nosing around behind him to find out about the often disturbing things that happened during and after the last battle. Now, I had clearly crossed into his business and he took no offense. This was no small accommodation between two men.

The decision on whether to dig these two sites rested at the headquarters in Hawaii since the new locations were not on the schedule. They could authorize the digs on this trip or slip them to next year. If JTF-FA included it in this cycle, they would likely have to extend the mission. I was pleased, though I did need to get home to California, so my publisher could reach me regarding updates to this manuscript, which we had anticipated doing prior to my departure for Cambodia.

Back in town that evening, I finally figured out a way to send and receive email at the local phone company site in Sihanoukville. To my surprise, Teleah Cross, Danny's childhood friend, had emailed me:

Dear Mr. Wetterhahn
I don't know if you remember me or not, but I'm the person you talked to in Williamstown, W.V. about Danny Marshall. I just wanted to know if you found out any more info on Danny, Joe and Gary on your last trip. I talked to Danny's brother this fall when he came in and he has talked to all his sisters and his brother and they are not going to tell their mother anything about what I found on the Wall on the Web, or about what you are trying to do. Somewhere in her mind she still thinks Danny is alive, and somehow that is the only thing that keeps her going. I understand how they feel. I watched my mother and father go through hell when my

brother passed away in 1980. But I guess if
you don't know all there is to know it makes
it a little more easy to deal with.

But whatever you have found out, I would
like very much to know, because I would like
to know what has happened to my Dear Friend
Danny G. Marshall.

I replied that I was in Cambodia, observing the current recovery effort. When I got back to the hotel, Captain Velez informed me that JTF in Hawaii has just approved the two new digs on the west beach, time permitting.

On Tuesday, January 16, 2001, I caught a helicopter ride to the island and spent the day roaming the west beach. I located the bunker position where the Khmer Rouge took on Lieutenant McDaniel's patrol. Shell casings were scattered everywhere. Perfect spot for an ambush.

Six days went by with slow progress being made on the east beach site. A little note from Teleah was awaiting me in Sihanoukville.

Dear Ralph,
First I want to thank you for writing back so
soon and all the info you gave me, the info
was a little harder to take than I thought it
would be because this means at last My Dear
Friend is gone and will never be coming home
again. On May 15th, it will be 26 years that
have gone by not knowing. Maybe on May 15th
this year we can lay Danny to rest at last
and just remember the good times we all had
growing up in that little town. I miss him
even more now than before, now that you think
his remains have been found, because if in
fact they are Danny's, that means it is all
over and that we know where he is, well at
least hope he is with God.

But I would like to ask you a small favor,
is there anyway before you come back to the

States could you place some flowers on the
grave site with a little note (Danny, Love
You and Miss You, Teleah) it would mean so
much to me for him to have something from
someone from home.

> Thank You Very Much,
> Teleah Cross

As of Tuesday, January 23, 2001, the JTF team had found nothing. I figured they would not finish the east beach site before February 4, the close of the mission. I had jury duty—already delayed once— awaiting me, and an anxious editor, so I decided to start heading for Long Beach. Two U.S. embassy staffers were at the hotel, intending to return by car after breakfast to Phnom Penh. I could hitch a ride with them.

So, I rose at 5:00 A.M., went outside and found a maintenance man already up, watering flowers. He let me pick a few. I walked to the roadside and hailed a motorcycle taxi, hopped on the rear and used hand signals to direct him on into the darkness. Twenty minutes later, we rolled to a stop at a place called Kah Pos. The driver parked behind an abandoned hotel. I walked the short deserted distance in the bleak gray of dawn. My steps took me down the path to the beach. Then I moved south along the shore to what the recovery team calls "the grotto," the sandy alcove where Danny was placed after he died. I stood above on the rocks and began to toss the flowers I had brought. First a yellow chrysanthemum—yellow ribbons being the symbol of the missing-in-action. Then I tossed a red flower for Teleah, wanting it to be a rose, but there were none available. Then I tossed a purple and white orchid for all the tears shed, the pain he suffered, the days and nights Danny never knew. Finally, I took out the letter she asked me to write. I had added some thoughts of my own, about her and how she still thought of him. I placed the letter inside an envelope and dropped it into the grotto. As I looked up, the sun began to paint a high thin cirrus deck in pinks and vermillion. Then a sweep of incoming surf spent itself, gently placing the letter on the sand. I looked and in the brightening moments of daylight read on the envelope, To Danny.

On February 2, 2001, I was back in Long Beach when Lieutenant Colonel Childress called. The team had managed to finish the east beach dig and had gotten to the first of Em Son's two sites on west beach, the one where Ashton Loney was reportedly buried. "Good news!" Childress said.

Captain Velez had sent the following:

> We found him by the beach, just like the witness said. We were on our last dig day. By luck, I was doing the final touches on the grid and spotted bone. I thought it was turtle—I had seen turtle bone earlier—but then, long bones were surrounding it. We found him just as the witness indicated.

If the DNA and dental comparison holds up, Lance Corporal Ashton Loney will have come home. For Joseph Hargrove—or possibly Gary Hall, if Em Son's latest identification is accurate, and my instincts are off—the wait to return will be a little longer.

President Ford considers the *Mayaguez* Incident the high point of his administration. He stated, "I think this is a clear, clear indication that we are not only strong, but we have the will and the capability of moving." As recently as the 2000 Republican Convention, the *Mayaguez* Incident was cited as a triumph for President Ford and the country.

Off the shores of Cambodia, the strategic imperatives of showing a "clear, clear" American victory resulted in the conscious abandonment of three marines. But our country has sacrificed men and women before in pursuit of the common good. Some fifty-eight thousand were lost during the failed course of the entire Vietnam War. One can argue that from the outcome of the *Mayaguez* Incident emerged a great benefit for America in our show of strength and the effect this had in the Communist world.

But what was lost in the flag waving were the lessons to be learned from the mistakes that occurred. The Marine leadership had decided to send to the crisis area the lesser trained of the two available battalion landing teams. I found no admission that highlighted the need to ensure the most combat-ready unit be tasked during a contingency. During the ground combat phase, they had only one fatality, Ashton Loney. It could be argued that the marines had acquitted themselves well once they set foot on the island. Overlooked apparently were the forty-three wounded, twenty eight with minor injuries, and the three who were left behind.

Regarding the abuse of the excellent communications between the White House and the combat troops, it was never properly addressed by the General Accounting Office in their report or by the Pentagon, except for streamlining the mechanics of the intelligence dissemination process.

Lieutenant Colonel Austin cited in his report, "There were no direct radio communications between [himself] and the Commander of the Task Group, Colonel Johnson." He went on to point out, "Not all ordnance delivery was cleared with [me], the ground commander. The most glaring example was the use of a fifteen-thousand-pound bomb dropped in mid-afternoon with absolutely no prior notice to or clearance from [me]."

The problem of improper training and bad communications would rear its head again during the Iran Crisis five years later, when poorly trained helicopter pilots had to be replaced midway in the preparation period. A fatal helicopter crash at *Desert One* ended that operation before the forces even reached the target. Eight casualties were left behind. An internal military report later stated, "The isolation of tactically knowledgeable commanders from one another and from responsible operational planners seems to have been deliberately fostered in the Iranian episode. Confused and divided lines of command and tactical micromanagement from Washington were very much in evidence."

Not only was information on the missing withheld after the *Mayaguez* Incident, but the sacrifice of the twenty-three men lost in the helicopter crash in Thailand was quickly dismissed as incidental and not connected to the operation. The information on these twenty-three losses was not released to the media at the time, failing to even show up in either *Time* or *Newsweek* editions of May 26, 1975, a full ten days after the end of hostilities. To this day, these casualties are rarely included in the total count for the incident, even though they were clearly part of it. For those who did return, their lives were forever changed by the incident. For some, like the troubled private from Chicago, K.O. Taylor, his discharge papers were withdrawn and he remained in the Marine Corps until voluntarily separating the next year. For others, the trauma of that day has remained, manifesting itself in emotional problems that have affected their marriages and jobs. Few came away unscathed.

The Khmer Rouge fared no better although ambiguity exists as to the number of Cambodian casualties. Estimates range from as many as twenty-five killed to as few as thirteen. After the dust cleared, many of the Khmer leaders involved in the incident were "sent up" during the next few months as the leadership in Phnom Penh dealt with perceived reactionaries. Sam Sok, an infantryman who had fought on the east beach, stated that the question among all the troops was, "How deep in the ranks will they go?" For those taken to Phnom Penh, the prison at Toul Sleng was the end of the line. Called "Hill of the Poisoned Tree," Toul Sleng was the converted school where the errant were interrogated, then, along with all family members, executed and buried in the Killing Fields at Choeng Ek, twelve miles south of Phnom Penh.

As for Em Son, he continued fighting until 1988 when his right leg was blown off by a mine, his eighteenth wound. Incredibly, he was engaged in close-combat one month later and saw two additional actions before being withdrawn from combat service. By that time, he had also lost two brothers and one sister in the fighting.

To this day, neither Lance Corporal Joseph N. Hargrove, Private First Class Gary L. Hall, nor Private Danny G. Marshall has received a posthumous award for their heroism beyond the automatic issuance of the Purple Heart.

Hargrove lost a brother to the war in 1968, saved his siblings the next year from their father's arson, and finally held off a Khmer Rouge attack while helping many marine buddies reach safety in 1975. One can surely say that whatever he might have held against the Marine Corps, he served his family, his Corps, and his country above and beyond the call of duty. For Hall, the big kid from Covington, Kentucky, his high school chum said poignantly, "Our backyard wars were the games of children, which as we grew older came to an end.

This was all we knew of war until Gary became a real marine. Gary never came back to that backyard, and we learned what wars were really like." Indeed, Gary became a "real marine" who, like many others, never returned. As for Danny Marshall—the tough kid from Waverly, West Virginia—his actions on Koh Tang surely marked his moment of redemption. He threw himself into the fray for his buddies, as always.

They did their duty, these three. No one can argue otherwise. The evidence indicates they did a whole lot more.

The struggle on Koh Tang was, in a sense, a metaphor of the entire Vietnam War: an action begun for what seemed a good and noble purpose, which quickly degenerated into an ugly, desperate fight, micromanaged from no less than the office of the president of the United States. While Gerald Ford and Henry Kissinger improvised tactics, confusing political expedience with military reality during a black-tie dinner, Americans lay bleeding and dying needlessly on a distant spit of sand. In so many ways, the *Mayaguez* Incident mirrors the outcome of the Southeast Asian conflict itself.

In the end, the majority of our troops and the entire crew of the *Mayaguez* got out. However, of the forty-one that gave their lives during the *Mayaguez* Incident, only twenty-three of the deceased were sent home for burial in 1975. The remains of nine lost on Koh Tang were returned to next of kin in 2000. For nine others, including the three who were captured, even that dignity has been delayed. Hargrove, Hall, and Marshall have become the *Private Ryans* of the Vietnam War, except unlike in the fictional World War II movie, nobody came back to save them.

As for the battered old hulk of the *SS Mayaguez*, she was still black-sided and rusty four years later in 1979, but her days of hauling cargo had come to an end. After thirty-five years plying the sea-lanes, men with blowtorches cut the ship into segments and ripped her insides out. Her steel bones were sold for scrap and scattered. In a matter of days the *Mayaguez* had vanished.

Appendix A

Mitochondria DNA (mtDNA) science has been used to identify many of the casualties of our nation's wars. The technique has found notoriety lately, the most notable mtDNA success story being that of the investigation done on remains disinterred from the Tomb of the Unknown Soldier in Washington, D.C. The bones were positively identified as those of First Lieutenant Michael Blassie, an air force pilot shot down in 1972. The identification process required analysis of hardy mitochondria DNA from deep within the bone specimen, then matching it with blood, saliva, or even skin samples of DNA taken from maternal relatives of the missing. Because mtDNA matching is not as statistically accurate as standard DNA comparisons, the Department of Defense typically delays announcing results until all the remains from a given case have been recovered and examined. This delay is needed to preclude misidentification due to the probability, low though it might be, of later discovering that two of the deceased have nearly identical mtDNA profiles.

At this point, however, the Department of Defense has split the *Mayaguez* case into two groups: the thirteen men missing from *Knife 31*, downed off the eastern shore on the morning of May 15, 1975, and the five servicemen lost on the western side of the island that day and later.

The process of case closure in each instance is painstakingly slow. In fact, maternal relatives of four of the missing servicemen were not even located until June of 1998. Within a few months of that development, nine mtDNA matches were obtained. The families were not notified because efforts to recover more remains were still in progress. The casualty office for each service is concerned that a family might be told too soon that their son's remains had been recovered and were being sent to them for interment. The family might go through the ordeal of revisiting their loss, a funeral, and a burial. More bones found would mean more trauma for families. As a result, case closure is a carefully controlled process starting with the recovery teams from the Joint Task Force for Full Accounting (JTF-FA) and Central Identification Lab in Hawaii (CIL-HI). Their finds are sent to DNA specialists at the Armed Forces DNA Identification Lab (AFDIL) in Maryland. The results are sent for review by civilian, board certified consultants. This is done, according to public affairs specialist at CIL-HI, army staff sergeant Earl Bushong, "so that independent, nonmilitary confirmation of our findings are made." If the civilian review validates the AFDIL findings, the appropriate casualty offices are notified, then the individual families, at which time a military review board authorizes public release of the names.

For the nine mtDNA matches so far obtained, the civilian review board completed its approval. Next-of-kin notifications followed, as did public announcements. All nine of the servicemen were aboard *Knife-31*. Thus far, none of the IDs included any of the missing three-man machine-gun team.

Here is how the AFDIL determined the identity of remains through MtDNA testing.

Human cells contain two kinds of DNA. The type found in the nucleus inside the chromosomes is a mixture of DNA from an individual's mother and father. Also inside each cell are hundreds of tiny mitochondria, the cell's energy producers. These contain DNA only from an individual's mother (mtDNA). According to forensic anthropologist David Rankin at CIL-HI, "When a living organism dies, DNA inside the cells begins immediately to degrade from the body's own enzymes. Then heat, humidity, ultraviolet rays from the sun, and soil contaminants such as bacteria continue the breakdown process." Each cell has only two copies of chromosomal DNA, and it decays rapidly after death. The mitochondria are much hardier, and thus are more likely to survive than the nuclear DNA. With mitochondria, however, the DNA sequences are not nearly as unique as those found in the chromosomes. According to Mitch Holland, AFDIL's resident expert on mtDNA, "There are probably more than 100,000 different mtDNA sequences in the population, but we won't know until we have more data." The database is currently nearly ten thousand sequences. For example, in one test of 650 samples, the same sequence was not seen in the same region AFDIL has selected, making the probability of confusion of that sample less than 1 in 650 in the general population. If samples from relatives of all the known deceased at a given site are obtained and none are repetitive, then matched sequences with a maternal relative's mtDNA provide a very compelling argument for the identification of those skeletal remains. Because the probability for error is statistically higher with mtDNA than with pure DNA from chromosomes, the importance of obtaining samples from relatives of all the MIAs associated with any one site cannot be overstated.

The mtDNA in question are contained in long, paired strands of genetic material consisting of 16,569 base pairs of nucloetides. These are bonded to a base, forming what looks like the rungs of an immensely long, circular ladder. The seemingly random series of rungs (pairs) are actually arranged in a unique and identifiable order in individuals who are maternally related. AFDIL selects one particular segment, which contains 610 pairs of the four nucleotides: adenosine, thymidine, guanosine, and cytidine. For ease in differentiating, these are lettered A,T,G, and C (see Figure 1). Each bonds to its base mate as shown: A to T and G to C.

SEGMENT OF A MITOCHONDRIA DNA STRAND

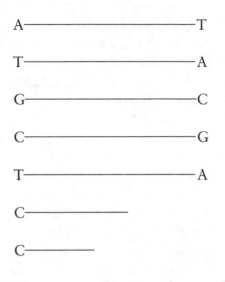

FIGURE 1

The sequence of these pairs is what is compared with mtDNA obtained from any maternal relative: grandmother, mother, great-aunts and great-uncles on the grandmother's side, maternal aunts and uncles, children of sisters, children of maternal aunts, and so forth.

The process of analyzing mtDNA from remains is difficult and time-consuming. The first step is preparing the sample. A fragment, usually about two inches in length, is cut from skeletal bone mass. The segment is sanded to remove surface contaminants such as bacteria. Then it is washed in alcohol and distilled water. A hammer and chisel are used to break the specimen into smaller pieces, which are then placed in a commercial blender that pulverizes the sample. A fine, portland cement–like mixture results.

Next, the mixture is placed in a chemical bath. Using salts and buffers, the cells are broken open to release the DNA strands or ladders. A centrifuge is used to separate the DNA from cell debris, which passes through a membrane and sinks to the bottom.

POLYMERASE CHAIN REACTION

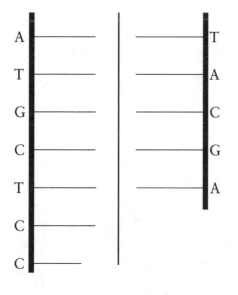

FIGURE 2.

Once the strands have been separated, an amino acid sequence is introduced containing all four of the nucleotides, which serves to duplicate the unique DNA sequence. This process, called a polymerase chain reaction (PCR)(see Figure 2), acts like a copy machine as the separated rung pairs attach or anneal to new nucleotides, thereby making many identical copies of the original mtDNA sequence (see Figure 3). This is needed to provide enough of a sample to examine.

ANNEALED MITOCHONDRIA DNA STRAND

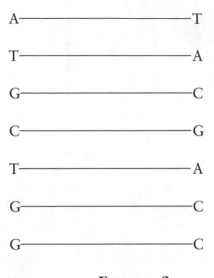

FIGURE 3

The nucleotides are then tagged with a phosphorescent chemical dye that comes in the Perkin Elmer Sequencing Kit. Different colors of dye attach themselves to the nucleotides. The tagging allows a laser to be used to detect the sequence of tagged pairs. Once the base (victim) sequence has been determined, it is projected on a computer screen and compared with mtDNA from potential maternal relations of the deceased.

A match would appear as shown in Figure 4. The sequence is what is matched against donor samples. Sample No. 2 is a match with the base sequence. A probability of high confidence can be made regarding the source of the base mtDNA sample if the No. 2 sample was a maternal relative of one of the servicemen missing on Koh Tang.

MITOCHONDRIA NUCLEOTIDE COMPARISON WITH SAMPLES

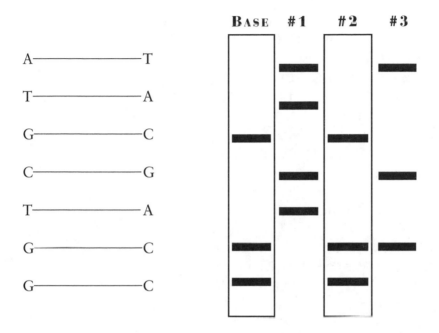

FIGURE 4

Now that some of the servicemen are believed to have survived the battle, the mtDNA identification becomes even more important. It will serve to verify or contradict witness statements and focus the recovery team's search for those missing servicemen.

After AFDIL completed its work on the bone samples already recovered, the results were sent back to CIL-HI in Hawaii, where maternal donor samples were compared to the ones found at Koh Tang. An mtDNA sequence matched one provided by the sister of Lieutenant Richard Vandegeer. Tooth restorations found on a section of jawbone also matched X rays from Second Lieutenant Vandegeer's dental file, doubly confirming the results and validating the mtDNA process. Thus far, of the eighteen servicemen missing from the *Mayaguez* Incident, nine have been declared killed in action and their remains returned to next of kin.

These include, according to the Defense POW/Missing Personnel Office, the following nine servicemen:

BENEDETTE, DANIEL A., PFC, USMC
BLESSING, LYNN, PFC, USMC
COPENHAVER, GREGORY S., LCPL, USMC
GARCIA, ANDRES, LCPL, USMC
GAUSE, BERNARD, JR., HM1, USN
MANNING, RONALD J., HN, USN
SANDOVAL, ANTONIO R., LCPL, USMC
TURNER, KELTON R., PFC, USMC
RICHARD, VANDEGEER, 2/LT., USAF

Awaiting identifications are:

BOYD, WALTER, PFC, USMC
LONEY, ASHTON N., LCPL, USMC
HALL, GARY L., PFC, USMC
HARGROVE, JOSEPH N., LCPL, USMC
JACQUES, JAMES J., PFC, USN
MARSHALL, DANNY G., PVT, USN
MAXWELL, JAMES RICKEY, PFC, USMC
RIVENBURGH, RICHARD W., PFC, USMC
RUMBAUGH, ELWOOD EUGENE, S/SGT, USAF

Also repatriated immediately after the incident were the twenty-three crewmen from the downed helicopter in Thailand.

COLLUMS, BOBBY G., SGT, USAF
COYLE, GERALD A., S/SGT, USAF
DWYER, THOMAS D., SGT, USAF
FORD, BOB W., SGT, USAF
FRITZ, GERALD W., SGT, USAF
FROEHLICH, LAWRENCE E., 1/LT, USAF
GLENN, JACKIE D., T/SGT, USAF
HAMLIN, DARREL L., SGT, USAF
HANKAMER, GREGORY L., SGT, USAF

Higgs, David A., SGT, USAF
Ilada, Faleagafulu, SGT, USAF
Kays, James G., CAPT, USAF
Lane, Michael D., SGT, USAF
London, Dennis W., SGT, USAF
Mathias, Robert P., SGT, USAF
Moran, Edgar C., II, AMN, USAF
McKelvey, William R., SGT, USAF
McMullen, George E., T/SGT, USAF
Nealis, Tommy R., SGT, USAF
Raber, Paul J., SGT, USAF
Ross, Robert W., SGT, USAF
Weldon, Robert P., SGT, USAF

Appendix B

AC-130

Mission: The Lockheed AC-130 gunship provides close air support for troops in contact with opposing forces, interdiction tasks conducted against preplanned or targets of opportunity, and missions providing air base and facilities defense.

Features: These aircraft incorporate side-firing weapons integrated with sensor, navigation, and fire control systems. The AC-130 provides accurate firepower or area saturation during extended loiter periods, day or night and in adverse weather. The sensor suite consists of a television, infrared detector, and radar. These allow the gunship to visually or electronically identify friendly ground forces and targets any place, any time.

Armament: AC-130: 40-mm cannon, 105-mm cannon, and two 20-mm guns.

Power Plant: Four Allison T56-A-15 turboprop engines.

Crew: Five officers (pilot, copilot, navigator, fire control officer, electronic warfare officer) and nine enlisted (flight engineer, TV operator, infrared detection set operator, loadmaster, five aerial gunners).

A-7 CORSAIR

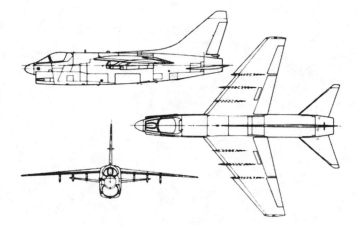

Mission: Built by Vought, the air-refuelable Air Force A-7D was designed for close air support plus long-range interdiction and strike missions. The A-7E Navy version had the additional ability of delivering nuclear weapons.

Features: These aircraft incorporate integrated navigation and fire control systems. The avionics suite consists of a heads-up display, an inertial navigation platform, mapping and terrain-following radar, and a computer-controlled bombing and strafing system. These allow the pilot to identify ground targets visually or via radar, which are then designated to the computer. The computer solves the ballistic geometry needed to allow the intended weapon to hit the target. The computer projects a symbol on the heads-up display for the pilot to follow until automatic bomb release.

Armament: One M-61A-1 20-mm gatling gun with five hundred rounds, two fuselage stations and six wing stations capable of carrying air-to-air and air-to-surface missiles, bombs, rockets, gun pods, and fuel drop-tanks.

Power Plant: One Allison TF-41 turbojet engine with 14,500 pounds of thrust.

Crew: One pilot.

F-4 PHANTOM

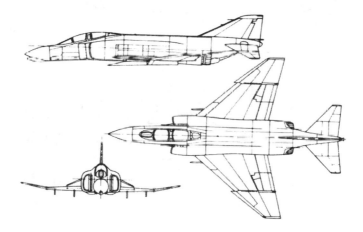

Mission: Designed by McDonnell-Douglas as an all-around combat aircraft, the F-4 could perform interceptor, conventional bomb, and nuclear missions.

Features: These aircraft incorporate integrated navigation and fire control systems. The avionics suite consists of an inertial navigation platform, air-intercept radar, and a computer-aided bombing system.

Armament: The air force F-4E version carries one internal M-61A- 1 20-mm gatling gun, and has five fuselage stations and two wing stations capable of carrying air-to-air and air-to-surface missiles, bombs, rockets, gun pods, and fuel drop-tanks. The Navy version, the F-4J, has no internal gun.

Power Plant: Two General Electric J-79 turbojet engines produce seventeen thousand pounds of thrust in afterburner.

Crew: One pilot and one radar/systems operator.

F-111 ARDVARK

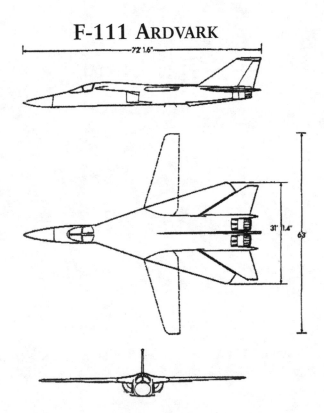

Mission: Designed by General Dynamics in the early 1960s as a multirole fighter that was to replace virtually all air force and navy fighters of the time. The plane was expected to perform interceptor, conventional bomb, and nuclear missions in all weather conditions, but design problems with the engines, range, and weight prevented it from being accepted by the navy.

Features: These aircraft incorporate integrated navigation and fire control systems. The avionics suite consists of an inertial navigation platform, mapping and terrain-following radar coupled to the autopilot, and a computer-controlled bombing system. These allow the pilot to identify ground targets visually or via radar, which are then designated to the computer. The computer solves the ballistic geometry needed to allow the intended weapon to hit the target. The computer projects a symbol on the instrument panel for the pilot to follow until automatic bomb release. The wings sweep to seventy degrees for high-speed flight and the crew sit side by side in a cockpit capsule that protects them during high-speed ejections.

Armament: One M61A-1 20-mm gatling gun, one fuselage station and six wing stations capable of carrying air-to-air and air-to-surface missiles, conventional and nuclear bombs, rockets, gun pods, and fuel drop-tanks.

Power Plant: Two Pratt & Whitney TF-30 turbojet engines with 18,500 pounds of thrust in afterburner.

Crew: One pilot and one systems operator.

OV-10 BRONCO

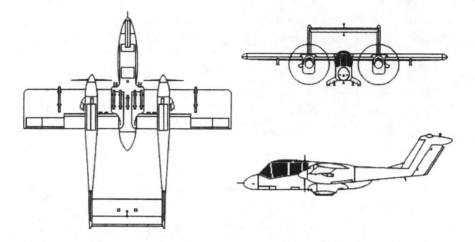

Mission: Counterinsurgency operations to include reconnaissance, helicopter escort, forward-air-controller duties, and limited close air support pending arrival of tactical fighters.

Features: The OV-10 has a high-aspect wing allowing extended loiter times over lightly defended targets. Excellent visibility is provided by the wrap-around windscreen. The avionics suite includes VHF-FM and UHF radios.

Armament: Four M-60C 7.62-mm machine-guns carried two per wing-mounted sponson, one fuselage station and four wing stations capable of carrying air-to-air Sidewinder missiles, bombs, rockets, flare pods, and fuel drop-tanks.

Power Plant: Two 715-horsepower Garrett AiResearch T-76-G turbo-props.

Crew: One pilot and one observer.

CH-53 AND HH-53 HELICOPTERS

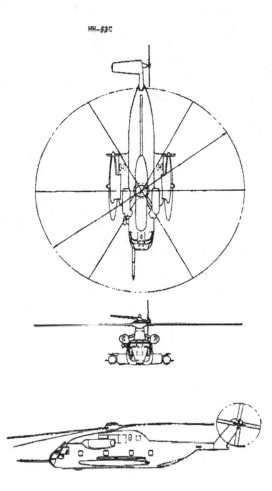

HH-53C

Mission: The HH-53C was designed as a long-range aircrew recovery helicopter. The CH-53C was designed for covert operations in enemy territory, to include delivery and pickup of road-watch teams and ground parties. Both have similar external appearance but have significant internal differences.

HH-53C Features: The HH-53C is fitted with jettisonable 450-gallon external fuel tanks mounted on stub wings. The tanks are fitted with explosion-retardant polyurethane foam. The aircraft also has a hydraulic operated rescue hoist, titanium armor-plate protection, and an air-to-air refueling probe. Avionics includes a doppler navigation system, low-light-level television for night operations, and a full radio suite.

HH-53C Armament: The HH-53C carries three 7.62-mm Gatling-type miniguns mounted in the crew door, the left forward cabin window, and on the cargo ramp. The rate of fire can be adjusted to either 2,000 or 4,000 rounds per minute.

CH-53C Features: The CH-53 is fitted with jettisonable 650 gallon fuel tanks which have no explosion-retardant foam inside. The aircraft is not air-to-air refuelable. It carries a hydraulic operated rescue hoist and titanium armor-plate protection. Avionics includes a doppler navigation system, low-light-level television for night operations, and a full radio suite.

CH-53C Armament: The CH-53C carries two 7.62-mm Gatling-type miniguns mounted in the crew door and the left forward cabin window. The rate of fire can be adjusted to either 2,000 or 4,000 rounds per minute.

Powerplant: Two General Electric T-64 turboshaft engines.

Crew: HH-53: pilot, copilot, two flight mechanics, and two pararescuemen.
CH-53: pilot, copilot, three flight mechanics.

Appendix C

CHRONOLOGY OF THE *MAYAGUEZ* INCIDENT

DATE/TIME (approximate)

CAMBODIA	WASHINGTON	ACTION
MAY 12	MAY 12	
2:10-2:18 P.M.	3:10-3:18 A.M.	SS *Mayaguez* intercepted by Cambodian gunboat.
2:18 P.M.	3:18 A.M.	John Neal receives mayday call in Jakarta and contacts U.S. Embassy.
3:54-5:55 P.M.	4:54-6:55 A.M.	U.S. Embassy, Jakarta, alerts White House, CIA, NMCC, DIA.

CAMBODIA	WASHINGTON	ACTION
MAY 12	MAY 12	
4:55 P.M.	5:55 A.M.	SS *Mayaguez* anchors near Poulo Wai Island.
6:02 P.M.	7:02 A.M.	NMCC notifies Pacific Command to ready reconnaissance aircraft and crews.
6:30 P.M.	7:30 A.M.	JCS orders Pacific Command to send reconnaissance aircraft to locate ship.
6:40 P.M.	7:40 A.M.	President Ford is briefed on seizure.
8:57 P.M.	9:57 A.M.	P-3 aircraft launches from Thailand to locate ship.
8:37 P.M.	9:37 A.M.	CINCPACFLT directs USS *Holt* to the area.
11:05 P.M.	12:05 P.M.	President convenes National Security Council (NSC) meeting #1.
MAY 13		
12:50 A.M.	1:50 P.M.	White House announces seizure of ship.
1:12 A.M.	2:12 P.M.	USS *Coral Sea* is ordered to the incident area.
3:30 A.M.	4:30 P.M.	Representative from Liaison Office, Peoples Republic of China, refuses to accept State Department message for Cambodia captors, ordering release of ship.
5:00 A.M.	6:00 P.M.	*Voice of America* broadcast to Cambodia carries news story of SS *Mayaguez* seizure.
5:24 A.M.	6:24 P.M.	USS *Wilson* is underway toward seizure area.
8:16 A.M.	9:16 P.M.	P-3 aircraft identifies SS *Mayaguez* anchored off Poulo Wai Island. P-3 takes battle damage in tail.
8:43 A.M.	9:43 P.M.	SS *Mayaguez* gets underway to northeast.
8:44 A.M.	9:44 P.M.	US 7th Fleet directs marine amphibious group to prepare to deploy.

CHRONOLOGY OF SS *MAYAGUEZ* INCIDENT

CAMBODIA	WASHINGTON	ACTION
	MAY 13	
11:10 A.M.	12:10 A.M.	US Liaison office in Peking delivers message to Cambodian embassy and Chinese Foreign Ministry.
11:30 A.M.	12:30 A.M.	Mariners warning to avoid the incident area goes out to shipping.
1:26 P.M.	2:26 A.M.	P-3 Aircraft reports SS *Mayaguez* dead in the water off Koh Tang.
3:00 P.M.	4:00 A.M.	Thai premier informs US: Thailand will not permit use of Thai bases for US action against Cambodia.
3:45 P.M.	4:45 A.M.	A-7 aircraft strafe in front of SS *Mayaguez* to signal ship not to get under way.
4:40-5:00 P.M.	5:40-6:00 A.M.	SS *Mayaguez* crew board fishing boats and anchor off Koh Tang. Aircraft report Caucasian personnel on board.
5:33 P.M.	6:33 A.M.	Pilot reports crew is disembarking onto Koh Tang. Heavy anti-aircraft fire observed during pass. Number of personnel moving inland is unknown.
8:00-9:00 P.M.	9:00-10:00 A.M.	Cambodian guards take Captain and chief engineer back to SS *Mayaguez* to examine cargo. US aircraft drop flares and group returns to island anchorage, where they spend the night.
9:30 P.M.	10:30 A.M.	President Ford convenes NSC #2.
11:10 P.M.	12:10 P.M.	JCS orders all boats to/from island intercepted. USAF Security police are directed from Nakhon Phanom to U-Tapao. All H-53 helos are ordered to U-Tapao. Two marine platoons are ordered from the Philippines to U-Tapao and a marine battalion from Okinawa is ordered to prepare to deploy.

CAMBODIA	WASHINGTON	ACTION
MAY 14	MAY 13	
2:06 A.M.	3:06 P.M.	C-130 aircraft receives antiaircraft fire from island. Two companies from Philippines deploy to Thailand.
2:12 A.M.	3:12 P.M.	USMC battalion from Okinawa is ordered to deploy.
4:06 A.M.	5:06 P.M.	Battalion landing team begins airlift from Okinawa.
4:46 A.M.	5:46 P.M.	USS *Holt* estimated arrival off Koh Tang is set for 11:00 P.M. Cambodia time on the 14th.
5:30 A.M.	6:30 P.M.	NMCC confirms 23 Americans died in helicopter crash; 18 were security police en route to U-Tapao.
5:45 A.M.	6:45 P.M.	Two marine companies from the Philippines arrive at U-Tapao.
6:00 A.M.	7:00 P.M.	Fishing boat with SS *Mayaguez* crew departs Koh Tang, headed for the Cambodian mainland. Three patrol boats proceed ahead of the trawler.
7:12 A.M.	8:12 P.M.	JCS relays president's decision to sink patrol boats.
7:20 A.M.	8:20 P.M.	Cambodian patrol boat sunk by A-7 aircraft.
7:35 A.M.	8:35 P.M.	Rescue helicopter launched from Thailand to attempt to save survivors of sunken patrol boat. No survivors are found.
7:45 A.M.	8:45 P.M.	Vessel spotted with what look like Caucasians aboard. Riot control gas fails to turn it around.
9:30 A.M.	10:30 P.M.	President assembles NSC meeting #3.
10:00 A.M.	11:00 P.M.	President relays decision to use only riot control agents on vessel with Caucasians aboard and to sink patrol boats.

CAMBODIA	WASHINGTON	ACTION
MAY 14	**MAY 13**	
10:10-11:30 A.M.	12:30 A.M.- 11:10 P.M.	Riot control gas fails to stop fishing boat which proceeds into Kompong Som harbor, anchors, the moves south and anchors off coast.
	MAY 14	
11:20 A.M.	12:20 A.M.	RF-4 reconnaissance plane photographs fishing boat with SS *Mayaguez* crew visible, huddled in bow.
11:29 A.M.	12:29 A.M.	U.S. aircraft sink one patrol boat and damage four.
11:48 A.M.	12:48 A.M.	JCS orders planning for recovery of ship at sunrise, May 15. Marines are to simultaneously attack Koh Tang and board the SS *Mayaguez*.
12:20-3:00 P.M.	1:20-4:00 A.M.	Fishing boat with SS *Mayaguez* crew proceeds to Rong Sam Lem island, anchors, and crew is put ashore.
1:45-3:35 P.M.	2:45-4:35 A.M.	U.S. aircraft observe a fishing boat depart coast, then proceed to Rong Sam Lem. Information is never passed to White House.
2:00 P.M.	3:00 A.M.	Marine BLT from Okinawa arrives at U-Tapao.
3:54 P.M.	4:54 A.M.	State Department receives Middle East U.S. embassy message that a senior Chinese diplomat related that his government was using its influence with Cambodia to obtain release of the SS *Mayaguez* and crew.
3:00 -5:00 P.M.	4:00- 6:00 A.M.	U-21 aircraft with marine officers aboard overflies Koh Tang at 4:00 P.M. to identify landing zones.
4:00 P.M.	5:00 A.M.	Thai Prime Minister protests arrival of marines at U-Tapao despite his position that Thai facilities not be used.

CAMBODIA	WASHINGTON	ACTION
MAY 14		
5:20 P.M.	6:20 A.M.	SS *Mayaguez* captain is told to select crewmembers and return to ship to radio U.S. authorities to stop bombing. When crew refuses to board gunboat, Cambodians tell SS *Mayaguez* captain that entire crew will remain on Rong Sam Lem overnight and be released the next morning.
MAY 15		
1:06 A.M.	2:06 P.M.	U.S. aircraft sink another patrol boat near Koh Tang.
2:52 A.M.	3:52 P.M.	President convenes NSC meeting #4.
3:00-5:00 A.M.	4:00-6:00 P.M.	Khmer Rouge hear approach of USS *Holt*.
3:45-4:10 A.M.	4:45-5:10 P.M.	President orders military operations to be used to recover SS *Mayaguez* and crew, including naval air attacks on Kompong Som and Ream Naval facility. B-52s are withheld, but remain on alert.
4:14 A.M.	5:14 P.M.	Launch command is passed to marines at U-Tapao, who delayed departure awaiting approval. First helicopter wave with marines takes to the air.
5:40 A.M.	6:40 P.M.	Congressional leaders are briefed on operation.
6:00-6:22 A.M.	7:00-7:22 P.M.	Three helicopters offload marines onto deck of USS *Holt*. Marines will board SS *Mayaguez*, deck-to-deck.
6:07 A.M.	7:07 P.M.	Phnom Penh radio announces SS *Mayaguez* will be released.
6:06-6:20 A.M.	7:06-7:20 P.M.	Khmer Rouge on Koh Tang hear approaching helicopters and run toward fighting positions.
6:20-7:00 A.M.	7:20-8:00 P.M.	First wave helicopters and marines attack Koh Tang. Three helicopters are immediately shot down.

CAMBODIA MAY 15	WASHINGTON MAY 14	ACTION
6:30-7:00 A.M.	7:30-8:00 P.M.	SS *Mayaguez* crew signs "manifest" and departs Rong Sam Lem island for the ship.
7:06 A.M.	8:06 P.M.	First navy strikes launch from USS *Coral Sea*.
7:10 A.M.	8:10 P.M.	USS *Wilson* arrives on scene.
7:25 A.M.	8:25 P.M.	USS *Holt* pulls alongside the SS *Mayaguez*.
7:29 A.M.	8:29 P.M.	President Ford and Secretary of State Kissinger discuss Cambodian overture to release ship. Ford refuses to halt operation unless Cambodians also release the crew.
7:45-11:00 A.M.	8:45 P.M.-12:00 A.M.	Navy attacks begin against mainland targets.
8:15 A.M.	9:15 P.M.	White House releases statement acknowledging Cambodian message about release of SS *Mayaguez*. President Ford offers to cease military operations if crew is included in release.
8:30-9:15 A.M.	9:30-10:15 P.M.	USS *Wilson* plucks marine survivors from sea.
9:35 A.M.	10:35 P.M.	P-3 aircraft sights fishing boat with Caucasians aboard waving white flags, heading for Koh Tang.
9:49 A.M.	10:49 P.M.	USS *Wilson* intercepts fishing boat. All 40 crewmen are taken safely aboard.
	MAY 15	
11:27 A.M.	12:27 A.M.	President Ford announces recovery of SS *Mayaguez* and crew.
11:55 A.M.	12:55 A.M.	JCS orders cessation of all military operations. Second wave of marines turns around.
12:06 P.M.	1:06 A.M.	SS *Mayaguez* crew reboards ship which is under tow by USS *Holt*.

CAMBODIA	WASHINGTON	ACTION
MAY 15		
12:10-12:35 P.M.	1:10-1:35 A.M.	Second wave reverses course back to Koh Tang and inserts troops on west beach.
3:45 P.M.	4:45 A.M.	Thai Premier presents diplomatic note protesting use of Thai territory for launching military operations against Cambodia.
4:20-6:15 P.M.	5:20-7:15 A.M.	OV-10 FAC aircraft arrive over Koh Tang and assume control of naval gunfire and airstrikes. One partially submerged gunboat is silenced by air and naval firepower.
6:15-6:30 P.M.	7:15-7:30 A.M.	Withdrawal from east beach completed.
6:35 P.M.	7:35 A.M.	BLU-82 15,000 lb. bomb is dropped near west beach.
6:40-8:30 P.M.	7:40-9:30 A.M.	Withdrawal from west beach completed.
11:00 P.M.	12:00 P.M.	Marine officers determine 3 marines left behind.
MAY 16		
6:30-10:00 A.M.	7:30-11:00 pm.	USS *Wilson* circles Koh Tang looking for survivors.
10:00 A.M.	11:00 P.M.	JCS orders all forces to depart Cambodian waters. Efforts to recover dead and missing are terminated.

Notes

Histroical details dealing with actions involving the *Mayaguez* crew were primarily condensed, edited, and revised using *The Four Days of Mayaguez* by Roy Rowan, published by W.W. Norton in 1975; tape recorded transcripts of crew interviews maintained at the Gerald R. Ford Library in Ann Arbor, Michigan; and from clarifying details revealed by Khmer Rouge veterans. Specifics regarding the battle on Koh Tang were similarly edited and updated primarily using *Americans at War* by Daniel P. Bolger, published by Presidio Press in 1985; *A Very Short War*, by John F. Guilmartin, Jr., published by Texas A&M University Press in 1995; and *Fourteen Hours at Koh Tang* by Thomas D. Des Brisay in USAF Southeast Asia Monograph Series, Vol. 3, published by the U.S. Government Printing Office in 1977, all of which provide excellent reading. My reporting on diplomatic and military decisions made during the four National Security Council meetings held during the *Mayaguez* Incident is based on the recently declassified NSC minutes maintained at the Ford Library.

NUMBER BEFORE ENDNOTES INDICATES PAGE IN BOOK

CHAPTER 1

11. "Found with the remains . . . an armory's worth of ammunition": Regarding the .38-caliber revolver found at the site, marines were issued .45-caliber pistols during that period. The air force issued .38-caliber revolvers. Second Lieutenant Vandegeer was the only air force member to have died in the helicopter crash.

16. "witness report from 1985. A Cambodian source had related that an American had been wounded sometime after the Koh Tang assault and was then executed": Taken from JCRC Report T88-060, *One American Survivor of* Mayaguez *Incident Executed by Khmer Rouge During May 1975*. From JCRC Liaison, Bangkok, Thailand, February 24, 1985, p. 2.

CHAPTER 2

25. Grotius, *Mare Liberum (Free Sea,* 1609), Based on the Roman legal principle: Quoted from "Freedom of the Seas," Microsoft® Encarta® Online Encyclopedia 2000.

25. "In her hold . . . at Sattahip in Thailand": Roy Rowan, *The Four Days of Mayaguez* (New York: W. W. Norton, 1975), p. 15.

26. "Hush Puppies spattered with paint drippings": Coombes debrief, Roy Rowan notes, *Mayaguez* Papers, Gerald R. Ford Library, p. 1.

26. "Rumors of oil deposits . . .": Daniel P. Bolger, *Americans at War 1975–1986, An Era of Violent Peace* (San Francisco: Presidio Press, 1985), p. 22.

26. "At 2:18 in the afternoon . . . navigation fix": *Seizure of the Mayaguez*, Reports of the Comptroller General of the United States, Committee on International Relations, U.S. Government Printing Office, Washington, D.C., 1976, p. 25.

26. "As he finished . . . picked up the phone": Roy Rowan, *The Four Days of Mayaguez*, p. 17.

26. "Sixty-two-year-old captain . . . counting out $5,000 in shore pay.": Miller debrief, Roy Rowan notes, *Mayaguez* Papers, p. 1.

26. "He was still spry . . . taking the steps two at a time from his cabin to the bridge.": Roy Rowan, *The Four Days of Mayaguez*, p. 18.

27. "Coombes knew . . . an SOS would have little value.": Miller debrief, Roy Rowan notes, *Mayaguez* Papers, p. 13.

27. "Twice before Greenlin had been in a tight spot.": Roy Rowan, *The Four Days of Mayaguez*, p. 27.

28. "The Swift boat fleet seized . . . vessels on May 6.": Daniel P. Bolger, *Americans at War 1975-1986, An Era of Violent Peace*, p. 22.

29. "Sereno released the ladder . . . it stretched toward water.": Roy Rowan, *The Four Days of Mayaguez*, p. 38.

29. "The first Cambodian . . . battalion commander Sa Mean.": Em Son, interview, Phnom Penh, October 2000. Sa Mean was of equivalent rank as Em Son, commanded the garrison at Poulo Wai, and captured the ship. According to Em Son, Sa Mean was killed in 1978 in Prevang Province. The *Mayaguez* crew never knew the name of the man they called the "Ensign."

29. "An AK-47 . . . and he carried a U.S. Army field-pack radio.": Roy Rowan, *The Four Days of Mayaguez*, p. 40.

30. "Third Mate David C. English was . . . shot twice during combat in Vietnam.": Roy Rowan, *The Four Days of Mayaguez*, p. 42.

31. "'Things can't be that bad, mate,' replied the Australian.": Roy Rowan, *The Four Days of Mayaguez*, p. 46.

32. "He made a call . . . after which he said to Miller, 'Okay.'": Miller debrief, Roy Rowan notes, *Mayaguez* Papers, tape III, p. 7.

CHAPTER 3

33. "Neal notified the U.S. embassy . . . dispatch reached the National Military Command Center (NMCC) in Washington.": Daniel P. Bolger, *Americans at War 1975-1986, An Era of Violent Peace*, p. 23.

34. "'We've got a little crisis,' . . . after a weekend of golf, tennis and swimming.": Roy Rowan, *The Four Days of Mayaguez*, p. 66.

34. "The president also had recently learned . . . executions were being expanded to include virtually anyone with 'bourgeois' education.": Henry Kissinger, *Years of Renewal* (New York: Simon and Schuster, 1999), p. 551.

34. "Over in the State Department . . . Kissinger closed the meeting with, 'I know you damned well cannot let Cambodia capture a ship a hundred miles at sea and do nothing.'" Henry Kissinger, *Years of Renewal*, pp. 547-48.

35. "Ford announced . . . he alone had the responsibility for the tough calls.": Ron Nessen, *It Sure Looks Different from the Inside* (New York: Simon and Schuster, 1978), p. 118.

35. "Shortly after nine-thirty . . . Jones was substituting for JCS chairman General George S. Brown who was in Europe on a NATO inspection.": Henry Kissinger, *Years of Renewal*, p. 551.

36. "Colby reported . . . 'would be in or near the port now.'": National Security Council Minutes, May 12, 1975, Top Secret (declassified), Gerald R. Ford Library, p. 3.

36. "At that point, Schlesinger piped in . . . 'ten miles out.'": National Security Council Minutes, May 12, 1975, Top Secret (declassified), p. 3.

36. "Later Kissinger would remark . . . 'a detailed intelligence briefing by Colby . . . wrong in every detail.'": Henry Kissinger, *Years of Renewal*, p. 552.

36. "Kissinger and Schlesinger began an exchange . . . Kissinger opened with . . . 'I also suggest some show of force.'": National Security Council Minutes, May 12, 1975, Top Secret (declassified), p. 5.

37. "Kissinger pegged Schlesinger . . . being the same as procrastination.": Henry Kissinger, *Years of Renewal*, p. 558.

37. "The absence of General Brown . . . direct access to the president, which is the chairman's prerogative by law.": Henry Kissinger, *Years of Renewal*, p. 558.

37. "'There is an old Chinese saying . . . and that is the impression that we should convey.'": National Security Council Minutes, May 12, 1975, Top Secret (declassified), p. 8.

37. "He felt the need to personally turn it into *specific* action and on *his* order . . . 'we will mine.'": National Security Council Minutes, May 12, 1975, Top Secret (declassified), p. 8.

37. "'Henry was an incorrigible signal-sender . . . ' Schlesinger later recalled.": Walter Isaacson, *Kissinger* (New York: Simon and Schuster, 1992), p. 650.

38. "Kissinger leaned forward . . . 'we are not to be trifled with.'": National Security Council Minutes, May 12, 1975, Top Secret (declassified), p. 11.

38. "The president pronounced it 'judge-a-ment . . . the Italian pronunciation.'": *Newsweek*, May 26, 1975, p. 15.

39. "Ford ignored . . . he did not 'give a damn about offending their sensibilities.'" Gerald A. Ford, *A Time to Heal* (New York: Harper and Row, 1979), p. 277, and Daniel P. Bolger, *Americans at War 1975-1986, An Era of Violent Peace*, p. 27.

39. "Kissinger summed up . . . 'I am more in favor of seizing something, be it the island, the ship, or Kompong Som.'": National Security Council Minutes, May 12, 1975, Top Secret (declassified), p. 15.

40. "Nessen issued a press release stating that the president 'considers the seizure an act of piracy.'": *Time*, May 26, 1975, p. 12.

40. "While taking questions, Nessen covered . . . cargo (unknown commercial).":
News Conference #211, At the White House with Ron Nessen, Gerald R. Ford
Library, pp. 1-3.

40. "Schlesinger expanded . . . okaying the preparation of sea mines . . . approved for
use in any recovery attempt.": Daniel P. Bolger, *Americans at War 1975-1986, An Era
of Violent Peace.*

40. "The Government . . . in Phnom Penh will be responsible for the consequences.":
Henry Kissinger, *Years of Renewal*, p. 555.

41. "Kissinger offered to cancel . . . but Ford . . . told Kissinger to go.": Walter
Isaacson, *Kissinger*, p. 649.

CHAPTER 4

43. "*U.S. pilots . . . 'can't even bomb an outhouse without my approval.'* Lyndon B.
Johnson": William C. Westmoreland, *A Soldier Reports* (Garden City, N.Y.:
Doubleday, 1976)

44. "Peterson then relayed the disturbing message to Subic that his 5-inch gun was
out of service": Roy Rowan, *The Four Days of Mayaguez*, p. 73.

44. "On April 30 . . . would be the final shots fired at an American vessel during the
collapse of South Vietnam.": Roy Rowan, *The Four Days of Mayaguez*, p. 74.

CHAPTER 5

47. "Be sure you are right, then go ahead. The motto of David Crockett in the War
of 1812": John Bartlett, comp., *Familiar Quotations*, 9th ed. (1901).

47. "Miller . . . began handing out apples and oranges to the Khmer gunmen.": Miller
debrief, Roy Rowan notes, *Mayaguez* Papers, tape III, p. 10.

48. "Miller pointed at the bucket . . . 'these fellas are getting a little friendlier.'": Roy
Rowan, *The Four Days of Mayaguez*, p. 60.

48. "English worked out a two-part plan . . . .so he dialed the engine room and started gabbing.": English debrief, Roy Rowan notes, *Mayaguez* Papers, English—
vignettes during the seizure, p. 1.

48. "English scanned the deck. 'Let's find out . . . what they're armed with.'": Roy
Rowan, *The Four Days of Mayaguez*, p. 61.

49. "They would not let anyone . . . they believed it might be used for sending messages.": *Time*, May 26, 1975, p. 17.

49. "The Khmers showed misgivings . . . avoiding the mashed potatoes altogether.": Roy Rowan, *The Four Days of Mayaguez*, p. 62.

49. "The Cambodian escorted him to his cabin . . . and while Miller slept he feared the two might enlist the other crew members.": Miller debrief, Roy Rowan notes, *Mayaguez* Papers, tape III, p. 8.

49. "The task group . . . got the first warning order at 8:00 P.M.": Daniel P. Bolger, *Americans at War 1975-1986, An Era of Violent Peace*, p. 24.

50. "The U-Tapao pilot raised his gear handle . . . fifteen minutes later when the Orion Le Doux had launched from U-Tapao began painting Poulo Wai on radar.": Daniel P. Bolger, *Americans at War 1975-1986, An Era of Violent Peace*, p. 24.

50. "Messegee had imposed . . . 'play heads up!'": Daniel P. Bolger, *Americans at War 1975-1986, An Era of Violent Peace*. p. 25.

51. "The new Orion . . . read the name in white block letters on bow and stern: MAYAGUEZ.": Daniel P. Bolger, *Americans at War 1975- 1986, An Era of Violent Peace*. p. 29.

CHAPTER 6

53. "*Hold the fort! I am coming! Gen. William T. Sherman, as signaled to General Corse in Allatoona from the top of Kenesaw, October 5, 1864*": John Bartlett, comp., *Familiar Quotations*, 9th ed.

53. "Captain Miller got orders . . . a 022 degree course to the northeast . . . instead aimed at a chain of small islands on the way to the mainland": Roy Rowan, *The Four Days of Mayaguez*, p. 82.

54. "Minutes later . . . Sanchez pounded his fists together. 'We're going to get help now.'": Roy Rowan, *The Four Days of Mayaguez*, p. 82.

54. "Burns directed . . . his command post divert them anyway. By radio, Bogard was instructed to proceed to the . . . southeast and began a climb.": Daniel P. Bolger, *Americans at War 1975-1986, An Era of Violent Peace*, p. 30.

57. "Shutting down the power plant caused a short burst of steam . . . it was thought the *Mayaguez* might be preparing to get under way. The A-7s were told to make a low pass for a closer look.": Daniel P. Bolger, *Americans at War 1975-1986, An Era of Violent Peace*, p. 30.

58. "Miller watched the gunboats return to the ship . . . heading back for the five thousand dollars Miller had left in the safe.": Roy Rowan, *The Four Days of Mayaguez*, p. 94.

59. "Myregard looked . . . 'Let's just wait, Jerry. I don't want to get anyone in this crew shot and killed if we don't have to.'" Roy Rowan, *The Four Days of Mayaguez*, p. 96.

60. "The fishing boat pulled alongside, then . . . a plane spilled out a string of flares as it passed overhead.": Roy Rowan, *The Four Days of Mayaguez*, p. 99.

CHAPTER 7

61. A sizeable rescue force . . . USS *Coral Sea* . . . USS *Holt* . . . USS *Wilson* . . . .USS *Okinawa* . . . would not reach Koh Tang until the eighteenth at the earliest.": John F. Guilmartin, *A Very Short War* (College Station, Tex.: Texas A&M University Press, 1995), p. 47.

62. "There they were told that Colonel John M. Johnson . . . was designated as commander of Task Group 79.9.": John M. Johnson, Randall W. Austin and David Quinlan, *The Koh Tang Mayaguez Operation*, final report, 1975, p. 5.

62. "One of the last times U.S. marines had retaken a ship was during the Civil War blockades.": *Official Records of the Union and Confederate Navies in the War of Rebellion*, Cornell University Library, Series 1, Vol. VI, p. 195, and Vol. XII, p. 346, 709, et al.

62. "Major Raymond E. Porter . . . assisted by Captain J. P. Feltner . . . would assume on-scene command . . . . D Company might be going into action, but none like they had ever imagined.": Daniel P. Bolger, *Americans at War 1975-1986, An Era of Violent Peace*, p. 33.

62. "Most of 1st Battalion, 9th marines . . . could not be extended except in case of an emergency. The III MAF sought authorization . . . but it was denied.": George R. Dunham and David Quinlan, *U.S. Marines in Vietnam 1970-75, The Bitter End*, p. 251.

64. "Hargrove exhibited 'homesickness and a deep longing for his wife.' His adjustment problems were serious . . . but the medical officer . . . found Hargrove 'fit for duty.': *Investigation to Inquire into the Circumstances Surrounding the Missing in Action Status in the Case of USMC Lance Corporal Joseph N. Hargrove*, June 7, 1975, 3D Marine Division, Fleet Marine Force, FPOSF 96602, p. 3.

64. "Marshall . . . had been 'busted by four Japanese police and a Marine captain' ten days earlier . . . it was only a matter of time before the Marine Corps . . . dug up his past, and sent him to prison.": Anonymous diary entry, pp. 7-8.

65. "But Taylor had worked well . . . Davis broke regulations, stuffing the papers in a drawer as he turned to other matters.": John F. Guilmartin, *A Very Short War*, p. 51.

66. "Though there were plenty of people with problems . . . no one was cut from the deployment roster.": Mykle Stahl, interview, San Antonio, Texas, August 2000, tape 1, side 1.

CHAPTER 8

69. *"He was damn good with an M-60 machine-gun, and he carried a pocket Bible into combat.":* Lt. James Davis notes.

70. *"Mount Olive Tribune* . . . January 3, 1969, issue I found an article headlined, 'Beautancus Home Gutted by Fire.'": *Mount Olive Tribune*, "Area Man Bound over to Court," January 3, 1969, p. 3.

72. "But Rudolph . . . waited until . . . the witching hour that cold night, he set a fire . . . and the fire department came.": *Mount Olive Tribune*, "Area Man Bound over to Court," January 3, 1969, p. 3.

73. "On August 27, 1969, Rudolph Hargrove was sentenced to eight to ten years for unlawfully burning a dwelling.": *Mount Olive Tribune*, "Duplin Man Gets Prison Term for House Burning," August 29, 1969, p. 8.

73. "he met Gail . . . got married right after receiving orders to report to Okinawa .": From interviews with brother Kochise Hargrove, sister-in-law Sandy Hargrove, and mother Charlotte, January-November 1999, Mount Olive, North Carolina, and other locations.

CHAPTER 9

75. "The 21st Special Operations Squadron was equipped with . . . CH-53 had guns located in the crew door and left forward cabin window. The Rescue HH-53s had those and a third gun .": John F. Guilmartin, *A Very Short War*, p. 43.

77. "All operable . . . helicopters were loaded and . . . seven CH-53s launched toward U-Tapao along with five HH-53s.": John F. Guilmartin, *A Very Short War*, pp. 13-14.

78. "Initial thoughts were that . . . whoever had gotten back aboard was now scurrying off the ship.": Roy Rowan, *The Four Days of Mayaguez*, p. 102.

78. "At 2:11 A.M. on May 14, General Brent Scowcroft awakened President Ford. The *Mayaguez* was under way, headed for the mainland.": Ron Nessen, *It Sure Looks Different from the Inside*, p. 121.

79. "Rockefeller was not swayed. 'The issue is how we respond. Many are watching us, in Korea, and elsewhere . . . . I think we need to respond quickly.'": National Security Council Minutes, May 13, 1975, 10:22 A.M., Top Secret (declassified), p. 11.

80. "Ford was mindful . . . of the USS *Pueblo* crew back in '68 . . . . He ordered the air force to stop any Cambodian boats from moving either to or from Koh Tang and the mainland.": Ron Nessen, *It Sure Looks Different from the Inside*, p. 121.

80. "Obvious to Ford . . . 'I am very concerned about the delay in reports . . . .There must be the quickest possible communication to me.'": National Security Council Minutes, May 13, 1975, 10:22 A.M., Top Secret (declassified), p. 7.

81. "Kissinger later confided, 'The risks were greater than the benefits and the benefits were really domestic.'": Roy Rowan, *The Four Days of Mayaguez*, p. 92.

81. "Schlesinger had argued against the use of the big bombers, which were so widely tied . . . to the unpopular cause in Vietnam.": Ron Nessen, *It Sure Looks Different from the Inside*, p. 122.

81. "Kissinger drew a confident smile and said: 'I know your magazine's deadline. I think we can meet it.'" Roy Rowan, *The Four Days of Mayaguez*, p. 92.

CHAPTER 10

84. "Gary was a tall, clumsy kid who was the target for most of our jokes and put-downs.": David Sammons, interview, childhood friend of Gary Hall, Covington, Kentucky, August 26, 2000.

85. "'Strict is what he was. You knew exactly what the man had in mind when he spoke.'": David Sammons, interview, childhood friend of Gary Hall, Covington, Kentucky, August 26, 2000.

86. "No, I'm not signin' no papers while you're still under eighteen.": Norma Hall, interview with Gary's mother, Covington, Kentucky, August 28, 2000.

86. "'When we got to Parris Island . . . .Mosquitoes were eating me alive . . . . "Don't touch them mosquitoes. They got a right to eat too!'": Larry Barnett interview, Parris Island recruit, Phnom Penh, October 2000.

87. "Gary Hall . . . looked you right in the eye when he spoke, and there was none of the clumsiness . . . he had when he left for boot camp.": Barbara and David Jones, interview, childhood friends of Gary Hall, Covington, Kentucky, August 25, 2000, and David Sammons, childhood friend of Gary Hall, Covington, Kentucky, August 26, 2000.

CHAPTER 11

89. "A sailor's life was tough on a wife and marriage. . . . He wondered if she was in for a really extended period of his 'absence.'": Roy Rowan, *The Four Days of Mayaguez*, p. 119.

90. "Dave English had spread his 250 pounds over the same fish net . . . listened to the plane grinding away the hours, a few thousand feet above.": Roy Rowan, *The Four Days of Mayaguez*, p. 123.

91. *"Pull something like that, and we all may get our heads chopped off*, thought Miller.": Roy Rowan, *The Four Days of Mayaguez*, pp. 104-30.

92. "Then a four-engine turboprop joined. . . . Flashes of cannon fire spit from its side ports above where the lone patrol boat still headed northeast.": Daniel P. Bolger, *Americans at War 1975-1986, An Era of Violent Peace*, p.41.

CHAPTER 12

95. "Even the right decision is wrong if it's made too late.": Lee Iacocca, *Iacocca, An Autobiography*, with William Novak, (New York: Bantam Books, 1984), p. 54.

96. "The link passed information . . . directly connected to real-time events.": John F. Guilmartin, *A Very Short War*, p. 55.

96. "Robotoy . . . sawed off the end of the boat. It sank so fast that an inbound RF-4C reconnaissance plane could only photograph an ominous slick in the water.": Daniel P. Bolger, *Americans at War 1975-1986, An Era of Violent Peace*, p. 42.

97. "'Thirty to forty possible Caucasians are huddled in the bow.'": Reports of the Comptroller General of the United States, Seizure of the *Mayaguez*, Part IV, U.S. Government Printing Office, Washington, D.C., October 4, 1976, p. 118.

97. "But the president was torn with the other possibility . . . he might kill them all.": Roy Rowan, *The Four Days of Mayaguez*, p. 143.

97. "At 10:30 P.M. the council members joined Ford . . . assumed that if the fishing boat with those crew members got ashore, the odds were against getting them back unharmed. . . . Schlesinger urged caution arguing.": National Security Council Minutes, May 13, 1975, 10:40 P.M., Top Secret (declassified), p. 2.

97. "Ford looked around . . . 'Do we let them go into port?'": National Security Council Minutes, May 13, 1975, 10:40 P.M., Top Secret (declassified), p. 3.

98. "I gave the order . . . .I cannot understand what happened on that order.": National Security Council Minutes, May 13, 1975, 10:40 P.M., Top Secret (declassified), p. 4.

98. "Jones . . . 'Our communications are so good that we can . . . make the decisions from here.'": National Security Council Minutes, May 13, 1975, 10:40 P.M., Top Secret (declassified), p. 4.

99. "'I have to get the word out,' Scowcroft interrupted. 'What should I tell them?'": National Security Council Minutes, May 13, 1975, 10:40 P.M., Top Secret (declassified), p. 5.

99. "Ford spoke. . . . 'do not attack it.'": National Security Council Minutes, May 13, 1975, 10:40 P.M., Top Secret (declassified), p. 5.

99. "'I think the pilot should sink them," Kissinger said . . . . 'He should destroy the boats and not send situation reports.'": National Security Council Minutes, May 13, 1975, 10:40 P.M., Top Secret (declassified), p. 5.

99. "One Chinese official did hint . . . in the event the United States, undertook military measures.": Daniel P. Bolger, *Americans at War 1975-1986, An Era of Violent Peace*, p. 43.

99. "Henry Kissinger. . . . 'I am thinking not of Cambodia, but of Korea, and of the Soviet Union and of others.'": National Security Council Minutes, May 13, 1975, 10:40 P.M., Top Secret (declassified), p. 11.

100. "Jones presented five. . . . The fifth alternative . . . was to bomb additional mainland targets twenty-four hours after attacking Cambodian shipping.": Possible Scenarios for Recovery of Ship and Crew, Top Secret (declassified), briefing by General Jones to NSC, pp. 1-4.

102. "H-hour wound up being set by the Pentagon for just before sunrise, May 15, Cambodia time.": Daniel P. Bolger, *Americans at War 1975-1986, An Era of Violent Peace*, p. 43.

102. "Should the exact timing of the attack have been left up to the marine commander . . . ?": A review of Lieutenant Colonel John F. Guilmartin, Jr.'s *A Very Short War*, includes a scholarly discussion of this very issue on p. 58.

CHAPTER 13

103. "I accepted the realization that . . . its objective could no longer be rescue, only retaliation.": Lloyd M. Bucher, *Bucher: My Story*, with Mark Rascovich (New York: Doubleday and Company, 1970), p. 211.

104. "Major Porter's D Company . . . briefing turned out to be more like a quiz session. . . . 'questioned as to the feasibility of a helo assault directly onto the deck of the Mayaguez.'": Daniel P. Bolger, *Americans at War 1975-1986, An Era of Violent Peace*, p. 40.

105. "Small gray cartridges . . . spewing clouds of white tear gas.": Roy Rowan, *The Four Days of Mayaguez*, p. 146.

105. "Then the smoke cleared. . . . *Now's the time*, thought English . . . . Second Engineer Juan Sanchez, unconscious on the deck.": Roy Rowan, *The Four Days of Mayaguez*, p. 147.

107. "His message was that this was a navy problem that should be dealt with on navy territory.": Em Son, interview, Takeo Province, Cambodia, October 2000.

107. "This guy don't look Cambodian to me. I think he's Thai.": Roy Rowan, *The Four Days of Mayaguez*, p. 157.

108. "The pilot had no idea of the significance . . . nor did anyone in the film-analysis room . . . when the film was developed an hour and a half later.": Reports of the Comptroller General of the United States, Subcommittee on International Political and Military Affairs, Seizure of the *Mayaguez*, Part IV, p. 77.

108. "Welcome to Cambodia.": Roy Rowan, *The Four Days of Mayaguez*, p. 160.

CHAPTER 14

111. "Shortly after 2:00 P.M. . . . Burns decided the idea of a direct helicopter assault onto the *Mayaguez* was pointless. . . . Porter's men stood down.": Daniel P. Bolger, *Americans at War 1975-1986, An Era of Violent Peace*, p. 22.

112. "General Burns got word of the decision . . . to proceed with option four . . . at 5:42 A.M., four minutes before sunrise on Thursday, May 15, the next morning.": John F. Guilmartin, *A Very Short War*, p. 59.

112. "Still not yet considered . . . the break of day began some thirty minutes before sunrise.": U.S. Naval Observatory, *The Nautical Almanac for the Year 1975*, pp. 99, 258.

113. "General Burns told him that the mission commander . . . aircraft 'will coordinate the strike activities and receive directions from [me].'" George R. Dunham and David Quinlan, *U.S. Marines in Vietnam 1970-75, The Bitter End*, p. 245.

113. "Admiral Gayler in Hawaii advised Burns that *he* was retaining control of the marines.": George R. Dunham and David Quinlan, *U.S. Marines in Vietnam 1970-75, The Bitter End*, p. 240.

113. "The physical separation . . . was a source of particular irritation to Johnson.": Austin Johnson and David Quinlan, *The Koh Tang* Mayaguez *Operation*, after-action report, May 1975, p. 11.

113. "while he, Colonel Johnson, supposedly in charge and only two hundred miles from the fight, could not.": George R. Dunham and David Quinlan, *U.S. Marines in Vietnam 1970-75, The Bitter End*, p. 245.

113. "Due to the scarcity of helicopters, Colonel Johnson . . . effectively relinquishing his on-scene control to Lieutenant Colonel Randall W. Austin.": George R. Dunham and David Quinlan, *U.S. Marines in Vietnam 1970-75, The Bitter End*, p. 245.

111. "In any event, Johnson decided . . . G Company, headed by Captain Davis, to hit the beach first.": Austin Johnson and David Quinlan, *The Koh Tang* Mayaguez *Operation*, after-action report, May 1975, p. 11, and John F. Guilmartin, *A Very Short War*, p. 72.

115. "'Do any members of your crew work for the CIA?' . . . 'We can only talk to commercial radio stations or to other ships.'": Roy Rowan, *The Four Days of Mayaguez*, p. 163.

117. "Then the commander got on the microphone . . . the English- speaker told Miller that . . . his crew would return to the ship. . . . Harrington . . . wanted two shifts. 'Seven, Captain,' he said.": Roy Rowan, *The Four Days of Mayaguez*, p. 168.

118. "Myregard . . . 'I'm not going by gunboat. Our own planes will blow that thing out of the water.'": Roy Rowan, *The Four Days of Mayaguez*, p. 169.

119. "Colonel James M. Shankles . . . on the ground at U-Tapao during the critical planning period, but no one from his staff was brought to the meeting.": John F. Guilmartin, *A Very Short War*, p. 79.

120. "Regardless, there were those above the level of the planning group at U-Tapao who did know . . . but did not as yet know what the marine attack plan entailed.": George R. Dunham and David Quinlan, *U.S. Marines in Vietnam 1970-75, The Bitter End*, p. 245.

121. "Colonel Alfred Merrill . . . approached . . . General Baxter, with his concerns. Baxter . . . dismissed him.": John F. Guilmartin, *A Very Short War*, p. 79.

121. "Private K. O. Taylor . . . problem marine . . . would go in with Davis on the first wave.": John F. Guilmartin, *A Very Short War*, p. 81.

122. "General Burns . . . approved the plan and called it in to Admiral Gayler in Hawaii.": General John J. Burns interview, Long Beach, CA, July 27, 1999.

122. "When the security-police option had been briefed . . . the attack should be made from U.S. destroyers with sufficient gunfire to cover a boarding party.": Robert T. Hartmann, *Palace Politics*, 1980, p. 326.

122. "So Gayler trumped the idea of a simultaneous ship and island assault.": Daniel P. Bolger, *Americans at War 1975-1986, An Era of Violent Peace*, p. 55.

123. "Henry Kissinger . . . 'My recommendation is to do it ferociously. We should not just hit mobile targets, but others as well.'": National Security Council Minutes, May 14, 1975, 3:52 P.M., Top Secret (declassified), p. 18.

123. "Schlesinger agreed. 'We will destroy whatever targets there are.' Ford added, 'And they should not stop until we tell them.'": National Security Council Minutes, May 14, 1975, 3:52 P.M., Top Secret (declassified), p. 18.

213. In fact . . . at his request, the president had allowed him a leave of absence to go back to Phnom Penh.": David Kennerly, telephone interview, December 13, 1999.

124. "'Has anyone considered . . . that he might not have gotten his orders from Phnom Penh?'" David Kennerly, as read to during telephone interview, December 13, 1999.

124. "'But I was in Cambodia. . . . We don't even know who the leadership is. Has anyone considered that?'": Daniel P. Bolger, *Americans at War 1975-1986, An Era of Violent Peace*, p. 56, and interview with David Kennerly, by telephone at his residence, December 13, 1999.

CHAPTER 15

126. "Eugene Marshall had no job.... 'Gene sure could drink a bit, though.'": Interview with nearby neighbor who declined to be identified, Waverly, West Virginia, September 1, 2000.

127. "'Meet me at the park at noon,' was a common challenge issued by Danny.": Roger McPherson, interview with childhood friend, Waverly, West Virginia, August 31, 2000.

127. "'They took every darn ornament off the tree I decorated in the front yard. Didn't leave a one.'": Interview with nearby neighbor who declined to be identified, Waverly, West Virginia, September 1, 2000.

127. "Danny nodded at the tool, 'you can have her.' The boy backed off . . . never making a move toward Teleah.": Teleah Cross, interview with childhood sweetheart, Williamstown, West Virginia, August 31, 2000.

128. "Danny somehow became the proud owner of an old blue-and-white Plymouth. He . . . 'would drive the thing two days, then work on it for ten.'": Teleah Cross, interview with childhood sweetheart, Williamstown, West Virginia, August 31, 2000.

128. "Joe Marshall was working on the machine by the side of the house.": Teleah Cross, interview with childhood sweetheart, Williamstown, West Virginia, August 31, 2000.

128. "He clubbed Huggins up the side of the head, then shoved White to the ground.": Teleah Cross, interview with childhood sweetheart, Williamstown, West Virginia, August 31, 2000.

128. "White and Huggins . . . obliged Danny with his own set of handcuffs.": Teleah Cross, interview with childhood sweetheart, Williamstown, West Virginia, August 31, 2000, and Roger McPherson, interview, childhood friend, Waverly, West Virginia, August 31, 2000.

129. "According to . . . Teleah, Danny's hometown was rid of 'the orneriest little white boy the Waverlians ever seen.'" Teleah Cross, interview with childhood sweetheart, Williamstown, West Virginia, August 31, 2000.

CHAPTER 16

132. "Em Son knew simply that . . . the increasing amount of American air traffic did not bode well for the future.": Em Son, interview, Tang island, Cambodia, March 1999.

133. "Ki was also responsible for patrols around the seven-mile island.": Em Son, interview, Phnom Penh, Cambodia, October 2000.

133. "The unit took their orders by radio from III Division Headquarters on the mainland at Ream, commanded by Meas Mut.": JTF-FA message P 071840Z, May 1999, Additional Information Report 991C-001 Concerning Tang Island Priority Case 1998 and Cases 2002, 2003, and 2038, p. 4.

134. "The gun pits were well stocked and ammunition bunkers were easily reached.": Rot Leng, interview, Kompong Som and Tang Island, Cambodia, February 1997.

134. "'Take them to Kompong Som,' Em Son had told Sa Mean.": Em Son, interview, Phnom Penh, Cambodia, October 2000.

135. "'As long as the ship stays far from the island, do nothing,' came the reply. 'Our naval force is not strong enough to counter it.'": Em Son, interview, Phnom Penh, Cambodia, October 2000.

CHAPTER 17

138. "Only . . . Em Seng and his sister Em Sao were allowed to remain to care for the property.": Em Sao and Em Seng interview, Takeo Province, Cambodia, October 2000.

139. "Em Son was quick to learn . . . prisoners except for brief question-and-answer sessions that ended in executions.": William Shawcross, *Sideshow, Kissinger, Nixon and the Destruction of Cambodia* (New York: Simon and Schuster, 1979), pp. 248-49.

141. "Em Son ordered the village evacuated to the mainland as he began preparations to defend the island from attack.": Em Son, interview, Takeo Province, Cambodia, October 2000.

Chapter 18

143. "In those cases . . . no helicopter from Nakhon Phanom had been lost, even though confusion ruled the day.": John F. Guilmartin, *A Very Short War*, pp. 18-24.

144. "He told the assault force . . . the opposition to consist of between eighteen and thirty irregulars.": George R. Dunham and David Quinlan, *U. S. Marines in Vietnam 1970 to 75 The Bitter End*, p. 248, and John F. Guilmartin, *A Very Short War*, p. 84.

145. "Major Porter's boarding party would embark on *Jolly-11, Jolly-12,* and *Jolly-13* HH-53s.": John F. Guilmartin, *A Very Short War*, p. 84.

145. "For the next hour and a half the men worked with Anders, 'feverishly' assembling the details into a workable structure.": Kawanami, *History of 3rd Tactical Fighter Wing*, pp. Kenneth K. Kawanami, U.S. Government Printing Office, 1975, 55-57.

146. "'you'll set up a defensive perimeter and you'll shoot any enemy assaulting down the beach and any gunboats that try to come around behind us.'": Gale Rogers, interview, February 1999.

146. "Stahl had a problem . . . chose to move his second machine-gun crew, Hargrove, Hall, and Marshall, to another helo.": Mykle Stahl, interview,. September 2000.

146. "It was then," McNemar was to say years later, "that we knew we were going into shit.": John F. Guilmartin, *A Very Short War*, p. 86, and phone interview with Lester McNemar, December 2000.

Chapter 19

149. At 6:10 P.M. . . . President Ford . . . brushed right past James Cannon . . . trying to stop him to sign a letter to Mayor Beame denying financial aid to nearly bankrupt New York City.": Ron Nessen, *It Sure Looks Different from the Inside*, p. 123.

150. "Senator Mike Mansfield asked why the bombing of Kompong Som . . . since he heard that some members of the crew were believed to be there.": Roy Rowan, *The Four Days of Mayaguez*, p. 179.

150. "The bombing was designed to prevent the launch of a counterattack by some twenty-four hundred troops stationed around Kompong Som.": Ron Nessen, *It Sure Looks Different from the Inside*, p. 124.

151. "Not mentioned by Ford was the fact that the oil storage facility at Kompong Som was also targeted in each of the four planned raids.": John F. Guilmartin, *A Very Short War*, p. 211.

151. "Senator John McClelland . . . 'Do we have to do it all at once? Can't we wait to see if the Cambodians attack before we attack the mainland?'" Ron Nessen, *It Sure Looks Different from the Inside*, p. 124.

152. "James Eastland . . . 'Blow the hell out of 'em.'": Milton R. Benjamin, Paul Brinkley-Rogers, Bernard Krisher, Ron Moreau, and Lloyd H. Norman, "Ford's Rescue Operation," *Time*, May 26, 1975, p. 25.

CHAPTER 20

153. "the last of the CH-53 *Knives* and three more *Jolly Green* helicopters lifted off for Koh Tang, a total of eleven in all.": U-Tapao status board, May 15, 1975, official USAF photograph of the helicopter status board showing launch and recovery times.

155. "'Everybody up!' Miller shouted . . . 'Come on, everybody. Get up!'" Roy Rowan, *The Four Days of Mayaguez*, p. 184.

155. "Standing nearby was Dave English. . . . 'More goddamn lies.' He turned and walked away.": Roy Rowan, *The Four Days of Mayaguez*, p. 186.

156. "Davis . . . *We should be hitting the beach now*! As he breathed, he felt the lump from the photographs tucked inside his flak vest. . . . *Here we go again*, he thought.": John F. Guilmartin, *A Very Short War*, p. 86.

156. "Captain Walter Wood looked out at an 'incredibly small helo pad.'" Daniel P. Bolger, *Americans at War 1975-1986, An Era of Violent Peace*, p. 60.

157. "Up, up, everyone up!" Em Son shouted. . . . Men came tumbling out of barracks buildings and from inside makeshift tents.": Rot Leng, interview, Kompong Som, Cambodia, February 1997, and Em Son, interview, Phnom Penh, Cambodia, October 2000.

157. "'Oh, my God, here we go again.'. . . Em Son took a deep breath, set himself, then yelled for his men to get to their positions.": Em Son, interview, Phnom Penh, Cambodia, October 2000, tape 1, side 1.

158. At 6:10 A.M . . . . on nearby Rong Sam Lem . . . the English-speaker said. 'The high commander in Phnom Penh has not given them permission to release the crew.": Roy Rowan, *The Four Days of Mayaguez*, p. 187.

158. Denham's helicopter came in low and fast. . . . Suddenly, tracers whipped in front of Denham's eyes. . . . Twenty marines shouted as they ran out the open ramp for cover.": John F. Guilmartin, *A Very Short War*, p. 89.

160. "Captain Davis . . . reached up and felt blood oozing between his fingers.": John F. Guilmartin, *A Very Short War*, p. 88, and Wyatt, interview, Los Angeles, May 2000, tape 1, side 1.

160. "Wyatt, bleeding from his left ear. . . . Liquid was sloshing around on the floorboards, but he didn't smell fuel. It was leakage from damaged water barrels.": Wyatt, interview, Los Angeles, May 2000, tape 1.

160. "*Knife-21* settled into the water. . . . Sergeant Rumbaugh was nowhere in sight above the swirling, hissing surface.": Daniel P. Bolger, *Americans at War 1975-1986, An Era of Violent Peace*, p. 64.

160. "Two helicopters were sliding in from the left toward the east beach. Phat Kheng took aim.": Rot Leng, interview, Kompong Som, Cambodia, March 1999.

163. "The wounded sergeant was the last to reach safety as the helicopter disintegrated and explosions ripped the air.": Larry Barnett, notes, series of e-mail interviews, September 2000.

163. "flames that swept in through the gun port while bullets cut through the fuselage 'like green fire flies.'" Timothy Trebil, telephone interview, September 24, 2000.

164. "Once outside . . . Gregory S. Copenhaver and two other marines charged the beach.": John F. Guilmartin, *A Very Short War*, p. 90.

164. "the last man to leave the helicopter alive.": Timothy Trebil, telephone interview, September 24, 2000.

166. "Ralston thought it was marker dye. Then he realized the stain was human blood.": Daniel P. Bolger, *Americans at War 1975-1986, An Era of Violent Peace*, p. 66.

CHAPTER 21

167. "navy medic began to work on Barschow's leg.": Larry Barnett, e-mail notes, September 2000.

168. "The airborne controller in *Cricket* . . . was attempting to maintain contact with survivors of a downed aircraft.": John F. Guilmartin, *A Very Short War*, p. 91.

169. "McDaniel . . . guessed, and had managed to overrun one 60-mm mortar position.": George R. Dunham and David Quinlan, *U.S. Marines in Vietnam 1970-75, The Bitter End*, p. 251, and John F. Guilmartin, *A Very Short War*, p. 89.

170. "'*Cricket,* do you want me to insert my marines in the same LZ where *Knife-Twenty-three* and -*Thirty-one* have gone down? . . . ' All the *Jolly*s were also diverted to west beach.": John F. Guilmartin, *A Very Short War*, p. 90.

170. "Then *Jolly-42* . . . saw neither marines nor signs of friendly activity around the landing zone.": John F. Guilmartin, *A Very Short War*, Texas A&M University Press, College Station, Texas, 1995, p. 91.

171. "the air force sergeant who manned the gatling gun. The sergeant fell back, bright arterial blood bubbling from his shattered chest.": Daniel P. Bolger, *Americans at War 1975-1986, An Era of Violent Peace*, p. 67.

172. "Clark . . . took a moment to relish the fact that he was still alive, then . . . the air support that Lieutenant McDaniel had been coordinating showed up.": Dale Clark, interview tape, January 31, 1999.

172. "Lieutenant Colonel Austin gathered his troops and . . . had only four M-16 rifles ": James McDaniel, video interview tape, Henninger Productions, *Seized at Sea*, Discovery Channel documentary, March 2000.

172. "Austin was far from the fighting . . . and the men began inching from one fighting position to another along the beach.": Daniel P. Bolger, *Americans at War 1975-1986, An Era of Violent Peace*, p. 77.

173. "Tutele and Staff Sergeant Serferino Bernal were ordered to take out the Khmer machine gun.": John F. Guilmartin, *A Very Short War*, p. 92.

173. "Greer had been under fire before and as rounds impacted the helicopter, they initially mistook the thumping for the sound of marine boots on the ramp entry.": John F. Guilmartin, *A Very Short War*, p. 101.

175. "The two marines in front and directly behind McDaniel moaned in pain. . . . Loney, a few yards ahead, lay motionless.": James McDaniel, video interview tape, Henninger Productions, *Seized at Sea*, Discovery Channel documentary, March 2000.

CHAPTER 22

178. "'What kind of manifests?' 'I will tell you what they are.'. . . 'You write them down.'": Roy Rowan, *The Four Days of Mayaguez*, pp. 187-88.

178. "'The compound commander . . . Chhan.' . . . 'My name is Samkol'. . . . Manifest number one . . . two . . . three . . . no bombs shooting, no airplanes fly over Cambodia.'": Roy Rowan, *The Four Days of Mayaguez*, p. 188.

179. "Miller paused . . . but more important, he wanted to finish this and get back to his ship. Again, he wrote it down as spoken.": Roy Rowan, *The Four Days of Mayaguez*, p. 189.

180. "'You're not signing a confession for me. It's against my principles.'": Charlie Miller, interview, Miller VII, Roy Rowan notes, *Mayaguez* Papers, p. 5.

181. "'When I get mad, I get pissed . . . .' Tom LaBue shut his mouth.": Roy Rowan, *The Four Days of Mayaguez*, p. 192.

CHAPTER 23

183. "Sir: I have to state . . . that I have taken a valuable prize . . . now called the Susan Jane. . . .": Official Records of the Union and Confederate Navies in the War of Rebellion, Cornell University Library, Series 1, Vol. VI, p. 195.

183. "During the night the USS *Holt*'s maintenance crew had finally managed to jury-rig a power supply for their 5-inch gun . . . he and his crew were ready.": Robert A. Peterson, telephone interview, November 2000.

184. "The *Holt*, one hundred feet shorter than the *Mayaguez*, would use the . . . O-1 deck just above the *Holt*'s main deck. . . . A-7s would strafe near the ship . . . while the *Holt* pulled alongside.": Robert A. Peterson, telephone interview, November 2000, and Daniel P. Bolger, *Americans at War 1975-1986, An Era of Violent Peace*, p. 60.

185. "The *Holt* had rope fenders . . . the maneuver would be dicey, and Peterson would probably have only one chance to succeed.": Daniel P. Bolger, *Americans at War 1975-1986, An Era of Violent Peace*, p. 61.

185. "Captain Wood and his boarding party were positioned on the O-1 deck . . . every M-16 pointed at the hijacked ship.": Robert A. Peterson, telephone interview, November 2000, and Roy Rowan, *The Four Days of Mayaguez*, p. 196.

185. "Captain Wood . . . raced below with his squad, arriving near the bow on the main deck just as the *Holt* slid abeam.": George R. Dunham and David Quinlan, *U.S. Marines in Vietnam 1970-75, The Bitter End*, p. 246.

185. "At 7:25 A.M., the hulls came together. . . . ": Reports of The Comptroller General of the United States, *Seizure of the Mayaguez*, Part IV, Appendix 7, p. 124.

186. "'marines over the side!' . . . Wood and Coker found themselves alone on a vessel. . . . 'Corporal Coker and I worked feverishly at the lines and the two ships were made fast.'": Daniel P. Bolger, *Americans at War 1975-1986, An Era of Violent Peace*, p. 61.

186. "The vessel was deserted.": Daniel P. Bolger, *Americans at War 1975-1986, An Era of Violent Peace*, p. 62.

CHAPTER 24

187. "propaganda minister Hu Nim was picked up by the CIA's Foreign Broadcast Information Service in Bangkok.": Roy Rowan, *The Four Days of Mayaguez*, p. 202.

187. "'Wishing to provoke no one . . . but we will not allow the U.S. imperialists to violate our territorial waters . . . or force us to release their ships whenever they want by applying threats.'": Roy Rowan, *The Four Days of Mayaguez*, p. 204.

187. "The CIA's translators delivered . . . 'an impressive demonstration of the intelligence agency's abilities.'" Ron Nessen, *It Sure Looks Different from the Inside*, p. 125.

188. "Kissinger was monitoring the operation . . . when word of the Cambodian dispatch reached him . . . at around 8:15 P.M.": Ron Nessen, *It Sure Looks Different from the Inside*, p. 125.

188. "A decision had to be made. . . . First Kissinger phoned . . . to inform the National Military Command Center that the planes . . . should proceed on course but drop no ordnance until notified by the president.": Henry Kissinger, *Years of Renewal*, p. 568.

188. "Ford wanted clarification . . . promising to call off military operations as soon as the crew members were freed.": Ron Nessen, *It Sure Looks Different from the Inside*, p. 125.

189. "Nessen took the call in his office. 'Come down here right away,' Kissinger ordered . . . then hung up.": Ron Nessen, *It Sure Looks Different from the Inside*, p. 125.

189. "Scowcroft . . . burst into Nessen's office . . . and . . . pulled him to Kissinger's office.": Ron Nessen, *It Sure Looks Different from the Inside*, p. 125.

189. "We have heard. . . . As soon as you issue a statement . . . we will promptly cease military operations.": Henry Kissinger, *Years of Renewal*, p. 569.

190. "'Relations between the Western democracies . . . have . . . been strained in recent years by . . . to help them solve their immense problems.'": Office of the White House Press Secretary, Exchange of Toasts, Edward J. Savage Files, Gerald R. Ford Library, May 14, 1975, pp. 3-4.

190. "The prime minister made clear . . . he did not consider military force the appropriate way to solve political problems.": Henry Kissinger, *Years of Renewal*, p. 566.

190. "The strike force jettisoned their bombs . . . and headed back to the carrier.": John F. Guilmartin, *A Very Short War*, p. 211.

191. "At 9:15 P.M., Nessen found himself . . . in the press briefing room. . . . "'There are no bigger stories than international military confrontations.'": Ron Nessen, *It Sure Looks Different from the Inside*, p. 126.

191. "'Look!' Nessen shouted. 'What I have to say . . . there is some urgency about it. . . . The newsmen rushed to their phones...cameras.": News Conference #219, At The White House with Ron Nessen, 9:15 P.M. ETD, Gerald R. Ford Library, May 14, 1975, p. 1.

CHAPTER 25

193. "Rogers scanned the crescent-shaped beach. . . . South of the burning helicopter, he spotted a gunboat, partially submerged in the cove.": Roy Rowan, *The Four Days of Mayaguez*, p. 199.

194. " . . . one of his lookouts called out that he saw a head in the water off the port bow.": Roy Rowan, *The Four Days of Mayaguez*, p. 200.

194. "Underneath the ballooning cloud bobbed another head. . . . The gig was armed with two M-60 machine-guns and manned by Petty Officers First Class Alvin Ellis and Thomas Noble.": Roy Rowan, *The Four Days of Mayaguez*, p. 200.

195. "'the medic was right on top of me giving me morphine. Boy, did that feel good.'": Timothy Trebil, telephone interview, September 24, 2000.

195. At 7:29 A.M . . . his crew boarded a fishing boat, the *Sinvari.*": Roy Rowan, *The Four Days of Mayaguez*, p. 206.

196. "'You will contact the American government when you get on your ship. Tell them to stop the jets.'": Roy Rowan, *The Four Days of Mayaguez*, p. 207.

196. "'We free,' he yelled. . . . He started prancing around, and the other four Thais began whooping it up.": Roy Rowan, *The Four Days of Mayaguez*, p. 208.

197. "He . . . pulled five U.S. twenty-dollar bills from the folds of the undergarment.": Roy Rowan, *The Four Days of Mayaguez*, p. 209.

197. "Miller . . . even had Omar doff his white mess jacket.": Roy Rowan, interview notes, Charlie Miller, Tape VII, Gerald R. Ford Library, *Mayaguez* collection, p. 9.

198. "The Orion swung low, three engines running, as it circled the boat.": Roy Rowan, interview notes, Charlie Miller, Tape VII, Gerald R. Ford Library, *Mayaguez* collection, p. 10.

199. "'Captain . . . ' Rogers said, 'you're just about an hour late. They've already started bombing Kompong Som.'" Charles Miller, *Mayaguez* captain, after-action notes on rescue during the *Mayaguez* Incident, Gerald R. Ford Library Archives, p.11.

199. "the time was 11:10 P.M., just minutes after the conclusion of what Kissinger later described as 'the den Uyl fiasco.'": Henry, Kissinger, *Years of Renewal*, p. 570.

199. "Ford came half out of his chair . . . 'They're all safe,' Ford whooped . . . 'We got them all out, thank God. It went perfectly.'" Ron Nessen, *It Sure Looks Different from the Inside*, p. 127.

CHAPTER 26

201. "The shouting sounded as though they were taunting him.": McDaniel, interview, Henninger Productions, *Seized at Sea*, Discovery Channel Documentary, March 2000.

202. "The entire southern flank came alive with gunfire . . . as the two forces converged to within fifteen yards of each other.": John F. Guilmartin, *A Very Short War*, p. 95,

203. "Nessen rushed back to the Oval Office. . . . 'Look, we have one thing that Laitin doesn't have,' Nessen argued . . . .'Why doesn't the president go out and announce the recovery . . . in the middle of the *Johnny Carson Show?*'" Ron Nessen, *It Sure Looks Different from the Inside,* p. 128.

203. "When asked about casualties, Schlesinger stalled.": Robert T. Hartmann, *Palace Politics* (1980), p. 328.

204. "Kissinger interrupted, 'but tell them to bomb the mainland. . . . Otherwise they'll attack us as the ship leaves.'" Ron Nessen, *It Sure Looks Different from the Inside,* p. 129.

204. "At my direction, the United States forces tonight boarded. . . . I have now received information that the vessel has been recovered. . . . I wish to express my deep appreciation . . . for their sacrifice.": Ron Nessen, *It Sure Looks Different from the Inside,* p. 129.

205. "The president took another round of congratulations. Then . . . announced, 'I'm . . . going to bed.'": Ron Nessen, *It Sure Looks Different from the Inside,* p. 129.

205. "Ford turned to the major. 'Say, Bob, how did Baltimore do tonight?'" Robert T. Hartmann, *Palace Politics*, p. 329.

CHAPTER 27

208. "Most of the men inside *Knife-22* erroneously assumed they were in Cambodia. . . . McNemar returned to the downed helicopter and shot up the instrument panel, rendering the machine unflyable.": Suzanne Crotty, letter home, June 3, 1975, describes the landing near the Thai border: "The helicopter that landed in Trat wasn't sure if they were in Thailand or Cambodia, and they came out ready to fight. . . . The one in Trat couldn't be repaired and was trucked back to U-Tapao about a week later."

209. "*Knife-51* and *Knife-52* arrived after being brought to flight status. . . . *Knife-51* was loaded and launched . . . only to be recalled. . . . ": John F. Guilmartin, *A Very Short War*, p.97.

209. "Inside the helicopter operations . . . the battalion staff . . . were . . . assigning the proper infantry units to the remaining helicopters.": John F. Guilmartin, *A Very Short War*, p. 105.

209. "Colonel Johnson was vehement about reinforcing the men on the island before any thought of pulling out would be entertained.": John F. Guilmartin, *A Very Short War*, p. 97.

210. "'You want to go back in with us?' McNemar asked. 'No,' Wyatt replied. McNemar stared hard at him for a moment, then said, 'Yes, you do.'": Wyatt, interview, Los Angeles May, 2000, tape 1, side 1, and telecon Lester McNemar, December 2000.

210. "250 marines to be inserted in the second wave, only 127 men could be squeezed into the . . . helicopters.": John F. Guilmartin, *A Very Short War*, p. 106.

210. "As they headed south . . . the *Specter* AC-130 gunship passed by overhead, returning to U-Tapao to refuel.": George R. Dunham, and David Quinlan, *U.S. Marines in Vietnam 1970-75, The Bitter End*, p. 257.

211. "An information bottleneck had developed as reports . . . were being processed inside *Cricket*, the EC-130 command ship.": John F. Guilmartin, *A Very Short War*, p. 107.

211. "Staffers at every level . . . tried to update their commanders with tail numbers, sortie counts, battle damage reports, and other minutiae.": John F. Guilmartin, *A Very Short War*, p. 108.

212. "Then came word . . . 'disengage and withdraw all forces from operating areas as soon as possible.'": JCS to CINCPAC message, 150455Z (1155G). Urey W. Patrick, *The Mayaguez Operation*, p. 62, asserts that the initial order was issued at about 1030-1045, despite a COMUSSAG/7th Air Force situation report to the contrary.

212. "Bullshit, there are marines down there. Who's going to take them off?" Mykle Stahl, interview, September 2000, tape 1, side 1.

213. "The marine protests were passed to 7th Air Force, and within fifteen minutes the order was rescinded.": John F. Guilmartin, *A Very Short War*, p. 112.

213. "Stahl scampered out of its way, falling again before reaching the sand.": Mykle Stahl, interview, San Antonio, Texas, September 2000, tape 1, side 1.

213. "Meanwhile marines from Davis's G Company were coming toward them carrying five wounded men . . . .": *Air War Vietnam*, Mayaguez *extract*, Headquarters, Pacific Air Force, p. 134.

214. "Scattered firing was coming from Khmer positions and men in black attire were seen running south.": Curtis Myrick, interview, August 2000, tape 1, side 1.

214. "navy medic Poore had hypodermic needles in his mouth and one hand, and his .45 pistol within grasp of the other, working feverishly to get morphine into the screaming wounded.": Curtis Myrick, interview, August 2000, tape 1, side 1.

214. "second lieutenant . . . then drained it in one long guzzle.": Steven Poore, telephone interview, November 2000.

215. "Finally a marine grabbed Stahl . . . .Captain Stahl ceased to be fully effective as a commander.": Mykle Stahl, interview, San Antonio, Texas, September 2000, tape 1, side 1.

217. "All together, they had three rocket-propelled grenade rounds, about 300 AK-47 rounds, a handful of mortar rounds, and some hand grenades.": Rot Leng, interview, Kompong Som, Cambodia, March 1997, tape 1, side 1.

217. "John S. Standfast . . . had positioned the M-60 crew, without Anderson's knowledge.": John S. Standfast, testimony from *Investigation to Inquire into the Circumstances Surrounding the Missing in Action Status in the Case of Private First Class Gary C. Hall, Lance Corporal Joseph N. Hargrove, and Private Danny G. Marshall*, completed on June 7, 1975, p. 1.

218. "Anderson . . . set up three trip flares to warn the men should the Khmer Rouge decide to try infiltrating in the dark.": Investigation of Inquiry, July 1975, Sergeant Carl C. Anderson, sworn statement, p. 1.

218. "Finally, Davis made up his mind. ' . . . we're not going to take this island.'": John F. Guilmartin, *A Very Short War*, p. 116.

CHAPTER 28

219. "Colonel Harry Goodall . . . picked four pilots and had maintenance prepare . . . . OV-10 aircraft for launch.": John F. Guilmartin, *A Very Short War*, p. 112.

220. "Major Robert W. Undorf . . . former fighter pilot.": John F. Guilmartin, *A Very Short War*, p. 112.

220. "orders arrived from 7th Air Force to launch the OV-10s 'ASAP.'": John F. Guilmartin, *A Very Short War*, p. 120.

220. "*Nail-68* and *Nail-47* were airborne minutes later.": John F. Guilmartin, *A Very Short War*, p. 121.

220. "an attempt to pull out Cicere's twenty-five-man unit by helicopter would be tried first.": Daniel P. Bolger, *Americans at War 1975-1986, An Era of Violent Peace*, p. 78.

221. "*Jolly-43* . . . was silhouetted against a white background.": John F. Guilmartin, *A Very Short War*, p. 117.

221. "Sergeant Thomas Bateson as he tried to return fire from the ramp minigun, the only one still operating.": Thomas D. Des Brisay, *Fourteen Hours at Koh Tang*, in USAF Southeast Asia Monograph Series, Vol. 3, U.S. Government Printing Office, Washington, D.C. 1977, p. 137.

221. "*Jolly-43's* . . . volatile mixture that streamed behind the fleeing helicopter for 150 yards.": John F. Guilmartin, *A Very Short War*, p. 117.

222. "Major Undorf, and his wingman who had finally arrived at 4:20 P.M.": John F. Guilmartin, *A Very Short War*, p. 121.

222. "The platoon sergeant got off two more rounds, also missing the Khmer who disappeared before anyone else could take a bead.": Larry Barnett, interview notes, Koh Tang, Cambodia, October 2000, and Cicere, interview, via email, December 2000.

223. "After twenty-one more rounds were fired, the gunboat was . . . silenced for good.": John F. Guilmartin, *A Very Short War*, p. 122.

223. "Khmer casualties up to that point had been inflicted primarily by 20-mm aircraft cannons . . . .": Rot Leng, interview, Kompong Som, Cambodia, March 2000.

223. "the able-bodied Khmer troops had gathered well south of the two beaches.": Em Son, interview, Koh Tang, Cambodia, March 1999.

223. "Lieutenant Colonel Austin felt that his position was defendable overnight, and . . . his men were in good shape.": John F. Guilmartin, *A Very Short War*, p. 115.

224. "At the time . . . Undorf could only count on three armed helicopters, *Jolly-11, Jolly-12,* and *Knife-51.*": John F. Guilmartin, *A Very Short War*, p. 130.

224. "Em Son received word that 'the American leader had been killed and the invaders were preparing to depart.'": Mao Run, interview, Phnom Penh, Cambodia, March 2000, and Rot Leng, interview, Kompong Som, Cambodia, March 2000, Henninger Productions Interviews.

225. "The rest of the thirty-two-man contingent were dug in north of the machine-gun.": Carl C. Anderson, sworn testimony, *Report of Inquiry*, Headquarters, Fleet Marine Force, Pacific, Camp H. M. Smith, Hawaii, July 22, 1975, p. 2.

225. "None of the machine-gun crew was injured . . . .": Robert K. Atkins, sworn testimony, *Report of Inquiry*, Headquarters, Fleet Marine Force, Pacific, Camp H. M. Smith, Hawaii, July 22, 1975, p. 1.

225. "Em Son decided it was 'too dangerous for the moment to proceed with the flanking maneuver.'": Em Son, interview Koh Tang, March, 1999.

226. "To his amazement, they had recovered their ammunition cache unscathed.'": Rot Leng, interview, Kompong Som, Cambodia, March 1997.

226. "Cicere looked at . . . Barnett. "You have to stay, too. Pick ten men.' . . . For Barnett, seeing those hands in the air was the proudest moment . . . " Barnette, interview, Koh Tang, Cambodia, October 2000 and Cicere, interview, via email December 2000.

227. "Backlund requested . . . 'hard stuff,' as he put it, to . . . at least make them keep their heads down.": John F. Guilmartin, *A Very Short War*, p. 123.

227. "'It's time to get the action going.' Undorf got the message.": Daniel P. Bolger, *Americans at War 1975-1986, An Era of Violent Peace*, p. 80.

227. "7th Air Force ordered the dropping of the first of these weapons.": John F. Guilmartin, *A Very Short War*, p. 124, and R. W. Austin, *Koh Tang Assault/Operation* Mayaguez *Report*, December 9, 1975, p. 5.

228. "It exploded just beyond the whirling tail rotor.": Daniel P. Bolger, *Americans at War 1975-1986, An Era of Violent Peace*, p. 82.

229. "Its position was given away by a line of waterspouts that trailed from the beach toward the escaping helicopter.": John F. Guilmartin, *A Very Short War*, p. 124.

229. "The marines . . . dreading the thought that they might be sent out to retrieve it.": Larry Barnett, e-mail notes, September 2000, and Gale Rogers, taped interview, June 1998, tape 1, side 1.

230. "The effect of the BLU-82, if any, was to induce the Cambodians to inch closer to the American lines.": Daniel P. Bolger, *Americans at War 1975-1986, An Era of Violent Peace*, p. 81, and Em Som, interview, Phnom Penh, Cambodia, October 2000.

230. "'We heard it, but we . . . ignored it.'": Em Son, interview, Phnom Penh, Cambodia, October 2000.

230. "The device dangled beside the open door on the partially submerged helicopter.": George R. Dunham and David Quinlan, *U.S. Marines in Vietnam 1970-75, The Bitter End*, p. 259.

231. "Then a piece of rubber tubing was inserted over the two open pipe ends and secured with radiator clamps.": John F. Guilmartin, *A Very Short War*, p 120.

CHAPTER 29

234. "Coordination complete, Undorf . . . began the west-beach extraction . . . after the futile search . . . for the lone survivor on the east side.": John F. Guilmartin, *A Very Short War*, p. 131.

234. "tracers streamed into the perimeter and bounced around like flaming popcorn.": Daniel P. Bolger, *Americans at War 1975-1986, An Era of Violent Peace*, p. 83.

234. "tripping . . . the body of Lance Corporal Loney as they stumbled in the flickering light from the helicopter, with wind and sand from rotor wash swirling about them.": Carl C. Anderson, sworn testimony, *Report of Inquiry*, Headquarters, Fleet Marine Force, Pacific, Camp H. M. Smith, Hawaii, July 22, 1975, p. 3 of Anderson testimony.

235. "A Khmer rocket-propelled-grenade streaked across the blackness . . . beyond the helicopter.": Thomas D. Des Brisay, *Fourteen Hours at Koh Tang*, in *USAF Southeast Asia Monograph Series*, Vol. 3, U.S. Government Printing Office, Washington, D.C. 1977, p. 142.

235. "Hargrove and Marshall then led the way . . . Sergeant Anderson and Private First Class Rios following.": Carl C. Anderson, sworn testimony, *Report of Inquiry*, Headquarters, Fleet Marine Force, Pacific, Camp H. M. Smith, Hawaii, July 22, 1975, p. 2 of Anderson testimony.

235. "Private Mario Gutierrez saw them . . . and heard Hall yelling for more ammunition.": Mario Gutierrez, sworn testimony, *Report of Inquiry*, Headquarters, Fleet Marine Force, Pacific, Camp H. M. Smith, Hawaii, July 22, 1975, p. 1 of Gutierrez testimony.

235. "McNemar had already sent his M-60 teams off the island.": Lester McNemar, telephone interview, December 2000.

236. "A mortar flare lit up the night sky.": Em Son, interview, Phnom Penh, Cambodia, October 2000. The mortar battery under his command had flare rounds and used them during the extraction as his men tried to flank the marine position.

236. "Private First Class David M. Wagner gave Hall all the M-60 ammunition he had just prior to boarding a helicopter.": David M. Wagner, sworn testimony, *Report of Inquiry*, Headquarters, Fleet Marine Force, Pacific, Camp H. M. Smith, Hawaii, July 22, 1975, p. 1 of Wagner testimony.

236. "HM3 Steven Poore waded through the surf assisting. . . . As he did so . . . fragments slammed into his knee. Bloodied, Poore limped to shore and began putting a battle dressing on the freshly wounded marine.": Steven Poore, telephone interview notes, November 2000.

237. "Seventy-nine marines remained on the west beach.": John F. Guilmartin, *A Very Short War*, p. 132.

238. "Forty-four marines hustled off the helicopter before Blough lifted off at 7:08 P.M., headed once again for Koh Tang.": Thomas D. Des Brisay, *Fourteen Hours at Koh Tang*, in *USAF Southeast Asia Monograph Series*, Vol. 3, U.S. Government Printing Office, Washington, D.C., 1977, p. 143.

238. "two recently arrived OV-10s, *Nail-69* and *Nail-51*, piloted by Captain Seth Wilson and First Lieutenant Will Carroll": John F. Guilmartin, *A Very Short War*, p. 133.

239. "*Specter-21* circled overhead . . . to locate Cambodian gun emplacements.": John F. Guilmartin, *A Very Short War*, p. 133.

239. "They're all around us," Davis radioed. . . . Radio transcript from *Specter-21*.

240. " Willy J. Overton and Emelio Trevino . . . 'tail-end charlie' on the left flank, also remained in their foxholes, overlooked by Davis.": Emilio Trevino, and Willy J. Overton, sworn testimony, *Report of Inquiry*, Headquarters, Fleet Marine Force, Pacific, Camp H. M. Smith, Hawaii, July 22, 1975, p. 1 of Trevino and Overton testimony.

240. "The helicopter began drifting backward toward the tree line and above dug-in marines. Brims added power.": John F. Guilmartin, *A Very Short War*, p. 141.

241. "Overhead, *Specter-21* answered . . . with a fusillade of 20-mm and 40-mm rounds that streamed from the AC-130 in a curtain of fire.": John F. Guilmartin, *A Very Short War*, p. 141.

241. "Hargrove, Hall, and Marshall . . . were to hold the flank . . . and wait for a whistle . . . Stahl was gone. So was the whistle.": William L. Thornton, telephone interview, November 1997.

242. "Up they stood, one by one, then staggered toward the roaring noise, lights, and blowing sand near the helicopter.": Clark Hale, interview, Kompong Som, Cambodia, October 4, 2000, and Lester McNemar, interview, December 2000.

243. "Sprawled in front of him were Trevino and Overton, trying to claw their way aboard in the blackness.": Emilio Trevino and Willy J. Overton, sworn testimony, *Report of Inquiry*, Headquarters, Fleet Marine Force, Pacific, Camp H. M. Smith, Hawaii, July 22, 1975, p. 1 of Trevino and Overton testimony, and John F. Guilmartin, *A Very Short War*, p. 142.

244. "Sergeant Fisk saw muzzle flashes coming from the north side, so he sent short bursts from his GAU-5 in response.": Wayne Fisk, interview, January 2001.

244. "Fisk landed on top of Davis, and the two men wrapped arms in an embrace.": John F. Guilmartin, *A Very Short War*, p 143.

244. Brims radioed, "Some of the marines. . . . exactly what we're looking for.": from radio transcripts record by *Specter-21*.

CHAPTER 30

249. "Stahl inspected all returned equipment . . . matched those from weapons issued to the missing men. None were found.": Mykle Stahl, interview, San Antonio, August, 2000, tape 1.

250. "Stahl fell asleep believing he would be awakened in a few hours, once the means to return to the island had been determined.": Mykle Stahl, interview, San Antonio, August, 2000, tape 1.

250. "The admiral halted the meeting and asked all the others except Davis and Austin to leave the room.": Lester McNemar, telephone interview, December 2000.

250. "A short while later, Captain Stahl was awakened in his stateroom and told the plan to go back to Koh Tang was off.": Mykle Stahl, interview, San Antonio, August, 2000, tape 1.

251. "Rodgers could hear their shouts so . . . the Khmer Rouge could easily hear his . . . messages in English, French, and Khmer.": J. Michael Rogers, letter to author, September 1996, p. 2.

251. "The *Wilson* then departed the area as ordered by Admiral Gayler's staff in Hawaii.": J. Michael Rodgers, letter to author, September 1996, p. 2.

252. "By week's end more than fifteen thousand letters, telegrams, and phone messages had been received.": Ron Nessen, *It Sure Looks Different from the Inside*, p. 129.

253. "Captain Miller attributed their release to the jet strikes . . . and the marine assault on Koh Tang.": Ron Nessen, *It Sure Looks Different from the Inside*, p. 130.

253. "For five days . . . the Pentagon doggedly stuck to its original story that only one marine had been killed": Congressional Record, May 21, 1975, p. 15,752.

253. "to require nine days to get a final casualty tally through to that same White House contact? Yet that is how long it took.": John Osborne, *White House Watch* (Washington, D.C.: New Republic Books, 1977), p. 141.

254. "'These crews admitted that they were agents of the CIA who had to establish contact with other agents in hiding on Cambodian soil.'": *New York Times*, May 16, 1975, p. 1.

255. "seizure of the *Mayaguez* was initiated by a local commander and that authorities in Phnom Penh learned of it many hours later.": Reports of the Comptroller General of the United States, Subcommittee on International Political and Military Affairs, Committee on International Relations, *Seizure of the Mayaguez, Part IV*, U.S. Government Printing Office, Washington, D.C., October 4, 1976, p. 102.

255. "Kennerly. . . . he was not to make a habit of it.": David Kennerly, telephone interview, December 1999.

255. "Nations outside the Communist bloc handled the issue with relief or indifference.": Henry Kissinger, *Years of Renewal*, p. 573.

255. "Ford interrupted the meeting and had Henry Kissinger step outside the Cabinet Room with him.": Henry Kissinger, *Years of Renewal*, pp. 571-72.

256. "Schlesinger . . . never gave the president the data . . . as to how the orders got mishandled.": Walter Isaacson, *Kissinger, a Biography*, p. 651.

256. "Ford . . . dismissed it as Monday-morning quarterbacking by those who never had to make life-and-death decisions under pressure of time and incomplete information.": Ron Nessen, *It Sure Looks Different from the Inside*, p. 131.

257. "the GAO review . . . was hampered at every turn by its inability . . . in obtaining access to other records and to key personnel involved in the crisis.": Reports of the Comptroller General of the United States, Subcommittee on International Political and Military Affairs, Committee on International Relations, *Seizure of the* Mayaguez, *Part IV*, U.S. Government Printing Office, Washington, D.C., October 4, 1976, pp. 63, 98.

257. "The correct image was discovered after an hour-long search. . . . Twenty-nine persons could be counted crammed on the forward deck.": Reports of the Comptroller General of the United States, Subcommittee on International Political and Military Affairs, Committee on International Relations, *Seizure of the* Mayaguez, *Part IV*, U.S. Government Printing Office, Washington, D.C., October 4, 1976, pp. 78-80.

257. "Admiral Gayler's headquarters . . . ensure acknowledgment of critical intelligence by all concerned commands.": Reports of the Comptroller General of the United States, Subcommittee on International Political and Military Affairs, Committee on International Relations, *Seizure of the* Mayaguez, *Part IV*, U.S. Government Printing Office, Washington, D.C., October 4, 1976, p. 104.

258. "requiring a senior administration official to observe . . . deliberations during crises, and provide Congress with full information on ongoing matters.": Reports of the Comptroller General of the United States, Subcommittee on International Political and Military Affairs, Committee on International Relations, *Seizure of the* Mayaguez, *Part IV*, U.S. Government Printing Office, Washington, D.C., October 4, 1976, p. 136.

259. "Ford did a damn good job, but I just want to thank those marines.": Roy Rowan, *Time*, May 26, 1975, p. 17, and Henry Kissinger, *Years of Renewal*, p. 575.

259 "The troops were assembled and told . . . under pain of court-martial.": William L. Thornton, telephone interview, November , 1997, and Barnette, Larry, interview, Phnom Penh, Cambodia, October 2000.

260. "Hargrove, Hall, and Marshall, were intentionally left out.": 2nd Battalion, 9th Marine Regiment, 3rd Marine Division pamphlet, *Service in Remembrance of United States Marine Corps and United States Navy Personnel Killed-in-Action, Operation Mayaguez, 15 May 1975.*

260. "No mention was made of the missing-in-action.": *Okinawa Marine*, May 23, 1975, pp. 1-3.

260. "Hargrove's mental state as a contributing factor, yet indicated he was 'fit for duty.'": *Investigation to Inquire into the Circumstances Surrounding the Missing in Action Status in the Case of Private First Class Gary C. Hall, Lance Corporal Joseph N. Hargrove, and Private Danny G. Marshall*, completed on June 7, 1975, p. 2, item 17, and p. 3, items 2 and 7.

260. "Had it not been for a momentary delay . . . five, not three would have been abandoned.": Emilio Trevino, and Willie J. Overton, testimony, *Investigation to Inquire into the Circumstances Surrounding the Missing in Action Status in the Case of Private First Class Gary C. Hall, Lance Corporal Joseph N. Hargrove, and Private Danny G. Marshall*, completed on June 7, 1975, p. 1, both documents.

261. "I heard Hall yell for ammo, so I gave him mine.": David M. Wagner, testimony, *Investigation to Inquire into the Circumstances Surrounding the Missing in Action Status in the Case of Private First Class Gary C. Hall, Lance Corporal Joseph N. Hargrove, and Private Danny G. Marshall,* completed on June 7, 1975, p. 1.

261. "defend the flank with your M-16s if necessary.": Mykle Stahl, interview, San Antonio, August 2000.

261. "'The last helicopter would swing around to their position and pick them up.'": William L. Thornton, telephone interview, November 1997.

CHAPTER 31:

263. "two magazine articles.": *"Left Behind on Koh Tang"* appeared in *The Retired Officers Magazine*, August 1996 and *"Mayaguez, Forgotten Battle"* appeared in *Soldier of Fortune* in May 1996.

264. "'We'd have had to go back,' Captain Davis said.": James Davis, interview, *Seized at Sea*, Henninger Productions, Discovery Channel documentary, May 14, 2000.

264. "Captain Stahl . . . wrote to Hargrove's wife and . . . his explanation that the men did not survive had no firsthand confirmation in fact.": Letter to Gail Hargrove, wife of Joseph N. Hargrove, May 1975.

264. "Joseph Hargrove's Purple Heart had not yet been presented to his next-of-kin.": Hargrove's Purple Heart was presented to his widow, Gail Hargrove, in Raleigh, North Carolina in November 1999 as a result of the increased media attention brought on by the August 1998 *Popular Science* article, "Missing in Action." A local USMC Reserve officer did research and determined that the medal had never been presented. He contacted next of kin.

265. "at least seven different witnesses related information pertaining to . . . American soldiers after the battle for Koh Tang.": JCRC Reports T86-127, April 7, 1986; T88-060, February 24, 1988; Evaluation of report T-86-127, February 9, 1987; Evaluation of report T-88-060, April 11, 1988; Summary Report October 14-23 and October 25, 1991; Additional Information Report, T88-060, December 5, 1995; Detailed Report of Investigation For Case 1998, June 5, 1996, and many others.

273. "Later, I obtained Em Son's full debriefing report from JTF-FA upon my return to the States.": JTF-FA Additional Information Report 991C-001, concerning Tang Island Priority Case 1998, and Case 2002, 2003, 2038, May 7, 1999.

277. Ralph Wetterhahn, *The Russians of MiG Alley, The Retired Officers Magazine*, August 2000, pp. 68-75, and *Nguyen Van Bay and the Aces from the North, Air & Space,* November 2000, pp. 44-51.

CHAPTER 32:

277. "Now we save our bullets . . . . We have other ways of punishment.": Al Santoli, *To Bear Any Burden* (New York: Ballantine Books, 1985), p. 247.

277. "His brigade commander . . . instructed Em Son to . . . capture alive any Americans still on Koh Tang.": JCRC Report T88-060, *One American Survivor of Mayaguez Incident Executed by Khmer Rouge During May 1975*, February 24, 1985, p. 2.

279. "When I order them what to do, that's exactly what they do.": Em Son, interview, Phnom Penh, Cambodia, October 2000, tape 1, side 2.

279. "He had found an American M-60 machine gun a few yards from where the captive American had been taken.": Rot Leng, interview, Kompong Som Harbor, Cambodia, February 21, 1997, and Em Son, interview notes, Phom Penh, Combodia, October 2000.

280. "Em Son ordered the men to bury the body . . . .They threw some sand to cover the body.": Em Son, interview notes, Phnom Penh, Cambodia, October 2000, and Rot Leng, interview, Seaside Hotel, Kompong Som, Combodia, February 20, 1997.

280. "The prisoner was tall and thin, had light-colored hair and stubble on his chin.": Em Son, interview, Phnom Penh, Combodia, October 2000, tape 1, side 1.

281. "The American did not attempt to run . . . so he shot him again in the chest and the American died.": JCRC Report T88-060, *One American Survivor of Mayaguez Incident Executed by Khmer Rouge During May 1975*, February 24, 1985, p. 2.

282. "Em Son confirmed that only two members of his unit had pistols, he and Platoon Commander Soeun.": Em Son, interview, Phnom Penh, Combodia, October 2000, tape 2, side 1.

282. "The American was 'dragged beside a mango tree nearby and buried.'" Em Son interview, Phnom Penh, tape 2, side 1, October, 2000.

283. "These matched . . . Hall (brown hair, six-foot-two and 220 pounds) and . . . Marshall (sandy blond hair, five-foot-three, tall and 130 pounds).": *Narrative,* Joint Casualty Resolution Center case 1998-0-01 thru 03, NAS Barbers Point Hawaii, 1998, p. 1–2.

285. "The men threw dirt and rocks over the feet.": JTF-FA report, Additional Information report 991C-001 Concerning Tang Island Priority Case 1998 and Cases 2002, 2003 and 2038, May 7, 1999, p. 6.

285. "There he tied the loose end of the rope to vines. . . . A month later, he checked. . . . Bones . . . were bleaching in the sun.": JTF-FA report, Additional Information Report 991C-001 Concerning Tang Island Priority Case 1998 and Cases 2002, 2003 and 2038, May 7, 1999, p. 6–7.

CHAPTER 33:

291. "We had entered Indochina to save a country, and ended by rescuing a ship.": Henry Kissinger, *Years of Renewal*, p. 575.

311. "President Ford considers the *Mayaguez* Incident the high point of his administration. . . . 'we have the will and the capability of moving.'" Henry Kissinger, *Years of Renewal*, p. 575.

312. "Forty-three were wounded, and twenty-eight had minor injuries. Three were left behind.": Randall W. Austin, Koh Tang/Mayaguez Historical Report, December 9, 1975, p. 5, and New Briefing, CINCPAC REP Philippines, Subic Bay, May 19, 1975, p. 3.

313. "How deep. . . . will they go?" Sam Sok, interview, Kompong Som, Cambodia, March 1999.

313. "By that time he had also lost two brothers and one sister in the fighting.": Em Son, interview, Takeo Province, Cambodia, October 2000.

312. "'The most glaring example was the use of a fifteen-thousand-pound bomb . . . with absolutely no prior notice to or clearance from [me].'": Randall W. Austin, *Koh Tang/Mayaguez Historical Report*, December 9, 1995, p. 5.

314. "Gary never came back to that backyard, and we learned what wars were really like.": David Sammons, interview notes from his written account, childhood friend of Gary Hall, Covington, Kentucky, August 26, 2000.

Index

ABOUT THE AUTHOR

Ralph Wetterhahn is an accomplished journalist, widely read in *Air & Space/Smithsonian, Popular Science, Leatherneck Magazine,* the *Bangkok Post, Soldier of Fortune, The Retired Officers Magazine, Vietnam,* the U. S. Air Force Academy magazine, and *Checkpoints,* among other publications. He is a former U. S. Air Force fighter pilot who served combat tours during the Vietnam War with both the Air Force and the Navy, completing 180 combat missions. His combat decorations include the Silver Star, Distinguished Flying Cross, Navy Achievement Medal, Air Force Commendation Medal, the Air Medal with eighteen oak leaf clusters, and credit for downing one MiG-21. He is fluent in Thai, has traveled to and written extensively about Vietnam, Russia, Thailand, Laos, and Cambodia. He lives in Long Beach, California.